Edward Schillebeeckx

Thomas Eggensperger / Ulrich Engel /
Angel F. Méndez Montoya (Hg. / Eds.)

Edward Schillebeeckx

Impulse für Theologien im 21. Jahrhundert ·
Impetus Towards Theologies in the 21st Century

Matthias Grünewald Verlag

Wir danken Drs. Hadewych Snijdewind OP (Nijmegen) für die Vermittlung der Abdruckrechte des Umschlagfotos.
We express our gratitude to Drs. Hadewych Snijdewind OP (Nijmegen) for arranging the photo publishing rights.

MIX
Papier aus verantwortungsvollen Quellen
FSC® C003147

Für die Schwabenverlag AG ist Nachhaltigkeit ein wichtiger Maßstab ihres Handelns. Wir achten daher auf den Einsatz umweltschonender Ressourcen und Materialien. Dieses Buch wurde auf FSC®-zertifiziertem Papier gedruckt. FSC (Forest Stewardship Council®) ist eine nicht staatliche, gemeinnützige Organisation, die sich für eine ökologische und sozial verantwortliche Nutzung der Wälder unserer Erde einsetzt.

Bibliografische Information der Deutschen Nationalbibliothek
Die Deutsche Nationalbibliothek verzeichnet diese Publikation in der Deutschen Nationalbibliografie; detaillierte bibliografische Daten sind im Internet über http://dnb.d-nb.de abrufbar.

Alle Rechte vorbehalten
© 2012 Matthias Grünewald Verlag der Schwabenverlag AG, Ostfildern
www.gruenewaldverlag.de

Umschlaggestaltung: Finken & Bumiller, Stuttgart
Umschlagabbildung: Edward Schillebeeckx OP, Berg en Daal, 8.9.2008, © Mirjam Ates-Snijdewind
Druck: CPI – buchbücher.de, Birkach
Hergestellt in Deutschland
ISBN 978-3-7867-2935-8

INHALT | TABLE OF CONTENTS

Thomas Eggensperger / Ulrich Engel / Angel F. Méndez Montoya
Einführung | Introduction   9

Johann Baptist Metz
Geleitwort | Preface   15

Robert J. Schreiter
Indicators of the Future of Theology in the Works of Edward Schillebeeckx   21

Alessandro Cortesi
Das Heil der Menschheit in einer Welt der vielen Religionen
Anregungen aus dem Werk von Edward Schillebeeckx   39

Stephan van Erp
Incarnational Theology
Systematic Theology after Schillebeeckx   53

Christian Bauer
Heiligkeit des Profanen?
Spuren der „école Chenu-Schillebeeckx" (H. de Lubac)
auf dem Zweiten Vatikanum   67

Vera Donnelly
The Sacramentality of Schillebeeckx's Theological Journey   84

Bernadette Schwarz-Boenneke
Die Widerständigkeit der Wirklichkeit als erstes Moment des Erfahrens   94

Geraldine Smyth
Forgiveness between the Theological and Social
Invitation to Reconciling Grace 110

Pierre-Yves Materne
Metz und Schillebeeckx – Mystik und Politik
Komponenten für eine verantwortliche Theologie 138

Angel F. Méndez Montoya
Performing the Reign of God
The Mystical and the Political Co-Existing in Edward
Schillebeeckx's Philosophical Theology 148

Bernhard Kohl
Jenseits des Diskurses
Ethische Anstöße bei Edward Schillebeeckx 156

Thomas Eggensperger
„Weil Politik nicht alles ist" – sondern?
Eine sozialethisch ausgerichtete Relecture und Neubesinnung 170

André Lascaris
Schillebeeckx in an Age of „The Immanent Framework" 180

Maximilian Halstrup
Theologie 2.0!
Faktizität und Selbstrealisierung als Basiskategorien einer
lebensweltlich verpflichteten Hermeneutik des Glaubens 192

Manuela Kalsky
Heil im alltäglichen Leben
Weiterdenken mit Edward Schillebeeckx in einer multireligiösen
und multikulturellen Gesellschaft 211

Erik Borgman
„... like a sacrament"
Towards a theological view on the real existing church 230

Ulrich Engel
Dominikanische Predigt
Eine hermeneutische Rekonstruktion in ekklesiopraktischer
Absicht   252

Stefan Knobloch
Edward Schillebeeckx' Trilogie als Denkanstoß meiner Theologie
Eine Dankesbezeugung   269

Mitarbeiter/-innen | Contributors   276

Thomas Eggensperger / Ulrich Engel / Ángel F. Méndez Montoya

EINFÜHRUNG | INTRODUCTION

Ende 2009 verstarb im niederländischen Nijmegen der flämische Konzilstheologe Edward Schillebeeckx OP (12.11.1914 – 23.12.2009).[1] Anlässlich des ersten Jahrestages seines Todes veranstaltete das Institut M.-Dominique Chenu – Espaces Berlin (IMDC) der Dominikaner zusammen mit der Philosophisch-Theologischen Hochschule der Kapuziner in Münster und dem Lehrstuhl für Dogmatik an der Katholisch-Theologischen Fakultät der Universität Münster ein internationales Symposium.[2] Es war zugleich das V. Treffen von Theologiedozentinnen und -dozenten des Predigerordens in Europa.[3]

Theologische Fortschreibungen in der Spätmoderne

Unter der Überschrift „Impulse für Theologien des 21. Jahrhunderts" gingen die ca. 30 Wissenschaftlerinnen und Wissenschaftler aus dem (Umfeld des) Dominikanerorden(s) der Frage nach, in welchen Hinsichten die vielfältigen Facetten der Theologie Edward Schillebeeckx' auch für die Zukunft fruchtbar gemacht werden können. Für den Hauptvortrag hatte der US-amerikanische Systematiker Robert J. Schreiter C.PP.S.

---

[1] Zu Biographie und Werk vgl. U. Engel, Edward Schillebeeckx. Gotteserkenntnis und Gotteserfahrung, in: ders., Gott der Menschen. Wegmarken dominikanischer Theologie, Ostfildern 2010, 113–134.

[2] Vgl. u. a. M. Tumbrink, In memoriam Edward Schillebeeckx OP. Bericht über ein internationales Symposium in Münster, in: *Ordenskorrespondenz* 52 (2011), 213–216; dies., In memoriam Edward Schillebeeckx OP. Internationales Symposium der Dominikaner in Münster, in: *Wort und Antwort* 52 (2011), 87–89; dies., Symposium: In memoriam Edward Schillebeeckx op (1914–2009). Münster, 9–11 december 2010, in: *Tijdschrift voor Theologie* 51 (2011), 327–328; Th. Eggensperger / U. Engel, Theologische Impulse für das 21. Jahrhundert. Internationales Schillebeeckx-Symposium in Münster, in: *Kontakt* 39 (2011), 54–55.

[3] Nach Huissen/NL 2002, Salamanca/E 2004, Pistoia/I 2006 und Louvain-la-Neuve/B 2008.

zugesagt. Schreiter gilt als einer der besten Kenner der Theologie des Dominikaners; von 2000 bis 2006 hatte er den Lehrstuhl für Theologie und Kultur der Edward Schillebeeckx-Stiftung an der Theologischen Fakultät der Universität Nijmegen inne.

In einem von vielen Studierenden der Philosophisch-Theologischen Hochschule und der Universität besuchten Abendgespräch erinnerte der Münsteraner Fundamentaltheologe Johann Baptist Metz an Person und Werk seines Kollegen Edward Schillebeeckx. Neben einer langjährigen Zusammenarbeit im Rahmen der internationalen Zeitschrift *Concilium* verband beide das theologische Engagement für eine weltoffene, dem Geist des Zweiten Vatikanischen Konzils verpflichtete kritische Kirche.

Die Diskussionen der zum Symposium versammelten Theologinnen und Theologen aus insgesamt neun Ländern (Deutschland, Niederlande, Belgien, Frankreich, Italien, Kroatien, Irland, Mexiko und USA) fragten, ausgehend von der im Zentrum des Schillebeeckx'schen Denkens verankerten Idee einer Korrelation zwischen *Erfahrung* und *Tradition*, nach dem Ort der Theologie heute. Beide, *Situation* und *Überlieferung*, stehen in einem Wechselverhältnis, denn „die jeweils aktuelle Situation, in der wir leben – die zweite Quelle –, [ist] ein inneres konstitutives Element des Verstehens von Gottes offenbarendem Sprechen in der Geschichte Israels und in der Geschichte Jesu [...], der von Christen als Heil von Gott her von und für die Menschen bezeugt wird – die erste Quelle."[4]

Es kann also in der Theologie, so der Tenor der meisten Symposiumsbeiträge, nicht darum gehen, die biblische Botschaft ‚einfach so' auf die heutige Situation *anzuwenden*. Nach Maßgabe der Hermeneutik gilt vielmehr: Was die evangelische Botschaft *heute für uns bedeutet*, ist nicht zu ergründen, außer *in Beziehung zu unserer heutigen Situation*. Ohne den konstitutiven Bezug zu den Erfahrungen der (post-)säkularen Menschen wäre der Rekurs auf Schrift und Tradition bloß fruchtlose und letztlich irrelevante Wiederholung.

In diesem Gedanken wird die Theologie Edward Schillebeeckx' auch in spätmoderner Zeit anschlussfähig[5] – und zwar hinsichtlich der zentralen christologischen, ekklesiologischen, sozialethisch-politischen und pastoralen Herausforderungen! Fast alle Beiträge der Tagung, die für die Drucklegung zumeist wesentlich überarbeitet wurden, liegen hiermit

---

[4] E. Schillebeeckx, Menschliche Erfahrung und Glaube an Jesus Christus. Eine Rechenschaft. Aus dem Niederländischen von H. Zulauf, Freiburg/Br. 1979, 14.
[5] Vgl. auch L. Boeve / St. van Erp / F. Depoortere (Eds.), Edward Schillebeeckx and Contemporary Theology, London 2010.

nun vor. Wir verbinden diese Publikation mit dem Wunsch nach breiter Rezeption und engagierter, gerne auch kontroverser Diskussion.

Dank

Ein besonderer Dank für eine rundum gelungene und ausnehmend unkomplizierte Organisation des Symposiums gebührt dem Sekretariat der Philosophisch-Theologischen Hochschule Münster in Person von Marion Bäumer und ihrem Mitstreiter Christian Föller. Den Mitarbeiter/-innen am Lehrstuhl für Dogmatik an der Katholisch-Theologischen Fakultät der Universität Münster – Agnes Wiedemeier, Franzis Rewer, Marion Tumbrink, Florian Kleeberg und Marcellus Goldbeck – sei für vielfältige Unterstützung im Vorfeld der Tagung gedankt. Frank Ewerszumrode OP danken wir für manch bilinguale Hilfestellung während der Münsteraner Zusammenkunft. Tracy Rammler, Rebecca Pohl, Sabine Schratz, Michael Lauble und Bernhard Kohl OP gilt ein besonderes Dankeschön für die Übersetzungen im vorliegenden Buch. Für die finanzielle und logistische Unterstützung des Kongresses sei dem Lehrstuhl für Dogmatik an der Katholisch-Theologischen Fakultät der Universität Münster, der Niederländischen Provinz des Dominikanerordens und ihrem Provinzial Ben Vocking OP sowie der Philosophisch-Theologischen Hochschule Münster in Person ihres Rektors Thomas Dienberg OFMCap gedankt. Ohne die Hilfe der Flämischen Provinz des Dominikanerordens und ihrem Provinzial Marcel Braekers OP hätte das vorliegende Buch nicht veröffentlicht werden können; auch hier sagen wir von Herzen: „Dankeschön"! Last but not least gilt unser Dank dem Matthias-Grünewald-Verlag in Person von Gertrud Widmann und Volker Sühs für die professionelle und unkomplizierte Zusammenarbeit.

* * *

At the end of the year 2009 the Flemish conciliar theologian Edward Schillebeeckx OP (11/12/1914 – 12/23/2009) died in the Dutch town of Nijmegen.[6] The Dominican Institute M.-Dominique Chenu – Espaces Berlin (IMDC), the Philosophical-Theological Seminary of the Capuchins in Münster, and the Chair for Dogmatics at the Catholic Theological

---

[6] Concerning biography and works cf. U. Engel, "Edward Schillebeeckx: Gotteserkenntnis und Gotteserfahrung", op. cit.

Faculty of the University of Münster held an international symposium in honor of the first anniversary of his death.⁷ This was also an occasion for the 5th meeting of theology scholars from the Order of Preachers in the European Union.⁸

Theological Developments in Late Modernism

Under the title "Impetus Towards Theologies in the 21st Century" approximately 30 scholars both members and associates of the Dominican Order pursued the common task of creating a fruitful dialogue between Edward Schillebeecx's multi-faceted theology and the issues of future theology. The U.S. American systematic theologian, Robert J. Schreiter, CPPS, graciously presented the main talk of this symposium. Schreiter held the Chair for Theology and Culture at the Edward Schillebeeckx Foundation of the Theological Faculty at the University of Nijmegen from 2000 to 2006, and he is credited to be one of the most important experts on the theology of the Dominican thinker E. Schillebeeckx.

In addition, the systematic theologian, Johann Baptist Metz, from the University of Münster, reflected upon the life and work of his colleague, E. Schillebeeckx. Metz shared his thoughts with many students of the Philosophical and Theological College from this University. Metz recalled how he and Schillebeeckx were closely connected with each other through both their long-standing cooperation in the international journal *Concilium* as well as in their dedication to the promotion of an open-minded, critical church committed to the spirit of the Second Vatican Council.

Theologians from a total of nine different countries (Germany, the Netherlands, Belgium, France, Italy, Croatia, Ireland, Mexico, and the United States) gathered at the symposium under a common purpose of discussing the position of current theology, assessing the relevance of discussions of the focused on the position of theology today, recurring back to the central idea of Schillebeeckx's thought, primarily focusing

---

[7] Cf. M. Tumbrink, "In memoriam Edward Schillebeeckx OP. Bericht über ein internationales Symposium in Münster", op. cit.; idem, "In memoriam Edward Schillebeeckx OP. Internationales Symposium der Dominikaner in Münster", op. cit.; idem, "Symposium: In memoriam Edward Schillebeckx op (1914–2009)", op. cit.; Th. Eggensperger / U. Engel, "Theologische Impulse für das 21. Jahrhundert", op.cit.

[8] After Huissen/NL 2002, Salamanca/E 2004, Pistoia/I 2006 and Louvain-la-Neuve/B 2008.

upon the correlation between *experience* and *tradition*. Both *actual experience* and *handed-down tradition* interact with each other, for, as Schillebeeckx points out, "the given situation in which we live – the second source – an inner constitutive element of understanding divine revelation within the history of Israel and throughout the history of Jesus who is testified by Christians to be the salvation to all people coming from God – the first source."[9]

Most speakers at the symposium agreed upon a common understanding that the aim of theology is not making a straightforward *application* of biblical texts to modern contexts. Instead, the task of theological hermeneutics must claim that what the evangelists may *mean for us today* cannot be determined unless they are understood *in relation to today's situation*. Without a constitutive reference to the experiences of (post-)secular people, the recourse to word and tradition is but an unrewarding, and ultimately an irrelevant repetition.

In light of this position, theologians at this symposium argue that the theology of Edward Schillebeeckx– regarding his central Christological, ecclesial, socio-political, and pastoral challenges – can indeed engage with the context of late modernity.[10] With this publication we hope to create a wide reception, as well as invite the reader to engage into critical discussions.

Acknowledgements

Special thanks for the successful and exceedingly uncomplicated organization of the symposium must be given to the secretary's office of the Philosophical and Theological College at the University of Münster, under the representation of Marion Bäumer and her colleague Christian Föller. To the staff of the Chair for Dogmatics at the Catholic Theological Faculty at the University of Münster – Agnes Wiedemeier, Franzis Rewer, Marion Tumbrink, Florian Kleeberg, and Marcellus Goldbeck – we express our gratitude for your great support in preparing for this symposium. Frank Ewerszumrode OP was very helpful with bilingual challenges at the Münster gathering. Tracy Rammler, Rebecca

---

[9] Cf. E. Schillebeeckx, Menschliche Erfahrung und Glaube an Jesus Christus, op. cit., 14. There is no English translation of this book. It is planned to include it in the last volume of Schillebeeckx' Collected Work in English; Inquiry of E. Borgman to U. Engel.

[10] Cf. also L. Boeve / St. van Erp / F. Depoortere (Eds.), Edward Schillebeeckx and Contemporary Theology, op. cit.

Pohl, Sabine Schratz, Michael Lauble and Bernhard Kohl OP deserve a special thanks for the translations of this book. We also wish to express our gratitude to the Chair of Dogmatics at the Catholic Theological Faculty at the University of Münster, to the Dutch Province of the Dominicans represented by Provincial Ben Vocking OP, and to the Rector of the Philosophical Theological College in Münster, as well as to Thomas Dienberg OFMCap, for their financial and logistical support. This book would not have been published without the help of the Flemish Province of the Dominicans represented by Provincial Marcel Braekers OP; again a sincere "thank you"! Last but not least the Matthias-Grünewald-Verlag, represented by Gertrud Widmann and Volker Sühs, deserve our thanks for the professional and uncomplicated cooperation.

Translation from German: *Tracy Rammler*

Berlin – México D.F., 15.11.2011
Fest des hl. Albertus Magnus
Feast of St Albert the Great   *Die Herausgeber – The Editors*

Johann Baptist Metz

GELEITWORT | PREFACE

Bei dem hier dokumentierten Symposium zum Gedenken an Edward Schillebeeckx hat mich etwas besonders beeindruckt: die Teilnahme verhältnismäßig vieler junger theologischer Referenten und Zuhörer. Schillebeeckx starb 2009 im Alter von 95 Jahren. Woher die anhaltende Neugierde, das durchstechende Interesse in einer Atmosphäre des überbeschleunigten Generationenwechsels?

Im postmodernen Abschied vom modernen Zeitalter der Kritik, speziell der Ideologie-, der Religions- und Kirchenkritik, ist das Leben in der Kirche und gerade die Situation für junge Theologen keineswegs leichter geworden. Die kaum verarbeiteten kritischen Vorbehalte gegenüber Religion und Kirche sind nämlich inzwischen nicht einfach verschwunden, sondern aus der öffentlichen Diskussionswelt ins alltäglich-allgemeine Bewusstsein abgesunken. Der Dualismus zwischen Glaubenstradition und individueller Lebensgeschichte, zwischen Bekenntnis und Erfahrung, zwischen Glaubenswelt und Argumentationswelt hat sich nicht gemildert, sondern existenziell verschärft. Zunehmend klafft eine Lücke zwischen einer weiterhin gepflegten Bereitschaft zur festlich-feierlichen, zuweilen eventartigen Lebensrahmung durch die Kirche und dem kirchlichen Einfluss auf die individuelle Lebensgestaltung. Nicht zuletzt unter jungen Katholiken lauert die Gefahr einer schizophrenen Kirchlichkeit. Die ursprünglich erwartete und gesuchte Lern- und Reformbereitschaft in der Kirche ist eben nicht nur durch einen mangelnden Umkehrwillen der Glaubenden behindert, sondern auch durch eine augenscheinlich allzu abgehobene Lern- und Erfahrungsunwilligkeit der kirchlichen Hierarchie.

Lässt sich denn die gegenwärtige Krisensituation ausschließlich mit der Gefahr der „Verweltlichung" des kirchlichen Lebens (Benedikt XVI. bei seinem Deutschlandbesuch im September 2011) erläutern und kritisieren? Waren sich gerade Kirche und Jugend nicht schon einmal näher –

vor allem in der unmittelbaren nachkonziliaren Zeit (in der es noch keine Weltjugendtage gab)? Das konziliare *aggiornamento* zielte nicht auf eine undialektische Verweltlichung der Kirche, nicht auf eine fahrlässige Preisgabe ihrer konstitutionellen Ungleichzeitigkeit gegenüber dem „Zeitgeist". Es galt vielmehr – endlich – dem Versuch einer produktivkritischen Auseinandersetzung mit dem Geist der Moderne, um die inzwischen aufgebrochenen und aufgestauten kritischen Fragen nicht unter ihrem Niveau zu behandeln. Zu den theologischen Konzilsberatern, die an diesem kirchlichen Erneuerungsversuch maßgeblich beteiligt waren, gehörte vor allem auch Edward Schillebeeckx.

Seinen Namen hörte ich erstmals in Karl Rahners Vorlesungen Anfang der 1950er Jahre. Schillebeeckx war für uns damals der besonders interessante flämische Dominikaner mit dem nur schwer zu buchstabierenden Namen. Persönlich lernte ich ihn im Herbst 1963 kennen – bei den ersten Planungen einer von meinem holländischen Verleger Paul Brand angeregten internationalen theologischen Zeitschrift. Ihr Name – *Concilium* – war gleichzeitig ein zentraler Programmpunkt: die theologisch gestützte Fortführung des Reformansatzes im Zweiten Vatikanischen Konzil. Gewiss sind die Themen und Probleme dieses Konzils nicht einfach die Themen und Probleme der heutigen Kirche. Aber ebenso gewiss ist, dass sich das Ringen in der Kirche um ihren künftigen Weg an der Art entscheidet, wie dieses Konzil im Leben der Kirche gegenwärtig bleibt. Wird sich eine betont offensive oder eher eine rein defensive Form der Treue zu diesem Konzil und überhaupt der Rettung von kirchlichen Traditionen durchsetzen? Karl Rahner, selbst einflussreicher Konzilstheologe, sprach von diesem Konzil als dem „Anfang eines Anfangs", als dem allen Patinareformen widerstehenden keimhaften Aufbruch in eine neue Epoche der Kirchengeschichte, dem in wagender Treue Rechnung zu tragen sei.

Edward Schillebeeckx war einer der wichtigsten theologischen Vertreter dieser Treue. Dazu wenigstens ein paar Hinweise. Der biblisch und philosophisch kundige Systematiker entfaltete eine theologische Hermeneutik, die nicht nur für die Christologie der Kirche bedeutsam ist, sondern auch – in der Gestalt einer sog. Anerkennungshermeneutik – für den kirchlichen Umgang mit einer religiös und kulturell pluralistischen Weltöffentlichkeit. Für Schillebeeckx war das Gottesthema – wie auch für Rahner und auch für mich – nie nur ein kirchlich verschlüsseltes Thema, sondern ein Menschheitsthema, an dem sich der besondere Charakter der heute herrschenden Krisen erkennen lässt.

Nach meiner Verantwortung für die Sektion „Fundamentaltheologie" in der Zeitschrift *Concilium* habe ich über eine Reihe von Jahren zusammen mit Edward die Sektion „Dogmatik" betreut. Die Behandlung von Themen wie beispielsweise „Autorität der Glaubenden" in der Kirche oder „Recht der Gemeinde auf Eucharistie" könnte verdeutlichen, wie „orthopraktisch" bzw. wie „dialektisch" (im Sinne der Dialektik von Theorie und Praxis, von Erinnern und Vergessen) wir hier die ekklesiologischen Themen zu behandeln suchten. Es ging z.B. um die wachsende Bedeutung der „Mündigkeit" der Glaubenden, die angesichts des Zerfalls von lebensprägenden Traditionen sich selbst an einer Alphabetisierung beteiligen müssen, in der sie sich auch miteinander über ihre Glaubenserfahrungen und ihre Glaubensnöte austauschen können. So sollte „Gemeinde" gerade auch als zur Eucharistie versammelte Erinnerungs- und Erzählgemeinschaft praktisch werden. Dieses Gemeindebild widersteht freilich den gegenwärtigen Versuchen, den Beteiligungsschwund am kirchlichen Leben durch einen Zusammenschluss von territorialen Großpfarreien zu kaschieren, in denen womöglich alles noch sprachloser, beziehungsloser, gewissermaßen „unpersönlicher" zu werden droht. Hier sollte man durchaus die Überlegungen von Schillebeeckx zu einer basisgestützten Kirchenreform noch einmal nachlesen.

Ein neugierig sortierender Rückblick auf sein theologisches Werk kann gerade für junge Theologen und Theologinnen zum ermutigenden Ausblick auf jene befreite Freiheit im Glauben werden, von der Paulus den Korinthern (1 Kor 3,21–23) sagt: „Alles gehört euch, Paulus, Apollos, Kephas [...] – alles gehört euch; ihr aber gehört Christus, und Christus gehört Gott".

* * *

One of the things that particularly impressed me of the symposium commemorating Edward Schillebeeckx that is documented in this volume was the participation of a comparatively high number of young theological presenters and audience members. Schillebeeckx died in 2009 at the age of 95. Where does this continuing curiosity, this piercing interest come from in an atmosphere of overly accelerated generational change?

Life within the Church and above all the situation for young theologians, has by no means been made any easier by the postmodern farewell to the modern age of critique, especially ideological, religious and Church critique. This is because the critical reservations towards religion and the

Church, barely having been accommodated, have not simply disappeared in the meantime, but have sunk from the public realm of debate into everyday mundane consciousness. The dualism between a tradition of faith and individual life stories, between creed and experience, between the world of faith and the world of debate rather than mellow, has intensified existentially. A gap is becoming increasingly visible between people's continuing readiness to solemnity, ceremonially framing their lives with Church events, and the Church's influence on individual life choices. The danger of a schizophrenic churchliness lurks, not least among young Catholics. The willingness to learn and to reform, initially expected from and sought in the Church is hindered not only by believers´ unwillingness to reverse course, but also by the Church´s hierarchy´s unwillingness to learn and experience, which is due to the fact that it is apparently far too aloof.

Can the current crisis then be explained and critiqued solely through the threat of "secularising" of Church life (as stated by Pope Benedict XVI on his visit to Germany in September 2011)? Have not the Church and youth in particular been closer to each other in the past – especially in the time immediately following the Second Vatican Council (when World Youth Days did not yet exist)? The conciliar *aggiornamento* was not aimed at the undialectical secularisation of the Church; it was not aimed at the reckless surrender of its constitutive non-synchronicity with the "Zeitgeist". On the contrary, it was intended – finally – to be a productive and critical engagement with the spirit of modernity in order to treat the critical questions that had meanwhile been fractured and pent-up at their due level. Edward Schillebeeckx was above all one of the theological consultants at the Council who played a considerable role in this attempt to regenerate the Church.

I first heard of Edward Schillebeecx in Karl Rahner's lectures in the early 1950's. To us at the time, Schillebeeckx was that particularly intriguing Flemish Dominican with the name that was difficult to spell. In the autumn of 1963 I met him in person during the preliminary planning phase for an international theological journal initiated by my Dutch publisher Paul Brand. The journal´s name – *Concilium* – was simultaneously crucial to its agenda: the theologically supported continuation of the approaches to reform begun by the Second Vatican Council. Certainly, the concerns and issues of that Council are not straightforwardly the same concerns and issues regarding the current Church. But, just as certainly, the struggles within the Church concerning its future path will be decided by the ways in which this Council remains present in the life of the Church. Will a markedly offensive or rather a purely defensive mode of loyalty to this Council and to the preservation of ecclesiastical traditions prevail more generally? Karl Rahner, himself an influential theologian of the Council, called this Council the "beginning of a beginning", sowing the seeds of the awakening of a new era in Church history, an era resistant to all patina-coated reforms, a beginning that demands to be accompanied by a daring faithfulness.

Edward Schillebeeckx was one of the most important theological representatives of this faithfulness. At least a few remarks need to be made on this matter. The systematic theologian, knowledgeable of both the Bible and philosophy, developed a theological hermeneutics that is not only significant for ecclesiastic Christology, but also – in the shape of a so-called hermeneutics of recognition – for Church dealings with a public world characterised by religious and cultural plurality. To Schillebeeckx – as well as for Rahner and for myself – the question of God was never merely an issue encoded by the Church, but also an issue for humanity, an issue that demonstrates the specificity nature of the current crisis.

After my responsibilities for the section "Fundamental Theology" in the journal *Concilium*, for a number of years I edited the "Dogma" section together with Edward. The treatment of topics such as "The Authority of Believers" in the Church, or "The Congregation's Right to the Eucharist" might illustrate how "orthopraxis" or how "dialectical" (in the sense of a dialectic of theory and practice, of remembrance and forgetting) our engagement with these issues sought to be. One issue, for instance, was the increasing significance of the "maturity" of believers, who, faced with the disintegration of formative traditions, have to engage in a literacy process in which they can also share their faith experiences and crises with each other. It was thus hoped that the "congregation" would become practicable, specifically as a community of remembrance and of story-telling gathered around the Eucharist table. Admittedly, this notion of congregation resists the current attempts to conceal the dwindling participation in Church life by merging large territorial parishes in which, if anything, things are threatening to get even more speechless, unconnected, in a sense more "impersonal." In this context, Schillebeeckx's ideas on grassroots-based Church reform absolutely merits a re-reading.

Particularly for young theologians, an inquisitive, discriminating review of his theological work can turn into an encouraging prospect of a liberated freedom within faith of which Paul says in Corinthians (1 Cor

3:21–23): "For all things are yours; Whether Paul, or Apollos, or Cephas, [...] all are yours; And ye are Christ's; and Christ is God's."

Translation from German: *Rebecca Pohl*

Robert J. Schreiter

INDICATORS OF THE FUTURE OF THEOLOGY IN THE WORKS OF EDWARD SCHILLEBEECKX

1. Introduction

Since his death in December of 2009, the impact of the work of Edward Schillebeeckx on the future of theology has been a contested area. An obituary reflection in the Vatican's *L'Osservatore Romano* spoke of a "sunset" of his work and influence.[1] The author, an auxiliary bishop who had written his dissertation on Schillebeeckx some thirty years ago, tied Schillebeeckx to Eric Hobsbawm's concept of the "short" twentieth century – a century that lasted from the outbreak of war in Europe in 1914 to the collapse of the Soviet Union in 1991[2] – and concluded that Schillebeeckx's thought had now disappeared below the horizon, much as had the defining events of the twentieth century.

In the Netherlands and elsewhere, voices were raised to note the continuing importance of his work for theology in the twenty-first century.[3] Already in 2008, a symposium had been held in Leuven, consisting principally of younger scholars who had written doctoral dissertations on Schillebeeckx, that sought to explore Schillebeeckx's theological signific-

---

[1] F. Brambilla, "In morte di Edward Schillebeeckx: Una teologia tramontata con il 'secolo breve'", in: *L'Osservatore Romano*, 29 dic. 2009.

[2] E. Hobsbawm, *The Age of Extremes: The History of the World, 1914–1991*, New York: Pantheon Books, 1995.

[3] St. van Erp (Ed.), *Trouw aan Gods toekomst. De blijvende betekenis van Edward Schillebeeckx*, Amsterdam: Boom, 2010. This also appeared as a special issue of *Tijdschrift voor Theologie* in the first issue for 2010. In March, 2010, a symposium was held in Chicago that examined the continuing impact of his work. The papers from this event (by R. Schreiter, E. Chia, and A. Sison) may be found on the Schillebeeckx Foundation website at: ru.nl/Schillebeeckx.

ance for contemporary theology.[4] And this symposium is examining the same topic as well.

Why the contestation of the continuing relevance of Schillebeeckx for theology? To be sure, because of the advanced age to which he lived, he was not theologically active in publishing for the last ten or so years of his life. In addition, his books are now out of print in the major European languages, which could indicate that he is no longer being read. Then, too, he made a point frequently, especially in his later years, that he did not intend to found a "school" that would serve to perpetuate his theological insights and ideas. Rather, he exhorted younger scholars to take up the burning issues of their times much as he had tried to do in his own. In a letter addressed to the participants in the 2008 symposium in Leuven, he wrote: "I thank you all for your willingness to take my thought as the starting point for doing theology for the 21st century – but only as a starting point." Certainly in the second half of his career (but also notably already from his earliest writings), Schillebeeckx was engaged with the issues of his day. For that reason, he has been called a "pastoral" theologian – one who always wanted his theology to make a difference for contemporary men and women – even though his style of writing would have precluded non-scholars from immersing themselves in his thought. While such concern for current issues has great pastoral value, one might query whether this will make a theologian's contribution lasting beyond its contemporary exposition. As an old proverb puts it: he who takes opportunity as a bride may find himself a widower tomorrow.

Yet there is also considerable evidence that Schillebeeckx's thought and influence will continue well into the twenty-first century. Most notable is the steady and continuing flow of doctoral dissertations on his theology, especially from Rome (where international students are writing on him) and in North America. To this point, more than eighty such dissertations have appeared, and there are more still coming.[5] No doubt too, the eleven-volume edition of Schillebeeckx's major works announced by the Edward Schillebeeckx Foundation in 2009 will only spur more young scholars to take up his work again.

Secondly, a number of authors have noted that some of the methods that Schillebeeckx introduced into Catholic theology have now become

---

[4] L. Boeve / St. van Erp / F. Depoortere (Eds.), Edward Schillebeeckx and Contemporary Theology, London: T. & T. Clark, 2010.
[5] R. Schreiter, "De invloed van Edward Schillebeeckx – Dissertaties over zijn werk", in: *Tijdschrift voor Theologie* 50 (2010), 153–165.

so widely used that we tend to forget how novel and even revolutionary these were at the time. His wide-ranging use of different philosophical approaches, his introduction of contemporary hermeneutics into Catholic theology, his early use of correlation theory to bring together faith and culture (although he moved beyond this in his later work), his recasting of how christology should be approached by a systematic theologian, and his use of critical social theory associated with the Frankfurt School are all examples of this. He opened up Catholic theology to new methods in ways that other theologians have not done. In so doing, he set his stamp on a way of doing theology that continues to work itself out in many authors today.

So how would one best address this question of Edward Schillebeeckx's relevance to theology in the coming years, weighing both the negative and the positive aspects of the evidence? I have chosen to approach this in three moves. In a first part, I would like to examine the assertion of Schillebeeckx being very much a theologian of the twentieth century, and what that portends for the immediate future. There are already marked discontinuities between the twentieth and the twenty-first century, but there are also continuities. Both the discontinuities and the continuities need to be noted if one is to make a fair assessment of Schillebeeckx's contribution to both.

In a second part, I want to look briefly at his methods for doing theology and what that might tell us about how his thought and influence will endure into the twenty-first century. Are these methods still relevant to the pursuit of theology, or do they represent an important, but short-lived, experiment that is now superseded or marked by a return to other, earlier methods? We cannot answer such a question definitively for our current century, since we are barely into its second decade. But trying to address it in some way, however briefly, may help us gauge where theology finds itself at this point in time.

And in a third part, I would like to take up four issues (or challenges or questions) that theology faces at the current time. These four points by no means constitute an exhaustive list; nor, some might argue, even the most central ones facing theology today. But I doubt that few would argue that they need not be addressed in some measure. However one may think about them, they at least illustrate how Schillebeeckx's own theology might be engaged with issues about which he did not, in his own lifetime, take up in the forms in which we now face them.

2. Edward Schillebeeckx: A Theologian of the Twentieth Century?

It was noted at the beginning of this presentation that an obituary linked the theology of Edward Schillebeeckx closely to the "short" twentieth century. The implication was that, just as that short century had now ended, so too had Schillebeeckx's theological project disappeared in its wake. In line with a certain restorationist style of thinking that is now in vogue in some circles, the theology that had characterized that short century was an interruption of or deviation from the larger trajectory of theology, and now it had mercifully passed, so that we could return to theology as it should be undertaken.

This contentious – or even contemptuous – way of reading the twentieth century and its theology seeks to elevate theology from its being situated in a given time and place, a finite undertaking by equally finite men and women who are trying to grasp the infinite. I would like to undertake a brief reading of Schillebeeckx's life and thought as indeed very much intertwined with the events of the twentieth century – not so much to prove its superficiality or attention to the wrong kind of detail, but rather to show that such involvement and engagement connotes the true task of the theologian.

Hobsbawm spoke of the twentieth century as the "short century," extending only from 1914 to 1991. If one looks at the idea of "century" from the perspective of events that have had great impact on one another, and so could be drawn together to create a certain pattern of coherence, then one could argue that the twentieth century was indeed a short century. Hobsbawm contrasts this with the "long" nineteenth century, which according to him extended from the French Revolution in 1789 to the beginning of the First World War in 1914. If the French Revolution was a portent of the end of the rule monarchy and empire in Europe, than the First World War was indeed the beginning of the end of that century. In that war, three of the great monarchies of Europe were to fall, and a fourth – the British Empire – began the decline that led to its fall some forty years later. The twentieth century was an epoch beset by great ideologies that emerged in the wake of the First World War – notably in the rise of Communism in Russia and National Socialism in Germany. Although the Nazi regime came to an end in 1945, the Soviet regime continued for nearly half a century, and its end marked a profound turning point – although not the "end of history," as American Francis Fukuyama declared at that time.⁶

The beginning and ending dates of this short twentieth century certainly found echo in Schillebeeckx's own life and thought. His birth in November of 1914 was also marked by a disruption. His parents and family were evacuated from their home in Kortenberg to the relative safety of Antwerp ahead of the advancing Germany army. Although they were able to return to Kortenberg a few months later, this interruption was a portent of endings and beginnings that would mark Schillebeeckx's life and thought.

His education as a young Dominican in nearby Leuven came at a time of growing ferment in the intellectual life of the Church. He was fortunate there to be under the tutelage of fellow Dominican Dominicus De Petter (1905–1971), whose philosophy was bringing about a departure from the arid Scholasticism of the time by bringing Thomism into conversation with newer philosophical streams, especially that of phenomenology. De Petter's thought would forge the possibility of a departure from the regnant Neo-Scholasticism that marked Catholic philosophy and theology at the time. De Petter's concept of "implicit intuition" created space for non-conceptual possibilities within theology in a time that found a theology heavily rationalistic in tone. This theme that Schillebeeckx expounded upon in a 1952 essay, that marked Schillebeeckx's own maturing into a different way of doing theology.⁷ Like his Jesuit counterpart in Leuven at about the same time, Joseph Maréchal (1878–1944), who also was bringing the Thomism of the time into contact new currents in philosophy and ultimately also with that of Immanuel Kant, De Petter was laying the groundwork for a kind of Thomism that would break with the immediate past and lay the groundwork for something different. In the case of Schillebeeckx, the concern with the non-conceptual moment in the act of faith would create the space for the development of narrative as a special vehicle for theology.

If the First World War interrupted the domestic peace of the Schillebeeckx family at the time of his birth, the Second World War postponed Schillebeeckx's study of theology. The post-war Paris he entered after the War was a place of ferment as well. Phenomenological and existential

---

⁶   F. Fukuyama, The End of History and the Last Man, New York: Free Press, 1992.
⁷   E. Schillebeeckx, "Het niet-begrippelijk kenmoment in onze Godskennis volgens Thomas van Aquino", in: *Tijdschrift voor Filosofie* 14 (1952), 411–453; and later, idem, "Het niet-begrippelijk kenmoment in de geloofsdaad: probleemstelling", in: *Tijdschrift voor Theologie* 3 (1963), 167–194.

philosophy were shaping the intellectual scene in such figures as Maurice Merleau-Ponty, Jean-Paul Sartre and Albert Camus. Schillebeeckx's sojourn in Paris at Le Saulchoir put him into contact with two important streams of thinking: the *nouvelle théologie* of the *ressourcement* movement, as well as the vision of Incarnation and history of Marie-Dominique Chenu. Both of these have been well commented upon by others.[8] But the work going on at Le Saulchoir, as at its Jesuit counterpart La Fourvière in Lyons, marked a keen sense of wishing to engage the larger Christian Tradition with contemporary concerns. Suffice it to say here that both of these contributed to Schillebeeckx's ongoing preoccupation with both tradition and contemporary context, as would be evident in his retrieval of sacramental theology in the 1950s, and his quest for epistemological methods in the 1960s and 1970s. It might be added that the concern for context, of course, would be a hallmark of later twentieth-century theology.

Schillebeeckx's appointment to the Professorship of Dogma and the History of Theology at the Catholic University in Nijmegen in 1957 took him out of the relative security of the Dominican Studium in Leuven and put him on the national stage in the Netherlands. The Second Vatican Council followed shortly thereafter. The encounter there with other European theologians certainly widened his purview, and brought him into the center of the defining moment for twentieth-century Catholicism. The history of the Catholic Church in the twentieth century continues to be periodized as "before" and "after" the Council. The aftermath of the Council, in all its vicissitudes, would mark the rest of his career as a theologian – down to the obituary in *L'Osservatore Romano* already cited.

His first journey to North America in 1966 opened him to an encounter with secularization in a form not yet quite as prevalent in northwestern Europe at the time. The response to secularization and the modernity that made it possible would provide the backdrop for the rest of the theology he would write from that time onward.

The impact of twentieth-century thought upon how theology was to be undertaken showed itself particularly strongly in Schillebeeckx's theology in the years after the Council. German and French hermeneutics,

---

[8] See E. Borgman, Edward Schillebeeckx: Een theoloog in zijn geschiedenis. Deel I: Een katholieke cultuurtheologie (1914–1965), Baarn: Nelissen, 1999. On Chenu and the Saulchoir, see also J. Cooper, Humanity in the Mystery of God: The Theological Anthropology of Edward Schillebeeckx, London: Continuum and T. & T. Clark, 2009, as well as J. Mettepenningen, Nouvelle Théologie – New Theology: Inheritor of Modernism, Precursor of Vatican II, London – New York: Continuum – T. & T. Clark, 2010.

Anglo-Saxon analytic philosophy, and the Critical Social Theory of the Frankfurt School all left their epistemological mark on his work from the late 1960s onward. The profusion of methodological implications (or the *confusion* of them, as their critics would say) marked Schillebeeckx as a theologian supremely attuned to the intellectual currents of the second half of that century.

The Berlin Wall fell in 1989, marking the beginning of the end of the twentieth century, as Hobsbawm would have it. 1989 also marked the publication of Schillebeeckx's so-called third volume of his trilogy on christology, *Mensen als verhaal van God*.[9] It was in that volume that his phrase *"extra mundum nulla salus"* would first appear. An obvious play on the medieval *"extra ecclesiam nulla salus,"* it summed up in a significant way Schillebeeckx's own theological project for the twentieth century. He returned to the phrase in his letter to the 2008 Leuven symposium on the ongoing significance of his work. He noted at that time that his critics had complained that he was too focused upon the *"mundum"* at the expense of the more theological *"salus"* – so much so that he was allowing the world to set the agenda for theology, rather than seeing what salvation meant for a sinful world. He denied that such was the case. He saw them rather as mutually determining and mutually defining: one could not understand the meaning of salvation without examining the world for which God had intended it; nor could one understand the destiny of the world apart from God's plan for creation.

So was Edward Schillebeeckx a theologian of the twentieth century? He most certainly was – shaped (but not determined) by his biography and the areas of theology that he tried to engage. But was he more than that? Was he more than the product of the forces that surrounded him and that have, in the minds of some, now subsided? Yes, I believe he was more than that. Indeed, he was more than a passing chimera of a now exhausted age, precisely because he did engage his age as profoundly as he did. In a way, his theology is grounded in the theological event of the Incarnation that was so important to his teacher Chenu, and which echoes throughout his own theology, especially his anthropology and his Soteriology. It is in the Logos' taking flesh and becoming one of us that Christ's ongoing meaning for us and for the world is to be found. Only by embracing the particular may we find the genuine universal. Throughout all creation we find the traces, the *vestigia*, of Trinitarian particularity and universality revealed over and over again, as St. Augustine reminded

---

[9] Baarn: Nelissen, 1989.

us already so long ago. The heavenly Jerusalem is not intended to float above the earth, but is intended to come down to it.

The twenty-first century will no doubt be characterized at some future point as departing from its immediate predecessor in many ways. But its development cannot be understood apart from its origins. I believe that, even as the twenty-first century engages themes and challenges that seem distant or different from those of the twentieth, we can learn from the themes Schillebeeckx chose to engage, as well as the methods he utilized for that engagement. Before turning to some themes and challenges of the twenty-first century, let me first reflect on Schillebeeckx's contribution to method.

3. Theological Methods for the Twentieth Century – and the Twenty-First

It has already been noted that through the course of his theological work, Schillebeeckx engaged a host of methods, from historical methods of research through philosophical methods such as phenomenology, hermeneutics, analytic philosophy, and critical social theory. In his unpublished lectures on hermeneutics, one will find structuralist, post-structuralist, and semiotic methods as well. Here I wish to focus on three dimensions of his reflections on method that, to my mind, will continue to have relevance in the twenty-first century for theology.

The first is his use of an *inductive* approach. Theology has often been more inclined to work with a deductive approach, especially evident in more propositionally construed theology. Deduction comes, as it were, rather naturally to theology. If theology is indeed knowledge about God, who is both Creator and Revealer, then one would start with what has been revealed and deduce further knowledge of God from that. Moreover, a certain theology of creation would support a deductive approach, since the world God has created is deemed to be meaningful and logically coherent. The God-given powers of human reason would only affirm such use of deduction. When theology has been construed as something that can be reached by the disputational procedures of a *quaestio*, this would likewise appear to make deduction pre-eminently suitable for theological discourse.

No doubt the early influence of phenomenology on Schillebeeckx's philosophical development would have predisposed him to look to experience as a source for theology, as did his hearing of the lectures of Merleau-Ponty in Paris in the post-War years. His theology of "encounter" in his work on the sacraments is clearly the legacy of his engagement with phenomenology. To begin with experience as a basis for theology was hardly a foregone conclusion in early twentieth-century theology. On the Protestant side, the work of the Erlangen School and the whole of Liberal Theology as it was indebted to Schleiermacher would have raised warning signals on the Catholic horizon. Moreover, an anthropology that was haunted by human sinfulness would make experience a doubtful category for beginning theology, especially the experience of those not belonging to a spiritual elite.

Human experience as a starting point on the journey of faith is already well established in Schillebeeckx's theology by the time of the 1970s, as is evidenced especially in the second volume of his christology. That volume begins with a long reflection on human experience as it relates to God's revelation and to the development of a theology. To be sure, in looking back on that work, one might find the concept of experience presented there as somewhat undifferentiated and innocent of the effects of social location. The potential differences of experience for women and for men, in different cultural settings, and in different epochs of human history would be more quickly brought to the fore in any twenty-first century description of human experience. Yet rather than allowing these often divergent voices to cancel one another out, they might be heard together symphonically as at least articulating enduring questions if not providing absolute answers. Listening to experience is more than listening to an individual or a group; echoes of their location in culture and in society resound here as well. This is humanity in all its concreteness, something that Catholic theology affirms again and again in the discourse of the Incarnation. Christ has become one of us, not as a universal archetype, but as one of us in all our specificity and limitations.

Certainly one of the dividing elements in theology and in the Church itself today can be found in the differing experiences that people are articulating. Those experiences recount not only differing worldviews, but also the play of power and the anguish of human suffering. Schillebeeckx's own concern about the nature of human suffering – a feature that has been very attractive to students who are coming from backgrounds of poverty and oppression – is one of the dimensions of his theology that has been distilled from his attention to human experiences.

A second feature of Schillebeeckx's concern for method that will continue to have relevance for theology is one closely related to experience; namely, the primacy he gives to narrative. The word "narrative" (or *verhaal*) occurs in two of the three titles of his Jesus-books – as a subtitle to the first volume ("*het verhaal van een levende*"), and in the principal title of the third volume ("*Mensen als verhaal van God*"). Schillebeeckx's interest in narrative would appear to be a direct result of his focus upon human experience, since human experience is most often related in narrative. Indeed, in oral cultures, narratives have precedence over more analytic accounts, and continue to prevail even in predominantly literature cultures in art and literature.

Schillebeeckx did not develop any elaborated account of his predilection for narrative in his hermeneutical writings or lectures as far as I know. It appears to have been more of an instinctive, intuitive response.[10] It appears to spring rather as a natural consequence of his interest in human experience and his commitment to uncovering histories. The fact that narrative figures so strongly in the Bible and especially in the Gospels would only seem to corroborate his intuition.

Of course, a concern for narrative did not lead Schillebeeckx to abandon more analytic modes of thinking; far from it. Yet he clearly saw the limits of the conceptual, something that De Petter's work had already intimated in the 1930s, for conveying the experience of God that human beings could have.

If anything, the enduring importance of narrative as a vehicle of human communication is even more evident in the twenty-first century than it was in the twentieth. The role of narrative in histories of the Holocaust, the power of narrative testimony in Truth and Reconciliation Commissions that have been carried out as a means of national reconstruction after conflict, and the narration of significant national and international figures all point to narrative's enduring significance – not just in society as a whole, but in theology in particular.

It was Schillebeeckx's capacity to hold together the significance of both narrative and analytic thought that leads to the third characteristic of his methodology that I would like to hold up. His willingness to engage both the past and the present critically – no matter where that critical

---

[10] I remember a conversation we had around 1974 when he asked me to supply him with some bibliographical references about how theologians in the United States were using narrative. He clearly grasped the significance of narrative, but was still looking for the theoretical underpinnings of it.

quest might lead him – that made him such an imposing figure for those seeking new insights, and such a threat to those who wanted to maintain relationships of power as they still stood. His investigations by the Congregation of the Doctrine of the Faith often turned on his use of history and critical analysis to lay bare the sometimes ideological construals of doctrine or practices that were by no means as eternal and unchanging as they were being presented. Schillebeeckx was fearless in his commitments to truth and seeking out the truth. He had a confidence in the working of God's grace in creation that meant the faith and the Church need not fear what might be revealed by critical and careful investigation. Triumphalist or obscurantist readings found no weight with him. Surely this is a methodological insight we will continue to need in this century.

4. Four Areas of Challenge for Theology Today

Jennifer Cooper pointed out in her recent dissertation how much Schillebeeckx was a pastoral theologian.[11] By that is meant how concerned for and engaged in the issues pressing upon believers today he was throughout his life: from a revitalized approach to the sacraments, through human and doctrinal issues such as marriage, the Eucharist, the figure of Christ, ministry, and even ecology (at the end of his life). Were he still with us, what issues would he be addressing? In the brief compass of this presentation, it would be impossible to draw up a taxative list. Rather, I would like to focus on four of these issues in the final part of this presentation. These four are chosen because they represent widespread concerns at this point in time and all, I believe, could be illuminated by Schillebeeckx's own work. Given the limitations of space, they can only be treated briefly. They are: (1) the resurgence of religion in the world; (2) what is coming after postmodernity; (3) the enduring importance of addressing suffering; and (4) concern for the environment and care of the earth. Of these, the first two are closely related. The third and fourth are challenges that Schillebeeckx did address in his published works, yet continue to take on new forms for us.

---

[11] J. Cooper, Humanity in the Mystery of God, op. cit.

4.1. The Resurgence of Religion

God is Back is the provocative title of a book published by two editors of the British journal *The Economist* in 2009.[12] The title of the book comes from the fact that the same journal, in a 2001 editorial, had declared that God was dead. In the book, the authors recant, as it were, (one is a Roman Catholic, the other an atheist), because they now see evidence of a vibrant belief in God, even in highly secular societies, and in spite of the New Atheism being debated in Europe and North America. Their vision is professedly not a naïve one; they realize that this revival of religion has also given voice in violence in many parts of the world, and is not always a benevolent presence. They acknowledge too that secularization has not withered or gone away; indeed, it is still vigorous in Europe, North America, and Australia.

By saying that "God is back" the authors are catching up to something that sociologists have been noticing since the early 1990s; namely, a profound questioning of the secularization hypothesis. That hypothesis once suggested that as countries modernized, they would become increasingly secular. Religion would retreat from the public sphere to the private realm, and then would gradually disappear altogether. Northern Europe was seen as the paradigm and vanguard of this movement, which the rest of the world would then follow in turn.

Today, Europe is now seen by those same sociologists as more the exception than the rule. Ever since Max Weber posited the secularization hypothesis more than a century ago, religion has managed time and again to find a way back. Indeed, the authors from *The Economist* admit that the world in its entirety is probably more overtly religious in its practices and beliefs than it was twenty years ago. Again, this religious resurgence is not an unalloyed good. But its vitality in its myriad forms is something that cannot be discounted or overlooked.

Nor is secularization disappearing in Europe and North America; if anything, it appears to be moving forward inexorably. But in those places new models are being put forward to understand the societies on those two continents. In Europe, the German philosopher Jürgen Habermas – himself an agnostic – stunned many with his affirmation in 2001 that Europe could not be understood apart from its religious roots. He has since

---

[12] J. Micklethwait / A. Wooldridge, God is Back: How the Global Revival of Faith is Changing the World, London and New York: Penguin, 2009.

suggested that Europe is now becoming a "post-secular" society.[13] By that he means that secularization has not disappeared, but that secularity and religion now are living side by side. This is not just the case with the immigrants arriving in Europe (some of whom themselves become more secular in succeeding generations), but Europeans themselves are showing more openness to religious impulses than previously thought. Secularity can therefore no longer be considered utterly dominant and unilaterally governing the rules of public discourse, but must share the public podium with religion.

The Canadian (and Catholic) philosopher Charles Taylor has put forward a somewhat similar point, albeit in a different way. In his book, *A Secular Age*[14] he presents a narrative of the rise of secularization in the West, and sees three realities living side by side today; namely, secularity, religion, and the remnants of European Romanticism, embodied in nineteenth century utopian ideologies and Nietzschean nihilism. By ideologies, he means socialism, communism, and nationalism.

Schillebeeckx was preoccupied with the impact of secularization on Christian thought from the latter 1960s onward, especially as it became an increasingly defining factor in the Low Countries. Students of Schillebeeckx's thought, especially in Leuven, have continued to trace these features in his work.

Can Schillebeeckx's work offer some way forward in seeing this phenomenon of resurgence of religion in the wider world in general, and in the realigned of secular and religious forces in Europe in particular? Taking a cue from Charles Taylor's narrative of the rise of secularity in the West, with a consequent move from what he calls the "porous self" (i.e., a self and a society open to and in communication with unseen or spiritual forces surrounding them in their day-to-day world) to the "bounded self" (i.e., a secularity that denies or ignores such outside intrusions on the empirical reality in which one lives), I think a revisiting of Schillebeeckx's understanding of sacrament might be helpful here. Sacraments mediate seen and unseen realities. The considerable debate around the relationship of nature and grace that was so prominent in European theology in the 1930s and 1940s provides something of a framework into rethinking a sacramental imagination in a post-secular world. Just as de Lubac and others came to see grace not as something extrinsic to creation,

---

[13] See his collection of essays, Zwischen Primitivismus und Naturalismus, Frankfurt/M.: Suhrkamp, 2005.
[14] Cambridge, MA: Belknap Press of Harvard University Press, 2007.

but given already with creation, so too the interpenetration of grace and creation – a feature of Schillebeeckx's theology in the 1950s and 1960s – might be revisited today to rethink how religion and secularity might more fruitfully relate to each other. This would take Schillebeeckx's frequent allusion to the secular reality in which we live beyond affirming the positive aspects of it (regarding emancipation and affirmation of the human in and of itself) to a more intricate pattern of interaction.

Schillebeeckx did of course consider revisiting the theme of sacraments in the 1990s. But what he seemed especially concerned about was incorporating the results of interdisciplinary research into ritual and performances of celebration. I think that there is a profitable angle to looking once again at the mediating character of sacraments as a way of understanding the resurgence of religion in the world.

4.2. What Comes after Postmodernity?

A second field of endeavor closely related to the religion and secularity discussion now going on is the end of postmodernity. "Postmodernity" was something widely discussed in highly modern societies in the 1980s and 1990s, although the term came to have a range of different meanings. The "postmodern" could mean something coming after modernity; it could mean the final stages of the modernist project that still needed to be achieved (as it does to Habermas); or it could mean the collapse of modernity from its internal contradictions and a revitalization of the premodern (as it does to the proponents of Radical Orthodoxy in the English-speaking world).

Here I would like to pursue postmodernity in the sense accorded it by Jean-Francois Lyotard in his 1979 study for the Province of Quebec in Canada.[15] The postmodern was characterized by a fragmentation of previous coherences, the breakdown of a shared vision of society, a pluralism that could not be reduced to any kind of unity, and a general instability kept in motion by late capitalism or – in its subsequent manifestation – by globalization. In Lyotard's own characterization, this fragmentation and pluralization was marked by the death of any master narrative (*grand récit*) holding a society together.

While this could be a fairly accurate picture of certain strata of highly modern societies, especially in their middle and upper classes, the strains of such increasing pluralization have become increasingly evident.

---

[15] La condition postmoderne. Rapport sur le savoir, Paris: Éditions de Minuit, 1979.

Worldwide migration has been creating multicultural societies in those same postmodern settings that the inherited postmodern models of multiculturalism cannot sustain. While reaction to this fragmentation and pluralization has found voice from the political right (in figures such as Thilo Sarrazin in Germany and Geert Wilders in the Netherlands), there is a growing sense that there may be limits to how much plurality a society can sustain.[16]

Alongside talk of a post-secular society, there is talk of a "Second Modernity" by sociologists such as Ulrich Beck.[17] Among the youngest generation coming of age, in at least some parts of the highly modern world, a "searching for the whole" has come much more into evidence. This takes the complexity and plurality of the contemporary world seriously, yet seeks out patterns of coherence and direction within them. Globalization has only made this quest more urgent: the speed of communication and how it has compressed time and space, as well as the pluralization of our cities, call out for a vantage point from which to navigate this astounding variegation.

Here some return to some measure of a master narrative seems imperative. (Ironically, the statement "There is no master narrative" carries within itself a contradiction, just as does "absolute relativism") Schillebeeckx's concern for narrative might be a way of probing the nonconceptual qualities of the current situation – including what has been called the "geopolitics of emotion"[18] – that are shaping public discourse today.

4.3. *The Enduring Importance of Addressing Suffering*

The theme that has captured the most attention among the youngest generation of scholar researching Schillebeeckx's work has been that of suffering. No fewer than six doctoral dissertations have been published in the last ten years devoted to one or other aspect of this topic.[19] The geo-

---

[16] P. Berger explored this already in the 1990s in his book: Die Grenzen der Gemeinschaft, Gütersloh: Bertelsmann Stiftung, 1998.

[17] The September 2010 issue of *The British Journal of Sociology* is devoted to this topic once again.

[18] D. Moisi, La géopolitique de l'emotion, Paris: Flammarion, 2009.

[19] K. McManus, The Place and Meaning of Suffering in the Theology of Edward Schillebeeckx (Toronto 1999); E. Tillar, Suffering for Others in the Thought of Edward Schillebeeckx (Fordham 1999); D. Simon, Provisional Liberation, Fragments of Salvation: The Practical Critical Soteriology of Suffering of Edward Schillebeeckx (Ottawa 2001); A. Rego, Suffering and Salvation: The Salvific Meaning of Suffering in the Later Theology of Edward Schillebeeckx (Melbourne 2001); A. Sison, Political Holiness in Third Cinema: The Crystallization

graphic provenance of the six authors is also significant: two from Asia (the Philippines and Malaysia), two from the United States, and one each from Canada and Australia.

As has already been noted, suffering has been a theme central to Schillebeeckx's writing since the second volume of the christology trilogy. The contrast experience produced in suffering expresses itself in protest: this is something that should not be! Schillebeeckx in no way glorifies suffering or sees Christ's suffering as an appeasement of divine wrath or a necessary expiation. Rather it is Christ's solidarity with suffering humanity and a cry for liberation. Because his treatment of the "ecumene of suffering" has touched such a wide and diverse audience, it is likely to be an enduring contribution of Schillebeeckx's thinking well into the twenty-first century.

4.4. Concern for the Environment and Care of the Earth

The dangers of environmental degradation have been signaled already for half a century, arguably since the appearance of Rachel Carson's *Silent Spring*.[20] While much of the theological writing remains in a hortatory model of "shoulds" and "should nots" it is increasingly taking on a more profound form. Schillebeeckx addressed ecological issues directly already in the 1990s.[21]

What may be of more enduring significance for theological reflection on the environment and care for the earth was the discovering of the centrality of theme of creation for his theology, articulated first by Philip Kennedy in his 1993 Fribourg dissertation, *Deus humanissimus* and retrieved again in Jennifer Cooper's theological anthropological investigation of Schillebeeckx in his early theology. In both Kennedy's and Cooper's work, the authors made note of the fact that Schillebeeckx never produced a full treatise on creation or on theological anthropology. But both authors were able to reconstruct from his lecture notes and his writings the framework for a fuller articulation of those themes. This is suggestive of how Schillebeeckx's work is being seen by younger scholars

---

of Edward Schillebeeckx's Eschatological Perspective in Kidlat Tahimik's "Perfumed Nightmare" (Nijmegen 2004); and M. Teng, Be Merciful: The Tragedy and Productive Power of the Suffering *humanum* in E. Schillebeeckx and the *Analects* of Confucius (Alphonsiana 2009).

[20] New York: Houghton and Mifflin, 1962.
[21] E. Schillebeeckx, "Plezier en woede beleven aan de schepping", in: *Tijdschrift voor Theologie* 33 (1993), 325–346.

and its theological potential for the coming years. The sheer volume of his writing, and his commitment to central themes of the Christian mystery, are likely to continue to yield new insights for theology in the years to come. Given the continued interest in emerging scholars in his work, there is a great likelihood that this theologian of the twentieth century will continue to speak to us well into the twenty-first.

* * *

Zusammenfassung des Beitrags von Robert J. Schreiter

In einem Nachruf auf Edward Schillebeeckx, der im *L'Osservatore Romano* erschien, wurde die Vermutung geäußert, dass die Bedeutung Schillebeeckx' für die Theologie gleichzeitig mit dem „kurzen" zwanzigsten Jahrhundert, wie Eric Hobsbawm es bezeichnet hatte, verschwunden ist. Schillebeeckx selbst betonte ja regelmäßig, dass er keine Schule gründen, sondern die brennenden theologischen und pastoralen Fragen seiner Zeit angehen wolle. Dieser Beitrag versucht deswegen Indikatoren dafür auszumachen, wie es Schillebeeckx' Œuvre im 21. Jahrhundert ergehen könnte.

Der erste Teil beschäftigt sich mit der Frage, wie Ereignisse der europäischen Geschichte mit Schillebeeckx' Leben verknüpft sind, beginnend mit seiner Geburt im ersten Jahr von Hobsbawms „kurzem Jahrhundert" (1914). Den Grundstein während seiner theologischen Ausbildung legten das „*ressourcement*" (Auseinandersetzung mit den Originalquellen der Theologie) und die „*nouvelle théologie*". Das Zweite Vatikanische Konzil und dessen Nachwirkungen im 20. Jahrhundert formten sein Denken in einer unverwechselbaren Weise. Der hieraus zu ziehende Schluss lautet, dass Schillebeeckx ganz und gar ein Theologe des 20. Jahrhunderts war. Aber genau diese Art von Involviertheit sollte die Arbeit eines Theologen ausmachen.

Der zweite Teil widmet sich der bleibenden Bedeutung einiger Elemente der theologischen Methodologie, die Schillebeeckx zum theologischen Diskurs beigesteuert hat und die das 21. Jahrhundert weiterhin prägen werden. Drei werden genauer untersucht: seine Betonung der menschlichen Erfahrung, die Wichtigkeit von Narrativität und seine Aufmerksamkeit für die Verbindung von narrativem und kritischem Denken. Der abschließende Teil greift vier Gebiete auf, die die Theologie des 21. Jahrhunderts momentan kennzeichnen: das Wiederaufleben der Religion, die Frage danach, was auf die Postmoderne folgt, der bleibende Kampf um das Verständnis von Leid und die Sorge für die Umwelt. Hierzu werden Elemente aus Schillebeeckx' Denken vorgeschlagen, die die jeweiligen Felder näher beleuchten können. Die Schlussfolgerung besteht darin, dass sein Vermächtnis ohne Zweifel auch für die Theologie des 21. Jahrhunderts von Bedeutung bleibt.

Übersetzung aus dem Englischen: *Bernhard Kohl*

Alessandro Cortesi

DAS HEIL DER MENSCHHEIT IN EINER WELT DER VIELEN RELIGIONEN

Anregungen aus dem Werk von Edward Schillebeeckx

Mit diesen Ausführungen möchte ich einige Linien des Denkens von Edward Schillebeeckx nachzeichnen, ausgehend von seinem Buch *Menschen. Die Geschichte von Gott*[1], das einen Dreh- und Angelpunkt seines theologischen Denkens und, wie mir scheint, einen überaus anregenden Beitrag zu den theologischen Fragen darstellt, welche die heutige Debatte aufwirft.

In diesem Werk werden die Begriffe „Heil", „Menschheit", „Geschichte", „Identität des Christentums" und „Religionen" in ihrem wechselseitigen Bezug im Rahmen eines faszinierenden Vorschlags dekliniert, der einiges zur Erneuerung des *intellectus fidei*, aber auch der kirchlichen Praxis beizutragen hat.

Im Vorwort des Bandes bietet Schillebeeckx in wenigen Zeilen eine ernüchterte Analyse der kirchlichen Geschehnisse in den letzten zwanzig Jahren seit dem II. Vaticanum, gleichzeitig aber nimmt er diese missliche Erfahrung im heutigen Kontext zum Anlass, seine Bemühung um kritische Glaubenseinsicht noch einmal darzustellen. Dazu muss er wieder zum Kern des Evangeliums und des christlichen Glaubens vorstoßen und auf das schauen, was jenseits der vorwiegend innerkirchlichen Fragen authentisch und einzigartig ist.

So schreibt er: „[...] seit den 70–80er Jahren hat sich vor allem in der römisch-katholischen Kirche vieles verändert. Die Freude, zu dieser Kirche zu gehören, die während des Zweiten Vatikanischen Konzils und in

---

[1] E. Schillebeeckx, Menschen. Die Geschichte von Gott. Aus dem Niederländischen von H. Zulauf, Freiburg/Br. 1990.

den ersten Jahren danach stark zunahm, wurde in den letzten Jahren auf eine harte Probe gestellt. Diese Situation zwang mich nach langen Überlegungen, meinen ursprünglichen Plan für dieses Buch ziemlich gründlich zu ändern. Ich kam zu der Einsicht, dass es besser sei, nach dem Kern des Evangeliums und der christlichen Religion zu suchen, nach dem Eigentlichen und Einzigartigen derselben, als mich in einer Periode kirchlicher Polarisierung unmittelbar mit innerkirchlichen, im Grunde zweitrangigen Problemen hinsichtlich des christlichen Glaubensinhalts und der Frage, welche Aufgaben die Christen in dieser Welt haben, zu beschäftigen. Denn ist es nicht die christliche Kernbotschaft, an der auch jede Ekklesiologie gemessen werden kann und muss? [...] Gerade das, was im Zweiten Vaticanum ‚neu' gegenüber dem nachtridentinischen Kirchenverständnis und der entsprechenden Ekklesiologie war, hat in den 70er und 80er Jahren von Seiten der Amtskirche keine konsequenten institutionellen Strukturen erhalten."[2]

Aus dieser Passage spricht eine tiefe Enttäuschung, was die Träume vieler Leute in den 1960er und 1970er Jahren angeht. Es wurden keine institutionellen Maßnahmen ergriffen, um jene christliche Freiheit zu verwirklichen, die das Konzil so hoch geschätzt hatte, ja, der Konzilsgeist selbst ist ausgelöscht worden. Und so haben nun, wie Schillebeeckx bekümmert feststellt, „aus verschiedenen (oft kirchenpolitischen) Interessen kirchliche Hierarchen eine unkontrollierte Macht über unmündig gemachte Menschen Gottes, ‚Gottes Volk auf dem Weg'"[3].

Auch wenn diese Bewertung ein starkes Gefühl der Enttäuschung in Bezug auf die in der Konzilszeit geweckten Hoffnungen erkennen lässt, sieht Schillebeeckx dennoch einen Horizont der Hoffnung. Diese seine Perspektive resultiert aus einer Haltung tiefen Glaubens an den Gott der Offenbarung, der sein Heil in der Geschichte mitteilt. Schillebeeckx entdeckt insbesondere, wie dringlich es ist, den Kern des Evangeliums tiefer zu bedenken, das zu erfassen, was die Einzigartigkeit des christlichen Glaubens ausmacht, nämlich die Wahrnehmung, dass „die Menschen die Worte sind, deren Gott sich bedient, um seine Geschichte zu erzählen". In einem Kontext stößt er auf eine verborgen gegenwärtige evangelische Blüte, die ihn ermutigt zu einer Untersuchung über eine „Kirche von mit Gott verbundenen Menschen, die kritisch und solidarisch anwesend ist bei Menschen ‚in der Welt', bei ihren kleinen und großen Problemen und

[2] Ebd., 7f.
[3] Ebd., 8.

ihrer ‚profanen', echt-menschlichen und un-menschlichen Geschichte"[4] – in deutlichem Kontrast zu einer supranaturalistischen Sicht und einer Kirche, die der Welt entrückt ist.

Die Frage nach dem Heil

Wir haben es also mit einer Reformulierung des Ansatzes in der theologischen Frage des Heils, der für Schillebeeckx' gesamte Forschung zentralen Frage, zu tun.

Im ersten Kapitel seines Buches entwickelt der Autor seine Darlegung ausgehend von der Analyse der radikalen Kontrasterfahrung in der menschlichen Geschichte. Die negativen Erfahrungen und – gegen sie und zugleich mit ihnen – die Erfahrungen des Widerstands gegen die Ungerechtigkeit, die darauf ausgerichtet sind, eine menschlichere Welt zu schaffen, bilden den Ort einer Begegnung und einer tiefen Solidarität im gemeinsamen Lebenseinsatz von Männern und Frauen.

Das Heil, das von Gott kommt, ereignet sich nicht nur in einigen wenigen, von den Religionen gebildeten Räumen, vielmehr ist die menschliche Erfahrung an sich der Ort, an dem durch das Wirken Gottes Heilsgeschichte geschieht, und die Geschichte ist der Ort, an dem Gott seine Geschöpfe schafft und befreit.[5]

Schillebeeckx beseitigt die Identifikation des Heils mit der Religion, auch wenn er erklärt, die Religionen seien Orte, an denen ein Bewusstsein vom Heilshandeln Gottes bestehe. Die Religionen werden nach einer Seite hin relativiert: Sie sind nicht identisch mit dem geschenkten Heil. Andererseits haben sie eine sakramentale Dimension: Ihre konstitutive Dimension besteht im Zeichen-Sein. Sie schließen eine Valenz der Erinnerung an den universalen Heilswillen ein: „Die Kirchen leben aus dem Heil, das Gott in der Welt vollbringt."[6]

Für den gläubigen Christen hat die Erfahrung des Widerstands gegen alles, was sich als unmenschlich erweist, ihr Fundament in Jesus, der als

---

[4] Ebd., 9.
[5] Ebd., 34: „Man kann Heil-von-Gott-her [...] nicht auf die besonderen Stätten des Heils, die wir *Religionen* nennen, reduzieren. Heilsgeschichte lässt sich nicht auf die Geschichte der Religionen oder auf die Geschichte des Judentums und des Christentums reduzieren. Denn die gesamte Profangeschichte steht selbst schon unter der Leitung des befreienden Gottes der Schöpfung. Der erste Ort, an dem Heil oder Unheil vollbracht wird, ist daher unsere sogenannte ‚Profangeschichte', deren befreiender Schöpfer Gott ist, der aber auch [der Richter] über die von Menschen bewirkte Unheilsgeschichte ist."
[6] Ebd., 37.

Christus und Gottes Sohn, als menschliches Angesicht einer erhofften und nahe gekommenen Transzendenz, bezeugt wird. Dies dürfte eine wichtige Passage von Schillebeeckx' Vorschlag sein: Er unterstreicht, dass es für das Leben des Glaubenden von zentraler Bedeutung ist, Jesus in seiner geschichtlichen Erfahrung zu sehen und zu würdigen. Sein Versuch, das Proprium des Evangeliums in der heutigen Zeit zu identifizieren, konzentriert sich in einer christologischen Perspektive, die die Geschichte Jesu von Nazareth ganz ernst nimmt.

Derart tritt Schillebeeckx für die Überwindung des Bruchs ein, den viele Christen zwischen dem christlichen Glauben als Gehorsam gegen die Offenbarung Gottes einerseits und der im Raum des Menschlichen gelebten Erfahrung andererseits erblicken. Im Verhältnis zwischen den beiden Sphären herrscht weder Trennung noch Unabhängigkeit. Gestützt auf die Analyse der Struktur der Erfahrung weist der Autor auf, dass die religiösen Erfahrungen nicht neben oder jenseits, sondern in, mit und unter persönlichen menschlichen Erfahrungen gemacht werden, bei denen die religiöse Tradition eine Hilfe ist und eine Stütze der Interpretation bildet.

Dieser Ausgangspunkt, der den Glauben als Antwort auf das Offenbarungsereignis sieht, das uns in der Erfahrung des Menschlichen einholt, ist wichtig, wenn man das Spezifische der christlichen Erfahrung erfassen will: „In dieser Hinsicht liegt das Wesentliche der christlichen Offenbarung darin, dass die Jünger Jesu aus einem erfahrenen Umgang mit ihm behaupten, dass in diesem Menschen, in seinem Leben und seiner Botschaft, in seinem Handeln und in der Art seines Sterbens, in seiner ganze Person als Mensch, Gottes Absichten mit der Menschheit – und darin der ‚eigene Charakter' Gottes – in höchstem Maße zur Offenbarung, zum menschlichen Bewusstsein gekommen sind: Gemäß dieser Glaubenserfahrung ist Jesus der Ort, an dem Gott auf entscheidende Weise sich selbst als Heil von und für Menschen geoffenbart hat."[7]

Die Offenbarung enthält eine Dimension der Unsagbarkeit, andererseits wird sie ja stets in unserer Geschichte ergriffen und ist insofern beschreibbar. In diesem Sinn weist Schillebeeckx auf, dass es keine Offenbarung ohne Glauben geben kann.

Nicht nur die Erfahrungen von Sinn, sondern auch die Erfahrungen von Sinnlosigkeit, Ungerechtigkeit und ungerechtem Leid verlangen eine Bekehrung als Metanoia, als neue Weise des Verstehens, Handelns und Seins.

---

[7] Ebd. 50f.

Aus einer solchen Position ergibt sich eine bestimmte Art und Weise, den Kern der christlichen Identität zu verstehen: nicht als eine homogene Identität, welche die Nichtchristen ausschließt, diffamiert und diskriminiert. Vielmehr vollzieht sich in dem nie abgeschlossenen Interpretationsprozess der Relektüre der Bibel und der Glaubenstradition in immer neuen, unterschiedlichen Situationen die schöpferische Weitergabe dessen, was einer einzigen, in unterschiedlichen kulturellen Kontexten gelebten Glaubenstradition gemeinsam ist.

In diesem Sinne bezieht Schillebeeckx Stellung fern von der Position des Konzils von Florenz, das erklärte, in Christus sei der einzige Zugang zu Gott gegeben, und zwar in einem ausschließlichen und andere Glaubenspositionen ausschließenden Sinn. „Wir müssen auch heute, ohne die Konsequenzen und die Implikationen des Konzils von Florenz, nachweisen können, [...] warum wir von Herzen Christen sind und bleiben, ohne Nichtchristen zu verketzern oder zu diskriminieren; schließlich nachweisen, was wir dann, in nüchterner Demut und im theologischen Wahrheitszeugnis, mit Sendung oder Mission anfangen sollen."[8]

Komprimiert zeigt sich hier, dass Schillebeeckx in seinem Versuch, den Kern des Evangeliums zu identifizieren, die Auffassung vertritt, zentral in der christlich-religiösen Erfahrung sei die Wahrnehmung, dass Heil das Handeln Gottes ist, das nicht außerhalb, sondern innerhalb der menschlichen Erfahrung erlebt wird, und dass der Glaube das Einschwingen in eine Interpretationstradition ist, die die Heilserfahrung als Wirken Gottes auslegt. In dieser Perspektive ist die Menschheit die Geschichte von Gott.

Die geschichtliche Einzigartigkeit Jesu als Grundlage für eine universalistische Offenheit

Jesus hat in seinem geschichtlichen Handeln und in seiner Lehre eine Humanisierung angesagt und betrieben, die ‚Evangelium' über ihn selbst und über Gott und dessen Leidenschaft für die Menschheit ist. Dies ist im Leben Jesu und im Bezug auf seine Auferstehung von zentraler Wichtigkeit. Diese beschränkt sich nicht auf die Dimension seines Leidens und Todes, sondern begreift auch das Leben ein. Ein Blick in das Neue Testament zeigt die vier Evangelien neben den Briefen des Paulus. Während für Paulus das Bekenntnis von Tod und Auferstehung im Zentrum steht,

---

[8] Ebd., 70.

legen die Evangelien den Akzent auf den prophetischen Inhalt des öffentlichen Lebens Jesu.[9] Die Auferstehung ist Vollendung und Bestätigung von Seiten des Vaters dafür, dass die Lebenspraxis Jesu die Auferstehung bereits vorweggenommen hat. Das veranlasst uns dazu, im menschlichen Handeln Jesu das Geschehen einer Offenbarung Gottes zu erblicken, der sich mit dem Antlitz eines Gottes-für-die-Menschheit zeigt; in diesem Sinne unternimmt Jesus eine Neudefinition sowohl des Antlitzes Gottes als auch des Antlitzes des Menschen.

Die Tatsache, dass Jesus in seinem irdischen Leben die Zeichen für das Gottesreich als Heil für alle setzt (zum Beispiel die Seligpreisungen als Botschaft für den, der in Armut, Kummer und Unterdrückung lebt), repräsentiert die Konkretisierung des Glaubens an den Gott, der im Schöpfungsakt sein Vertrauen in die Menschheit gesetzt hat. Die Hinwendung zu Christus, die die Kirche vollzieht, indem sie nach der Auferstehung Christus in das Zentrum ihrer Botschaft stellt, ist keine Horizontverschiebung, sondern die Erkenntnis, dass sich gerade im historischen Geschick des Gekreuzigten die Manifestation Gottes ereignet hat. Auf diese Weise lässt sich der Übergang von der Theozentrik in der Verkündigung Jesu zur christozentrischen Botschaft der Kirche, die von Christus spricht, rechtfertigen.[10]

Auf dieser Ebene ortet Schillebeeckx die Wurzel der universalistischen Dimension der christlichen Botschaft, die gebietet, von der geschichtlichen Einzigartigkeit der Erfahrung Jesu auszugehen, um von daher die Möglichkeit einer Öffnung und des Bewusstseins von einem Heilsangebot an die ganze Menschheit zu erwägen.

„Doch bedeutet die Offenbarung in Jesus, wie sie uns das christliche Evangelium verkündet, keineswegs, dass Gott eine geschichtliche Partikularität (und sei es die Jesu von Nazareth) verabsolutiert. Aus dieser Gottesoffenbarung in Jesus lernen wir, dass keine einzige geschichtliche Singularität absolut genannt werden kann und dass deshalb, durch die in Jesus vorhandene Relativität, jeder Mensch Gott auch außerhalb Jesu begegnen kann, nämlich in unserer weltlichen Geschichte und in den darin entstandenen vielen Religionen. Auch der auferstandene Jesus von Nazareth weist über sich selbst hinaus weiter *auf Gott hin*. Man könnte sagen: Gott weist über Jesus Christus im Geist auf sich selbst als Schöpfer und Erlöser hin: als auf einen Gott der Menschen, *aller* Menschen. Gott

---

[9] Vgl. ebd., 151ff.
[10] Vgl. ebd., 164ff.

ist absolut, aber keine einzige Religion ist absolut."[11]

Die Betrachtung der geschichtlichen Singularität Jesu liefert einen Schlüssel zur Interpretation der Bewegung des christlichen Glaubens selbst. Mit diesem Rückbezug lässt sich nunmehr ein Weg beschreiten, auf dem den verschiedenen religiösen Traditionen besondere Aufmerksamkeit gilt. Es geht dabei nicht darum, die Unterschiede zwischen den verschiedenen Religionen aufzulösen, vielmehr tritt Schillebeeckx dafür ein, sie aufrechtzuerhalten und als Chance zu begreifen, indem man eine Vielfalt von Glaubenswegen identifiziert, die imstande sind, einen Beitrag zu einer volleren Erfahrung der Offenbarung Gottes zu leisten, die sich ja ihrerseits nicht auf die Erfahrung des historischen Christentums reduzieren lässt.

Gott kann nicht auf die Begrenztheit einer Erfahrungstradition reduziert werden, und so nimmt die Pluralität der Religionen eine Valenz des Reichtums an. Das Proprium des Christentums ist es, dass es die Beziehung zu Gott an die in der Zeit und im Raum situierte Singularität der Erfahrung Jesu von Nazareth bindet. „Das ist die Einzigartigkeit und Identität des Christentums, aber zugleich seine unvermeidliche geschichtliche Begrenzung."[12]

Das Herzstück der Identität des Christentums bildet die Haltung, die es ermöglicht, das Vorhandensein und die Unterschiedlichkeit der anderen Religionen in positiver Weise aufzunehmen. Gerade die Tatsache, dass das Christentum in der kontingenten, begrenzten Erfahrung Jesu von Nazareth wurzelt, bildet einen relevanten Punkt seiner Identität. Jesus als Offenbarung Gottes zeigt an, dass sich das Leben Gottes gegenüber der Menschheit in diesem partikulären, geschichtlich situierten Leben ereignet.

Schillebeeckx warnt vor der Gefahr, in der christologischen Reflexion Formen des Doketismus Vorschub zu leisten, und mahnt, die Menschheit Jesu ernst zu nehmen. Im aufmerksamen Blick auf das menschliche und geschichtliche Geschick Jesu lässt sich wahrnehmen, wie Gott ein partikuläres, geschichtliches Leben nicht absolut setzt, sondern vielmehr die Erkenntnis ermöglicht, dass auch Jesus über sich hinausweist. Sein ganz auf Gott und auf die Verkündigung des Gottesreichs ausgerichtetes Leben verweist auf den Gott des Heils, den *Deus humanissimus*, der einen Heilsplan für die ganze Menschheit hat. Die Betonung der Singularität Christi erlaubt so, eine Offenheit zu gewinnen, die für die christliche Er-

[11] Ebd., 213.
[12] Ebd., 214.

fahrung als Beziehung zu Jesus und als Nachfolge Jesu konstitutiv ist. Von daher können wir entdecken, „dass [...] durch die in Jesus vorhandene Relativität jeder Mensch Gott auch außerhalb Jesu begegnen kann, nämlich in unserer weltlichen Geschichte und in den darin entstandenen vielen Religionen. Auch der auferstandene Jesus von Nazareth weist über sich selbst hinaus weiter *auf Gott hin*. Man könnte sagen: Gott weist über Jesus Christus im Geist auf sich selbst als Schöpfer und Erlöser hin: als auf einen Gott der Menschen, *aller* Menschen. Gott ist absolut, aber keine einzige Religion ist absolut."[13]

In diesem Denkhorizont greift Schillebeeckx auf, was er im ersten Teil des Buches vertreten hat: Das Herzstück der christlichen Botschaft, „Heil-von-Gott-her in Jesus-Christus", kann von neuem in der Geschichte der Menschheit erfahren werden, und diese Erfahrung verweist auf eine Beziehung zu Gott, die sich nicht in den Grenzen einer religiösen Erfahrungstradition – auch nicht der christlichen – erschöpft. Schillebeeckx neigt entschieden dazu, die Vielfalt der Religionen nicht als zu meidendes und zu bekämpfendes Übel zu betrachten, sondern als Chance der Fruchtbarkeit und Offenheit für das von Gott kommende Heil. „Dabei wird wohl deutlich, dass (aufgrund der Gleichnisse Jesu und der Praxis des Reiches Gottes) der Gott Jesu ein Symbol der Offenheit, nicht der Geschlossenheit ist. Damit ist eine positive Beziehung des Christentums zu anderen Religionen gegeben, zugleich jedoch die Einzigartigkeit des Christentums gewahrt, und ist schließlich auch der christlichen loyalen Bejahung der Positivität der anderen Weltreligionen entsprochen."[14]

Die christliche Konzeption von den anderen Religionen im Sinne der Offenheit ist hier nicht so sehr von einer Betrachtung des dreieinen Gottes her motiviert, sondern vom Rückbezug auf die historische Singularität, auf die Kontingenz und auf die Begrenztheit Jesu von Nazareth, auf seine geschichtliche Erfahrung. Hier stehen wir vor einem Ort der Offenbarung Gottes, der der Menschheit Heil anbietet. Aber gerade diese Aufmerksamkeit für die geschichtliche Singularität Jesu von Nazareth wird zum Antrieb für die Geschichte der christlichen Gemeinschaft: Die verschiedenen historischen Formen, die das Christentum in der Geschichte annimmt, sind nichts Absolutes, sondern gestalten sich als offene Erfahrungen im Bezug zu Christus. Die Christentümer in der Geschichte bleiben der Bewegung der Inkarnation gehorsam und können in ihrer jeweiligen Erfahrung die Offenbarung Gottes nicht ausschöpfen.

[13] Ebd., 213.
[14] Ebd., 214f.

Orthodoxie, Orthopraxis, Mystik

Die Reflexion über die Identität des Christentums, das sich auf die Nachfolge des Propheten aus Nazareth gründet, hat Konsequenzen für die Beziehung zwischen Orthodoxie und Orthopraxis. Aus den Worten und den Taten Jesu ergibt sich der Begriff eines Gottes, der voller Leidenschaft für die Befreiung der Menschheit ist. Und dieser Gottesbegriff hängt wesentlich mit einer Praxis der Befreiung zusammen. Gott will nicht objektiviert werden, sondern er will, dass man ihm in einer Praxis der Befreiung begegnet. Das Heil schenkt sich in der Befreiungspraxis, die die Geschichte Jesu fortsetzt: „Das Heil, das als Verheißung für alle in Christus grundgelegt ist, wird universal, nicht dank der Vermittlung einer abstrakten und universalen Idee, sondern kraft seines kognitiven, kritischen und befreienden Charakters in einer und durch eine konsequente Praxis des Reiches Gottes. Es handelt sich also nicht um eine rein spekulative, theoretische Universalität, sondern um eine Universalität, die allein durch die Verbreitung der Geschichte von Jesus, den die Christen als Christus bekennen, und durch christliche Praxis in den fragmentarischen Gestalten unserer Geschichte realisiert werden kann."[15]

Damit steht in der Praxis die geschichtliche Manifestation des rechten Glaubens auf dem Spiel. „Die Korrelation zwischen einerseits dem christlichen Glauben (mit seiner eigenen narrativ-praktischen Struktur und der darin mitgegebenen kognitiven, kritischen und befreienden Kraft) und andererseits aktuellen Erfahrungen innerhalb einer modernen Gesellschaft wird letztlich nur auf der Basis einer Praxis produktiv durchgeführt werden können, die Heil für alle realisieren und dadurch die Wahrheit eben als universale zu ihrem Recht kommen lassen will."[16] Diese Betonung der Praxis steht ganz im Einklang mit der Idee der Mystik, wie Schillebeeckx sie entwickelt. Er folgt dabei einer Konzeption von Mystik, die Gottesverehrung und Befreiung vereint.[17]

Jesus zeigt in seiner Praxis und in seinen Worten ein Gesicht Gottes im Geist einer offenen Identifikation. Schillebeeckx sieht darin eine Verbindung mit einer betimmten Linie der Mystik, die wiederum eine Spannung zwischen zwei Richtungen einschließt: jener, die sich von der Welt abwendet, und jener, die Gott als unaussprechlichen Ursprung aller Schöpfung wahrnimmt und doch Rückzug und Verinnerlichung schafft.

---

[15] Ebd., 225
[16] Ebd., 227.
[17] Vgl. ebd., 219.

Dass man dafür offen ist, Gott in seinem Gott-Sein zu finden, führt nicht dazu, die geschöpfliche Dimension in ihrer Autonomie und Freiheit zu negieren, sondern sie neu zu entdecken und auf neue Weise zu würdigen. „In dieser mystischen Sicht will Er [Gott] denn auch der Geliebte der ganzen Schöpfung sein. Wer Gott als Gott in seiner inneren Eigenart finden will, kann die Geschöpfe nicht ausschließen. Und gerade in dieser Sicht wird konsequent die besondere, sogar einmalige Stellung des Menschen Jesus von Nazareth innerhalb der Weltgeschichte auch für nichtchristliche Formen der Mystik zumindest begreiflich und nachvollziehbar [...]. Diese Form der mystischen ‚Gelassenheit' [...] lässt sich mit dem prophetischen Christentum durchaus vereinbaren. Bei Jesus ist gerade seine mystische ‚Abba'-Erfahrung der Grund seines prophetischen Auftretens. Denn in solcher Mystik kann die Liebe zu allen Menschen und die allumfassende mitgeschöpfliche Liebe als Ausdruck der Liebe zu Gott voll zu ihrem Recht kommen. In dieser Mystik ist reichlich Raum für den Kampf für Gerechtigkeit und Liebe, für die Heilung der Schöpfung: für alles, was in dieser vergänglichen Welt lebt."[18]

Das Christentum wird Grund und Anlass für Begegnung und Dialog mit jeder Mystik finden können, die in der Aufmerksamkeit für Gerechtigkeit, Liebe und Schöpfung lebt, während es mit den Formen, die die radikale Verneinung des Endlichen vertreten, nie zu einer Synthese, sondern nur zu einem Dialog zwischen zwei nicht aufeinander reduzierbaren Religionen kommen kann.

Solche Sensibilität für die Mystik enthält immer auch die Aufforderung, die christliche Liebe in ihrer ureigenen Dimension zu verstehen: Insofern sie Gottesliebe mit mystischer und theologaler Tiefe ist, lässt sie sich nicht auf die ethische Dimension reduzieren, und dennoch drängt sie vermöge ihres konstitutiven Grundes zu einer Befreiung, die auch die soziale und politische Dimension umfasst.

Im Kreuz Jesu manifestiert sich die bedingungslose Treue zur Botschaft von der universalen Liebe Gottes zur gesamten Schöpfung, vor allem zu den Armen und Marginalisierten. Jesus hat eine mitreißende innere Freiheit gelebt, nicht in der Form der Resignation und der Gewöhnung an das Böse, sondern als Reaktion und radikale Opposition gegen die ruchlose Welt. „Deshalb kann der Christ sagen: Aufgrund des Evangeliums Jesu Christi bekenne ich, dass der Name Gottes zu Recht mit der evangelischen Utopie von Gerechtigkeit und Liebe, mit dem Traum einer Befreiung zu immer besserer Humanität verbunden wird und dass dieser

[18] Ebd., 230.

Name Gottes zu Unrecht mit der aktiven oder passiven Rechtfertigung (und sei es aus noch so göttlich mystischen Motiven) eines viele Menschen verletzenden und knechtenden gesellschaftlichen Wirtschaftssystems verbunden wird."[19]

Das Christentum muss sich daher in der Treue zu dem Gott Jesu Christi jede Flucht aus der Welt und jede passive Resignation versagen, weil Gott sich in der Schöpfung definitiv auf die Welt eingelassen hat. Konzis ausgedrückt: „Gott ist nicht ‚derselbe' vor und nach seiner Schöpfung!"[20] In dieser Perspektive weist Schillebeeckx auf einige neue Horizonte im Zusammenhang mit der Sendung der Kirche hin. Das Herzstück der Verkündigung ist der Gott aller Menschen und die endgültige Gottesherrschaft, die auf der Botschaft und dem Handeln Jesu gründet. Gott schafft Heil in der menschlichen Geschichte, den gläubigen Christen und der Kirche kommt nur der zweite Platz zu. Darüber hinaus ist zu beachten: „Die Gegenwart tritt in den Inhalt des Verständnisses des Evangeliums ein."[21]

Die Mission hat ihren Ursprung nicht in einem Gefühl der Überlegenheit, sondern vielmehr in einer Leidenschaft für das Gottesreich, für eine weiter ausgreifende Humanisierung und für eine Befreiung, die alle Aspekte des menschlichen Lebens betrifft.

„Christen sind gezwungen, von Jesus Christus zu zeugen, also das Evangelium hinauszutragen, weil sie Gottes Reich der Gerechtigkeit und Liebe in der ganzen Welt fördern wollen" (232 f.). In einer kurzen Rückbesinnung auf Jean Marc Ela, *Le cri de l'homme Africain*, drückt Schillebeeckx seine Zustimmung zu diesem Buch aus und präzisiert, die Hauptaufgabe der Mission bestehe nicht so sehr im Inkulturationsprozess, sondern vielmehr in der Suche nach dem Reich Gottes in der Gestalt einer solidarischen menschlichen Gesellschaft.

So zeichnet sich eine tief greifende Horizontveränderung ab: Vom Schema des Gegensatzes Licht – Finsternis, in dem das Licht das Christentum wäre und die Finsternis den heidnischen Religionen entspräche, müsste sich der Übergang zu einem anderen Typ von Kontrast vollziehen, in dem das Reich Gottes dem Reich dieser Welt gegenübersteht – wobei das letztere zu verstehen ist als die von Gott gut geschaffene Welt, die die Menschheit mit Unrecht erfüllt hat: „Die aktive Präsenz der christlichen Kirche an der Front dieser Konflikte ist die primäre missio-

---

[19] Ebd., 231.
[20] Ebd.
[21] Ebd., 232.

narische Tat. Man zeigt das Evangelium mit Hilfe seiner befreienden Früchte für den Menschen."[22] In diesem Sinn können die Kirchen Zeichen des Heils sein (identifizieren sich dabei aber nicht mit dem Heil), indem sie eine karitative und zugleich politische Diakonie entfalten. So werden die Christen Zeugen einer christlichen Botschaft sein können, und zwar indem sie sich bewusst als Minderheit in den Dienst an einer Mehrheit stellen, und nicht indem sie sich vor allem um die zahlenmäßige Vermehrung ihrer eigenen Anhänger sorgen. „Das Evangelium allen Notleidenden in der Welt zu bringen, nicht nur durch das Wort, sondern vor allem durch solidarisches Handeln und somit durch eine Befreiungspraxis, gehört zum Wesen des Christentums. [...] Die christliche Botschaft vom Reich Gottes mit ihrem Befreiungspotential bleibt in ihrer Eigenart ein Angebot an alle Menschen, zugleich auch eine Konfrontation mit anderen Religionen als solchen (und nicht nur mit ihren Mitgliedern). Auch die Kultur der Menschen, selbst ihre religiöse Kultur, kann evangelisiert werden, ohne dass diese Kulturen dadurch ihre spezifische Eigenart und Identität aufzugeben brauchen."[23]

Die christliche Botschaft vom Reich Gottes ist die Besonderheit des Christentums und wird der gesamten Menschheit angeboten. Es ist also christliche Art, sich an die anderen Religionen als komplexe Systeme und nicht nur an deren einzelne Mitglieder zu wenden; hier kann eine Dynamik der Akzeptanz des Evangeliums wirken, ohne dass dabei derjenige, der eine andere Religion lebt, auf seine eigene Besonderheit und Identität verzichten muss. Und dem Christentum kann geholfen werden, sich für noch nicht abgeschlossene Inkulturationsprozesse zu öffnen.

Schluss

Zum Schluss dieser Analyse möchte ich einige Elemente skizzieren, die mir in Schillebeeckx' Vorschlag für unsere Gegenwart wichtig scheinen.
– Die Betrachtung der Geschichte der Menschheit als Heilsgeschichte und der Funktion der Religionen als Gemeinschaften und Interpretationstraditionen, die die von Gott herkommende Heilsgeschichte, wie sie sich in der menschlichen Realität ereignet, explizit machen, ist eine mit den tiefsten Intuitionen des Zweiten Vatikanischen Konzils über-

[22] Ebd., 233.
[23] Ebd., 235.

einstimmende Perspektive; sie lässt zudem eine fruchtbare Offenheit gegenüber den Ansprüchen der heutigen Zeit erkennen.
- Die Analyse, die Schillebeeckx anstellt, ist nicht naiv-optimistisch, sondern behält stets das Geschick der Menschheit im Blick, das von Humanisierungsprozessen, aber auch von der Erfahrung des real existierenden „Inhumanen" geprägt ist. Gerade im Widerstand gegen alles, was an Inhumanem erfahren wird, wie auch im Streben nach Erfüllung und Aktualisierung der Menschenwürde und der Gerechtigkeit entdeckt Schillebeeckx eine Offenheit, in der Glaubende und Nichtglaubende einen gemeinsamen Horizont entdecken können. Dort identifizieren die an Christus Glaubenden die Gegenwart eines Heils-von-Gott-her, das in Christus offenbar geworden ist.
- Schillebeeckx bejaht die Positivität der unterschiedlichen religiösen Wege nicht in einer Optik pluralistischen Typs, sondern ausgehend von der Betrachtung des einzigartigen, geschichtlichen Geschicks Jesu von Nazareth. Sein Geschick ist Offenbarung Gottes und konkretisiert das Heil-von-Gott-her, und dennoch ist es ein Weiterverweis und stiftet eine Offenheit für Gott, der sein Heil in der Geschichte der Menschheit schenkt. In der Treue dazu wurzelt auch die Relativierung der geschichtlichen Erfahrungen der verschiedenen Aktualisierungen des Christentums.
- Die Entscheidung für das Evangelium, das spezifische Element des Christentums, führt auf einen Weg der Befreiung, der das Gottesbild selbst betrifft und Menschen Jesu eigene Option für die Armen übernehmen lässt. Schillebeeckx schlägt einen mystischen Horizont vor, in dem das Christentum heute zu leben sei. Es handelt sich dabei nicht um eine Art Mystik, die eine geringere Bereitschaft zur Begegnung mit den Religionen zur Folge hätte, sondern um eine solche, die in dieser Begegnung die Chance sieht, dass das Christentum als „Angebot" und damit als ein Dialog gelebt wird, der für die anderen Religionen offen ist.
- Die Perspektive, die der flämische Dominikaner entwickelt, konzentriert die Aufmerksamkeit auf den von Jesus beschrittenen Lebensweg als Weg des Heils und lenkt den Blick auf eine fruchtbare, gegenseitige Beziehung zwischen Orthodoxie und Orthopraxis. Im Anschluss an eine Anregung von A. Pieris betont Schillebeeckx: „Ohne Beziehung zu einer erlösenden und befreienden Praxis von Christen hängt die Erlösung, die damals von Christus gebracht wurde, in einer rein spekulativen, dünnen Luft. [...] Man muss den Lebensweg Jesu auch

selbst gehen; dann erhält der Lebensweg Jesu konkret eine universale Bedeutung."[24]

Übersetzung aus dem Italienischen: *Michael Lauble*

* * *

Abstract of the contribution of Alessandro Cortesi

This paper proposes an analysis of certain aspects of Schillebeeckx's thought with particular reference to his book *Church. The human story of God*. The consideration of the human history as history of salvation is linked to the consideration of the role of religions in the actual context. The experience of what is truly human and the 'contrast experiences' about what is inhuman in our life could open, in Schillebeeckx's thought, a common way to believers and non-believers in the search of salvation. In this context Schillebeeckx suggests a consideration of the positive role of different religious traditions not separated but linked with the historic experience of Jesus' life. The choice for the Gospel as peculiar element in Christian life becomes a proposal of a mystic: that means a movement in the direction of liberation which involves a liberation from traditional images of God and a movement towards the dialogue with different religions.

---

[24] Ebd., 215.

Stephan van Erp

INCARNATIONAL THEOLOGY

Systematic Theology after Schillebeeckx

Fifty years ago, Edward Schillebeeckx wrote an article on the new turn in the systematic theology of his day in the very first issue of his own journal, *Tijdschrift voor Theologie*.[1] This new turn consisted of a 'living attention to the historically new in confrontation with faith, as well as in the new states of thought, created by and in a human experience that is forever expressing itself anew in this world, for example in modern literature and in philosophy.[2] Schillebeeckx believed that this attention to the historically new will result in a double focus for modern theology. On the one hand, modern faith seems to indicate new theological modes of thought that need articulation and clarification. On the other, a changing faith forces us to reflect upon the renewals old theological achievements will undergo as a result of new influences. This is what gives modern systematic theology its double focus: on both the future and the past. Schillebeeckx repeatedly emphasises that the truth of old theology will not be lost as a result of the dynamics of a changing faith, but is instead purified and differentiated, and sometimes even corrected. He believes that systematic theology is the theological discipline *par excellence* to guide and reflect upon this growth. With that, the task of systematic theology has explicitly and fundamentally been determined as a historical one, ever since the middle of the twentieth century: both by safeguarding old theological truths and by reflecting on the experiences of the historically new in the present and the future.

---

[1] E. Schillebeeckx, "De nieuwe wending in de huidige Dogmatiek", in: *Tijdschrift voor Theologie* 1 (1961), 17–47.
[2] Ibid., 18.

What seemed to be a new and promising discovery to Schillebeeckx – allowing the content of theology to be codetermined by contemporary religious experiences and practices – may seem self-evident to the current generation of theologians, but has not lost its urgency. These times have become much more difficult to interpret by means of a theological scheme than any before them, however. There seems to be a virtually unbridgeable chasm with the past. Any attempt to bridge it seems to misinterpret the signs of the time or too hastily find similarities with the past. Systematic theology is the main theological discipline that risks making these mistakes, precisely because of the interwovenness of the historical and the topical. A survey of modern systematic theology will show that there are roughly two camps: one that seeks to safeguard old insights and one that mainly seeks the content of faith in our modern age. Fifty years on, Schillebeeckx's commitment to consider the interwovenness of present and past a central theme of systematic theology with a view to the future, seems to have become nearly impossible.

In this article, I will investigate the possibilities of a systematic theology after Schillebeeckx that interprets the modern condition of faith from the perspective of the history of the church and of theology and will reinterpret that history form the perspectives of the present. I will focus on developments in theology over the last fifty years. First, I will describe how the attention to the present did initially lead to a flourishing of modern systematic theology, contextual theology and a theology of culture (1). Next, I will outline the possibilities of a renewed influence of Schillebeeckx's theology on new generations of theologians (2).

1. The present as the motif for modern theology

1.1. *Anthropology and Christology*

Let us first take a look at Schillebeeckx's 'new turn.' One of the most important insights he derived from phenomenology of his day was the anthropocentric idea that human consciousness is a consciousness that has been incarnated in the world and in the body: 'it enters the world by means of the act in which it constitutes itself, in which it presents itself to this part of worldly reality that is our own biological-sensitive physicality.'[3] He used this non-dualist, constructive concept of the human

---

[3] Ibid., 26.

person realising itself in the world to outline the, as he saw them, 'revolutionary' consequences to modern systematic theology, particularly to Christology, Mariology, the doctrine of grace, ecclesiology and eschatology. He believes that the various different dogmatic tracts have undergone a radical change as a result of new ideas about the personhood of God and man and new ideas about the human experience of the relationship between God and man.

This 'antropologisation' of dogmatics has led to many misunderstandings and debates. The main misunderstanding, which also has been applied to Schillebeeckx's own theology, is that theology now supposedly gains an anthropological basis and will therefore entirely explain and constitute faith on the basis of human experience, as a consequence of which even theological concepts like revelation and grace are no longer considered the result of divine action, but subjective projections, devoid from any measure of reality. This is an incorrect inference, at least where Schillebeeckx's own theology is involved: "'In fact, the *locus theologicus*, even of the belief in creation, is the personal human history of the historical
Christ."[4] The incarnational pivot of the history of salvation must therefore be the precondition of faith and theology, he believes. Experiencing that history of salvation is not merely a human project, it is the result of divine action. This plan for salvation involves man in such a way that he can freely realize himself in it. So even in an anthropologically inspired theology like Schillebeeckx's, the primacy lies with divine revelation in history, even though this is always mediated by human experience. The anthropologisation of modern theology went hand in hand with a growing interest in Christology. According to Schillebeeckx, the first and most fundamental question is that for the mystery of faith, "the revelation of reality itself, with which we are confronted personally through the light of faith."[5] He believed that this revelation of reality was by definition historical, a key moment in the life and death of Jesus Christ. That is why the study of Christology offers the best insights into the relation between nature and grace.

The discussion about the foundations of faith has largely determined theological debate over the past fifty years.[6] It explains the great interest

[4] Ibid., 38.
[5] Ibid., 22.
[6] Cf. T. Guarino, Foundations of Systematic Theology, New York – London: T. & T. Clark, 2005.

in dogmatics at the beginning of the second half of the twentieth century. The deciding question whether revelation or experience comes first in theology, and what the special role of the historical person of Christ is, led to an entrenchment of different theological schools that determines the theological landscape to this day. The decision to either take revelation or history (including current experiences) as the foundation of theological debate does after all also determine the subject and the method of theological research.

1.2. Apologetics and the theology of culture

Subject and method of theology do not just change because of changing ideas about the foundations of faith, but also as a result of a growing awareness of the various different addressees of theology and the theologians' social position. In addition to the fundamental question of the relation between revelation and, the question for religious practices and audiences also became an important one. This, in turn, showed the importance of theological communication and perspective, which had dramatic consequences for the language of dogmatics. Communication and audience are aspects that seemed less urgent to Schillebeeckx in 1961 because the connections between church, university and society in catholic Nijmegen were much clearer and much more self-evident. The situation had changed dramatically twenty years later. The secularisation of western culture now posed a real problem to church and theology. It led to the development of applied theological communication in a changing, pluralist culture. That is why in the 1980s, David Tracy distinguished three types of audiences for theology – church, university, society – and arranged the various different theological disciplines and methods accordingly. It would mean, for example, a fundament theology that is rather more focussed on the discussion with other sciences and a practical theology that is rather more focussed on ecclesiastical developments.[7] The result was a multiplication of theological tasks, because the field of study was expanded outside the original religious community and tradition.[8]

---

[7] D. Tracy, The Analogical Imagination: Christian Theology and the Culture of Pluralism, New York 1981.

[8] Cf. L. Boeve, "Theology at the Crossroads of Academy, Church and Society", in: *ET-Studies: Journal of the European Society for Catholic Theology* 1 (2010), 71–90.

This attention to the diversity of theological audiences has not just influenced the development of different forms of theological communication and the adaptation of theological language and method depending on the discussion partner. Some believe that the expanded field of action of the theologian has also opened up new perspectives on the content of faith, which in turn has led to changing interpretations of theological concepts. After Schillebeeckx, this theological position has been developed further by Lieven Boeve and Erik Borgman in the Dutch-speaking countries. Boeve has used the concept of 'interruption,' which on the one hand describes God's actions in this world, particularly in a day and age in which the Christian story is no longer taken for granted. On the other hand, this divine interruption of history calls upon people to interrupt the world itself.[9] According to Boeve, this double interruption ultimately leads to a continuous recontextualisation of theology.

Borgman calls his project a 'theology of culture.' He claims to have derived its statute from Schillebeeckx's early theology and the theologies of Marie-Dominique Chenu and ultimately that of Thomas Aquinas.[10] What is at stake in this 'theology of culture' is a religious interpretation of contemporary culture, assuming that everything that exists is part of God's creation and as such part of the history of salvation. This theology does not regard tradition and the community of the church as a given that requires interpretation, but as living forms of community that are constantly renewed and provide the dynamic, ever-changing subject for theology. The result is a type of dogmatics that is focussed on the future and is inherently eschatological. As faith keeps renewing itself, dogmatics can never have the final say and is therefore, by definition, incomplete. It leads to a new style of theology that no longer presents integral, systematic tracts, but is instead essayist by nature.

1.3. Resourcement and retraditionalisation

---

[9] Cf. L. Boeve, "Edward Schillebeeckx & de actuele theologie: Een reflectie 'in media res'", in: *Tijdschrift voor Theologie* 50 (2010), 27–50, here 34. Cf. idem, Onderbroken traditie: Heeft het christelijk verhaal nog toekomst?, Kapellen 1999; idem, God onderbreekt de geschiedenis: Theologie in een tijd van ommekeer, Kapellen 2006.

[10] E. Borgman, Metamorfosen: Over religie en moderne cultuur, Kampen 2006, 19–22. Cf. idem, "Identiteit verwachten: Van theologische antropologie naar cultuurtheologie", in: *Tijdschrift voor Theologie* 42 (2002), 174–196; idem, ... want de plaats waarop je staat is heilige grond: God als onderzoeksprogramma, Amsterdam 2008.

Late-twentieth century theology has also seen a backlash against the development of anthropological and cultural theologies. Many wildly divergent theological schools harboured a discontent with the rise of historical and hermeneutical theology. Both theologians who build their work on Karl Barth's orthodox, ecclesiastical theology, and those who belong to new postmodern, neo-augustinian schools, are concerned with what they regard as the degeneration of dogmatics in modern theology.[11] Instead of culture or the contemporary, the religious practises of a religious community should determine the theological agenda.[12] There have been more and more orthodox, ecclesiastical, postmodern and restorationist theologians since the 1970s. Shortly after the Second Vatican Council, restorations movements started to emerge in the catholic church. In protestant theology, barthian theologians like C. Gunton, W. Placher, R. Jenson, T.F. Torrance and J. Webster, explicitly concentrate on the central doctrines of dogmatics, the doctrine of the trinity in particular. To the amazement of continental theologians, this has made a strong comeback in Anglo-American theology.[13] Followers of the most conspicuous theological school of the moment, *Radical Orthodoxy*, have fought the rise of social sciences within theology and made the case for a theological rather than a philosophical or social-theoretical foundation for the reflection on faith, in particular the idea of God's gift in creation.[14] In the 1990s, postliberal theologians turned against the rationalism of critical philosophy and claimed that theology ultimately has no rational foundation.

Regardless of the wide divergence of these schools, they all make extensive use of pre-modern sources, like the theologies of Augustine, Thomas Aquinas or John Calvin. For this reason, this theological trend could be regarded as an Anglo-Saxon continuation of the French *nouvelle théologie* from the 1940s and 50s. Another thing this resourcement has in common with *nouvelle théologie*, is its emphasis on the development of a constructive or positive theology.[15] There is, however, one important dif-

---

[11] Cf. J. Webster, "Theologies of Retrieval", in: J. Webster et al. (Eds.), The Oxford Handbook of Systematic Theology, Oxford 2007, 583–599.

[12] Cf. St. Hauerwas, With the Grain of the Universe: The Church's Witness and Natural Theology, Grand Rapids 2001.

[13] Cf. C. Gunton, The Promise of Trinitarian Theology, London 1997². See also G. van den Brink / St. van Erp, "Ignoring God Triune?: The Doctrine of the Trinity in Dutch Theology", *International Journal of Systematic Theology* 11 (2009), 72–90.

[14] J. Milbank, Theology and Social Theory: Beyond Secular Reason, Oxford 1990; J. Milbank et al. (Eds.), Radical Orthodoxy: A New Theology, London 1999.

[15] Cf. J. Mettepenningen, Nouvelle Théologie – New Theology: Inheritor of Modernism, Precursor of Vatican II, London – New York 2010.

ference with this catholic school. The theologians who together formed the *nouvelle théologie*, were interested in a stronger connection between theology and the contemporary church, and they were in favour of making tradition more dynamic. Instead, the recent resourcement movements are rather more interested in reviving the theological sources of the early church and what they consider to be original reflections of the Word of God.

Such a retraditionalisation in theology has almost entirely failed to establish itself in the Netherlands and Flanders. Had it managed to establish itself, it could have led to an increased interest in dogmatics in the Low Countries, albeit in a way that is diametrically opposed to the intention of Schillebeeckx's article of 1961. After all, his aim was the integration of the historically new in theological reflection without sacrificing the continuity with the past. In that case, mere resourcement will not suffice. Contemporary practises and experiences of faith continue to pose new theological questions, and ever since the Second Vatican Council there has been an explicit ecclesiastical order to take these questions seriously.

2. Edward Schillebeeckx's lasting influence

Next, we need to consider what exactly Schillebeeckx's influence on new generations of theologians can or could be, given the current theological context described above. Shortly after his death, some people claimed that Schillebeeckx's theology would soon be forgotten. Whether this will actually happen, remains to be seen, but we need to recognize that he lived in an age and a culture that was very different from ours. This is what motivated his biographer Erik Borgman to present Schillebeeckx's work against the background of his own history. By putting theological issues and controversies of the twentieth century in their cultural context, Borgman tried to offer an insight into the way in which Schillebeeckx was influenced by his age, and how he in turn has influenced that age. In doing so, the biographer presupposed that it would allow this theologian of a past age to become a discussion partner for the current generation again. Borgman believes that, although Schillebeeckx's ideas have become somewhat dated by later social and ecclesiastical developments, "they are essentially not superseded".[16] That is rather a categorical thing to say about a theologian who himself kept emphasising the inseparable connection between theological content and the cultural context in which it is developed. Taking Schillebeeckx's hermeneutics seriously, we may need to recognise that since the discovery of context and practise of faith as theological starting point, theology has constantly needed to reassess its stance towards the time in which it comes about. The logical conclusion would be that any theology that went before has therefore become superseded as soon the new theology is introduced. Is this the tragic consequence of hermeneutic theology: has it become superseded in accordance with its own principles of perspectivity and contextuality, as soon as the culture which produced it was over?

2.1. Dated, but not superseded: the obstinacy of Schillebeeckx's theology

The extent Schillebeeckx's influence on theology is not undisputed. Some regard his thinking as exemplary of the twentieth century which is now over. They see him as an adherent of the liberal theology that is now supposed to have failed; too partial to the historical-critical method and too concerned with the adaptation of Christian faith to the spirit of the times. This is the image that people usually have of Schillebeeckx: a liberal, modern theologian who, open to human experience and cultural context, has adapted theology to the modern age; somebody who paid more attention to the history of man than to the infinity of God; a theologian of practice, rather than of theory. Whether this is regarded as a positive or a negative description depends on the theological disposition and the theological school to which one belongs. Those polarising filters based on criteria like the importance of experience, practice and history have split theology after Schillebeeckx into schools and movements.[17] This compartmentalisation has also had consequences for the position of individual theologians. Schillebeeckx was deemed to belong to the liberal side, which meant that his work would be received by either a liberal sympathiser or a critical opponent. It meant that in the era after ideological criticism, theology became more and more ideological. Theology after Schillebeeckx became politicized to such an extent that

---

[16] E. Borgman, Edward Schillebeeckx: A Theologian in his History. Vol. 1: A Catholic Theology of Culture, 1914–1965, transl. by J. Bowden, London – New York: Continuum, 2003, 9–25, 23.

[17] Cf. H.W. Frei, Types of Christian Theology, New Haven CT: Yale University Press 1992, 28–55.

prior to a theological opinion, a fundamental-theological identification was required. The main question was whether one was orthodox or liberal, *foundational* or *postfoundational*, analytic or hermeneutic, historically critical or diachronous, scholarly or ecclesiastical, traditional or modern, etcetera. Such a forced positioning leads to an unfortunate reductionism when applied to a theologian like Schillebeeckx, because his theology cannot really be categorised in such a way.

The reception of Schillebeeckx's work was also vulnerable because it has never had a large following and because he never attempted to form a school, unlike people such as Karl Barth, Hans Urs von Balthasar, Karl Rahner and Dietrich Bonhoeffer. It is, however, much less common in theology than in philosophy to confess to a certain school or to explicitly declare oneself the follower of one individual thinker. Nevertheless, it is remarkable that Schillebeeckx has on the one hand influenced many different theological positions, yet on the other seems to have become marginalised because of this. I use the word 'seems,' because one of the reasons why the long-term effect of Schillebeeckx's ideas is so difficult to trace, is because they have become generally accepted. Meanwhile, the concepts of history and experience he helped to introduce as foundations for a theological method and as sources particular to theology, are now considered to be self-evident by many.

Few however fully consider the consequences of this self-evidence, namely the fact that it allows for a sacramental interpretation of the present and of practice. Many theologians in Flanders and in the Netherlands are – often without realising it – indebted to the historical and critical methods of thinkers like Schillebeeckx, but only few contemporary theologians know that these methods had a theological foundation. The result is a theology after Schillebeeckx that tries to relate to contemporary culture, just like he did. He tried to find new forms of what he called 'salvation-coming-from-God,' but this is no longer a criterion befitting 21st century theology. A new generation of theologians tries to find 'the theological' in culture, without actually knowing what to look for an where to look for it. This leads some to conclude that the theological is absent in modern culture. Others do see analogies of faith in modern cultural expressions and life styles, but those analogies are based on language and on phenomenons, instead of on a theory of divine intervention history, as Schillebeeckx saw them.

Although he has often been criticised for too strongly founding his theology on revelation, Schillebeeckx had even more often been criticised for the opposite. These critiques propose that he went too far in founding faith and the tradition of the church on human experience, as a result of which God's role would be finished. His emphasis on human experience is indeed the result of a fundamental philosophical consideration of modern epistemology and metaphysics and the theological recognition of the social-cultural and historical-political constellation as a source. In his earlier works, however, Schillebeeckx always reserves pride of place for the concept of *'revelation,'* and in his later works he increasingly qualifies this term with the concept of *'salvation.'* Revelation and salvation, like *history*, the *humanum* and *experience* are central concepts in his theology. The last three have to some extent played a leading part, because particularly at the council, they were presented to the church and world of his time as a challenge and an instruction to modern man. Revelation and experience were not regarded as a hierarchy, as each other's extension, however, but as a symbol of each other, inextricably connected, but not reducible to each other. The council and later also Schillebeeckx himself have undoubtedly theologically raised the status of the history of human experience, but always from the perspective of human existence as a sign of the love of God – a primarily *theological* idea therefore, which Schillebeeckx would later also provide with a solid Christological foundation.

Christology has also been a reason to be critical about the influence of Schillebeeckx's theology. His historical-critical method has caused a lot of criticism, which resurfaced in and as a result of the publication of Joseph Ratzinger's *Jesus Christ*. It should be mentioned that exegesis has strongly developed since the 1970s, and this has meant that the historical-critical method has lost its innovative force and has in fact been sidetracked. Schillebeeckx would probably have been the first to recognise this. He was not really an advocate of the historical-critical method, but he did believe that current developments in exegesis should have their consequences in dogmatics. His own use of the historical-critical method is not intended to give preference to the historical Jesus over the preached Jesus, it is an attempt to connect the theological question for *the truth of God* to the new developments in historical and empirical method. He took the scientific and scholarly developments of his day very serious, to such an extent that people now call his theology dated because of it. Nevertheless, the interest in texts and the history of the first century has boomed since his day. Had he lived in the 21st century, Schillebeeckx would surely have used the latest insights from those studies in his theology.

2.2. A theological understanding of faith now: the promise of Schillebeeckx's theology

So how do we continue to build on the work of Schillebeeckx who focused his theology on the culture and the age in which he developed it? He has left us a theological heritage that is rich in materials and subjects and urgently requires further investigation. Meanwhile, there have been over eighty doctoral theses on his work, and it seem likely that more are yet to follow. An eleven part collection of his works in English will soon be published, and it is likely that this will generate new research too. Further research into Schillebeeckx role and importance during and after the Second Vatican Council is needed, for example. In what way have Edward Schillebeeckx's lectures and articles influenced the documents of the Council? In what way has his interpretation of those council documents influenced his later theological hermeneutics and ecclesiology? What is the meaning of his theology of the universality of Christ in a religiously pluralistic culture? Has his emphasis on historicity, spirituality and experiences of suffering changed the study of religion and faith? As I have pointed out before, the main question for the evaluation of his theological point of view will remain whether Edward Schillebeeckx was a liberal or an orthodox theologian. How does his form of orthodoxy, orthopraxis, in his words 'the sought-after humanum, promised to us in Christ, which has to be performed,' relate to the current re-emergence of fundamentalism and neo-orthodoxy in theology and religion? And where does this Flemish theologian from Nijmegen fit into his time and age, among the great catholic theologians of the twentieth century, such as Karl Rahner, Hans Urs von Balthasar, Joseph Ratzinger, Henri de Lubac, Marie-Dominique Chenu, Hans Küng? Who will the new theological generation choose to be guided by? Schillebeeckx most certainly deserves to be considered for this role.

For his work to be suited for this role, the contextual difference between his time and ours needs to be bridged. The theological understanding of faith now is rather different from that of 1983, to moment at which Schillebeeckx held his valedictory speech upon leaving the Catholic University of Nijmegen. At a point in his life were he could have presented a retrospective of his work or a vision for the future of theology, Schillebeeckx explicitly chose to analyse the present. This choice is a direct result of the influence the documents of the Second Vatican Council have had on his theology. Particularly in its pastoral constitution *Gaudium et Spes*, this Council formulated a vision on the freedom and the responsibility of humanity in a changing world and on the role and the place of the church in solidarity with that world. The current states of faith, science and culture thus became a mission for church and theology. Schillebeeckx has allowed his theological agenda to be determined by those events. He did not do so by simply updating or adapting the content of faith to the times, like many of his contemporaries did, but by acknowledging the present as a source of theology. In keeping with the spirit of the Council, he considered the present itself to be the time and the place in which Gods creation is continued, in which Scripture and tradition are continued in new forms and a new language and in which the relationship between God and man gains a future. This present in which the Word of God can be heard in creation, Scripture and the living language of tradition and faith is the motif par exellance of modern theology, according to Schillebeeckx.

He defines the task of theology as finding a proper balance between tradition and situation. This does seem increasingly difficult to achieve in the current situation, however. Not only have the social-cultural and religious situation changed dramatically, tradition too has seen some radical changes. The most important difference with Schillebeeckx's day is perhaps that the church finds itself more and more compelled to present itself as a critical opposition to a materialist and relativist culture, and to oppose the religious point of view to others. The world has become a religious battleground and religious convictions have not just become the subject of criticism from other religious convictions, but also as religious convictions as such. Schillebeeckx's conflict avoidance strategy that aims to find a critical coherence of tradition and situation, may leave some space for diversity and discontinuity *in* tradition, but it might not be equal to a situation in which individual religious points of view are considered to be sparks that could set of the powder keg of a easily ignitable culture, and are therefore best kept private. The opening he tried to maintain between faith a culture now often seems to be closed. Contemporary theology can either position itself at one end of that opening or try to find openings that enable a new confirmation and realisation of the continuity between tradition and situation. The promise of Schillebeeckx's theology lies in the success of that constructive contribution to culture which contemporary theology itself makes.

Theology, as Schillebeeckx put it, moves between tradition and situation by means of reason, unlocking truth and criticising ideology.[18] And because he considered the situation, contemporary culture, to be the place where God acts, he deemed it of the utmost importance that theology should more extensively relate to philosophy, literary and historical sciences, religious sciences and social sciences. The exposition of his own theological frame of mind can thus be read as a programme for the future of theology in close cooperation with other sciences that have not lost their validity. As an analysis of the dynamic present – as the time and place of God in history – theology is not just a committed academic discipline, it is also a discipline that critically and constructively investigates the commitment of the sciences, church and society.

Schillebeeckx was convinced that theology could thus find a place in both the world of science and that of the church, and that it has its own special role in both these worlds. Amidst the other sciences, it uniquely takes its own practical and religious commitment as the subject of its investigation. Within the church, it reflects on its own commitment to God. As a scientific reflection, it does have its own, rightful place in the community of faith. By explicitly following these two tracks, by, on the one hand, taking its own religious commitment as the inspiration and subject of investigation, and on the other ensuring that this investigation meets the highest academic standards, Edward Schillebeeckx has shown that science and religion do not preclude each other. This is what makes him a shining example, even in a time of religious changes and conflicts that need clarification and understanding.

* * *

Zusammenfassung des Beitrags von Stephan van Erp

Seit Edward Schillebeeckx vor 50 Jahren die *Tijdschrift voor Theologie* ins Leben rief, hat die moderne Theologie Aufstieg und Fall erlebt. Mit seinem Eröffnungsartikel aus dem Jahr 1961 war er einer der Ersten, der die

---

[18] E. Schillebeeckx, Theologisch geloofsverstaan anno 1983. Afscheidscollege gegeven op vrijdag 11 februari 1983, Baarn 1983, 7.

Herausforderungen für die moderne Theologie in Worte fasste. Ihm zufolge liefert die ständig sich verändernde und somit jeweils neue Gegenwart das dynamische Material für die Theologie. Die Entdeckung der Geschichtlichkeit in ihren verschiedenen Formen von Vergangenheit, Gegenwart und Zukunft gab den Impuls zur Entwicklung neuer Theologien, welche sich seitdem als sehr einflussreich erwiesen haben. Das Konzept der Geschichtlichkeit trug zu einer neuen Verbindung von Anthropologie und Christologie bei. Darüber hinaus führte das Bewusstsein der Kontextualität und der Sozialität des Theologen zur Erarbeitung einer kommunikativen Theologie, die sich jeweils ihren Adressaten anpassen konnte. Kontextuelle Theologien entstanden, die dann in eine Theologie der Rekontextualisierung (L. Boeve) und eine Theologie der Kultur (E. Borgman) ausdifferenziert wurden. Eine gegen diese neuen anthropologischen und kontextuellen Entwicklungslinien gerichtete Reaktion stellten die neoorthodoxen und retradionalistischen Theologien dar, wie beispielsweise die Theologie Karl Barths und die radikale Orthodoxie von John Milbank, die sich derzeit als sehr einflussreich erweisen.

Der Autor dieses Beitrags schlägt die Inkarnation in ihrer geschichtlichen und eschatologischen Gestalt als neues Leitmotiv für die systematische Theologie nach Schillebeeckx vor. Dies wird damit begründet, dass am Ende weder die kritische Vernunft, noch die Hermeneutik (unabhängig davon, ob kontextuelle, biblische oder ekklesiologische), noch die Tradition Ausgangspunkt für eine dogmatische Theologie sein können – anders, als die fortlaufende geschichtliche Offenbarung Gottes in Jesus Christus, die sich in menschlicher Zeit und menschlichem Raum jeweils neu erweist. Auf der Arbeit von Schillebeeckx aufbauend wird eine systematische Theologie skizziert, die in einer Gemeinschaft verwurzelt ist, in welcher die geschichtliche Präsenz der Inkarnation eine Zukunft konstituiert, die Gottes Zukunft in dieser Welt ist.

Übersetzung aus dem Englischen: *Bernhard Kohl*

Christian Bauer

HEILIGKEIT DES PROFANEN?

Spuren der „école Chenu-Schillebeeckx" (H. de Lubac) auf dem Zweiten Vatikanum

Edward Schillebeeckx und das *Opus Dei* haben mehr gemeinsam, als auf den ersten Blick zu vermuten ist. Denn beide stehen für eine ganz bestimmte Form der Heiligkeit des Profanen. Edward Schillebeeckx für die theologische Heiligkeit der säkularen Welt, das *Opus Dei* für die spirituelle Heiligung des beruflichen Alltags[1]. Beide verorten das Heilige im Profanen, jedoch mit unterschiedlichen Akzenten: Schillebeeckx, um das Profane zu heiligen; das *Opus Dei*, um das Profane zu sakralisieren. Sakralisierung und Heiligung sind nicht dasselbe. Es handelt sich um verschiedene Strategien im konziliar-nachkonziliaren Kirche-Welt-Verhältnis. Sichtbar wird darin - um einen aktuellen kirchlichen Leitbegriff zu zitieren - auch die Entscheidungsfrage jeder missionarischen Pastoral: Geht es darum, das Profane zu sakralisieren? Oder aber Spuren des Heiligen darin zu entdecken? Zielt sie auf eine Ausweitung des kirchlichen Sakralbezirkes auf neue Personenkreise oder auf eine Selbstentgrenzung der Kirche auf ihren je größeren Gott, dessen Spuren in der Welt auch auf profanem Pflaster zu finden sind?

Um mit der hinter diesen Entscheidungsfragen stehenden Differenz von Heiligem und Sakralem theologisch weiterführend arbeiten zu können, genügt ein überschaubares Set von Begriffen: das Heilige, das Sakrale und das Profane. Es geht um eine Profanierung des Sakralem im Horizont des Heiligen, die auf dem Zweiten Vatikanum vor allem im Kontext der Pastoralkonstitution wirksam wurde und sich auf jenen Ursprung des

---

[1] Vgl. W. Krebber, „Ich bin der Weg ...". Notizen zur säkularen Spiritualität des Opus Dei, in: A. Zottl (Hrsg.), Weltfrömmigkeit. Grundlagen – Traditionen – Zeugnisse, Eichstätt – Wien 1985, 167–181, bes. 167–175.

Christentums selbst berufen kann, der auch im Zentrum des theologischen Werkes von Edward Schillebeeckx steht: Jesus von Nazareth.[2] Bündeln lässt sich die Problematik dieses Begriffstableaus in dem bereits genannten Begriff der profanen Heiligkeit, der im Umfeld des Konzils von namhaften Theologen wie den beiden Dominikanern Edward Schillebeeckx und M.-Dominique Chenu, aber auch von (Ex-)Jesuiten wie Hans Urs von Balthasar und Karl Rahner diskutiert wurde. Und zwar in der theologisch bedeutsamen Differenz von Heiligem und Sakralem, um die es im Folgenden gehen wird. Denn es gibt sie ja wirklich, die profanen Heiligen, jeder kennt sie: Menschen, die geben, ohne etwas zurückzuerwarten. Helden des Unmöglichen, die sich für andere einsetzen – bis hin zum Einsatz des eigenen Lebens. Der konzilstheologische Anteil dieses Sachverhaltes wird im Folgenden Thema sein. Zunächst im Kontext einer religionssoziologischen, dann auch einer theologischen Begriffsklärung. Und schließlich im Kontext zweier Konzilsinterventionen aus dem Jahr 1964 – eine von Schillebeeckx, eine von Chenu –, in denen es um den Stellenwert des Profanen in der Differenz von Heiligem und Sakralem geht. Abschließend werden noch einige Textpassagen benannt, mit denen sich eine entsprechende „école Chenu-Schillebeeckx"[3] in das Korpus des Zweiten Vatikanums eingeschrieben hat.

1. Das Sakrale, das Profane und das Heilige

Die grundlegende Unterscheidung des Religiösen besteht – zumindest in der französischen Religionssoziologie nach und im Gefolge von Émile Durkheim – in der Differenz von Sakralem und Profanem. Das eine wird vom anderen geschieden. Und diese Unterscheidung selbst wird mit einem potenziell gewaltproduktiven Tabu des Religiösen belegt. Man kann das sehr schön an der Etymologie des Profanen ablesen. Das *fanum* ist in

---

[2] Schon ein kurzer Blick auf die interne Geographie des damaligen Judentums zeigt: Jesus war weder ein Essener, der den Tempel spirituell in die Wüste verlegte, noch ein Pharisäer, der ihn in seinem Alltag verortete. Während die einen aus der profanen Welt flüchteten und in die Wüste gingen, zog Jesus durch die Dörfer Galiläas hinauf nach Jerusalem. Und während die anderen durch die häusliche Nachahmung von Tempelpraktiken ihre Alltagswelt sakralisierten, profanierte Jesus den Tempelkult, indem er die in Jerusalem vom Hohenpriester am Jom Kippur vollzogene Sündenvergebung auf den Straßen seiner Heimat praktizierte: „Jesus] [...] verlegte den Tempel [...] in den Alltag Galiläas." (M. Ebner, Jesus – ein Weisheitslehrer? Synoptische Weisheitslogien im Traditionsprozess [Herder Biblische Studien Bd. 15], Freiburg/Br. 1998, 413f.).
[3] H. de Lubac, Carnets du concile II, Paris 2007, 251.

der lateinischen Antike der vom übrigen Alltagsleben abgetrennte, sakrale Tempelbezirk. Alles, was vor ihm liegt, ist das *pro-fanum*, das Profane. Beides ist jedoch, allein schon über seine etymologische Wurzel, eng mit dem Begriff des ‚Fana-tismus' verbunden: einer fanatischen Absolutsetzung der Grenze zwischen Sakralem und Profanem. Roger Caillois, der mit seinen Mitstreitern des *Collège de Sociologie* eine ‚Sakralsoziologie' der Vergesellschaftung durch kollektive Erregungen betrieben hat, verfasste in der sozialen Gärung der 1930er Jahre das wichtigste Buch dazu: *L'homme et le sacré* (1939). In diesem Klassiker der Religionssoziologie wird das Religiöse über die Differenz von Sakralem und Profanem zum Thema gemacht. Diese Differenz ist geeignet, die verschiedensten religiösen Phänomene zu beschreiben. Für eine *theologische* Auseinandersetzung mit dem Thema jedoch reicht sie nicht aus. Dazu braucht es eine sprachliche Unterscheidung, die im Deutschen nicht auf den ersten Blick erkennbar ist: die Differenz von Heiligem und Sakralem. Denn das Heilige und das Sakrale sind nicht dasselbe. Das haben auch französische Intellektuelle wie Émile Benveniste[4], Emmanuel Lévinas[5] und Jacques Derrida erkannt. Letztgenannter schreibt im Rahmen seiner einschlägigen Capri-Diskurse über das religiöse Zeugnis: „Das pure Zeugnis [...] kann sich auf verschiedene Weisen aufteilen. Zunächst in die Alternative zwischen einer Sakralität ohne Glaube (Stichwort: Heidegger) und des Glaubens einer Heiligkeit ohne Sakralität [...] (Stichwort: Levinas, besonders als Autor von *Du sacré au saint*). [...] Man muss [...] das Heilige und das Sakrale voneinander trennen."[6]

Was im Deutschen meist unterschiedslos mit ‚heilig' übersetzt wird, heißt im Lateinischen *sacer* bzw. *sanctus* oder im Englischen *sacred* bzw. *saint*. Die deutsche Sprache kennt diese Differenzierung nicht und muss sich mit dem Fremdwort ‚sakral' behelfen, um sie zum Ausdruck zu bringen. Beim Begriff des Heiligen im Sinne von *sanctus* bzw. *saint* jedoch kann das Deutsche weiterhelfen. Dort ist das Heilige nämlich etymologisch an das Adjektiv „heil"[7] gebunden, was soviel wie ganz, gesund und unversehrt bedeutet. Der biblische Gott als der Heilige schlechthin steht für umfassendes Heil. Und Heil ist, wo ich ganz sein darf. Das schafft Identität in den Differenzen meines Lebens. Ich darf mit mir selbst identisch sein: im Sakralen genauso wie auch im Profanen. Die theologische

---

[4] Vgl. É. Benveniste, Le vocabulaire des institutions indo-européennes. Pouvoir, droit, religion. Vol. 2, Paris 1969.
[5] Vgl. E. Levinas, Du sacré au saint. Cinq nouvelles lectures Talmudiques, Paris 1977.
[6] J. Derrida, Foi et Savoir. Suivi de, Le Siècle et le Pardon, Paris 1996, 97f.
[7] Vgl. F. Kluge, Etymologisches Wörterbuch der deutschen Sprache, Berlin ²³1999.

Rede vom universalen Heilswillen Gottes kann somit zu einer zeitgemäßen, da differenztauglichen Spiritualität verhelfen – und damit zu einer Geisteshaltung, die Esoterik und Fundamentalismus gleichermaßen meidet. Beide haben mit der Setzung sakraler Differenzen zu tun: Banalisierung durch Esoterik negiert sie, Fanatisierung durch Fundamentalismus dehnt sie ins Extrem. Die wesentliche Kunst religiösen Lebens von heute besteht darum in einer entsprechend nichtbanalen wie unfanatischen Kultivierung von Religion.

Dieser komplexe Zusammenhang lässt sich anhand zweier liturgischer Praktiken des Christentums veranschaulichen[8]: Weihe und Segen. Etwas zu weihen heißt, es aus der Ordnung des Profanen herauszunehmen und mit einem Tabu des Sakralen zu belegen. Etwas zu segnen bedeutet, es jenseits der Differenz von Sakralem und Profanen in einen Horizont universalen Heils zu stellen. Kurz gesagt: Weihe schließt aus, Segen schließt ein. Während sich in der Weihe sakralisierende Teilungspraktiken bündeln, stellt der Segen den gesamten Alltag unter eine Verheißung heilvoller Ganzheit. So weiht zum Beispiel die römisch-katholische Kirche in der Regel vor allem zölibatär lebende Männer zu Priestern, segnet aber Osterspeisen, Wohnräume und sogar Motorräder. Es gibt aber auch paradoxe religiöse Gestalten wie zum Beispiel jene ersten französischen Arbeiterpriester[9], denen auch Edward Schillebeeckx nahestand. Sie verkörpern die sakrale Lebensform eines Heiligen *im* Profanen, das im Sinne des Konzils eher auf eine heiligende Assoziierung von Kirche und Welt als auf deren sakrale Dissoziierung zielt. Natürlich ist der Priester eine religiöse Gestalt des Sakralen. Genau darin ist er aber auch die Verkörperung eines christlichen Glaubens an das Heilige, der die herkömmliche

---

[8] Chenu bemerkt dazu: „Die Weihe hat eine eigene Dichte, die man in ihrer Originalität erst wertschätzen kann, wenn man sie zum Beispiel mit dem geringeren Akt einer einfachen Segnung vergleicht. Der Gegenstand wird in diesem Fall sicherlich in eine Beziehung zu Gott gesetzt [...], behält aber seine natürliche Funktion, seine irdischen Behandlungsweisen und seine nützliche Zielbestimmung. Gesegnetes Brot wird respektiert, aber gegessen." (M.-D. Chenu, Les laïcs et la ‚consécration' du monde, in: ders., Peuple de Dieu dans le monde, Paris 1966, 69–96, hier 77f.).

[9] Vgl. Ch. Bauer, Priester im Blaumann. Impulse aus der französischen Bewegung der Arbeiterpriester, in: R. Bucher / J. Pock (Hrsg.), Klerus und Pastoral (Werkstatt Theologie. Praxisorientierte Studien und Diskurse Bd. 14), Berlin 2010, 115–148; Ch. Bauer / V. Straßner, Kirchliche Präsenz in der Fabrik. Das Experiment der französischen Arbeiterpriester, in: M. Woyke (Hrsg.), Säkularisierung und Neuformierung des Religiösen. Religion und Gesellschaft seit der Mitte des 20. Jahrhunderts (Archiv für Sozialgeschichte Bd. 51), Bonn 2011, 187–208. Arbeiterpriester verweisen gerne auf das Beispiel Jesu, der Zeit seines irdischen Lebens nur eine ‚Messe' gefeiert, drei Jahre lang ‚Katechese' betrieben und die übrigen dreißig Jahre mit der Hand gearbeitet habe.

Hinordnung von Laien auf das Profane und von Klerikern auf das Sakrale überschreitet: „Seit der Erfahrung der Arbeiterpriester definiert man den Priester nicht mehr als einen Mann des Sakralen."[10] Er gelte nun als ein „Mann Gottes"[11], der für eine „Desakralisierung des Priestertums"[12] stehe – und dem man sogleich eine Reihe binnenkirchlicher Petitessen zum Vorwurf machte: „Pater X las die Messe im Overall. Anstatt *Dominus vobiscum* zu sagen, begrüßte Pater Y die Gemeinde mit ‚Salut, les copains' (‚Hallo, Leute'). Pater Z übersetzte *Ite missa est* mit ‚Auf, die Messe der Welt beginnt'."[13]

Der Begriff des Arbeiterpriesters verbindet ein profanes Außen („Arbeiter ...") mit dem sakralen Innen („... priester") zu einer nichtklerikalen Theologie des Priestertums. Jenseits exkludierender Teilungspraktiken des Sakralen (Stichwort: Priester im Talar) standen die ersten französischen Arbeiterpriester für inkludierende Ganzheitspraktiken des Heiligen (Stichwort: Priester im Blaumann). Auf diese Weise kam etwas Heiliges zur Darstellung, das Sakrales wie Profanes zugleich umfasst, durchdringt und verwandelt – und zwar in Richtung auf Heil. Zahlreiche katholische Meistertheologen des 20. Jahrhunderts wie Hans Urs von Balthasar[14], Karl Rahner[15], M.-Dominique Chenu[16] oder eben auch Edward Schille-

---

[10] Siehe M.-D. Chenu, Depuis l'expérience des prêtres-ouvriers, on ne définit plus le prêtre comme ‚homme du sacré', in: *Informations catholiques internationales* 472 (1976), 22–24.

[11] Ders., Le prêtre, handschriftliches Vortragsmanuskript vom 6.2.1968; Archives-Chenu/Paris, 1.

[12] Ebd., 2.

[13] P. Hebblethwaite, Johannes XXIII. Das Leben des Angelo Roncalli, Zürich 1986, 279. Im Brief eines Kurienkardinals war zu lesen: „Priester im Blaumann nahmen am Ende eines Essens mit ihren ‚Kumpels' aus der Fabrik das Brot und den Wein des Tisches, konsekrierten beides und verteilten es dann als Kommunion unter ihren Tischgenossen. In einem anderen Fall lehrte man den Gläubigen [...] eine einfache Antwort auf den liturgischen Gruß ‚Der Herr sei mit Euch': „D'ac!" [frz. ‚d'accord' = in Ordnung, okay]. Anderswo sprach man von Jesus nur als dem ‚großen Kumpel' oder man jubelte sich zu ‚Auf den tollen Burschen Jesus! Hip-hip Hurra!'." (zit. nach: Les Prêtres-Ouvriers. Documents, Paris 1954, 91).

[14] Der durch Thomas von Aquin ‚getaufte' Aristotelismus des Mittelalters ist für Balthasar eine „Geburtsstunde der modernen ‚Profanität'" (H.U. von Balthasar, Verbum caro. Skizzen zur Theologie I, Einsiedeln 1960, 99–200, hier 200): „Die hohe Scholastik [...] bedeutet den einzigartigen Kairos, in welchem die Theologie eben noch die sich verselbständigende Weltwissenschaft sakral zu verklären [...] vermag und damit den Profanwissenschaften ein Ethos mit auf den Weg gibt, das aus dem Bereich christlicher Heiligkeit stammt [...]." (ebd.).

[15] Rahner schloss sich in einem konzilsbezogenen Vortrag der Argumentation von Schillebeeckx an: „[Es ist] [...] noch deutlicher als bisher zu sagen, diese profane Welt [...] um eine Formulierung E. Schillebeeckx' aufzugreifen, zwar keine sakralisierte, aber doch [...] eine geheiligte ist. Das, was wir Gnade nennen [...], beginnt nicht erst dort, wo explizite Glaubensbotschaft, Kirche, Kult, Sakrament und geschriebenes Wort Gottes anfangen. All dieses explizit Sakrale ist vielmehr das [...] von Gott verfügte Zusichselbstkommen jener [...] Vergött-

beeckx[17] haben, wie bereits erwähnt, mit dieser Differenz von Sakralem und Heiligem gearbeitet. Schon die genannten Namen belegen, dass Schillebeeckx mit seinen Vorstellungen profaner Heiligkeit kein einsames theologisches Originalgenie war. Während der 1960er Jahre lagen die Themen „Desakralisierung und Heiligung"[18] vielmehr in der Luft. Heribert Mühlen spricht in diesem Zusammenhang von der Entsakralisierung als einem „epochalen Schlagwort"[19] und trifft damit den weltfreudigen kirchlichen Geist dieser Zeit. Schillebeeckx und andere hatten die richtige Nase, nahmen frühzeitig Witterung auf und haben sich auf eine theologisch noch immer anregende Weise damit auseinandergesetzt.

2. „École Chenu-Schillebeeckx" (H. de Lubac)

Der Autor dieses Beitrags ist kein Schillebeeckx-Fachmann. Er wurde mit einer Arbeit über M.-Dominique Chenu promoviert und kennt sich von dorther auch ein wenig in der *Nouvelle théologie* aus. Beide Größen, Chenu und die *Nouvelle théologie*, haben auch Schillebeeckx stark geprägt. Er selbst sagt über den Erstgenannten: „Er ist vielleicht der Mann, der mein theologisches Denken [...] am meisten inspiriert hat [...]. [...] Für mich war er die Verkörperung des dominikanischen Ideals [...]. Sein Büchlein ‚Le Saulchoir: eine theologische Hochschule' [...] hat mich stark inspiriert, später auch sein theologisches Geleit der Arbeiterpriester."[20]

lichung [...], in der Gott die ganze Welt [...] schon immer angenommen und geheiligt hat. Dieses sakralisierende Erscheinen der geheimen Angenommenheit der ganzen Welt ist gewiß selbst ein Moment [...] dieser Geheiligtheit der Welt von ihrem Ursprung her. Aber Erscheinung und Erscheinendes, Sakrament und Gnade decken sich nicht. [...] In ihrem Verhältnis zu der geheiligten, aber nicht sakralisierten Welt ist die Kirche noch sehr im Werden [...], weil sie [...] noch manches geschichtlich bedingt sakralisiertes Gelände aufgeben kann, das sie einst mit Recht bebaute [...]. Solche Besinnung auf das [...] Evangelium [...] und solche Freigabe der Welt in ihr Eigenes [...], bedeuten keine Kapitulation [...], noch den Rückzug aus einer [...] profanen Welt in einen bloß sakralen Bereich. Der von Gott immer geheiligten Welt sagt auch morgen das Evangelium ihr letztes Geheimnis zu." (K. Rahner, Der Mensch von heute und die Religion, in: ders., Schriften zur Theologie VI, Einsiedeln 1965, 13–33, hier 31ff.).

[16] Vgl. M.-D. Chenu, Les laïcs et la ‚consécration' du monde, a.a.O.
[17] Vgl. E. Schillebeeckx, Kirche und Welt im Licht des Zweiten Vatikanischen Konzils, in: ders., Gott – Kirche – Welt. Aus dem Niederländischen von H. Zulauf (Gesammelte Schriften Bd. 2), Mainz 1970, 228–242.
[18] C. Geffré, Désacralisation et Sanctification, in: *Concilium* 2 (1966), 93–108.
[19] H. Mühlen, Entsakralisierung. Ein epochales Schlagwort in seiner Bedeutung für die Zukunft der christlichen Kirche, Paderborn 1970.
[20] E. Schillebeeckx, Gott ist jeden Tag neu. Ein Gespräch, Mainz 1984, 32f.

Die beiden Dominikaner Dominic de Petter, der philosophische Lehrer von Schillebeeckx, und M.-Dominique Chenu, sein theologischer Lehrer (wenn auch Schillebeeckx nie im strengen Sinn sein Schüler war), sind durch eine markante Jahreszahl miteinander verbunden, die im Zusammenhang mit der Indizierung von *Une école de théologie* für beide den Verlust des Lehrstuhls (bzw. im Falle Chenus auch des Regentenamtes) bedeutete: 1942. In diesem Jahr wurden beide zum Gegenstand kirchendisziplinarischer Maßnahmen, die auch ihre jeweilige Hochschule betrafen. Nicht nur das Saulchoir, sondern auch die Hochschule der belgischen Dominikanerprovinz in Löwen, wo Schillebeeckx studierte und De Petter lehrte, musste sich 1942 einer Apostolischen Visitation unterziehen. Chenu blieb in den Jahrzehnten danach noch lange eine römische *persona non grata* und wurde erst durch Papst Paul VI. offiziell rehabilitiert.

Auf dem Konzil arbeitete er dennoch eng mit Schillebeeckx zusammen. Der Jesuit Henri de Lubac kritisierte in seinem Konzilstagebuch einige aus seiner Sicht „abenteuerlichen Theorien"[21] dieser dominikanischen „école Chenu-Schillebeeckx"[22]. Chenu und Schillebeeckx gäben zwar beide vor, im „Namen des Hl. Thomas zu sprechen"[23], verträten aber theologisch gefährliche Thesen – namentlich in ihrer Rede von einer „durch die Inkarnation gewirkten Konsekration der Welt"[24]. De Lubac schreibt: „Habe mit [...] dem Pfarrer von St.-Germain-des-Près [...] geplaudert. Er fragt mich, was ich über eine Theorie denke, die sich gerade in Paris [...] zu verbreiten beginne. Die Welt sei immer schon christlich. Und die christliche Offenbarung lasse uns das nur in einer einfachen Passage vom Impliziten zum Expliziten auch so aussprechen usw. Ich sage ihm, dass ich hundertprozentig gegen diese Meinung bin [...]. Père Schillebeeckx vertritt diese Theorie gegenwärtig sogar in Rom [...]. Und auch Père Chenu ist davon beeinflusst, wie ein kleiner Textbeitrag für die *Nouvelle Revue Théologique* über die ‚Consecratio mundi' zeigt."[25]

---

[21] H. de Lubac, Carnets du concile, a.a.O., 251.
[22] Ebd.
[23] Ebd.
[24] Ebd.
[25] Ebd., 218. Zur thomanischen Grundierung dieser Rede vom impliziten Christentum siehe Ch.J. Amor, „Schrankenloser Heilsoptimismus"? Ein thomistisches Schlaglicht auf *Gaudium et spes*, in: F. Gmainer-Pranzl / M.M. Holztrattner (Hrsg.), Partnerin der Menschen – Zeugin der Hoffnung. Die Kirche im Licht der Pastoralkonstitution *Gaudium et spes*, Innsbruck – Wien 2010, 239–263 (vgl. GS 22; LG 16) sowie zum Hl. Thomas auf dem Zweiten Vatikanum generell Ch. Bauer, Ortswechsel der Theologie. M.-Dominique Chenu im Kontext seiner Programmschrift *Une école de théologie: Le Saulchoir* (2 Bde.), Berlin 2010, 635–665.

2.1. Edward Schillebeeckx: Kirche und Welt

Um die beiden hier genannten Konzilsbeiträge von Schillebeeckx und Chenu wird es im Folgenden gehen.

Der von Kollegen wie Lubac[26] und Rahner[27] prominent wahrgenommene Vortrag von Schillebeeckx wurde an einem konzilsöffentlich wichtigen Anlass gehalten – bei der Eröffnung des neuen Gebäudes des Niederländischen *Documentatie centrum concilie* (DO-C) am 16. September 1964. Der Flame Schillebeeckx situiert sein Vortragsthema *Kirche und Welt im Licht des Zweiten Vatikanischen Konzils* dabei zunächst im Rahmen einer konzilstheologischen Prioritätenklärung: „Wie wichtig viele Konzilsentscheidungen über kirchliche Strukturen und Funktionen auch sein mögen, worauf es letztlich ankommt, sind die konkreten Menschen. Sie werden tagein, tagaus mit weltlichen Problem konfrontiert [...]. [...] Deshalb steht und fällt die säkulare Bedeutung des [...] Konzils mit dem Ergebnis von ‚Schema 13‘ [...]."[28]

Das Zweite Vatikanum steht nicht nur Chenu zufolge, sondern auch für Schillebeeckx im „geistigen Tiefenstrom von Chalzedon"[29]: „Das menschliche Dasein Christi mit all seinen geschichtlichen Bedingungen und Implikationen ist das [...] Leben Gottes [...] selbst. Damit sind die tiefsten, ungeahnten Möglichkeiten des Menschseins bloßgelegt. [...] Die irdische Geschichte wird somit nicht sakralisiert, denn sie behält ihre spezifische Eigenständigkeit, sondern geheiligt: aufgenommen in die absolute und ungeschuldete Gegenwart des Mysteriums. [...] Auch in unserem irdischen Leben sind wir bei Gott, nicht nur im Gebet, im kirchlichen Kult und in den Sakramenten."[30]

Schillebeeckx begründet dies mit der „weltliche[n] Säkularität"[31] des Schöpfungsauftrags Gottes an den Menschen: „Schöpfung ist [...] ein göttliches Setzen von Realitäten in ihrer profanen, nicht-göttlichen Eigenheit. Der Genesisbericht schildert in Abwehr gegen die [...] Schöpfungsberichte der Nachbarn Israels diesen göttlichen Akt als ein Handeln, das die Welt entmythologisiert und entsakralisiert, das die Welt an sich

---

[26] Vgl. H. de Lubac, Carnets du concile, a.a.O., 251.
[27] Vgl. K. Rahner, Der Mensch von heute und die Religion, a.a.O., 31f.
[28] E. Schillebeeckx, Kirche und Welt im Licht des Zweiten Vatikanischen Konzils, a.a.O., 228.
[29] M.-D. Chenu, Le rôle de l'Église dans le monde contemporain, in: G. Baraúna (Hrsg.), L'Église dans le monde de ce temps. Une analyse de la constitution ‚Gaudium et spes'. Bd. 2, Brügge 1968, 422–443, hier 440.
[30] E. Schillebeeckx, Kirche und Welt im Licht des Zweiten Vatikanischen Konzils, a.a.O., 230f.
[31] Ebd., 232.

selbst ausliefert, in die Hände des Menschen [...]. Und darin liegt beschlossen, dass aufgrund des immerwährenden Schöpfungsaktes Gottes die Geschichte der Menschheit eine stets weiter durchgeführte Entsakralisierung der irdischen Strukturen [...] zeigen wird."[32]

Es folgt jene Textpassage, welche die zitierte Kritik Lubacs auf sich zog. Schillebeeckx bezeichnet die Welt darin als „nicht sakral, aber geheiligt" (im Sinne einer First-order-Aussage) und die Kirche als den „eigens herausgehobenen Ausdruck dieser Heiligung" (im Sinne einer Second-order-Aussage): „In der heutigen Heilssituation der Inkarnation ist ‚die Welt' *implizites Christentum*, ein eigener, nichtsakraler, aber geheiligter Ausdruck der Lebensgemeinschaft des Menschen mit [...] Gott, während die Kirche als Heilsinstitution mit ihrem [...] Glaubensbekenntnis, ihrem Kult und ihren Sakramenten der eigens herausgehobene sakrale Ausdruck dieser Heiligung ist. [...] Anonymes, aber reales Christentum bedeutet in diesem Zusammenhang [...] die innerweltliche Lebensrealität, die in ihrer profanen Eigenständigkeit in die absolute und ungeschuldete Nähe des Mysteriums aufgenommen ist [...]."[33]

Schillebeeckx unterscheidet zwei „komplementäre Verwirklichungsformen des einen Christentums"[34]: einerseits den „sakralen, eigens gesetzten *kirchlichen* Ausdruck des theologalen Lebens der Gläubigen"[35] und andererseits den „*weltlichen*, nicht eigens gesetzten Ausdruck dieses Gnadenlebens"[36]. Und er präzisiert: „Nur insofern dieses theologale Leben selbst implizit und anonym bleibt und nicht zum eigentlichen Ausdruck in den spezifisch kirchlichen Gestalten kommt, können wir diese beiden Realisierungsformen des Christentums mit den Worten explizites und implizites Christentum bezeichnen."[37] In einer ergänzenden Fußnote fügt Schillebeeckx hinzu: „Es ist klar, dass der Status des impliziten Christentums von der Gnadenablehnung der Menschen durchkreuzt werden kann. Es liegt deshalb nicht in unserer Absicht, zu sagen, alle außerkirchlichen Menschen seien per se implizite Christen. [...] Es ist angebracht, dies kurz zu vermerken, weil der Einwand, es sei unverantwortlich, alle nichtkirchlichen Menschen zu impliziten Christen zu erklären, sicher zutrifft, wie

---

[32] Ebd.
[33] Ebd., 232f.
[34] Ebd., 232.
[35] Ebd.
[36] Ebd., 232f.
[37] Ebd., 233.

man übrigens genauso gut sagen muss, dass nicht alle expliziten oder Kirchenchristen schon per se wahre Christen sind."[38]

Wie in der Rede vom anonymen Christentum bei Karl Rahner[39], so geht es auch hier weniger darum, Nichtchristen gegen ihren Willen einzugemeinden, als vielmehr darum, den Christen ihre bisweilen allzu große Sicherheit in Sachen Gott zu nehmen. Es geht also weniger um anonyme oder implizite Christen, als um einen anonymen Gott[40], der sich unserem glaubenssicheren Zugriff immer wieder entzieht. Auch wir Kirchenchristen haben ihn nicht, auch wir müssen ihn erst noch suchen – und zwar auf vertrautem sakralem Gelände ebenso wie auf fremdem, im Wortsinn ‚heraus-forderndem' profanem Boden: „Aus dieser dogmatischen Sicht folgt, dass das Problem des ‚Schemas 13' nicht so gesehen werden darf, als ob die Kirche [...] nach der Konstitution über die Kirche [= LG], in der wir uns auf heiligem Boden befanden, jetzt eine ihr fremde, unheilige Welt beträte. Der Boden, den wir im Schema 13 betreten, ist *heiliger Boden*, auf dem schon Christi Erlösungsgnade wirksam ist, noch bevor die Amtskirche das rettende Wort Christi explizit an diese Welt richtet. [...] Die erste Aufgabe von Schema 13 liegt [...] darin, dass die Kirche die Heiligkeit des Bodens, den sie betritt [...], offiziell anerkennt."[41]

Schillebeeckx bezeichnet das implizite Christentum der Welt seiner Zeit als *das* „Arbeitsgebiet von ‚Schema 13'"[42]. Damit begebe sich die Kirche auf profanen Boden, um nach Spuren des Heiligen zu suchen: „Das schließt ihr Ja zur Eigengesetzlichkeit dieser Welt mit ein, da es nicht um eine Sakralisierung, sondern um eine Heiligung der weltlichen Wirklichkeit geht. [...] Deshalb hat die Kirche in Schema 13 dieser Welt nicht nur etwas zu sagen, sondern sie hat auch auf das zu hören, was das weltliche, implizite oder explizite, Christentum [...] anzeigt, sowohl in der außerkirchlichen ‚weltlichen' Welt als auch in den laikalen Erfahrungen seiner ausdrücklichen Gläubigen. [...] Und wenn die Kirche im Konzil ihr

---

[38] Ebd. – Siehe auch folgendes Augustinuszitat von Papst Benedikt XVI.: „Es sind viele draußen, die drinnen zu sein scheinen; und es sind viele drinnen, die draußen zu sein scheinen." (Benedikt XVI. / P. Seewald, Licht der Welt. Der Papst, die Kirche und die Zeichen der Zeit, Freiburg/Br. 2010, 20f.).

[39] Vgl. H.-J. Sander, Einführung in die Gotteslehre, Darmstadt 2006, 118–120; G.M. Hoff, Der fremde Ort des eigenen Gottes. Karl Rahners Theorie von den anonymen Christen als Grammatik theologischer Fremdsprachen, in: *Salzburger Theologische Zeitschrift* 11 (2007) 201–216.

[40] Vgl. Ch. Bauer, Gott und die Nebelkinder. Theologische Notizen über einen anonymen Berliner, in: Jahrbuch für das Erzbistum Berlin 2004, Berlin 2003, 72–78.

[41] E. Schillebeeckx, Kirche und Welt im Licht des Zweiten Vatikanischen Konzils, a.a.O., 234.

[42] Ebd., 234.

Ohr zum Hören öffnet, [...] dann hört sie nicht auf fremde Klänge, die von außen kommen, sondern sie erkennt darin die Stimme ihres eigenen Herrn wieder [...]. Dann hört sie auf die Frohe Botschaft, die [...] nicht nur aus der Schrift zu uns spricht, sondern ebenso aus jeder menschlichen Existenzerfahrung, die [...] mit der Huld des lebendigen Gottes konfrontiert wird."[43]

Schillebeeckx bringt in diesem Zusammenhang auch den Unterschied zwischen *Lumen gentium*, der bereits beschlossenen „Dogmatischen Kirchenkonstitution"[44], und *Gaudium et spes*, der zu diesem Zeitpunkt noch in einer kritischen Phase befindlichen „Pastoralen Kirchenkonstitution"[45] auf dem Punkt: „In der [dogmatischen] Konstitution über die Kirche spricht sie [= die Kirche] vor allem über die sakralen [...] kirchlichen Gestalten der Gnadensichtbarkeit; in Schema 13 behandelt sie die weltlichen und deshalb mehr verhüllten Ausdrucksformen [...] dieses Gnadenlebens: die weltliche Heiligkeit und die apostolische Säkularität."[46]

Die kirchliche Gestalt des Laien wird in dieser Perspektive zu einer Figur der christlichen Avantgarde in einer säkularen Welt: „[Das Schema muss] [...] aus den laikalen Existenzerfahrungen der Christen [heraus verfasst werden], die aufgrund ihrer Bindung an irdische Realitäten [...] die Frage [...] nach der Stellung der Kirche in ihrem Leben stellen. [...] Nur dann kann zu befreiendem Ausdruck kommen, wie die Kirche einerseits [...] Nicht-Welt ist, und wie andererseits die ‚Zusammenfassung aller Dinge in Christus als dem Haupt' im Gnadenleben des Menschen [...] wirklich eine weltliche Heiligkeit und eine apostolische Säkularität ins Leben ruft [...]. [...] Denn durch die gnadenvolle, aktive Gegenwart des Mysteriums [...] werden Natur und Gnade nicht sakralisiert oder ihrer profanen Bedeutung entzogen, sondern geheiligt [...]."[47]

2.2. M.-Dominique Chenu: Weihe der Welt

Eng mit diesen Überlegungen von Schillebeeckx verwandt ist Chenus 1965 erstmals veröffentlichter Beitrag *Les laïcs et la ‚consécration' du monde*, der ebenfalls auf eine entsprechende Konzilsintervention von 1964 zurückgeht und als eine theologische Auslegung von LG 34 veröffentlicht

---

[43] Ebd., 234f.
[44] Lat. „Constitutio dogmatica de Ecclesia".
[45] Lat. „Constitutio pastoralis de Ecclesia [in mundo huius temporis]".
[46] E. Schillebeeckx, Kirche und Welt im Licht des Zweiten Vatikanischen Konzils, a.a.O., 235f.
[47] Ebd., 239f.

wurde. Zunächst der Konzilstext: „So weihen auch die Laien [et laici ... consecrant], als Anbetende im heiligen Tun [adoratores sancte agentes], die Welt selbst Gott [ipsum mundum Deo]." (LG 34). Chenu beginnt seine Interpretation zunächst mit einer humanwissenschaftlichen Klärung der Begriffe: „Was ist genau unter einer ‚Konsekration' zu verstehen? [...] Es handelt sich um einen Akt, in dem der Mensch [...] eine Sache ihrem normalen Gebrauch oder eine Person ihrer ursprünglichen Bestimmung entzieht [...]. [...] Der auf diese Weise ausgesonderte sakrale Gegenstand ist beinahe in physischem Sinn unberührbar [...]. [...] Die Religionswissenschaftler beobachten dies [...] noch viel konkreter als die Theologen [...]."[48]

Chenu wechselt nun von einer religionswissenschaftlich-formalen zu einer theologisch-inhaltlichen Argumentation und trägt mit der Unterscheidung von Heiligem und Sakralem eine in diesem Zusammenhang wesentliche Differenz ein: „Das Sakrale erscheint in seiner ganzen Eigenart, wenn man es mit dem Heiligen vergleicht. Beide Begriffe unterliegen [...] konstanten Interferenzen [...]. Die Heiligkeit besitzt jedoch [...] andere Eigenschaften als die Sakralisierung. Gott ist zwar ‚heilig' [...], nicht aber im eigentlichen Sinn sakral. Die Heiligkeit ist jene überragende Würde, die man durch Teilhabe am göttlichen Leben annimmt. Trotz dieser Vereinigung mit dem Transzendenten sondert die Heiligkeit sich [...] nicht ab. Sie kann [...] in ihrer Initiation [...] sakrale Absonderungen erfordern, aber das sind nur irdische Bedingungen einer Gnade, die [...] das Sein in der vollen Wirklichkeit [...] seiner profanen Natur erfasst. Wenn das Profane auf die Seite des Sakralen tritt, dann hört es auf, profan zu sein. Das Profane aber, das heilig wird, bleibt profan."[49]

Der thomanisch geprägte Dominikaner Chenu, dessen implizite Theorie der Moderne von einer gottgewollten „Autonomie des Profanen"[50] ausgeht, begrüßt die moderne Entzauberung der Welt als eine wünschenswerte Desakralisierung: „Um einer gewissen panischen Angstvorstellung angesichts dessen entgegenzuwirken, was man den Atheismus der Industriekultur nennt, wollen wir festhalten, dass es in der innersten Gesetzmäßigkeit des Christentums liegt, die Welt zu desakralisieren, sie von ihren Göttern und Dämonen zu reinigen [...]. [...] Einer der tiefsten Charakterzüge im Denken des Konzils besteht in einem wachen Bewusst-

---

[48] M.-D. Chenu, Les laïcs et la ‚consécration' du monde, a.a.O., 76f.
[49] Ebd., 78.
[50] Ders., Le sacerdoce en question, maschinenschriftliches Manuskript o. J., Archives-Chenu/Paris, 6.

sein für [...] den Eigenwert der profanen Wirklichkeiten. [...] Man muss die Welt nicht sakralisieren, um sie zu heiligen."[51]

Eine solche Heiligung des Profanen braucht aus inkarnatorischen Gründen immer auch die kirchliche Ausdrücklichkeit des Sakralen: „In gewissem Sinn gibt es im Christen keine profane Wirklichkeit mehr [...], denn die Unterscheidung zwischen heilig und sakral ist überwunden. [Und doch] [...] gibt es die Notwendigkeit eines Kultes, in dem der Glaube an das Mysterium – in Anpassung an die *condition humaine* und an näherhin ‚religiöse' Bedürfnisse – seinen sinnenfälligen Ausdruck findet. [...] Ein solcher äußerlicher und sinnlich erfahrbarer Kult liegt in der Logik der Inkarnation. [...] Es ist daher legitim, den Begriff der Weihe [consécration] zu benutzen, um diesen speziellen Aspekt der Heiligung des Profanen durch die Gnade Christi zum Ausdruck zu bringen."[52]

Das Christentums hat eine doppelte Identität als Glaube *und* Religion – oder im Horizont der Inkarnationstheologie Chenus besser: als Glaube *in* Religion. Denn es gibt keinen christlichen Glauben ohne Religion.[53] Auch hinter dieser Verhältnisbestimmung steht eine „klassische Unterscheidung"[54] der Theologie, die diesmal sogar auf Thomas selbst zurückgeht. Ihm zufolge ist nämlich der Glaube eine göttliche Tugend, während die Religion nur eine Angelegenheit menschlicher Pflichten gegenüber Gott darstellt. In seinem Beitrag *Foi et religion* kommentiert Chenu kurz nach dem Konzil: „Der Glaube lässt dem Menschen seine [...] Welthaftigkeit, während die Religion einen Messerschnitt zwischen das Profane und das Sakrale setzt."[55] Unter dieser Differenz von Glaube und Religion fasste Chenu auch die „großen Themen des Konzils"[56] zusammen, dessen theologisches Zentrum ein mit dem Profanen solidarischer „Glaube, und nicht das Sakrale"[57] sei. Religion bestimmt sich im Christentum vom Zeugnis des Glaubens her und nicht umgekehrt. Von dorther entwickelte

---

[51] Ders., Les laïcs et la ‚consécration' du monde, a.a.O., 80f.
[52] Ebd., 88/90f.
[53] Das gilt ebenso für die Pastoral der christlichen Kirchen – weshalb Hans-Joachim Sanders häufig zitierte Unterscheidung zwischen Pastoral- und Religionsgemeinschaft auch ein wenig unglücklich erscheint. Christliche Pastoral umfasst beides: Glaube und Religion. Religiöse Praktiken vom weit gefassten Pastoralbegriff des Zweiten Vatikanums abzutrennen, halbiert nicht nur diesen Begriff, sondern entzieht das Religiöse auch dem religionskritischen Glaubenspotenzial des Pastoralen. Vielleicht wäre es im Anschluss an M.-Dominique Chenu besser, auf dem Boden eines entsprechend *inkarnierten* Pastoralbegriffs von einer Differenz von Glaubens- und Religionsgemeinschaft zu sprechen.
[54] M.-D. Chenu, Foi et religion, in: *Études philosophiques* 21 (1966), 357–369, hier 360.
[55] Ebd., 365.
[56] Ders, Le sacerdoce en question, a.a.O., 2.
[57] Ebd., 4.

Chenu die glaubensbezogene Theologie eines „profanen Christentums"[58], das einerseits an Dietrich Bonhoeffers Tegeler Skizzen eines „religionslosen Christentums"[59] erinnert und andererseits doch auch dem Inkarnationsbedürfnis des Menschen gerecht wird – inklusive entsprechender Folgen für religiöse Sakralgestalten[60] im Kontext des Konzils.

3. Spuren auf dem Zweiten Vatikanum

Schillebeeckx hat sich mit seiner Stellungnahme auf *Gaudium et spes* bezogen, Chenu auf *Lumen gentium*. Die aus beiden Konstitutionen bestehende Gesamtekklesiologie des Zweiten Vatikanums als einem weltbezogenen „Konzil der Kirche über die Kirche"[61] überschreitet die Unterscheidung von Sakralem und Profanen im Zeichen von Gottes universalem Heilswillen – und anerkennt somit auch eine „gerechte Autonomie der irdischen Wirklichkeiten" (GS 36). Der entsprechende Subtext des Gesamtkorpus aller sechzehn Dokumente ist von einer entsprechenden Differenz des Heiligen und des Sakralen durchzogen.

Man kann diese möglicherweise unbewusst vollzogene theologische Prägung im gesamten Vokabular des Konzils nachweisen. So bezeichnet sich das Zweite Vatikanum zum Beispiel gleich im Titel seines ersten großen Dokumentes, der Liturgiekonstitution, als *Sacrosanctum Concilium*. Diese Sakrales („Sacro-") wie Heiliges („-sanctum") umfassende Selbst-

---

[58] So eine Hauptthese von C.N. Salgado Vaz, Progresso humano e mensagem cristão, Braga 1974 (bes. Kap. VIII). Vielleicht sollte man etwas vorsichtiger (und damit auch theologisch korrekter) von einem *profanierenden* Christentum sprechen.

[59] D. Bonhoeffer, Widerstand und Ergebung. Briefe und Aufzeichnungen aus der Haft, Gütersloh ¹⁵1994, 140. P. Stockmeier resümiert: „Die These befruchtete zahlreiche theologische Strömungen der Gegenwart, von der ‚Gott-ist-tot'-Theologie bis zum Programm der Entsakralisierung [...]." (P. Stockmeier, Glaube und Religion in der frühen Kirche, Freiburg/Br. 1973, 10).

[60] Das Zweite Vatikanum verfügt über einen umfassenderen Begriff vom Priestertum als die damalige Römische Theologie mit ihrem ‚durchsakralisierten' Priesterbild (vgl. Ch. Bauer / V. Straßner, Kirchliche Präsenz in der Fabrik, a.a.O.). Das wird bereits deutlich, wenn man den Titel des konziliaren Priesterdekrets betrachtet, das die Arbeiterpriester ausdrücklich rehabilitierte (PO 8). Es heißt *Presbyterorum ordinis* und eben nicht *Sacerdotorum ordinis*. Presbyter und Sacerdos sind nämlich ebenso wenig dasselbe wie das Heilige und das Sakrale. Priester des Volkes Gottes sind zunächst einmal Presbyter eines Glaubens an das Heilige, dann erst Sacerdotes einer Religion des Sakralen. Oder inkarnatorisch zugespitzt: *Gerade als* Presbyter eines Glaubens an das Heilige sind sie *auch* Sacerdotes einer Religion des Sakralen.

[61] K. Rahner, Das Zweite Vatikanische Konzil. Allgemeine Einleitung, in: ders. / H. Vorgrimler, Kleines Konzilskompendium. Sämtliche Texte des Zweiten Vatikanums, Freiburg/Br. ²⁵1994, 13–33, hier 24.

bezeichnung bringt wohl am treffendsten die sakral-heilige Mischidentität des Konzils zum Ausdruck. Laut Priesterdekret ist dabei niemand anderes als Gott selbst jener eine und einzige „Heilige und Heiligmacher"[62] (PO 5) hinter allem Sakralen und Profanen, der mit Christus auch dessen „mystischen Leib" (PO 2) in der Welt „heiligt bzw. weiht"[63] (PO 12). Es kommt zu einer Übertragung von Fachtermini des Sakralen, die bisher für Priester, Diakone und Ordensleute reserviert waren, auf alle Christgläubigen überhaupt. Nicht nur die Kleriker „weihen"[64] (LG 34) die Welt für Gott, sondern auch – so die von Chenu ausgelegte Stelle – die Laien, indem sie in ihrem Alltag „heilig handeln"[65] (LG 34).

Das Konzil bezeichnet die Kirche in seinen beiden Konstitutionen *De ecclesia (in mundo hodierno)* als ein „universales Sakrament des Heils" (LG 1; GS 44), dessen pastorale Welt-Mission darin besteht, die Kulte und Riten der Völker desakralisierend zu „heilen" (AG 9). Mit dem Konzil entdeckt die Kirche auch „außerhalb ihres Gefüges vielfältige Elemente der Heiligung"[66] (LG 8), weshalb sie über andere Religionen sagen kann: „Die Kirche verwirft nichts von dem, was in diesen Religionen [...] heilig ist."[67] (NA 2). Das Heilige ist für das Konzil keine ‚sakralistisch' exklusive, sondern im Sinne der eingangs genannten Selbstentgrenzung eine missionarische Größe, welche die Kirche aus sich selbst herauslockt in die Welt. Überhaupt ist das Heilige ein verborgenes Grundthema des Zweiten Vatikanums. Ihr widmet es unter der Überschrift *Allgemeine Berufung zur Heiligkeit in der Kirche* sogar das gesamte fünfte Kapitel von *Lumen gentium*. Wenn es zu Beginn dieser Konstitution dann auch noch heißt, alle getauften und gefirmten Glieder des Volkes Gottes seien zu einer „heiligen Priesterschaft geweiht"[68] (LG 10), dann entgrenzt es damit höchstlehramtlich spezifisch sakrale Begriffe.

Das bedeutet vor allem eines: Priester haben im Volk Gottes genauso eine profane Sendung (Stichwort: ‚Weltdienst') wie die Laien eine sakrale Berufung (Stichwort: ‚Heilsdienst') besitzen[69] – und die gemeinsame Mis-

---

[62] Lat. „sanctus et sanctificator".
[63] Lat. „sanctificat vel consecrat".
[64] Lat. „consecrant".
[65] Lat. „sancte agentes".
[66] Lat. „elementa plura sanctificationis".
[67] Lat. „,in his religionibus [...] sancta sunt".
[68] Lat. „consecrantur in sacerdotium sanctum".
[69] E. Klinger betont, mit der Pastoralkonstitution habe das Konzil das „pastorale Wesen sozialer Tätigkeit und das soziale Wesen pastoraler Aufgaben" (E. Klinger, Betreuungspastoral, Mitgliederpastoral oder Sozialpastoral, in: *Imprimatur* 3 [1998], 117–125, hier 121) erschlossen. Eine entgegengesetzte Sichtweise trennt die „pastoralen von den sozialen Themen und

sion beider gilt dem einen Wohl der Menschheit. Das Konzil anerkennt damit nicht nur eine gewisse Autonomie des Profanen, das seinen Ursprung in „demselben Gott" (GS 36) habe wie das Sakrale, sondern es belegt auch jeden „künstlichen Gegensatz zwischen gesellschaftlicher Tätigkeit und religiösem Leben" (GS 43) mit dem einzigen ‚Anathema'[70], das es überhaupt ausspricht: „Von der Wahrheit weichen diejenigen ab [...] , die [...] meinen, [...] ihre irdischen Pflichten vernachlässigen zu können, ohne dabei zu beachten, dass sie gerade durch den Glauben [...] mehr zu deren Erfüllung gehalten sind. Nicht weniger aber irren jene, die umgekehrt meinen, sich so in irdische Geschäfte versenken zu können, als ob diese dem religiösen Leben ganz fremd seien, weil sie [...] meinen, dass dieses in bloßen Kultakten [...] bestehe. [...] Die Spaltung zwischen dem Glauben und dem täglichen Leben gehört zu den vergleichsweise schweren Verirrungen [graviores ... errores] unserer Zeit." (GS 43).

Was das für die von Papst Benedikt XVI. während seines Deutschlandbesuchs im September 2011 aufgeworfene Frage nach einer ‚Entweltlichung' der Kirche bedeutet, mag jede Leserin und jeder Leser selbst entscheiden.

* * *

ordnet sie ganz verschiedenen Personengruppen zu: Für das eine sind die Priester zuständig und für das andere die Laien." (Ebd., 118.)

[70] Diese Verurteilung trifft auch die Konzilsinterpretation von neokonservativen Salonkatholiken wie dem Journalisten Alexander Kissler. Dieser hatte anlässlich des Konflikts um die Piusbruderschaft am 24. März 2009 auf der Literaturseite der *Süddeutschen Zeitung* eine ‚Rezension' der sechzehn Konzilsdokumente veröffentlicht. „Muss ein ‚heiliges Konzil'", so fragt Kissler mit Blick auf *Gaudium et spes* maliziös, „sich Gedanken machen über Freizeit und Urlaub, über Verkehrsregeln und Währungen und Landwirtschaft?" In beispielloser Respektlosigkeit verkennt Kissler die lehramtliche Autorität der Pastoralkonstitution, weil er – wie auch deren Gegner auf dem Konzil und die Piusbruderschaft heute – den theologischen Rang des Profanen nicht anerkennt. Indem er menschliche Erfahrungen ins vermeintlich Belanglose verflacht (und damit zugleich auch einen vom Papst promulgierten Konzilstext lächerlich macht), unterschreitet er das Niveau der Pastoralkonstitution, die nicht nur von Freizeit und Urlaub handelt, sondern auch von Folter, Sklaverei und Völkermord. Wenn in diesem Zusammenhang von einem gottwidrigen Angriff auf „Leben selbst" (GS 27) die Rede ist, dann rückt das Konzil damit die von Giorgio Agamben in die Debatte gebrachte Gestalt des *Homo sacer* in den Fokus kirchlicher Aufmerksamkeit – und damit eine absolute Sakralisierung des Menschen im Doppelsinn des Wortes *sacer* (= sakral, verflucht), welche eine desakralisierende Theologie auf den Plan ruft, die für eine ‚Sanktifizierung' des *Homo sacer* im Zeichen der unteilbaren Würde aller Menschen eintritt.

Abstract of the contribution of Christian Bauer

The "école Chenu-Schillebeeckx" (H. de Lubac), which was developed during the Second Vatican Council, integrated a discussion on the notion of the non-sacral holiness of the profane. This essay explores two exemplary Council interventions (from 1964), both by Edward Schillebeeckx and M.-Dominique Chenu, whose desacralizing tendency made its way into the shaping of the Conciliar documents.

Translation from German: *Tracy Rammler*

Vera Donnelly

THE SACRAMENTALITY OF SCHILLEBEECKX'S THEOLOGICAL JOURNEY

"Life itself in the world then belongs to the very content of God's inner word to us [...] life itself becomes a truly supernatural and external revelation, in which creation begins to speak to us the language of salvation, in which creation becomes a sign of higher realities"[1]. This sentence set me thinking about the sacramentality of Edward Schillebeeckx's life.

He was born in 1914 the year the Great War broke out. In his youth he would have been aware of the injustice and horrific suffering caused by the ravages of war when as the poet wrote 'Flanders fields ran red with blood.' These experiences made a deep impression on Edward Schillebeeckx, and left enduring traces in his work. The tragedy of Flanders was a symbol for what occurs in cycles in human history – widespread and innocent suffering. Confrontation with such terrible suffering evoked what he called a 'contrast' experience; a term he used to express opposition to anything that does not concur with the search for a truly human life.[2] Consequently concern for the immensity of human suffering and oppression became a pervasive theme in the theologian's work since the 1960's, and it also influenced his thinking on soteriology.[3] When he wrote *Jesus* in (1974) and *Christ* in (1977)[4] he was motivated by the hope of providing a new focus for traditional western Christology, in the light of the

---

[1] E. Schillebeeckx, Christ the Sacrament of the Encounter with God, New York: Sheed and Ward, 1963, 8.
[2] Cf. idem, Church, the Human Story of God (English translation by John Bowden), London: SCM Press, 1990, 5–6; idem, Jesus an Experiment in Christology, London: Collins, 1979, 620–622.
[3] Cf. J. O'Meara, Salvation: Living Communion with God, in: M.Ch. Hilkert / R.J. Schreiter (Eds.), The Praxis of the Reign of God, New York: Fordham University Press, 2002.
[4] E. Schillebeeckx, Christ: The Christian Experience in the Modern World, London: SCM Press, 1980. English translation.

critical question whether it is still possible to experience Christian salvation in the ambiguities and paradoxes of the late 20th century.

In the book *Church* he develops more fully the identification between salvation and God's absolute presence in creation that is fundamental to his entire soteriology.[5] God's universal salvific intention for creation is realized whenever and wherever evil is resisted and good is furthered.[6] In chapter one Schillebeeckx establishes a clear distinction between salvation and revelation. Religion and churches are not salvation, but rather contexts in which and through which people become aware of God's saving activity in the whole of creation. For Christians, God is to be found in Jesus Christ, in whose life death and resurrection is disclosed the being of God as human salvation.[7] Schillebeeckx's understanding of the universality of salvation in, and through the liberating praxis of people is addressed in chapter three of *Church*. It is not just the drama of the death and resurrection of Jesus that tells us of God, but the entire ministry and life of Jesus, his "praxis of the reign of God." Only by allowing our own narratives to be engaged with that of Jesus can we hope to understand the experience of what God has done for us in Him.

The uniqueness of Christianity is found in the ways that the followers of Jesus continue to actualize the history and memory of Jesus' praxis of the kingdom, that is, the very being of God as salvation of men and women.

His concern for the ongoing suffering and oppression lead to his involvement with critical Christian communities, and later to his interest in liberation theology. He believed that the reality of such widespread suffering should make one realise that true holiness must include a political dimension that seeks not only the kingdom within, but should also forge bonds of solidarity with all who strive for a better, more human life. The coming of the kingdom of God is a grace, but a grace which is effective in and through human action and not outside it, above it, or behind it: "The transformation of the world, the outlining of a better society and a new earth which is worthwhile for all men and women to live in, has to be taken in hand by contingent human beings themselves. They therefore cannot expect God to solve their problems. Given a proper belief in creation, we cannot shift on to God what is our task in the world [...]. To

---

[5] The idea of creation is the oxygen and lifeblood of E. Schillebeeckx's theology. See "God and Creation" in: M.Ch. Hilkert / R.J. Schreiter (Eds.), The Praxis of the Reign of God, op.cit., Chapter 3.

[6] See E. Schillebeeckx, Church, the Human Story of God, op. cit., Chapters 1 and 5.

[7] See ibid., Chapter, 5.

overcome suffering and evil wherever we encounter them [...] is our task and our burden [...] it is not God's cause, except that this task of ours is within the absolute saving presence of God among us and thus as a human concern is also very close to God's heart."[8]

Schillebeeckx, turning around the usual adage "Outside the church there is no salvation" says "outside the world there is no salvation." He writes: "The world and human history in which God wills to bring about salvation for people are the basis for the whole reality of salvation. There is no salvation, not even religious salvation outside the human world."[9] God's saving power never breaks in from outside saving history. Rather, God's grace is present in the structure of historical human experience and praxis.

The quotation "Outside the world there is no salvation" with its emphasis on the concrete context for human religious life shows, that for Schillebeeckx, human experience has a sacramental character, and it also sums up his understanding of the relation between the sacred and the secular. Indeed, one can say that for him, there is continuity between the concepts of sacrament and of experience; in a sense they are both two sides of the same coin; both are explorations of what happens to people as they come into the presence of God. For him, experience has a sacramental character.

Modern theologians like Schleiermacher and Karl Rahner have argued that God is to be found in the depths of human experience, but dialectical theologians following the lead of Karl Barth in facing the realities of evil, suffering, and sin have argued that the transcendent and hidden God is revealed only in the Word of God – in Jesus Christ. Schillebeeckx proposes another possibility: God is revealed in human experience, but in a dialectical, rather than a direct fashion. The ultimate mystery of compassion at the heart of reality surprises us, as reality resists our human plans and expectations, and as efforts on behalf of those who suffer disclose "something extra" in human experience, the absolute presence of God. He believes that Divine revelation falls within human experience, but is not co-extensive with it. Revelation comes to us with the narrative of experience and history, but always opens us to something beyond that experience and history.

---

[8] Ibid., 231.
[9] Idem, On Christian Faith: The Spiritual, Ethical, and Political Dimensions, New York: Crossroad, 1987, 8.

The Incarnation of the Son of God is central to his thinking. He writes "The humanity of Jesus is concretely intended by God as the fulfilment of the promise of salvation."[10] The Incarnation (of the Son) itself redeems us, because it finds its completion in the supreme moment of the death, resurrection, and exaltation of Jesus.[11] Because God became human, bodiliness, concreteness, time and history take on a new light, a new meaning, nothing is secular anymore, everything is sacred.

The credibility of Christianity was one of Schillebeeck's constant preoccupations especially in the situation of post-war Europe, and with the growth of secularism which ensued. How to transcribe the message of Christ in a meaningful way for modern people was of perennial concern for him.[12] In his last major speech[13] where he talked about the challenges facing Dominicans today, he spoke about the transition which he as a theologian had undergone throughout his long theological career. He described this as a reversal of the classical adage (*fides querens intellectum*) faith seeking understanding, to (*intellectus querens fidem*) reason searching for faith. For him, this was not merely a play on words but rather the summary of a turnaround which typified the faith culture as a whole.

At the beginning of Schillebeeckx's theological life belief was accepted as a matter of course within wide sections of society. At that time the conviction that revealed truth was to be found in the Catholic Church was not questioned, and the function of the theologian was to explain, support, and nourish this faith. With the growth of modern sciences in (16th and 17th centuries) followed by the Enlightenment in the 18th century, the task of the theologian changed, and developed into a largely defensive one. This happened because the Church felt threatened by the new insights emerging from the modern sciences. However this defensive role did not sit easily with Schillebeeckx. Like a good Dominican, he realised that the work of the theologian should be in the service of the *kerygma* – the preaching of the good news of the salvation brought by Christ. Rather than fight against these new tendencies he embraced them and entered into dialogue with them to see what he could harvest from them to enrich his preaching in a meaningful way modern people.

During his philosophical studies in Louvain he was taught by D. de Petter who was one of the great intellectual influences in his life. He al-

---

[10] Idem, Christ the Sacrament of the Encounter with God, op. cit., 14.
[11] Ibid., 19.
[12] See idem, Church, the Human Story of God, op. cit., Chapter 2.
[13] From a talk given at the annual meeting of the Flemish Dominican family in 2003.

lowed him to read Kant, Hegel, and the phenomenologists,[14] something which would have been unusual for a seminarian at that time. De Petter also introduced him to St. Thomas as well as contemporary psychology and sociology. One important lesson Schillebeeckx learned from De Petter was the realization of the absolute priority of God's grace over human endeavour, the ultimate inability of any conceptual system to express completely the richness of human experience, and God's infinite love for creation. This broad foundation as we shall see was to stand him in good stead in his later work and writing, especially in his work on the sacraments.

After the war Schillebeeckx was sent for doctoral studies to Le Saulchoir, the Dominican faculty in Paris. This house was at the centre of the *Novelle Theologie* movement which promoted *ressourcement*. This movement was focussed on a return to the patristic and medieval sources of theology in preference to a dependence on later commentators and manuals of theology. Here, Schillebeeckx would also have been aware of outstanding Jesuit theologians involved in this movement, people like Henri de Lubac and Hans Urs von Balthasar, both opponents of neo-Scholasticism. In Paris he was privileged to be taught by people like Yves Congar, and Marie-Dominique Chenu, and under the guidance of the latter he completed his doctorate entitled *De Sacramentele Heilsecnomie*. Both Congar and Chenu had decidedly opted for dialogue with the prevailing culture, and their example made a lasting impression on Schillebeeckx. Chenu developed a new existential approach to the study of Thomas Aquinas. He critiqued the neo-scholastic Thomists for preferring a "philosophy of essences" over "the problems of existence, action, the individual, becoming and time."[15] Yves Congar was a great ecumenist, and "undoubtedly the greatest ecclesiologist not only of the 20th century but of the entire history of the Church as well."[16]

As a result of this experience the young theologian became convince that God's self-disclosure is not a mere occurrence of the past, but a continuing phenomenon mediated through contemporary cultural realities.

---

[14] Writers like Merleau-Ponty, Buytendijk, Binswanger (referred to by Schillebeeckx in his essay, "The Sacraments: an Encounter with God", in: D.J. Callahan / H.A. Obermann / D.J. O'Hanlon (Eds.), Christianity Divided, London: Sheed & Ward, 1962.

[15] F. Kerr, Twentieth-Century Theologians: From Neoscholasticism to Nuptial Mysticism, Oxford: Blackwell, 2007, 23.

[16] R.P. McBrien, I Believe in the Holy Spirit. The Role of Pneumatology in Yves Congar's Theology, in: G. Flynn (Ed.), Yves Congar: theologian of the Church (Louvain theological & pastoral monographs), Leuven: Peeters, 2005, 303–328, 305.

He also realised that the neo-Thomist revival which was in full swing at that time was very negative and defensive in its assessment of modern culture. In Paris he was also introduced to Albert Camus a protagonist of the new existential philosophical movement. For Schillebeeckx, all of these experiences were sacramental – providential signs – and he used them to good effect entering into dialogue with the culture of the times. This new theology aimed to connect with the real experience of people in order to win them over to Christ, something which is a feature of Schillebeeck's theology.

Reading these 'signs of the times' and influenced by this new thinking he realised that, in a secular postmodern world, it was in institutions and practices that symbolise the *sacred* in the world, namely the Church and the sacraments, that concrete emphasis and renewal was needed. He therefore chose sacraments as the theme of his doctoral dissertation. This was a 'masterful *ressourcement* work of traditional sacramental theology in the patristic and medieval authors, giving a fresh perspective on sacramental theology.'[17] In this work the Christological approach to sacraments is emphasized.

Building on his dissertation he developed another volume with the aim of producing a contemporary sacramental theology. This decision was undoubtedly prompted by the fact that questions about the relevance of Christianity were emerging with ever-increasing urgency.

Schillebeeckx realised that some ideas gleaned from the phenomenological approach could be used here to good effect especially the notion of "encounter." "Encounter" is the ground of interpersonal awareness and openness of existence that is, in fact co-existence. And the body is the locus for *the emergence and expression of meaning;* it is the sacrament of the self. "Human encounter proceeds through the visible obviousness of the body, which is a sign that reveals and at the same time veils the human interiority."[18] Obviously, this thinking had great potential for Christian, and especially for Catholic theology. Since salvation is a personal act of encounter between the human person and God through Christ; the Incarnation – God's assumption of flesh, and consequently of a human *body*, makes Christ therefore, the primordial (original) sacrament of God: "The man Jesus, as the personal visible realization of the divine grace of redemption, is *the* sacrament, the primordial sacrament." Jesus the Son of God himself is intended by the Father to be in his humanity the only way

---

[17] R.J. Schreiter (Ed.), The Schillebeeckx Reader, Edinburgh: T. & T. Clark, 1986, 3.
[18] See E. Schillebeeckx, Christ the Sacrament of Encounter with God, op. cit., 15.

to the actuality of redemption.[19] The English translation of this work is therefore, appropriately called *Christ the Sacrament of the Encounter with God*.[20] The focus is on Christ as the "primordial sacrament", the source from which all the sacraments flow: "Because the saving acts of the man Jesus are performed by a divine person, they have a divine power to save, but because this divine power to save appears to us in a visible form, the saving activity of Jesus is *sacramental*."[21]

Schillebeeckx roots this notion in his understanding of Christ whose Paschal mystery is meta-historical and trans-temporal,[22] in the sense that this mystery is experienced in the liturgy of the sacraments. He asserts the unique and once-for-all character of Christ's act of redemption, and complements it by stating that this mystery is always offered through sacraments to the Church. Christ is thus understood to be the central sacrament manifesting God's love to the world. The seven sacraments are specifications and manifestations of this original sacrament.[23]

The phenomenon of encounter also becomes operative in this approach since the Church encounters God through Christ; individual sacraments are occasions for this encounter to take place. He parallels his Christological treatment with an ecclesial understanding, which emphasizes that a sacrament is valid only when it is *ecclesial*: "Each sacrament is the personal saving act of the risen Christ himself, but realized in the visible form of an official act of the Church [...] a sacrament is the saving action of Christ in the visible form of an ecclesial action."[24] He again emphasises the ecclesial aspect: "The sacraments are therefore acts of the whole mystical body of Christ, and of his church. And indeed in this sense they are acts of Christ in and through his Church. Christ acts in the sacraments together with the people of God already realized and existing in the world."[25]

One can only adequately understand the sacramentality of individual sacraments only on the basis of the sacramentality of the Church. Schillebeeckx also writes about the Church as visible grace in human society, as sign or sacrament of God's presence in the world. It is the visible realization of Christ's saving mystery; The Church is a visible communion of

---

[19] Ibid.
[20] Ibid.
[21] Ibid., 15.
[22] Ibid., 56.
[23] Ibid., 54.
[24] Ibid.
[25] Ibid., 66.

grace. This communion, comprising members and a hierarchical leadership, is the earthly sign of the victory achieved by Christ. He stresses the fact that it is not only the hierarchical church, but also the believing people who belong essentially to the primordial sacrament which is the earthly expression of this reality.[26]

Schillebeeck's sacramental notion of the Church as a sign of God's presence in the world accords well with the theology of Church developed in the documents of the Second Vatican Council. They in a certain sense define each other. Indeed we can say without fear of contradiction that his influence on those documents was not inconsequential.

It is well known that during the Second Vatican Council he was one of the most active theologians, and had considerable influence even though he was not appointed as an official *peritus*. He drafted various council interventions for Dutch bishops such as Cardinal Alfrink, and gave conferences on theological *ressourcement* for many Episcopal conferences present in Rome. He was "ghost writer" of the Dutch bishops Pastoral Letter on the forthcoming Council in 1961, the contents of which rendered him suspect by the Holy office. One would not need to be a detective to see that Schillebeeck's finger prints are all over some of the documents.

For example in the various documents of the Council, the statement that the Church is the universal sacrament of salvation is referred to frequently, for example Dogmatic Constitution of the Church Chapter 7:48, "Christ [...] has through the Spirit instituted his body, that is the Church, as the universal sacrament of salvation." Again in the Pastoral Constitution on the Church in the Modern World, 1, 4, 45; and in The Constitution on the Liturgy 1, 5. We are all now accustomed to this type of ecclesiology, – we were brought up on it and take it for granted, but at the time it was written it signalled a shift from emphasizing Christ's presence in the sacraments, to the community's transformation through sacraments. It also marks a shift from emphasizing sacraments as things, or rituals, to sacraments as event, and meetings with Christ. It emphasizes the importance, indeed the indispensability, of the community model of church, in contrast to the institutional and pyramidal model of the Church, which was the dominant one up to the Council.

In the Foreword to his book *Church* Schillebeeckx has a quote which runs like this *"People are the words with which God tells his story."* What a mag-

---

[26] Ibid., 66–68.

nificent story his is and many lessons can be learned from it for us in the Church today.

Like Irenaeus, Schillebeeckx believed that "the glory of God is the human being fully alive." His life's work was a living out of that axiom. The Incarnation of the Son of God, and the coming of the kingdom was central to his thinking. Pastoral and social concerns were at the forefront of his theology from the beginning. His theological vision and method developed in response to the questions and experiences of contemporary believers, and extended to all those searching for meaning and purpose in life. Hence his attempt to rethink the story of Jesus and the Christian experience in the face of radical human suffering, and the growing crisis of credibility confronting Christian faith In the modern world. His investigations of the development of the Church's ministerial structures and theology in the early 1980's were prompted by concrete pastoral crises. For Schillebeeckx, the crisis of ordained leadership exists because of a failure to understand the implications of the sacramental nature of the Church as the place where the Spirit dwells and moves freely. He called for a more democratic church in today's social context, and for the exercise of ministerial authority in a way that is in keeping with the liberating authority of Jesus Christ.

* * *

Zusammenfassung des Beitrags von Vera Donnelly

Ziel dieses Artikels ist es, den Begriff der „Sakramentalität" als ein Kerncharakteristikum im Denken von Schillebeeckx aufzuzeigen. Schillebeeckx war davon überzeugt, dass nicht allein das Physische, sondern alles, was zum Menschsein gehört, als sakramentale Manifestation von Gottes Gegenwart erfahren wird. Dieser Gedanke zeigt sich in seiner Theologie und mehr noch in seinem Leben. Ich verwende „Sakramentalität" zunächst im allgemeinen Sinn von konkret sichtbaren Geschehnissen oder Ereignissen, die Sinn und Gnade konkret offenbaren und ausdrücken. Schillebeeckx verstand und verwandte die „Zeichen der Zeit". In einem zweiten Punkt wird aufgewiesen, wie diese sakramentale Denkweise zum Verständnis, ja zur Wiederentdeckung Christi als Ursakrament führte und wie sie für Christen heute einen neuen Zugang zur Kirche als Sakrament der Erlösung, zur Gnade und den Sakramenten eröffnete, die viel mehr sind als nur dinghafte Rituale: Sie sind persönliche Begegnung mit Christus.

Übersetzung aus dem Englischen: *Sabine Schratz*

Bernadette Schwarz-Boenneke

DIE WIDERSTÄNDIGKEIT DER WIRKLICHKEIT ALS ERSTES MOMENT DES ERFAHRENS

Im Zentrum der hermeneutischen Theologie von Edward Schillebeeckx steht die (Glaubens-)Erfahrung. So steht eine „bestimmte Erfahrung [...] am Ursprung des Christentums. Denn es begann mit einer Begegnung. Einige Menschen, Juden kamen in Berührung mit Jesus von Nazareth und blieben, von ihm fasziniert, bei ihm. Durch diese Begegnung und durch das, was in seinem Leben und später seinem Tod geschah, erhielt ihr eigenes Leben neuen Sinn und neue Bedeutung."[1] Dieses kurze Zitat birgt bereits die wesentlichen Elemente des Erfahrungsverständnisses, wie es Edward Schillebeeckx seinen theologischen Werken zugrunde gelegt hat. Dieses Erfahrungsverständnis wiederum bietet, so die These des vorliegenden Beitrages, die Grundstruktur seiner Theologie.

Die folgenden Überlegungen widmen sich somit dem Erfahrungsverständnis von Edward Schillebeeckx in den christologischen Prolegomena, genauer: den Werken „Christus und die Christen"[2] und „Menschen. Die Geschichte von Gott"[3]. Ausgehend von der gängigen Darlegung des Erfahrungsverständnisses bei Edward Schillebeeckx als „interpretierender Wahrnehmung"[4] wird es darum gehen, die Analyse des Erfahrungsverständnisses zu vertiefen und weitergehend die grammatikalische Struktur der Theologie bei Edward Schillebeeckx aufzuzeigen. In einem dritten

---

[1] E. Schillebeeckx, Die Auferstehung Jesu als Grund unserer Erlösung. Zwischenbericht über die Prolegomena zu einer Christologie, Freiburg/Br. 1979, 19.
[2] Ders., Christus und die Christen. Die Geschichte einer neuen Lebenspraxis, Freiburg/Br. 1977.
[3] Ders., Menschen. Die Geschichte von Gott, Freiburg/Br. 1990.
[4] Vgl. u. a. Ph. Kennedy, Edward Schillebeeckx. Die Geschichte von der Menschlichkeit Gottes, Mainz 1994, 54.

Schritt werden einige Korrektiva für die Verwendung des Begriffs „Erfahrung" entfaltet, die Konsequenzen für eine Theologie im Anschluss an Schillebeeckx aufzeigen.

1. Erfahren in Widerfahren und Benennen

„‚Erfahren' bedeutet ursprünglich: durch das Land fahren und so – durch Erkundung – in einen Lernprozeß aufgenommen werden. Erfahren heißt lernen durch ‚unmittelbaren' Kontakt mit Menschen und Dingen. Es ist die Fähigkeit, Wahrnehmungen zu verarbeiten. [...] Erfahrung vollzieht sich dialektisch: in einem Zusammenspiel von Wahrnehmung und Denken, Denken und Wahrnehmung. [...] Erfahrend identifizieren wir das Erfahrene, und wir tun dies dadurch, dass wir das, was wir erfahren, in schon bekannten Modellen und Begriffen, Schemata oder Kategorien unterbringen und sehen, ob es da hineinpasst oder nicht. Ich sehe etwas und sage: ein Stuhl. Dieses Ding erfahrend, interpretiere und identifiziere ich im Erfahren selbst. Denn ich interpretiere diese Ding nicht als einen Stuhl, ich sehe einen Stuhl, allerdings ist gerade dieses Sehen innerlich auch eine Interpretation."[5]

Schillebeeckx beschreibt Erfahren als einen dialektischen Prozess von Wahrnehmen und Interpretieren, einer vorsprachlichen und präreflexiven Wahrnehmung[6] sowie einer sprachlichen Erfassung und Einordnung.

Erfahrung wird bei Schillebeeckx und dessen – Formulierungen aufnehmend – in der Sekundärliteratur oft in einem zweifachen Sinne verwendet: Zunächst wird von Erfahrung im Sinne des vorsprachlichen Momentes der Erfahrung – und sodann im Sinne des Resultates aus Wahrnehmung und Interpretation gesprochen. Mit diesem uneindeutigen Sprachgebrauch bewegt man sich jedoch auf zwei verschiedenen Ebenen. Um dieser Sprachverwirrung eine differenzierende Alternative von Edward Schillebeeckx her anzubieten, aber vor allem auch um die Struktur der Theologie in den christologischen Prolegomena besser wahrzunehmen, lohnt es sich, das Erfahrungsverständnis eingehender zu betrachten.

---

[5] E. Schillebeeckx, Christus und die Christen, a.a.O., 25f.
[6] Vgl. ders., Was ist Theologie?, in: ders., Offenbarung und Theologie, Mainz 1965, 77–135.

1.1. Negative Erfahrungen als ursprüngliche und erste Erfahrungen

Über seine etymologischen Wurzeln weist das Wort „Erfahrung"[7] eine Verwandtschaft mit dem Griechischen ‚empeira' und ‚poreuesthai' sowie dem Lateinischen ‚periculum' auf. Etwas zu erfahren, bedeutet, etwas zu versuchen, sich auf den Weg zu machen, ein Risiko einzugehen, Vertrautes zu verlassen, etwas zu wagen. Erfahrungen zu machen, schließt mit Rückgriff auf die lateinische Wortwurzel Gefahr und Scheitern ein.

Wenn Schillebeeckx nun in seinen Darlegungen zum Erfahrungsverständnis erklärt, was es bedeutet, eine Erfahrung zu machen, dann setzt er bei Misserfolgen an. Man macht dort eine Erfahrung, „wo [...] Projekte blockiert werden und [Menschen] neu tastend beginnen, in sensibler Ehrfurcht und darin vor der Orientierung der Wirklichkeit."[8] Und an anderer Stelle schreibt er: „Es ist eine Tatsache, daß sowohl alltägliche als auch wissenschaftlich-experimentelle Erfahrungen einem ‚Widerfahren' viel zu verdanken haben: Erfahrungen von Widerständen und Widerspenstigkeit der Wirklichkeit, in der wir leben. Die Menschen leben von Mutmaßungen und Irrtümern, von Projekten und Konstrukten und deshalb von ‚trial and error'; ihre Projekte können ständig vom Widerstand der Wirklichkeit durchkreuzt werden, die sich nicht immer zu menschlicher rationaler Antizipation eignet."[9]

Dieser Ansatz bei den negativen Erfahrungen steht einem Erfahrungsverständnis entgegen, welches das eigene Planen und Forschen des Menschen im Erfahren in den Vordergrund stellt. Letzteres betont, dass der Mensch Erfahrungen macht, sich seine Welt erschließt und sie erforscht.[10] Schillebeeckx setzt einen anderen Akzent, wenn er als die ei-

---

[7] Vgl. F. Kluge, Etymologisches Wörterbuch der deutschen Sprache. 20. Aufl., bearb. von W. Mitzka, Berlin 1967, 171, 180, 239.
[8] E. Schillebeeckx, Christus und die Christen, a.a.O., 29.
[9] Ders., Menschen, a.a.O., 53.
[10] Vgl. G. Ebeling, Die Klage über das Erfahrungsdefizit in der Theologie als Frage nach ihrer Sache, in: ders., Wort und Glaube III, Tübingen 1975, 3–28, hier 3f.: „‚Erfahrung' – so lautet die Parole der Grenzüberschreitung und Horizonterweiterung, des Entdeckens und Eroberns, das Bewegungsprinzip der sogenannten Neuzeit, dieser sich selbst immer neu überbietenden Zeit. Von den Seefahrern des 15. Jahrhunderts bis zu den Raumfahrern des 20. erstreckt sich die Kette derer, die den buchstäblichen und zugleich geradezu magischen Sinn des Schlagworts ‚Erfahrung' sinnfällig repräsentieren. Hier vollzieht sich ein emanzipatorischer Aufbruch, aus der Bindung an das Herkommen in eine als offen erkannte Zukunft hinein, die eben dazu reizt, über sie zu bestimmen. Anstatt wie bisher auf die Tradition vertraut man auf die eigene Erfahrung. An die Stelle der Autorität überlieferter Texte tritt die Evidenz der Dinge selbst. Statt an spekulatives Denken hält man sich an das, was die Sinne wahrnehmen [...]. Der Umgang mit der Erfahrung wird nun methodisch diszipliniert. Das

gentliche Erfahrung die bezeichnet, in der etwas nicht so gelingt, wie es geplant ist.

Die eigentlichen Erfahrungen sind demnach die nicht die Erwartungen bestätigenden Erfahrungen, sondern negative Erfahrungen, also Widerfahrnisse und in Schillebeeckx' Terminologie Kontrasterfahrungen. Man geht in diesem Fall der „negativen" Erfahrungen von einer bestimmten Idee aus. Auf dem Weg der Realisierung stellt man fest, dass es anders kommt, sei es, dass etwas Gesuchtes sich als anders erweist oder dass ein Weg nicht weiterführt. In diesen Situationen zeigt sich in der Widerständigkeit die Wirklichkeit. Schillebeeckx verwendet hier Formulierungen, wie sie im hermeneutischen Zusammenhang der Schrift „Glaubensinterpretationen"[11] mit Bezug auf Heidegger bereits gebraucht wurden: Die Wirklichkeit gibt dem Menschen zu denken, sie entbirgt sich und lenkt die menschliche Wahrnehmung.[12]

1.2. Die kognitive Kraft der Erfahrung

Die Wirklichkeit, so Schillebeeckx in seiner Darstellung, wird hier zum Korrektiv des eigenen Planens und Projektierens. Sie ist es letztlich, die unser Denken bestimmt und seine Norm bildet: „[...] wo die Wirklichkeit diesen Entwürfen Widerstand leistet und sie implizit also indirekt lenkt, stehen wir im Kontakt mit einer von uns unabhängigen Wirklichkeit, dem von Menschen nicht Bedachten, nicht Gemachten oder Projektierten. Dort offenbart sich das Nicht-Manipulierbare, eine ‚transzendente' Macht, etwas, was ‚von anderswoher' kommt, sich gerade gegenüber unseren Projekten geltend macht und trotzdem alles menschliche Planen, Produzieren und Überlegen möglich macht und kritisch-negativ orientiert."[13]

Dieser lenkende Grund, wie im obigen Zitat benannt, begründet für Schillebeeckx, warum der Mensch trotz der Endlichkeit seines Denkens nicht in einen absoluten Skeptizismus verfällt. „Wie ein verborgener Magnet lenkt die Wirklichkeit ständig unser Planen und Sinnen: Wir wer-

zufällige Widerfahrnis wandelt sich in geplantes Experiment [...]. Der überwältigende Erfolg scheint diesem Vorgehen recht zu geben. Er wird zum Erfahrungsbeweis der Erfahrungswissenschaften."

[11] Vgl. E. Schillebeeckx, Glaubensinterpretation. Beiträge zu einer hermeneutischen und kritischen Theologie, Mainz 1971, 40ff.

[12] Siehe auch B. Schwarz-Boenneke, Erfahren in Widerfahren und Benennen. Zu Verständnis und Relevanz von Erfahrung in den christologischen Prolegomena von Edward Schillebeeckx (Studien zur systematischen Theologie und Ethik Bd. 48), Münster 2010, 118–121.

[13] E. Schillebeeckx, Christus und die Christen, a.a.O., 28.

den weiser durch das Leid der Mißerfolge, die uns neu orientieren. Dieses implizite Bewußtsein von dem verborgenen Magnet hat etwas außerordentlich Positives. Es ist ein Wissen, das nicht völlig verobjektivierbar und artikulierbar ist. Gerade dadurch ist die negative Kontrasterfahrung nie Zweck an sich selbst; sonst würde sie destruktiv und unproduktiv."[14]

1.3. Die kritische Kraft der Erfahrung

Von negativen Erfahrungen wird somit bei Schillebeeckx in einem dreifachen Sinn gesprochen: Auf einer ersten beschreibenden Ebene kann man unter „negativ" verstehen, dass etwas anders als erwartet verläuft – im Unterschied zu dem Positiven, wo ein Plan aufgeht und eine Erwartung sich bestätigt. Negativ meint auf dieser ersten Ebene: dass etwas nicht so verläuft, wie man es sich vorgestellt hat. Diese Ebene bezieht sich auf den Erkenntnisprogress.

Die zweite Ebene thematisiert die grundsätzliche menschliche Erkenntnisfähigkeit. Hier wird mit dem Negativen die Unzulänglichkeit und Endlichkeit menschlicher Erkenntnis umschrieben. Der Mensch hat und kann kein „absolutes Wissen" haben, weil er ein geschichtliches Wesen ist und in seiner leiblich-geschichtlichen Verfasstheit notwendig gebunden ist: „Dies weist darauf hin, daß menschliche Erfahrung endlich ist, daß der Mensch nicht Herr der Wirklichkeit ist trotz all seines Planens, ohne das anderseits Erfahrungen unmöglich wären. Absolute Erkenntnis ist dem Menschen nicht gegeben [...]."[15] Das Negative bezieht sich hier auf die Relationalität menschlichen Erkennens – und theologisch mit Bezug auf den sich zu erkennen gebenden Gott, der stets unaussprechliches Geheimnis bleibt, sowie auf das menschliche Unvermögen, Gott zu erfassen.

In der dritten Ebene siedelt sich das „negative" Moment auf der Ebene der praktischen Vernunft in den negativen Erfahrungen von menschlichem Leiden an, in denen sich das kritische Potential von Erfahrung zeigt, wenn diese verstanden werden als Kontrasterfahrungen und dann nicht nur 1) zu erkennen geben, dass es so nicht sein soll, sondern 2) auch einen positiven Sinngrund, ein menschliches Urvertrauen zu erken-

---

[14] Ebd., 29.
[15] Ebd.

nen geben in dem menschlichen Handeln gegen die Ungerechtigkeit und in der Veränderung der Situation.[16]

1.4. Mehrfache Offenheit der Erfahrung

Menschliches Erfahren zeichnet sich in dem dargestellten Sinne durch seine mehrfache Offenheit aus. Betrachtet man die strukturelle Ebene des Erkennensprozesses, dann zeichnet sich das Erfahren bereits durch das erste Moment des Widerfahrens als offen aus: Erfahrung ist in ihrer Struktur stets offen für und auf das, was widerfährt. Sie kann sich streng genommen nicht ‚von innen abschließen'.

Auf der Ebene des Erkenntnisprozesses unterstreicht „Erfahrung" die Dynamik und die Unabschließbarkeit des Prozesses. Sollen Erfahrungen lebendig bleiben, dann müssen sie sich im Alltag bewähren, dann entwickeln sie sich weiter durch Unerwartetes, wobei dieser Prozess die Person selbst beansprucht und verändert. Aus diesem Wissen um die Offenheit von Erfahrung und ihre Ausrichtung auf neue Erfahrungen entwickelt sich die Erfahrungskompetenz, die Schillebeeckx, Gadamer folgend, als eine Fähigkeit aus Erfahrungen für neue Erfahrungen[17] bezeichnet.

Zweitens bezieht sich die Offenheit auf die Relationalität der Erkenntnisfähigkeit, die Erfahrungen stets offen und ausgerichtet sein lässt auf die sich zeigende Wirklichkeit.

Drittens wird die Vorläufigkeit menschlichen Denkens hin auf seine prinzipielle Begrenztheit und Endlichkeit überschritten.

Die Offenheit auf der dritten Ebene lässt sich über das zweite Moment der Kontrasterfahrungen beschreiben, wenn sich nämlich Protest gegen eine ungerechte Situation erhebt. Der sich im Protest zeigende tragende Sinngrund und das menschliche Urvertrauen, das sich ansprechen lässt und in seinem Handeln antwortet, zeigt für Schillebeeckx eine Offenheit auf eine andere Situation, die uns und unser Tun in Anspruch nimmt. Die Verweigerung gegenüber dem Leiden „enthüllt eine Offenheit auf eine andere Situation hin, die durchaus Anspruch auf unser Ja hat."[18] Die Offenheit und das Ja auf das Unbekannte und Bessere hin werden getragen von partiellen Sinnerfahrungen.

---

[16] Vgl. E. Schillebeeckx, Theologie der Erfahrung – Sackgasse oder Weg zum Glauben?, in: HerderKorrespondenz 92 (1978), 391–397, hier 393: „Das Basisvertrauen ist nur gegeben im Zusammenspiel mit negativen Erfahrungen, es ist gegeben in diesen Kontrasterfahrungen und trotz dieser Kontrasterfahrungen, nicht vorher."
[17] Vgl. ders., Christus und die Christen, a.a.O., 32
[18] Ders., Menschen, a.a.O., 28.

Diese allgemeine Offenheit auf einen tragenden, wenn auch nicht positiv zu erfassenden Sinngrund, der die Matrix jeder religiösen Rede und Erfahrung ist, wird innerhalb einer religiösen Tradition mit dem eigenen Glaubensgut identifiziert und benannt: „Menschen, die an Gott glauben, geben dieser einen, zweiseitigen Grunderfahrung einen religiösen Inhalt. Das ‚offene Ja' erhält dann mehr Zielrichtung und Relief. Sein Ursprung ist nicht so sehr, oder zumindest nicht direkt, die Transzendenz ‚des Göttlichen' (die unaussprechlich und anonym ist, sich nicht in Worte fassen läßt) als vielmehr (wenigstens für Christen) das erkennbare menschliche Antlitz dieser Transzendenz, wie es unter uns im Menschen Jesus erschienen ist, den wir als Christus und Sohn Gottes bekennen."[19]

1.5. Das benennende Moment

Notwendig und untrennbar gehört somit zum ersten widerfahrenden Moment des Erfahrens sein zweites Moment, nämlich das interpretierende, sprachliche dazu. Erfahrung schließt eine sprachliche Einordnung ein: „Außerdem wird jeder neue Erfahrungsinhalt zur Sprache gebracht; eine neue Erfahrung ist auch ein Sprachgeschehen. Sprache ist ein Bestandteil der Erfahrung. In der uns vor-gegebenen Sprache, die wir dazu gebrauchen, ist aber schon eine ganze Erfahrungstradition gesammelt, und diese färbt auch unsere Erfahrungen."[20]

Wie nun aber ist das Zusammenspiel von „Erfahrung" und „Interpretation" zu sehen? In Auseinandersetzung mit den erkenntnistheoretischen Positionen von John Wisdom, Antony Flew, Richard M. Hare und John Hick[21] kommt Schillebeeckx zu der Überzeugung, dass jegliche Unterscheidung eines erfahrenden und eines interpretativen Momentes nur analytisch zu verstehen ist, sonst aber den fälschlichen Eindruck einer Trennung in eine reine und nichtsprachliche Erfahrung und einen interpretatorischen Überbau erweckt. Etwas zu erfahren bezeichnet nicht eine allgemeine Erfahrung, die dann je nach Traditionshintergrund verschieden gedeutet wird. Es meint aber auch nicht eine bestimmte religiöse Erfahrung in dem Sinne, dass das Religiöse eine bestimmte Qualität der Erfahrung sei. Etwas zu erfahren beschreibt vielmehr eine bestimmte Form der Weltbegegnung, einen dialektischen Prozess von Denken, Sprechen

---

[19] Ebd.
[20] Ders., Christus und die Christen, a.a.O., 26.
[21] Vgl. ebd., 42–47.

und „Erfahren"[22]. Es gibt somit „nie nicht interpretierte Erfahrung"[23]. Mit Bezug auf die Gestaltpsychologie beschreibt Schillebeeckx den dialektischen Prozess folgendermaßen: „Man sieht sie [die Konfiguration von gezeichneten Klötzchen, die man aus verschiedenen Richtungen je anders sieht] dann auch anders und interpretiert sie nicht nur anders. Wir sehen etwas vor einem Hintergrund oder Horizont. Das Struktur- oder Gestaltmoment wird nicht hinzugedacht, es ist ein inneres Moment der Wahrnehmung. Man sieht also etwas auf verschiedene Weise und interpretiert es nicht nur anders. Man kann die verschiedenen Perspektiven zwar zusammendenken, man kann sie aber nicht zugleich alle zusammen sehen! Das Identifikationsmoment liegt also in der Erfahrung selbst (man könnte sagen: Man sieht ‚die Interpretation'; besser: Wir sehen interpretierend). Es gibt keine neutrale Erfahrungsgegebenheit, denn alternative Interpretationen beeinflussen die Art und Weise, wie wir die Welt erfahren."[24]

In dieser Struktur des Widerfahrens und Benennens in der Erfahrung stellt Schillebeeckx Erfahrung als Zugang zur Wirklichkeit dar. Es fehlt in den späteren Werken eine stichhaltige Begründung dafür, warum etwas so und nicht anders benannt wird. An diesem Punkt ist Schillebeeckx sicher weiterzudenken.

Bedeutsam ist sein Ansatz, da er von alltäglichen Erfahrungen, also von einer allgemeinen Erkenntnistheorie ausgeht und nicht von der Struktur einer spezifischen, originären Begegnung mit dem Religiösen oder Heiligen in Form einer spezifischen Erfahrung.[25] Schillebeeckx zeigt auf, dass jeder Erfahrung eine „offenbarende" Struktur ausgehend von dem widerfahrenden Moment innewohnt.[26] Dies allein ist nicht hinreichend für eine religiöse Sinnstiftung.

In der Diskussion gegen ein rein materialistisches Verständnis des Menschen in bestimmten neurowissenschaftlichen Ansätzen vertritt der Psychiater und Philosoph Thomas Fuchs auf Basis der Phänomenologie eine ebensolche Erkenntnistheorie. Wirklichkeit zeigt sich demnach in einem Widerfahrnis, das wir leiblich, ja leibhaftig erfahren: „Man könnte auch sagen, das Wirkliche zeigt sich nicht im Gewohnten und Eingängi-

---

[22] Vgl. ders., Christus und die Christen, a.a.O., 42.
[23] Vgl. ebd., 46.
[24] Vgl. ebd.
[25] Vgl. H.-J. Höhn, Zeit und Sinn. Religionsphilosophie postsäkular, Paderborn 2010, 59.
[26] Vgl. Th. Fuchs, Der Schein des Anderen. Zur Phänomenologie virtueller Realitäten, in: C. Bohrer / B. Schwarz-Boenneke (Hrsg.), Identität und virtuelle Beziehungen im Computerspiel, München 2010, 59–73.

gen, sondern im Überraschenden, in der Enttäuschung oder Durchkreuzung unserer Erwartungen. Es weist ein Moment der Undurchdringlichkeit oder Fremdheit auf und erschließt sich oft erst in einem Prozess allmählicher Annäherung oder Auseinandersetzung."[27] Der Leib fungiert hier als Resonanzkörper der Begegnung mit der Wirklichkeit. Für den theologischen Zusammenhang ist mit diesem Widerfahrnis Erfahrung auf ein Anderes aufgebrochen. Die Denkbewegung in der Erfahrung wandelt sich von der Bewegung vom Subjekt auf das Objekt hin zu einer Bewegung vom Objekt zum Subjekt.

2. Die grammatikalische Grundstruktur der Theologie von Edward Schillebeeckx in Offenbaren und Glauben

Erfahrung konstituiert sich in einem dialektischen Prozess von Widerfahren und Benennen – und zeigt damit eine Strukturparallelität zum dialogischen Prozess von Offenbarung und Glaube auf: Gott offenbart sich dem Menschen. Das Angebot der Gnade aber manifestiert sich erst in der religiösen Antwort: „Das Angebot der Gnade und die gläubige Antwort sind die beiden Facetten ein und derselben reichen Wirklichkeit, so dass man mit Lévinas sagen kann: ‚L'Appell s'y entend dans la réponse.'" Das widerfahrende, offenbarende Moment tritt in Korrelation mit der menschlichen benennenden und bekennenden Glaubensantwort – bei aller Begrenztheit der menschlichen Sprache. „Dieses Sprechen – mag es noch so menschlich sein – ist daher keine eigenmächtige menschliche Initiative, es erfolgt aus Vollmacht und Mandat, kraft der Wirklichkeit. Der Mensch ist nicht Herr, sondern Verwalter der Wirklichkeit. Daraus geht wiederum hervor, dass dieses Sprechen von Gott und seiner Offenbarung unlöslich mit unserer gläubig-interpretativen Erfahrung der Wirklichkeit von Mensch und Welt verbunden ist. [...] Im Selbstverständnis der Religion liegt, gleichursprünglich, ein bestimmtes, nämlich religiöses Welt- und Menschenverständnis. Gott ist immer größer als die Art und Weise, wie er sich in unserer Geschichte zu erkennen gibt, größer als das Heil des Exodus aus Ägypten, größer auch als das Gericht der babylonischen Gefangenschaft."[28]

Verfolgt man nun die Darlegungen Schillebeeckx' zu der Begegnung der Jünger mit Jesus, dem Christus, z. B. die Auferstehungserfahrung,

---

[27] Ebd., 61.
[28] Vgl. E. Schillebeeckx, Christus und die Christen, a.a.O., 49.

dann zeigt sich in diesen Darlegungen stets diese Struktur des widerfahrenden und benennenden Momentes, wie es in seinem Erfahrungsverständnis dargelegt wurde. „Die christliche disclosure-Erfahrung, Grund, Quelle und Erschließung eines wahrhaft christologischen Jesus-Bekenntnisses, setzt die Gesamtheit des Lebens Jesu voraus, also bis zu dessen Beendigung durch seine Hinrichtung. Auch theologisch gesehen ist nur dieses vollendete Leben die Offenbarung Gottes in Jesus von Nazaret. Erst mit dem Tod Jesu ist, was ihn ‚persönlich' betrifft, seine Lebensgeschichte zu Ende; erst dann kann unsere Geschichte von Jesus beginnen. [...] Wohl haben diese Jünger – in einem (historisch nicht mehr rekonstruierbaren) Bekehrungsprozeß – das Überwältigende ihrer eigenen disclosure-Erfahrung erfaßt: ihre ‚Erkennntis' und ‚Anerkennung' Jesu in seiner Lebenstotalität. Das nenne ich ‚Ostererfahrung', die auf verschiedene Weisen zum Ausdruck gebracht werden konnte: Der Gekreuzigte ist der kommende Richter (maranatha-Christologie); der gekreuzigte Wundertäter ist in seinen Jüngern gegenwärtig; der Gekreuzigte ist auferstanden. Und dann kann man in der Tat sagen: In diesem Augenblick entsteht die Erfahrung, daß sie erst jetzt wirklich Jesus sehen, den Grund dessen, was bei den Ostererscheinungen ausgedrückt wird: Jesus ‚gibt sich zu sehen' (oophtè); nach seinem Tod wird er erst ‚epiphan'; d. h. transparent; im Glauben begreift man, wer er ist. Diese Erkenntnis der Jünger ist dann zugleich ein wiedererkennendes und doch neues Sehen Jesu – Jesu von Nazaret; nicht eines anderen, auch keines Mythos. Jesus, wie sie ihn erlebt hatten, bleibt das einzige Kriterium sowohl für ihre Erinnerungen als auch für ihre neuen Erfahrungen nach seinem Tod."[29] Die *disclosure*-Erfahrung, die die Jünger machen, umfasst den Schock der Jünger, eine Intuition und die Formulierung in eschatologischer Sprache.[30] Wirklichkeitserfahrung und sprachlicher Ausdruck sind auch hier aufeinander bezogen – und der Glaube an die Auferstehung beruht auf dieser Korrelation. Was die Jünger erfahren haben, beschreibt Schillebeeckx über die Analyse des Bekehrungsprozesses in den Erscheinungen sowie die Frage, was sie zu dieser Umkehr bewegt hat. Für Schillebeeckx ist klar, dass die Umkehr nicht allein Ergebnis einer Reflexionsleistung und einer Erinnerung der Jünger an Jesus sein kann. Vielmehr wird diese provoziert durch ein Widerfahrnis. Sie ist eine Glaubenserfahrung, die ihren Ursprung in der Initiative eines Anderen hat: „Über den auferstandenen Jesus spre-

---

[29] Ders., Jesus. Die Geschichte von einem Lebenden, Freiburg/Br. 1975, 342.
[30] Vgl. ebd., 306.

chen impliziert eine persönliche Erfahrung, die gerade als Initiative des anderen, Jesus selbst, interpretiert wird."[31]

Schillebeeckx Theologie geht aus von einer negativen Erfahrung im Sinne eines Widerfahrnisses, das hindeutend identifiziert wird, wissend darum, dass die Wirklichkeit selbst das Erfahrene und Bekannte übersteigt. Schillebeeckx theologischer Ansatz kann somit als eine negative Theologie gelesen werden, welche die drei Wege, der *via affirmativa*, der *via negativa* und der *via eminentiae*, beschreitet auf der Basis der Offenbarung Gottes in Jesus Christus.

Theologie ist notwendig offen auf die Wirklichkeit Gottes, die das menschliche Erfassen übersteigt, allerdings ist dies, wie dies in den Darlegungen zur kognitiven Kraft der negativen Erfahrungen angedeutet wurde, keine Flucht in ein rein negatives Reden über Gott oder ein radikales Schweigen erlaubt. Theologie bewegt sich in einer Dialektik von Negativem und Positivem, von Verborgenem und Offenbarem.[32]

3. Korrektiva für einen Gebrauch des Wortes „Erfahrung" und Konsequenzen aus dieser Differenzierung für eine Theologie der Gegenwart

Ausgehend von Schillebeeckx' Entfaltungen des Erfahrungsverständnisses in den christologischen Prolegomena möchte ich folgenden Vorschlag unterbreiten, Erfahrung nicht allein als einen dialektischen Prozess des Wahrnehmens und Interpretierens zu verstehen, sondern als Dialektik von Widerfahren und Benennen.

Aus dieser Differenzierung folgen dann in einem weiteren Schritt einige Korrektiva für das Erfahrungsverständnis, die ich abschließend thesenartig vorstellen möchte:
1. In Schillebeeckx' Werken und in der Sekundärliteratur, z. B. bei Lieven Boeve[33] oder Louis Dupré[34], trifft man wiederholt auf die Formulierung einer Korrelation von „Erfahrung" und „Interpretati-

---

[31] Ebd. 312; vgl. ebenso ebd., 322.
[32] Vgl. A. Halbmayr / G.M. Hoff (Hrsg.), Negative Theologie heute? Zum aktuellen Stellenwert einer umstrittenen Tradition (Quaestiones disputatae Bd. 226), Freiburg/Br. 2008.
[33] L. Boeve, Experience According to Edward Schillebeeckx: The Driving Force of Faith and Theology, in: ders. / L.P. Hemming (Eds.), Divinising Experience: Essays in the History of Religious Experience from Origen to Ricoeur, Leuven – Paris – Dudley 2004, 199–225, hier 216.
[34] L. Dupré, Experience and Interpretation: A Philosophical Reflection on Schillebeeckx's Jesus and Christ, in: *Theological Studies* 43 (1982), 30–52.

on". „Erfahrung" wird hier – entsprechend dem alltagssprachlichen Gebrauch – in einem zweifachen Sinne verwendet. Man spricht von „Erfahrung" erstens im Sinne des nichtsprachlichen Momentes der Erfahrung und zweitens im Sinne des Resultates dieses Erkenntnisprozesses.

Die Unterscheidung zwischen einem Widerfahrnis als dem ersten Moment des Erfahrens, dem Moment des Aufmerkens bzw. des nichtsprachlichen *Momentums*, und der Erfahrung – im Sinne des Erkenntnisprozesses und des Erkenntnisprogresses, vermeidet zunächst eine sprachliche Konfusion. Vor allem aber hat sie inhaltliche Folgen gerade für einen sachadäquaten Rezeptionsprozess.

2. Schillebeeckx unterscheidet Erfahrung sehr deutlich von einem Erlebnis[35] oder einem Event. Erfahrung beinhaltet ein Moment der Dauer sowie der Bewährung im Alltag, während ein alltags- und erst recht umgangssprachlicher Gebrauch „Erfahrung" auf ein kurzes „Erlebnis" oder ein „Event" reduziert.

Eine Reduktion aber dürfte die erschließende inhaltliche Dimension des Widerfahrnisses nicht mehr aufstörend und entbergend wirken lassen[36].

Ich verweise an dieser Stelle auf die Kritik von Otto Hermann Pesch[37] an Schillebeeckx' Erfahrungsverständnis, das seiner Leseweise nach zu sehr den projektierenden bzw. sinnstiftenden Vollzug des wahrnehmenden Subjektes betont, einer Öffnung auf ein Anderes aber ermangelt. Die vorgeschlagene Differenzierung des Erfahrungsverständnisses entschärft diese Kritik. Ferner liegt dieser Vorschlag eines über das Subjekt hinaus offenen Erfahrungsverständnisses in der Linie neuerer religionspädagogischer Werke, wie z. B. von Bernhard Grümme[38]. Grümmes Kritik richtet sich darauf, dass Schillebeeckx zwar auf hermeneutischer Ebene einen kritischen Ansatz ver-

---

[35] Vgl. E. Schillebeeckx, Christus und die Christen, a.a.O., 23.
[36] Vgl. L. Boeve, Experience According to Edward Schillebeeckx, a.a.O., 215.
[37] O.H. Pesch, Glaube – Erfahrung – Theologie. Einblick in einen ökumenischen Diskussionsstand. Eckdaten einer Klärung, in: *Freiburger Zeitschrift für Philosophie und Theologie* (2003), 5–49, hier 33.
[38] Vgl. hierzu die berechtigte Kritik Grümmes an der Korrelation von Glaube und Erfahrung bei Edward Schillebeeckx, die basierend auf einem rein hermeneutischen, den Interpretationsrahmen bestätigenden Erfahrungsverständnis es verunmöglicht, den bisherigen Erfahrungen widerstrebende Erfahrungen einzugliedern. Eine Erfahrung des Anderen und des Fremden bleibt nicht als solche in ihrer Radikalität erhalten. B. Grümme, Vom Anderen eröffnete Erfahrung. Zur Neubestimmung des Erfahrungsbegriffs in der Religionsdidaktik, Freiburg/Br. 2007, 140f.

folgt, aber über seinen Erfahrungsverständnis kritische Moment dahingehend aufhebt, als dass eine Wahrnehmung sich in einen bestehenden Interpretationszusammenhang einzufügen hat. „Hatte Schillebeeckx mit seinem, in den Rahmen von kritischer Korrelation und Interrelation eingebundenen Erfahrungsbegriff gerade die Gebrochenheit, das Fremde, die völlig unerwartete Neuheit und so auch die kritischproduktive Andersheit möglicher Erfahrungen für das Erfahrungssubjekt wahren wollen, so fällt er damit hinter seine Intention zurück. Erfahrungen von Andersheit, die den Menschen verstören, die ihn desintegrieren, die ‚eine Kluft in unseren Erfahrungsstrukturen' provozieren, die nicht mehr in der Verstehensdialektik hermeneutisch einzubergen und damit von ihm verarbeitet und bewältigt werden können, radikale überraschende Neuheitserfahrungen, Erfahrungen, die den Menschen über sich hinausrufen, Irritationen, durch die hindurch sich möglicherweise Gottes Anruf ereignen will: all dies wird abgeblendet."[39] Grümme sieht hier deutlich eine Schwierigkeit, die sich auch in Schillebeeckx' Benennung seines Erfahrungsbegriffes spiegelt. Schillebeeckx arbeitet mit der Korrelation von Wahrnehmung und Interpretation. Er weist z. B. nachdrücklich darauf hin, dass die Begegnung mit Jesus die bisherigen Erfahrungen und Deutungen irritierte. Nichtsdestotrotz drängt gerade auch dieses Widerfahrnis nach einer Benennung, welche in Rückgriff auf bestehende Begriffe erfolgt, diese aber in ihrer Bedeutung bricht und übersteigt.[40] Genau dieses Moment muss der Erfahrung erhalten bleiben, will sie heute das Glaubensgut nicht auf das jeweilige Denken reduzieren. Zugleich bedarf aber auch eine Erfahrung der Andersartigkeit eines Bezugspunkts zum eigenen Denken. Das radikal Andere muss als dieses Andere erkenn- und benennbar sein. Grümme hat klar aus religionspädagogischer Perspektive den Vorwurf der Assimilation des Glaubens an die lebensweltlichen Erfahrungen vor Augen. Seine Kritik daran, dass Schillebeeckx seinem eigenen Ansatz – und damit seiner Intention, einen rein hermeneutisch begründeten Erfahrungsbegriff aufzubrechen nicht durchhält – und letztlich wohl auch hinter seiner Intention, Tradition als eine lebendige zu verstehen, zurückbleibt.

---

[39] Ebd., 140.
[40] Vgl. E. Schillebeeckx, Jesus, a.a.O., 111, 159–206. Schillebeeckx stellt Jesus in dessen jüdischer Situation und Lebenswelt vor. So erfüllt Jesus zwar die Erwartungen seiner Zeitgenossen, bricht und übersteigt sie doch zugleich.

Das Moment des Widerfahrnisses der sich zeigenden Wirklichkeit kann aber gegen dieses Kritik stark gemacht werden, hat Schillebeeckx dies doch dezidiert angeführt, um Erfahrung von einem rein subjektiven Verständnis zu befreien.[41] Das Erfahren vollzieht sich vielmehr in einem Zusammenspiel von objektivem Widerfahrnis und subjektivem Benennen.

3. Auf dem Markt der Spiritualitätsangebote wird eine „spirituelle Erfahrung" nur allzu leicht zu einer „Selbst-Erfahrung" und kann in einer Nabelschau enden. Das dargelegte Erfahrungsverständnis kann hier als ein kritisches Korrektiv wirken, da es widerfahrend stets ein Anderes außerhalb des jeweiligen Subjekts und seiner Verfügbarkeit bedeutet.

4. Schillebeeckx spricht auch nicht von Erfahrung im Sinne einer religiösen Transzendenzerfahrung, z. B. einer Privatoffenbarung, wie dies in mehr esoterischen Kreisen unterschiedlicher Couleur und Ausrichtung geschehen mag. Wenn von religiöser Erfahrung gesprochen wird, dann von einer Glaubenserfahrung im Alltag.

Dies bindet einerseits „religiöse Erfahrung" sehr nüchtern und nachgerade pragmatisch an die widerfahrende, nicht vollends verfügbare Wirklichkeit an. Andererseits erhält gerade das religiös Alltägliche eine fundamentale Bedeutung.

Gerade in Zeiten von reduktiven Restrukturierungen bei katholischen Institutionen und der Konzentration auf das so genannte Kerngeschäft ist dann dem Alltäglichen Raum zu geben, das die Mauern etwa einer Sakristei weit überschreitet.

5. Erfahrung ist nie nur unmittelbare, „reine" Erfahrung. „Religiöse Erfahrung" ist damit immer an eine bestimmte Tradition gebunden, sie ist Teil einer bestimmten Weltsicht.

Gerade diese Einsicht wird durch einen scheinbar natürlich gottlosen Pragmatismus bestätigt. Es handelt sich um einen je verschiedenen Zugang zur Wirklichkeit. Auch wenn dies allzu bekannt scheinen mag, so ist es dadurch doch nicht falsch und auch nicht irrelevant geworden in Hinsicht etwa auf ein Gespräch zwischen unterschiedlichen Weltanschauungen in der Gesellschaft.

Dies spricht dann auch gegen eine vorschnelle Einverleibung gegenwärtiger Strömungen als religiös – gerechtfertigt durch die These einer Rückkehr der Religion. Es spricht für einen gelassenen Umgang mit der Pluralisierung einer Gesellschaft, die keinen übergeordneten

---

[41] Vgl. ders., Christus und die Christen, a.a.O., 26.

und für alle verbindlichen oder gleichermaßen zugänglichen Standpunkt kennt.[42]

Aus dieser Einsicht in die Vermitteltheit von Erfahrung folgt eine Leitlinie für den kirchlichen Auftrag zur Verkündigung – auch jenseits „traditionell katholischer" Milieus mit ihren Strukturen und Weltsichten, wie etwa kirchliche Entwicklungen im Bistum Erfurt oder auch wissenschaftliche Drittmittelprojekte an der dortigen Universität dies zeigen.

6. Zugleich erlangt über dieses Erfahrungsverständnis Tradition eine hohe Relevanz. Ohne einen identifizierenden, benennenden Sprach- und Traditionszusammenhang kann das Widerfahrnis nicht rezipiert werden. Tradition ist jedoch mit Schillebeeckx ein lebendiger Prozess. Eine Vereinnahmung von Tradition durch Traditionalismus oder eine kirchenpolitische Vernutzung z. B. für neokatechetische Tendenzen gefährdet somit Tradition vielmehr da sie ihre entscheide und tragende Bedeutung untergewichten können.

Edward Schillebeeckx bietet somit eine Theologie, welche in christologischer Fundierung ein lebendiges Weiterdenken notwendig begründet.

* * *

Abstract of the contribution of Bernadette Schwarz-Boenneke

Edward Schillebeeckx articulates a dialectical notion of experience. The first and 'objective' instance of experience is reality's resistance, which is imposed on every experiencing agent. This first instance only becomes a holistic experience when it integrates another instance of interpretation, which is based on a sense-giving activity and adaptation within a framework of language and thought. Experience develops in the acts of encountering and naming.

---

[42] Schillebeeckx spricht an einer Stelle davon, dass es keine anonymen Christen gibt. Inklusivisten sind alle in dem Sinne, dass man erkenntnistheoretisch notwendig an die eigene Position gebunden ist. Vgl. E. Schillebeeckx, Glaubensinterpretation, a.a.O., 108f.; ders., Theologie der Erfahrung – Sackgasse oder Weg zum Glauben?, a.a.O., hier 394: „Ich mache christliche Erfahrungen, weil ich in einer christlichen Tradition stehe."

The dialectics of encountering and naming, as studied in the "Christologische Prolegomena," forms the grammatical structure of Schillebeeckx's theology: the first instance of experience is always a gift of reality that affects the perceiving agent, triggers the event of interpretation and, furthermore turns into an impetus for transformation. According to Schillebeeckx, the first instance of Christian experience is the gift of reality revealed in and through Jesus, the Christ. However, this gift of revelation is only completed in the act of naming and professing our human answer to Christ's own gifting. In this way, encountering and naming, revelation and faith are necessary complements of Christian practice.

This essay argues that a critical analysis of Schillebeeckx's understanding of experience and of the grammatical structure of his theological discourse can bring up helpful pathmarks for modern theology.

Translation from German: *Tracy Rammler*

Geraldine Smyth

FORGIVENESS BETWEEN THE THEOLOGICAL AND SOCIAL

Invitation to Reconciling Grace

Introduction and Contexts

Often it is the poet, the prophet or the sage that most fully embody the complexities involved in the reciprocal dynamics of the inflicting and suffering of violence, the transcendent move of interrupting the cycle of revenge, and the graced experience of forgiving and being forgiven. Michael Longley, the Irish poet, writing in the midst of the sectarian conflict that raged in Northern Ireland for more than three decades, reflected on the costs of the violence and on the grace of forgiveness by dramatising a moment of transcendence from ancient wars of Greece and Troy. We glimpse here something of the grace and graciousness that Edward Schillebeeckx also knew and portrayed in a different idiom – that there is nothing abstract, escapist or disembodied in such experiences of grace given and received, but rather a depth of passionate suffering love. Paradoxically, it is in letting go to empathy, a more than human self-transcendence opens out, and an interhuman solidarity overcomes the ineluctable pattern of vengeance.

The poet recalls a self-transcending moment between arch-war-enemies, Achilles of Greece and old King Priam. Hector, Priam's son, has just been slain by Achilles. There is nothing platonic in the relationship, nothing that can be sublimated as the two enemies confront one another over the mutilated body of the young Hector. Facing Priam, Achilles somehow sees beyond the figure of the enemy to the face of a stricken fellow man; the bereft father discloses the face of his own father. The moment of empathy breaks down their enmity and forges a bond so strong that it can withstand the public manifestation of vulnerability. Both break down in contrite weeping, "until their sadness filled the building."[1]

Then Achilles ensures that the rituals of washing and clothing of the corpse are observed with all dignity –

"Laid out in uniform, ready for Priam to carry

Wrapped like a present home to Troy at daybreak."[2]

Then a parting meal is shared and we are told that they are "full of conversation, who earlier had sighed,"[3] facing each other now like lovers rather than sworn enemies. Only the words of Priam are given us (in a two-line final stanza – just half the length of the previous three stanzas and devoid of punctuation:

"'I get down on my knees and do what must be done

And kiss Achilles' hand, the killer of my son.'"[4]

Taking such a long view back into ancient Greek tragedy, as indeed of the Hebrew Prophets, or the parables of Jesus, one finds a transparent interplay between the personal, political and religious understanding of these themes. While in Western Europe and North America, the prevailing Christian focus on forgiveness and on reconciliation has been linked to the private, religious sphere, this too has increasingly changed over past decades, with political leaders and popes re-inscribing their public significance.[5] Such figures as Nelson Mandela and Ang San Suu Kyi, come to mind. The emergence of post-conflict truth and reconciliation commissions, from South Africa to Latin America, has brought system and formality to such discourse, with the intent of enabling former enemies to

---

[1] M. Longley, "Ceasefire", in: idem, Collected Poems, Cape Poetry, London: Jonathan Cape, 2006, Stanza I, 225.

[2] Ibid., Stanza II, 225.

[3] Ibid., Stanza III, 225.

[4] Ibid., Stanza IV, 225.

[5] L.G. Jones, Embodying Forgiveness: A Theological Analysis, Grand Rapids: Eerdmans, 1995, 73–118; M. Minow, Between Vengeance and Forgiveness: Facing History after Genocide and Mass Violence, Boston: Beacon Press, 1998. See also, L. Accattoli, When a Pope Asks Forgiveness: The Mea Culpas of John Paul II, transl. J. Aumann, New York: Society of St Paul, 1998; also, The Roman Catholic Church International Theological Commission Report, Memory and Reconciliation: the Church and the Faults of the Past, in: Origins, no 48, 16.3.2000, whose publication virtually coincided with a special Day of Pardon. Hereby, church leaders, politicians and erstwhile combatants assumed the spirit of dialogue, reconciliation and forgiveness (par 5.1). Cf. also G. Smyth, "Telling a Different Story: Hope for Forgiveness and Reconciliation in Northern Ireland", in: P. Rothfield / C. Fleming / P. Komesaroff (Eds.), Pathways to Reconciliation: Between Theory and Practice, Aldershot: Ashgate, 2008, 67–78. I will draw further here on some parts of that text.

confront the past interrelationally and with a view to shaping a different, more inclusive future.[6] In the context of decades of violent conflict in Northern Ireland, there is no lack of inspiration – from Gordon Wilson, to Michael McGoldrick – "ordinary" men and women who, through their Christian faith turned personal loss and violent bereavement into life-paths of peace and reconciliation.[7]

In recent centuries, forgiveness in the western Church figured most prominently in terms of the individual's relationship with God, as overseen by the Church through a forensic emphasis on sin and the institutional practice of confession. Paradoxically, there was a reduced scope for the personal. In recent decades, however, the sacramental understanding of forgiveness (theologically in terms of the forgiveness of sin, and anthropologically in terms of human repentance and the forgiveness of "enemies"), the Catholic Church has emphasised the personal, interpersonal, socio-political and liturgical, where, prior to the Second Vatican Council, the legal and institutional were to the fore. The documents of Vatican II manifest this changing emphasis, with more scope given to a deeper, nuanced theological anthropology and in the new significance given to social and historical context and culture. At the same time, the renewal in biblical studies – including a turn to salvation history and new methodologies – historical-critical, hermeneutical and liberational – made their impact on social forms of faith, theology, and of the Church in the midst of the modern world. One can discern the fingerprint of Edward Schillebeeckx on all these fronts. His work during the preceding and subsequent decades bore its own fruit.[8]

---

[6] See R.I. Rotberg / D. Thompson (Eds.), Truth v. Justice: The Morality of Truth Commissions, Princeton N.J.: Princeton University Press, 2000; also R. Daye, Political Forgiveness: Lessons from South Africa, New York: Orbis Books, 2004.

[7] Gordon Wilson lost his only daughter in the IRA bombing of a Remembrance Day Service, 1987, and bore witness as much by the depth of love for his daughter, comforting her in her dying moments and repeating her name – 'Marie', as by his avowing of forgiveness and commitment to peace in the name of Christ. Michael McGoldrick, lost his son in a random Loyalist attack, just days after he graduated from a Belfast university. Speaking at his son's burial he said, "How can I *not* forgive the people that killed my son. If I did not, I could no longer pray the 'Our Father', and then, I might as well go down there into that grave with my son." He dedicated the next ten years of his life organising visits of solidarity to Romania and caring for orphans there over several visits a year. It was on such a mission of mercy that he died in 2010.

[8] Cf. E. Borgman, Edward Schillebeeckx: A Theologian in his History. Vol. 1: A Catholic Theology of Culture, 1914–1965, transl. by J. Bowden, London – New York: Continuum, 2003, for a through historical exposition of Schillebeeckx's contribution to *ressourcement théologie*, affirming and reconstructing neglected biblical and patristic understandings of creation, God's mercy, *metanoia*, the Kingdom of God, together with contemporary perspectives from

Within the realm of the secular, this more holistic theological approach to forgiveness has made an influence in varied political and social contexts such as in the field of post-war reconciliation, and in transitional justice contexts in Latin American countries, and in Ireland. This can be seen too in the paradigm of ethics in international relations, but it is even visible within the theories of the realist school of political science, when irresolvable warfare yields to an acknowledgement of the impasse of a no-win situation. Particularly in intra-state conflict between different ethnic or cultural groups, the bitterest of enemies have found it necessary to construct a resolution beyond victory and defeat, endeavouring to negotiate between the claims of the state and its military force and those of all other combatants, even paramilitary resurgents.

But, *mutatis mutandi*, theology has in turn been impacted by the developing disciplinary field of Conflict Resolution and Peace Studies. The insights of the human and social sciences have challenged and assisted theologians to rethink and broaden out the understanding of forgiveness and reconciliation, and to re-examine the theological categories of righteousness, reconciliation and restorative justice. Australia in 2008 introduced its national *Sorry Day*; one of the first steps of the new South African government led by Nelson Mandela was to enshrine in the constitution a *National Day of Reconciliation*, and New Zealand has pioneered models of Restorative Justice towards its Maori populations, which have been drawn upon elsewhere. In many such cases, church bodies and charismatic Christians and groups, often in partnership with political institutions and civic organisations, forged a path in instituting and ritualising these processes of repentance, forgiveness and reconciliation.

In ways that recall the biblical symbol structure of God's all-embracing *Shalom*, the discipline of Peace Studies provides analytic evidence that ending a war is about more that ceasing hostilities, but involves a longer, deeper, more inclusive process. One hears now of "DDR" – disarmament, demobilisation and reintegration – positing the need for sustainability and a fresh start rather than merely a return to the *status quo ante*, with its implicit likelihood of repeating the cycle of violence. The possibility of letting go of the past, of healing memories and of a reconciling justice is fraught with difficulty, and its complexities will not be engaged *tout court* by peace treaties alone nor by the rules of "Track One Diplomacy." Something more is needed that takes better account of

---

phenomenology, anthropology and culture. See also E. Schillebeeckx, God and Man, New York: Sheed and Ward, 1969, 160–209.

the human condition and the interplay of culture and history – and religion. Peace needs to be "received" if we might borrow a word from Ecumenics, and become incarnated in the dynamics of civic relationship and freshly imagined institutions. Political agreements cannot provide for reconciliation, nor can forgiveness be managed.

When it comes to the possibility of forgiving enemies, exemplars can be cited (as above) of self-transcendence and of a superhuman generosity that many adjudge sheer folly. The notion and theological vocabulary of grace comes into view, and indeed Schillebeeckx's own words (imbued with the spirit of Aquinas), when he speaks of grace making humans more human and more than human.[9] Our own efforts alone will never suffice to bring meaning or wholeness or peace to life. Rather, life turned on the "'reversal' of tragic human existence 'into a glad, bold and free trust in God'"[10]. The natural and the supernatural come together but originate in God and are sustained by grace.

I will speak more fully below about the fundamentals of forgiveness from the perspective of Christian faith and practice, and particularly in relation to the utterly gracious gift at the core of Jesus Christ's life, death and resurrection, but so too I argue that we must acknowledge forgiveness in the secular world, within its own natural sphere and autonomy. We can be inspired by Schillebeeckx's commitment to the theology of culture and his method of correlation, built upon subsequently by others like David Tracy, Walter Brueggemann and Paul Ricœur, to bring the insights of faith into mutually critical correlation with the secular, seeking to live out the Gospel not as over against the world but *as God's hope for the world*, hope within history. Schillebeeckx's insistence is as important now as when he voiced it in the 1930s, upon creation as the location of God's revelation – *within* culture, history and existential struggle, though insisting even more strongly on not reducing grace to the scale of cultural attainability; insisting – and here we speak specifically about the forgiving of enemies – upon the divine source and origin of grace made manifest

---

[9] Schillebeeckx's early theology of grace was worked out in the context of his dialogue with the writings of Karl Adam, whose strong affirmation of creation and culture, however laid him open to the ideology of Nationalist Socialism. Schillebeeckx challenged Adam's noncritical synthesis of faith and culture, insisting on the absolute priority of the divine initiative of grace in the life of human beings, and the paradox that with freedom intact, human beings may through grace be gathered into the supernatural life of God: E. Schillebeeckx, "Natuur en Bovennatur", in: *Biekorf* 1942 (no number) and 1943 no. 4., 5, cited in E. Borgman, Edward Schillebeeckx, op. cit., 91 and 92; 395, n. 61, also 93ff. Cf. E. Schillebeeckx, Jesus: An Experiment in Christology, London: Collins, 1979, 42ff and 52ff.

[10] E. Schillebeeckx, as cited in: E. Borgman, Edward Schillebeeckx, op. cit., 92.

within the human, and in ways utterly beyond human knowing, imagining or capacity.[11] We need to wrestle further with this *aporia*.

A good dictionary definition of forgiveness reveals its religious traces and theological nuance. It is cognate with the old English *for-giefan* (the *for* prefix implying something utterly intensive), with the meaning – to give away, overlook an offence or debt, and still stronger, to show mercy and compassion.[12] The insistent interrelational dynamic and the suggestion of prior harm done is matched with the idea of something gratuitously offered, beyond desert and with a view to interrupting revenge. At an existential level, there is an implied giving away of oneself to another in a superlative gesture that opens the possibility of mutual re-orientation and new beginning. There are encouraging dimensions here for a renewed theological anthropology of forgiveness, and likewise, the potential for locating certain theses about forgiveness within the socio-theological and political contexts.

Michael Hurley (1934–2011), founder of the Irish School of Ecumenics, elucidates a distinction between the focus and method of secular and religious approaches to reconciliation – presupposing the reality that forgiveness and reconciliation discourse has indeed returned to the public sphere. Regarding the "secularization of reconciliation," he notes the concentration there on the reconciling of differing positions, based on justice and redress. By contrast, Hurley interprets the religious understanding as more personal, encouraging a change of heart animated by charity and the *superhuman act of forgiveness*. Doubtless, there are methodological challenges to be tackled in bringing Christian theological perspectives into this renewed public discourse, given the public repudiation of the categories of faith, but also because churches too often hold aloof from the norms of secular debate, holding to *a priori* assumptions, and reluctant to collaborate with those who do not share these.

The churches need to reflect critically on their readiness to acknowledge the autonomy of the secular in respect of their own authority; whether their current articulations of forgiveness and reconciliation are

---

[11] E. Schillebeeckx, Jesus, op. cit.: The author speaks of faith and grace here in terms of trust. "Why, in the end, anyone should put their trust in a given person is a mystery. One can adduce various factors having to do with psychology, biography, sociology, cultural history and the family; and they are relevant [...]. But they leave intact the mystery of the person of every person, and can never explain the trust motivated by faith. No more is an appeal to God's grace envisaged as an explanation. To speak of God's work of grace is to speak in the language of religious affirmation about the human mystery of trusting in someone" (673).

[12] See The Chambers Dictionary: New 9th Ed., Edinburgh: W. & R. Chambers, 2003, reprinted 2005.

adequate and accessible to culturally divided, politically complex societies; and the extent, in pluralist or divided contexts, to which they have evaded their social responsibilities and failed to develop a public theology that is at once modest, practical and capable of inspiring fresh vision of the new life that reconciliation signifies.[13] Clearly, a degree of theological precision is needed if there is to be a mutually fruitful encounter between a sociopolitical approach and that of Christian faith.

This essay continues in two further steps: the first explores the mutually fructifying understandings of forgiveness within the Christian tradition, while stressing its importance for public discourse – appealing to both an intrinsic and extrinsic hermeneutic. Thus, the insistence upon the pre-eminence of God's grace and the ineffable newness of Christ's salvation requires an examination of the biblical and doctrinal discourse of forgiveness in its own terms, *ad intra* and *ad extra*, bearing in mind with Schillebeeckx[14] that creeds and doctrines are more than closed cognitive systems, but patterns of whole ways of life in community, open to the face of God and to the face of the Other, bearing witness to the life and way of Jesus Christ and his offer of salvation for all – friend, stranger and enemy alike. This becomes doubly relevant when the contextual field of reference involves a society divided along politico-religious lines.[15] Northern Ireland is such a place where the dominant but divergent theologies clearly illustrate how faith and politics continue to intersect in specific and dialectical ways within and between the secular and religious domains.

The second, more contextual part of the essay will situate these understandings of forgiveness in relation to the practical work for reconciliation in Ireland emerging from four decades of conflict in and about Northern Ireland. It will engage the question as to how such a divided Christian community there might embody peace after the manner of Chr-

---

[13] Once finds a resonance here with Schillebeeckx's call for the church to adopt a "humble humanism" in its interactions with secular culture. The 1949 article of this name was reprinted in: E. Schillebeeckx, World and Church (Collected Works vol. 4), New York: Sheed and Ward, 1971, 19–31.

[14] The dialogue here with some key insights of Schillebeeckx will focus mainly on his book: Jesus: an Experiment in Christology, transl. H. Hoskins, London: Collins, 1979.

[15] Ireland, in the wake of centuries of politico-religious division in which the Christian religion played a prominent part, has for more than 80 years been divided into two jurisdictions – Northern Ireland, which is part of the United Kingdom, and the Republic of Ireland. The Good Friday Agreement of 1998 offered the basis for an inclusive political arrangement, which eventually led to a broadly accepted power-sharing Assembly in Belfast, Northern Ireland.

ist, who in the Johannine tradition speaks of himself as the way the truth and the life. The call to the churches is to encourage divided communities to live into the truth, to attend to the wounds of the other (person, community, church), to embrace life in fullness, but also themselves embodying in their own ecclesiology and ethic a New Creation that is forgiving, just and inclusive.

Forgiveness and Reconciliation in Public Life and Public Theology

Forgiveness cannot be understood in purely speculative terms, but rather through an approach grounded in the realities of the human condition as many-in-one, interrelational, historical/dynamic, and embodied. Not without irony, a purely speculative viewpoint short-circuits these human qualities, succumbing instead to the world of spectacle – reductionist, atomistic, speedy, and disembodied. Examples abound where the demands of a super-ordinate political ideology or the fascination of the media with high profile reconciliation drives the programming of public shows (in both senses of the word) of forgiveness and reconciliation. The political construction of certain historical commemorations come to mind, and a British Channel 4 TV series presided over by no less a figure than Archbishop Desmond Tutu, that brought a sister or mother face to face with the former soldier or paramilitary combatant who had decades previously, pulled the trigger or planted a bomb that killed their loved ones. Such programmes belie the fact that forgiveness cannot be arranged or managed and it is part of a larger process of reconciliation that requires time and mourning. The Church's ancient four-fold structure involving honest self-reflection, contrite acknowledgement, absolution and reparation embodies this sacramentally. Vamik Volkan, speaking from a psychoanalytic perspective on post-conflict reconciliation processes, decries publicly orchestrated accelerated enactments of post-war apology and forgiveness, without attending to the underlying causes and to a "significant amount of mourning" by the suffering group.[16] He observes the burgeoning interest in such enactments since Gorbachev's apology for the Soviet government role in the Katyn Forest Massacres in Poland.

---

[16] V. Volkan, Blood Lines: From Ethnic Pride to Ethnic Terrorism, Boulder, Colorado: Westview Press, 1997, 226.

"Stubborn large-group conflicts," Volkan asserts, "cannot be solved by an instant-coffee approach."[17]

I would venture that Hannah Arendt, writing as a secular Jewish philosopher, claiming that the "discoverer of the role of forgiveness in the realm of human affairs was Jesus of Nazareth," would have assented to the wisdom behind Volkan's provisos. Arendt avowed the connection between the religious and secular horizons: "that he made this discovery in a religious context and articulated it in religious language, [w]as no reason to take any less account of it in a strictly secular sense" with reference to socio-political transformation.[18] It should be noted also that whereas on the one side, moral philosophy has afforded scant critical attention to the conceptuality of forgiveness,[19] on the other hand, the idea of forgiveness has been saturated by religious experience and shaped by religious history and theology.[20] Therefore, while theology cannot lay exclusive claims or render its conceptualisation static, political thinkers and practitioners do well to explore something of the deep religious structure of forgiveness, and to open to its theological horizon as well as its "effective history."[21]

In its recent efforts to recover a consciousness of sin as social and structural, the Church is positing *ipso facto* a corresponding consciousness of grace. This is evidenced in the retrieval of such socio-politico-religious biblical symbols as "Covenant," "Jubilee," and "Kingdom of God."[22] Thereby, Christians are called by the Church to an intentional praxis of the Kingdom of God, a living out of grace through socio-political care

---

[17] Ibid.

[18] H. Arendt, The Human Condition: a Study of the Central Conditions Facing Modern Man, Chicago: Chicago University Press, 1958/1959, 238f.

[19] H.R. Mackintosh, Christian Experience of Forgiveness, London: Nisbet, 1954 (1927), 187.

[20] P. Ricœur, The Symbolism of Evil, Boston: Beacon Press, 1967.

[21] H.-G. Gadamer, Truth and Method, 2nd rev. ed., New York: Crossroads, 1989, 360. The author rightly stresses the living interplay between a tradition and its interpreters through active reception.

[22] Schillebeeckx for whom soteriology is the natural route into Christology, makes the "Kingdom of God" (the Lordship of Christ and the Kingdom as a site of God's copious life and mercy) in their concrete experiential, historical, political, soteriological and eschatological realities, a key hermeneutical focus in his magisterial work: Jesus: an Experiment in Christology. See, particularly, Part II, 105ff., 165ff., 207ff. and passim; also, idem, Interim Report on the Books *Jesus* and *Christ*, transl. J. Bowden, London: SCM Press – New York: Seabury Press, 1980, 99–102. The author's centralised the Parables of the Kingdom and of certain miracles of healing and forgiveness as liberating signs of the Kingdom here in the now. In his Lenten message, 2001, John Paul II linked forgiveness with the social reality of peace, and forgiveness as the way to peace, for individuals *and* nations, referring also to his own request for forgiveness for the sins of Roman Catholics over the centuries (cf. *Irish Times*, 10th February 2001).

and virtue as a corrective to the privatisation of sin and grace in the preceding era. The diminished popularity in the Catholic Church of individual auricular confession, signals a cultural rejection of the muscular Christianity of the 8th Century Irish penitential tradition.[23] The Reformation Churches repudiated the penitential aspects of display and arduous effort, but both traditions maintained the privatised emphasis.

By the mid 20th century, theologians like Edward Schillebeeckx, Johann Baptist Metz, Dorothee Sölle, Bernard Häring, Enda McDonagh, and documents from Latin American Bishops, following their meetings at Medellín (1968) and Puebla (1979), were making an impact in the reconstitution of the connection between salvation and social justice, de-emphasising forensic understandings of wrong-doing as individual moral delinquency, positing a more complex moral framework with greater account taken of collective systemic oppression, responsibility through solidarity, and Christ's preferential option for the poor. Such a turn to the social provides the external rationale for theological attention to the socio-political sphere of forgiveness. Theology provides a legitimate, finely tuned syntax and language whereby church members can contribute robustly to public discourse. As well as providing believers with an inspiring, (partially) integrating and challenging narrative and rationale, theological reflection must be able to communicate its message comprehensibly to those who live by other narratives and belief systems.[24]

There is also an intrinsic theological necessity for keeping "forgiveness" and "reconciliation" buoyed between the religious, interreligious and secular spheres. This derives from the nature of biblical revelation itself in its exploration of the interrelationship between God, humanity and the world. The Judaeo-Christian tradition discloses a constant interplay between a broad theological anthropology, as exemplified by the creation and wisdom traditions (with their allusion to beliefs held in common with neighbouring religions), and a specific soteriological narrative with a narrower interpretation of "salvation history" (with Exodus as its *ur*-text, together with particularist theologies of election and deliverance). *A fortiori*, looking to the future of theology in the context of late modernity, account must also be taken of the radically de-centred, destabilised field of all religious communication, the depth of ideological pluralism and suspi-

---

[23] J. Mahoney, The Making of Moral Theology: A Study of the Roman Catholic Tradition, Oxford: Clarendon Press, 1989 (1987), 5–17.
[24] See, J. D'Arcy May, "Political Religion: Secularity and the Study of Religion in Global Civil Society", in: B. Spalek / A. Imtoual (Eds.), Religion, Spirituality and the Social Sciences: Challenging Marginalisation, Bristol: Policy Press, 2008, 9–22.

cion of "grand narratives" and the hegemonic power derived from them, yet without construing pluralism as sheer randomness, and also acknowledging the role of faith in divine grace still strangely at work within creation, history and culture whatever the ambivalence, suffering and rupture, and calling for ecumenical listening and dialogue, inviting further search for communion.[25]

Thus, the concept of chosen people is oriented ultimately towards the saving of all nations.[26] Christians, within this paradoxical soteriological tradition, misread Christ's mission as an abrogation of the covenant with all creation, or the covenant with the Jewish people (Rom. 11), if they fail to discern the intrinsic unity of God's purpose, always mysteriously at work in history and culture, between the already and the not-yet of the New Creation. Authentic Christian theology upholds this unity of God's universal and particular purposes (as in Jewish teaching, albeit with its stronger eschatological emphasis), yet without claim to certainty about the whither and wherefore of the Holy Spirit. All human life and the whole cosmos are within God's reconciling embrace.[27] There should be no ugly ditch between sacred and profane, no split, as Schillebeeckx un-

---

[25] U. Luz, "Can the Bible Still be the Foundation for the Christian Church Today? The Task of Exegesis in a Society of Religious Pluralism", in: Studies in Matthew, transl., by R. Selle, Grand Rapids, Michigan – Cambridge, UK: Eerdmans, 2005, 314–332. See also, E. Schillebeeckx, Jesus, op. cit., 671–673, where Jesus' universal significance is reprised in these closing pages of the book, and is significantly correlated with *metanoia*.

[26] See, Y. Congar, "The Few Who Represent the Whole", in his book: The Wide World My Parish, transl. D. Attwater, Darton: Longman and Todd, 1964 (1961), 9–13. It should be noted, in the light of recent feminist hermeneutics that the biblical *pars pro toto* is problematic for many women. Within patriarchal culture, women did *not* represent tribes and nations (as for example in the two major biblical narratives of reconciliation: Esau and Jacob [Gen 33: 1–17]) and Joseph and his brothers (Gen. 45:1–8). No archetypal stories have been handed down of women who overcame mutual enmity and chose the way of reconciliation: D. Bergant, "Bearers of Reconciliation in Our World", unpublished lecture, Conference of the International Union of Superiors General, Rome, May 2004. But, adducing Jesus' example and teaching, she proposes: "This may well be the moment for women to assume the role of bearers of reconciliation."

[27] Jn. 1:11; Eph. 1:3ff; Acts 11:2ff. Different Christian denominations, adopt various methodological possibilities in correlating secularity and soteriology: for example, an approach of radical separation in the Calvinist tradition, seen for example in the early work of Karl Barth, linked to God's transcendence and universal mission (in this, not altogether different from the Roman Catholic tradition). Lutheranism's "Two Kingdoms" theory accords to each realm their relative independence. Theology requires dialectic and analogy. D. Bonhoeffer, reacting, like Barth, to Hegel's grand synthesis struggled to keep the difference of God and world anchored in their unity. See D. Bonhoeffer, Act and Being, London: Collins – New York: Harper, 1961 [1931], 168–169, 169.

failingly insists, between creation and redemption in Christian theological discourse.[28]

Forgiveness and Reconciliation: Clarifying Meanings and Ambiguities

It has been demonstrated that even secular dictionary definitions of forgiveness disclose theological hints of a transcending and transforming reciprocal action. In this view, there are clearly possibilities of sustaining an interrelational, socio-theological understanding of forgiveness in the context of a more radically open and engaged theological anthropology of reconciliation.

Gabriel Daly intimates this through some finely drawn linkages and distinctions. "Reconciliation" is thus the broader, more generative soteriological term, while forgiveness is its personally significant core.[29] Daly is at one with Schillebeeckx in stressing, additionally, the necessarily *symbolic* nature of such theological language; and in insisting upon a plurality of metaphors and models for meaningful theological communication.[30]

Paradox and Practice: Forgiveness as Gift, Inviting Reconciliation as Newness

In Christian theology, then, paradox is inescapable and always important if a functionalist reduction of forgiveness is to be avoided. This becomes clearer through a revisiting of the vexed relationship between forgiveness and repentance, where a paradoxical stance is required: first, in arguing

---

[28] E. Schillebeeckx, Interim Report on the Books Jesus and Christ, op. cit., 112–124: "Kingdom of God: Creation and Salvation" (chapter 6).

[29] See, G. Daly, "Forgiveness and Community", in: A.D. Falconer / J. Liechty (Eds.), Reconciling Memories, Dublin: Columba Press, 1998; *Reconciliation* is one of the classically preferred ways of describing the reality of salvation. *Redemption, justification, atonement*, and *sanctification* are others each with a specific historic and theological resonance. Such ascriptions to God are only by analogy, thereby avowing likeness and un-likeness between the divine and human expressions of such attributes as forgiveness.

[30] See, E. Schillebeeckx, Christ: the Christian Experience in the modern World, transl. J. Bowden, London: SCM Press, 1980, 477–514, where the author, adducing exegesis of successive NT texts, elaborates sixteen key soteriological concepts, including liberation, the defeat of death, reconciliation after dispute, opening into "a new way of life and a fulfilment, as redemption and the forgiveness of sins". Such models, however, were later construed in the more fundamental terms of "adoption" and "birth from God" (477). See also, Schillebeeckx's clarifying chapters on the hermeneutics of salvation, taking account of different world views, experience, tradition and interpretation: E. Schillebeeckx, Interim Report on the Books *Jesus* and *The Christ*, New York: Seabury – London: SCM, transl. J. Bowden, 1980, 3–39, and the significantly entitled chapter therein, "Living Tradition Thanks to Renewed Experience", 50–63.

that repentance is not a prior condition for forgiveness,[31] and that to assert otherwise would constrict the fundament of divine freedom, the universality of the salvation revealed in Christ, and the mysterious energy of the Holy Spirit within and beyond the Church. It would prefer a legalistic to a personal and interpersonal approach to forgiveness, and undermine the integral connection between salvation as an event, and the ongoing salvific process of conversion.[32] Paul Ricœur goes to the heart of the matter when he challenges the persisting tendency to confuse cause and effect in respect of forgiveness and repentance. Avowing the paradoxical relationship of forgiveness with repentance (the latter being our response), he stresses the contingent nature of repentance. Forgiveness is not tied to an instant, but rather, "it is the meaning of a whole life with its ups and downs, its crises but also its quiet display."[33] Schillebeeckx turns our attention frequently in recurring parts of *Jesus* to the synoptic theme of *metanoia* as belonging to the core of Jesus's preaching and *praxis* of the Kingdom of God. Such *metanoia* is not grounded on conditionality and constraint, but on gift, faith in a *kairos* invitation to decide for a new future of grace and newness.[34]

Grace in Double Pattern

Christian forgiveness implies a *turning away from sin*, but also, a *turning towards* relationship – with God and with others. Schillebeeckx, speaking of deliverance, justification and the implied relationship between forgiveness and *metanoia* asserts: "Deliverance, redemption, consists in so being re-

---

[31] Cf., L.G. Jones, Embodying Forgiveness, op. cit., who argues that repentance is not a prerequisite for forgiveness (against Swinburne's argument for prior repentance), 135–162; also, G. Smyth, "Brokenness, Forgiveness, Healing and Peace in Ireland", in: R.G. Helmick / R.L. Petersen (Eds.), Forgiveness and Reconciliation: Religion, Public Policy and Conflict Transformation, Philadelphia: Templeton Press, 2001, 329–359; also, P. Ricœur, "The Difficulty to Forgive", in: M. Junker-Kenny / P. Kenny (Eds.), Memory, Narrativity, Self and the Challenge to Think God, Münster: Lit Verlag, 2004. Ricœur insists that the inner consistency of the concept of forgiveness demands its *unconditionality* (explicitly in being *gift*) in respect to repentance "Repentance is not at all the condition of forgiveness [...]. If *there is* forgiveness, then *it remains* [...] It is our response that occurs in time [...]" (13ff.).

[32] See also, P.S. Fiddes, The Christian Idea of Atonement, London: Darton, Longman & Todd, 1989, 24–34.

[33] P. Ricœur, "The Difficulty to Forgive", op. cit., 13; also, B. Lonergan, Method in Theology, London: Darton, Longman & Todd, 1975, views conversion as recurring and interrelational, and involving the human capacity for self-transcendence (237–244); Lonergan speaks of "conversion as lived," and although "existential, intensely personal, utterly intimate," it has indeed a communal and historic reality" (130–131).

[34] E. Schillebeeckx, Jesus, op. cit., 207f., 672f.; also, idem, Christ, op. cit., 543.

conciled to one's past, that confidence in the future is again made possible."[35] Although the latter is not possible without the former, and forgiveness does not require repentance in advance, it does invite a new orientation to life with others as an enabling gift, amid the contingencies of history, and entering into the realities of human frailty and of human flourishing, calling us out of isolation into relationship. Also denoted here is the human possibility of "participative sharing" in the transcendent nature of forgiveness.[36] Both forgiveness and repentance are implied in the Matthean injunction (5:21): "Leave your offering there before the altar and go and be reconciled [...] and then come back and present your offering."[37] Jesus is demonstrating the inclusiveness of mercy, and exhorts his disciple that just as God's compassion is unbounded, so too their compassion is affirmed as participating in God's compassion.

More still, in Jesus' own teaching, God's forgiveness of us is co-implicated in our extending forgiveness to others (Mt. 6:12). Within the Christian pattern of reconciliation, we are to show mercy as God shows mercy (Lk. 6:36–37). Forgiveness opens the door to a fullness of life, the healing of relationship and the inclusion within one community of sinner and sinned against, as symbolised in the eschatological meal of God's reign (Mt. 22:10), in which just and unjust distinctions are overcome and apparently irreconcilable moral opposites are reconciled.

Paul is the classic exponent of forgiveness and reconciliation in the early Church. His teaching is shaped by his personal experience of the inbreaking grace of forgiveness, at the very time when he was persecuting the early Christian communities (Acts 4, 7, 9; 2Cor. 5–7; Col. 1:19–20, for example). In the narrative of the conversion of Saul, the double pattern stands out: the first moment describes how, in one blinding flash, without any expressed commitment to change, he experiences Christ's forgiveness. The second movement of repentance *followed* that experience (Acts 9:3–30). The first singular dramatic event is one moment within a larger sequence involving the wider community. Ananias, a member of that

---

[35] Idem, Jesus, op. cit., 672; also, idem, Christ, op. cit., 512–514.
[36] P. Ricœur, "The Difficulty to Forgive", op. cit., 13. Another Protestant theologian, H.R. Mackintosh, whose classic book on forgiveness has been cited above, makes a similar argument as going right back to the Hebrew Prophets and underwritten by Jesus, as "the contact between God and man [sic] which forgiveness is." He continues, "Because God is what they knew Him to be, He can *recreate a man's soul by taking him decisively into communion with himself* – an even which no immanent categories like law or evolution can ever explain." H.R. Mackintosh, Christian Experience of Forgiveness, op. cit., 179 (italics mine).
[37] This resonates with the Jewish prophets' repeated insistence on the integral link between worship and justice (e.g., Amos 5:21–24; Isaiah 1:11–17; Jeremiah 7:3–12).

community, in a pre-vision of the event, is given a mandate to welcome Saul the erstwhile enemy. At that point, we witness Saul's experience of the moment in which he is struck down, blinded, and forgiven. Then follows the fulfilment of that experience in his being welcomed into Ananias's house. Reconciliation is the graced matrix of forgiveness. Paul's conversion finds its radical starting point in his experience of forgiveness. Thence it opens out into the fullness of reconciliation, with worldwide and cosmic implications.

Theology Keeping Both Sides in View

Problems arise, not least a leaning towards Deism, whenever theological reflection on forgiveness and reconciliation are cut loose from their inherently inter-relational context. Here we should note the dominance of a certain legal model of soteriology, associated with Tertullian and Augustine, and by unbending neo-Scholastic interpretations of Aquinas's theology of grace. When hidebound by metaphors of the courtroom – strict punishment and legally imposed restitution – God's saving justice is cast in mechanistic modes that bear little resemblance to the personal forgiveness by which the biblical God reaches out in merciful pardon.[38] There is, however, another tradition associated with other Augustinian texts and with the Eastern Fathers, notably Irenaeus, whose intrinsically relational model of salvation, is expressed in metaphors of cleansing, the healing of sickness and the hope of being made whole.[39]

It would be false to claim an unequivocal bifurcation of the traditions of the Eastern and Western Church on this matter. Historically, neither is

[38] G. Daly, Creation and Redemption, Dublin: Gill and Macmillan, 1988, 184–186. Daly also adduces J. Hick, Evil and the God of Love, London: Macmillan, 1985 (1966). Hick identifies the Irenaean tradition as the "minority report" contrasting with the Augustinian "majority report" which won out in Western theology, 253, also, 205–218). E. Farley, Good and Evil: Interpreting a Human Condition, Minneapolis: Fortress Press, 1990, provides a useful literature overview of this tradition. Cf. ibid 33, n. 6.

[39] Irenaeus, Against the Heresies, IV.xxxviii.3; also, V. Lossky, In the Image and Likeness of God, eds. J. Erickson and Th. Bird, New York: SVS Press, 1985, 97–110, where Lossky contrasts the Western understanding of the ultimate human goal in terms of "redemption" (with sin as point of departure) and "the more positive definition of the same mystery" of the Eastern Church in terms of "deification" as "the ultimate vocation of created beings" (110). Although Augustine strove – against Pelagius – to underline the gratuitousness of grace, against reducing faith to an ethic of striving, the penal influence dominated in Christian history. Combining with the subsequent Celtic penitential approach to sin, this resulted in an undue emphasis on individualized repentance and on the significance of human expiation. See also, J. Mahoney, The Making of Moral Theology, op. cit., 224–231.

historically monolithic nor immune from patterns of assimilation to cultural power or prestige, ranging from the tribal to the imperialistic. Christianity in the West did, nonetheless, move into the systematization of laws and centralisation of ecclesial governance, causing it to elicit successive, though not entirely successful, historical challenges to reject the pomp and circumstance of its Constantinian and Carolingian trappings. In the past century, theologians in Western Europe, seeking to recover more dynamic, interrelational constructions of nature, sin and forgiveness, have fruitfully adduced the Eastern Orthodox tradition. Some of our Dominican theologians are among them, Yves Congar, for example, seeking to hold creatively the tension in understanding sin as *both* disobedience to the law and as a wounding of relationships. Salvation is experienced and expressed, tellingly, in bodily and with practical metaphors (breathing with both lungs or bi-focal vision).[40] Analogous insights from Primal Peoples, and from liturgical, ecological and feminist theologians, offer generative patterns for rethinking the theology of forgiveness and reconciliation in terms of historical, embodied, and joy-filled experiences of being healed and liberated.[41] So too, the renewal of ecumenical theology challenges us to seek always towards this "both-and," in openness to diversity-in-unity and unity-in-diversity, without fragmentation or totalisation. Both are needed, held together in an inflected, interdependent, ecumenical conversation.[42] Our theology and sacramental celebration of forgiveness has insufficiently inspired visions of new life, release out of sin and death into rebirth, community and New Creation. It centres unduly

---

[40] St.S. Harakas, from and Eastern Orthodox perspective, offers a schematic though still useful reading: the Reformation pattern stressing forgiveness and salvation as event centred on the once-for-all sufficiency of Christ's saving work (appealing to Heb. 9:25ff; Rom. 5:15–19), as grace appropriated by faith alone. Roman Catholic teaching is presented with its emphasis on human freedom in responding to grace (growth in grace through forgiving others, linked to the Pauline injunction to "work out your salvation in fear and trembling"). Isolated emphasis on the second reflects a Pelagian tendency, while exclusive stress on the former tends to a forensic interpretation of salvation. See, St.S. Harakas, "Forgiveness and Reconciliation", in: R.G. Helmick / R.L. Petersen, Forgiveness and Reconciliation, op. cit., 51–78.

[41] See, for example, S. McFague, The Body of God: An Ecological Theology, London: SCM Press, 1993, 133; also S. Frank Parsons (Ed.), The Cambridge Companion to Feminist Theology, Cambridge: Cambridge University Press, 2002, esp., Parsons' contribution, chapter 12 (206–223), "Redeeming Ethics", on the realigning of care, justice and the common good; P. Atkins, Memory and Liturgy: the Place of Memory in the Composition and Practice of Liturgy, Aldershot: Ashgate, 2004, e.g., chapter 7 (83–97), "Memories of Sin and Pain" and chapter 10 (126–139), "Memory, Imagination and Hope".

[42] See, G. Daly, One Church: Two Indispensable Values: Protestant Principle and Catholic Substance (Irish School of Ecumenics Occasional Papers vol. 4), Dublin: Dominican Publications, 1998, 11–13.

upon mortality and sin, disjoined from nature (natality) and grace. Schillebeeckx deeply grasped this in his constant return to the inextricable link in Jesus's own preaching in parables, table-fellowship, and miracles of healing, between the Kingdom already present and always anticipated in human transformation and promise. Theoretical soteriology must never disengage from God's merciful love as it is yearned for, creatively felt, and made exultantly manifest in the healing and joy animating the personal, historical lives of suffering and oppressed people.[43]

Forgiveness and Reconciliation in Northern Ireland

I have attempted to demonstrate that Christian forgiveness is predicated on the acceptance that human beings are constituted by and for relationship and new birth experienced in the throes of a history of human suffering, oppression and sin. When relations break down, forgiveness opens up an offer of a way back through the healing of relationships, and invites the protagonists into a wholly new reality, associated with metaphors of new birth, New Creation, the life of grace of love, with all the transforming possibilities and responsibilities of the gift of grace.[44] Paradoxically,

---

[43] Schillebeeckx makes this point trenchantly in Part II of his Jesus book (E. Schillebeeckx, Jesus, op. cit.), with the author's exegesis of the "praxis of the Kingdom of God" in terms of bringing Good News and making others glad. Particular focus is brought to the narration of Gospel parables, and the table fellowship and healings, associated with sinners, 124f., 140ff., 153f., 156ff., 185ff. The hermeneutical baseline is clear: that "through this community alone did it prove possible for the experience of salvation in Jesus with God as its source to develop after his death from a soteriological recognition of Jesus into a Christological conversion to Jesus the Christ" (219). It can be no different for his community of disciples today.

[44] E. Schillebeeckx, Jesus, op. cit., 124–127, 169. It is for this reason that theological accounts of forgiveness and salvation cannot stop short with the normative Chalcedonian summation as if theologically and evangelically exhaustive. Schillebeeckx urges a "searching Christology" and a soteriology rooted in good news for those who still cry out in pain and hope. Although criticised on this (e.g., re the absence of focus on sin and guilt, for example, or Walter Kasper's remonstrance that it led to a reductionism of salvation to mere human well-being and liberation), the Dominican mounts a redoubtable defence: Cf., E. Schillebeeckx, Interim Report on the Books *Jesus* and *Christ*, op.cit., 99–102. Directing "doubters" to his second book (Christ), and unequivocally avowing "objective redemption," he insists that, "redemption which has been achieved in Jesus needs to be presented in such a way that our history in fact remains ongoing human history [...] Christians believe in and through Jesus, that despite everything, the kingdom of God, as salvation for mankind, is still coming and will come; what has been achieved in Jesus Christ is the guarantee of this." Warning against forgetting the lessons of history, he calls for "'an anticipation in orthopraxis,' not only de-

the more impossible it seems the more necessary forgiveness becomes, because without it, people, communities and nations become trapped in an endless cycle of blame and revenge and nothing new can be born.

The withholding of forgiveness maintains un-freedom, as much for the sinned-against "victim" as the sinner or "perpetrator": "Without being forgiven, released from the consequences of what we have done," Arendt asserts, "we would remain the victims of its consequences forever."[45] Agency, reciprocity and responsibility are the alternative that forgiveness offers.

Yet, the "stubborn historicity" constantly enmeshes human capability in limitation, the ubiquity of resentment and blame, the pervasiveness of prejudice and fear, and for some, the overwhelming burden of suffering and evil. Here we confront the role of memory, where too, paradoxically, the incarnation of Jesus comes into view, as too his cross of suffering and death arises on the horizon of our vision, in its "scandalous particularity."

In my own particular context of Northern Ireland, the search for reconciliation dramatizes the struggle with that stubborn historicity at every level of life, but also the movements of inbreaking grace and of learning through dialogue across historically stubborn divisions, or through practical involvement with groups from other places of conflict, in collaborative projects of conflict resolution, the mending of memory, and exploration of the "promise" of newness – construed as co-remembering and "com-promise."

The journey out of violence towards peace has been painful and tortuous. Contesting opinions turn upon the tension between justice and reconciliation and upon the ambivalent views as to whether forgiving means forgetting,[46] bearing out what Martha Minow describes as the typical double concern which accompanies societies emerging from mass violence: "Too much memory or not enough; too much enshrinement of

---

spite but in suffering" (101f.); see also, idem, The Church with a Human Face, a New and Expanded Theology of Ministry, transl. J. Bowden, London: SCM Press, 1985, 10.

[45] H. Arendt, The Human Condition, op. cit., 237.

[46] On different modes of remembering, see, G. Smyth, "Sabbath and Jubilee", in: H. Ucko (Ed.), The Jubilee Challenge: Utopia or Possibility, Geneva: WCC, 1997, 59–76, particularly see, the Jewish tradition of the Sabbath of Remembrance, (*Shabbat Zachor*), 72; also, Interchurch Group on Faith and Politics, Remembrance and Forgetting: Building a Future in Northern Ireland (The Faith and Politics Group vol. 8), Belfast: Upper Crescent, 1998, which examines the interplay of such issues as memory in a contested space, memory and power, selective memory, the churches and memory, memory and biblical faith; see also, Interchurch Group on Faith and Politics, Forgive Us Our Trespasses: Reconciliation and Political Healing in Northern Ireland, Belfast, 1996, 8 and *passim*.

victim-hood or insufficient memorialising of victims and survivors; too much past or too little acknowledgement of the past's staging of the present."[47]

Paul Ricœur, speaking of the dynamics of memory observes that where memory is viewed as a debt to the past or duty to the ancestors, it is liable to become "a wheel of no release and – apposite to our purpose here –"Within memory lies the most secret resistance to forgiveness." For this reason, Ricœur prefers to address "the *work* of memory."[48] While there have been some outstanding examples of those who have spoken words of forgiveness from the depths of their own pain, there are many others for whom, forgiveness and the release it might bring, continues to pose intractable psychological, moral and spiritual challenges.

Some claim, God alone can forgive, often proof-texting with the out-of-context Gospel reference: "Who can forgive sins but God alone?" (Mk. 2:7b; Mt. 9:6–8; and Lk. 5:20–26). And yet, even behind feigned indignation, some trace of transcendence shows itself, as if hinting at the transcending power that inheres in the act of forgiving. True forgiveness is not cheap and its cost is counted in suffering, human suffering, but also the suffering of Jesus.[49]

One man I know – I shall call him Adam – who has recently been ordained within the Anglican Communion, as a young man, lost his Father and later his Uncle in separate assassinations by paramilitary Republicans in their fight for a united Ireland. Adam and I were part of a TV panel with Brian Keenan, the Belfast man who spent more than four years as a hostage in Beirut. He had been brutally tortured. We had been invited to reflect on whether some crimes are too heinous to forgive (as this text goes to press, similar debates are being tragically rehearsed in the wake of Anders Breivik's manic attacks in Norway in July 2011). Brian Keenan explained that the idea of forgiveness did not have any meaning for him, and that he had chosen to blot out from his mind the experiences of sustained brutality at the hands of his captors. Adam, in contrast, acknowledged that after decades of struggle with grief and loss and long vigils spent in the company of the suffering Jesus, he could now partially forgive the men who had robbed his youth and dismembered his family.

---

[47] M. Minow, Between Vengeance and Forgiveness, op. cit., 2.
[48] P. Ricœur, "The Difficulty to Forgive", op. cit., 15 (italics mine). He continues, stressing the need to let go of the claim to construct a story of our life without lacks or gaps, or of any expectation that we can repair all wounds (15). This has overtones of the Christian call to relinquish self-sufficiency in favour of actively opening one's life to salvation as gift.
[49] Cf., H.R. Mackintosh, Christian Experience of Forgiveness, op. cit.

"Now, finally, I can forgive what they did to me," he told me, "but I have not been able to forgive the suffering they inflicted on others in my family." He related to me later, over a meal, that his Mother had never got over the loss of her husband, followed by the death of her son (Adam's twin brother) who had ended his own life a few years later. He could not wholly find forgiveness within his human reach. In Schillebeeckx's terms, in that contrast experience of darkness and God's absence, Adam had known a fragmentary salvation even as he wrestled to make sense of his experience and of this utterly human history in the light of the Gospel of Jesus.[50] But Adam avowed that he still remained open to the *possibility* of a fuller forgiveness sometime in the future. The existential reality of pain-filled loss was beleaguered with impotence, since he never knew who had murdered his loved ones – he cannot envisage a face, a story, a conversation, or any kind of relationship with the perpetrators. Thus, his fractured life lacks access to a whole meaning, in his non-comprehension of the totality of the political context and the intractable system of enmity and division. He is denied the *experience* of a potential healing of relationships. Forgiveness in any full sense is humanly foreclosed. And yet in sharing the story of this brokenness and his ongoing grappling to interpret it in greater depth, Adam somehow bears witness to his discovery of a new path of life, of being himself forgiven, and, in ways not altogether clear to him, of the desire to participate in God's forgiveness through his ministry among other grieving families and a still traumatised society. In his existential context and experience of family devastation, and his human incapacity to find how forgiveness might have actual meaning, he has found himself drawn into the unknowable divine forgiving, both in its incarnate self-limitation and self-transcending power, drinking from the same cup as Jesus, and seeking to *practise* of the Kingdom of God on earth.

Clearly, discourse on the theological anthropology of forgiveness must take care not to speak facilely of forgiveness in the face of such "offending deaths" – occurring in the midst of humanly complex and historically protracted violent conflict. Yet, Douglas J. Davies, who coined the term, "offending deaths", while noting that they can fuel the cycle of revenge, also points up a paradoxical reality: the visible offence to social, moral values that emerges in the way the deaths are publically mourned, high-

---

[50] Is not Schillebeeckx's definition of revelation as given in E. Schillebeeckx, Christ, op. cit., à propos here? "So for believers, *revelation* is an *action of God* as *experienced* by believers and *interpreted in religious language* and therefore *expressed* in human terms, in the dimension of our utterly human history" (78).

lights the sacrificial aspect, while exposing the failures of those with public or political responsibility, and awakens conscientious resistance and civic protest for fundamental change.[51] In Adam's case, more than twenty years later it played no small contribution towards his decision to assume more fully his baptismal call as pastor, priest and prophet within ordained ministry. For me, meeting Adam and hearing his story and – as a perceived representative of the offending community – entering even briefly into his incalculable sorrow and struggle was a graced experience of solidarity in "forgiving-ness," over an evening meal when we shared his story and walked together through some of our shared painful history. In tasting together the bitterness of suffering, we knew again something of the Emmaus mystery of Christ's saving grace and of his communion, passion and pardon for every suffering creature.

The way God makes forgiveness real is hidden from us, but it surely involves a "supernatural" reality and experience, in a way that no nature can account for, involving "works which only God can do."[52] Exploring for those attributes in God which are revealed to the forgiven person, Mackintosh, striking a similar note to our Dominican theologian, identifies three particularly: the *experience of* "God disclosed as Personal, and as the Doer of a miracle [...] [and] the insight also reached by way of pardon that His very nature is sacrificial love."[53] Clearly visible is the Protestant

---

[51] D.J. Davies, "Offending Death, Grief and Religions", in: R.K. Fenn (Ed.), Sociology of Religion, Oxford: Blackwell, 2003, 404–417, 412.

[52] H.R. Mackintosh, Christian Experience of Forgiveness, op. cit., 184.

[53] Ibid., 184–191, 185. The author speaks of the analogy of unfathomable human suffering ("voyages of anguish") which are analogous with the forgiveness Christ imparts, "flowing from unmeasured expenditures of grief and will," not as some "changeless Absolute, but one who shares our grief and shame." He appeals to readers to make a supreme act of imaginative remembrance of an experience of a deep and great treachery at the hands of another, to drive home the idea that human forgiveness is never painless cheap or easy (187), but exacting and calling one into encounter with "sacrificial agony," re-experiencing the "indescribable repulsiveness" of the evil and the need for cleansing (188). This pain-filled human intercourse becomes a window on God's agonising exchange with us. Thus, does Jesus enter into communion with human misery, crossing the un-breachable gulf, numbered among the transgressors. Thus, "face to face with Jesus, we become aware [...] that the love in virtue of which He does this amazing and redeeming thing is positively the love of God Himself" (189). This is the "only conceivable medium of forgiveness," for in both instances, human-to-human and divine-to-human, the costing, saving grace confronts "the tragedy for both sides – *pain forming the necessary vehicle for forgiveness in an* experience in which nature is rent asunder" (189). It is from the depths of this self-abandoning "divine-human passion" that God forgives the world, and "to see into the unchanging heart of things, we must gaze upon the travail of the cross" (190).

currency of Atonement theology, but minted new, in the face of intense suffering as "the doctrine of *the cost* of the forgiving God.[54]

Do the Churches have a Role in enabling Forgiveness and Reconciliation?

To many in Ireland, in the wake of the appalling scandal of church involvement and collusion in sexual abuse of children over many decades, even to raise such a question would seem presumptuous, arrogant and out of touch with people's loss of trust, certainly in the Catholic Church. And yet the Church is the custodian of the *memoria Christi*, the memory of Christ's incarnation, teaching and celebration of divine forgiveness. Its mission is to be a sacramental embodiment of Christ's invitation to saving grace, though it belongs to the Holy Spirit to awaken faith and openness to that gift, and effect its transforming work among people and nations.

The Sacrament of Reconciliation shows a fourfold pattern, all within the gift of God and the power of the Holy Spirit – contrite acknowledgement of one's guilt; sincere confessing of sin before God; and the making good through assigned acts of healing penance the harm and damaged relationships vis à vis God, others and self (Acts of the Penitent), and the pronouncing of the words of absolution by the priest in the name of Christ (Role of the Confessor).[55] We may discern the underlying interrelationality and movement towards reintegration, but often there is no felt *experience* of the suffering, no sign of community lament and mourning. Strange to tell, one is more likely to encounter the visible work of reconciliation among community groups and civic organisations dedicated to the care and healing of victims-survivors. The churches need to work in

---

[54] Mackintosh notes that he had been able to trace the idea to H. Bushnell in his book: Forgiveness and Law, Grounded in Principles Interpreted by Human Analogies, (1874), Ann Arbor, MI: University of Michigan Library, 2005, 48, describing Bushnell in terms that remarkably recall Schillebeeckx's determination to keep the theological tradition of soteriology open for new experience and history: "[...] his [Bushnell] was an intelligence so free and rich [...]. No one was ever readier to lift the anchor and steer his own way" (H.R. Mackintosh, Christian Experience of Forgiveness, op. cit., 185–186).

[55] The former, according to Aquinas, constituted the matter of the sacrament and the latter its form. R.A. Duffy clarifies the changing emphases in contemporary theology, with a fuller integration of scripture, prayer and pastoral concern on the part of the confessor, and a more explicit Christological and liturgical context. See his entry s.v.: "Reconciliation", in: J.A. Komonchak / M. Collins / D. Lane (Eds.), The New Dictionary of Theology, Dublin: Gill and Macmillan, 1987.

partnership with such as these, recognising their expertise in such fields as political change, trauma-counselling, social renewal.[56]

There is evidence in Northern Ireland that the civic cooperation of the churches (though not control) is welcome. It must be acknowledged, however, that without facing up to the need to seek for mutual forgiveness and to live into the experience of broken communion in their own lives as churches, their witness will lack humanness, authenticity and credibility. Christians and churches as communities are called by Jesus to cross over to the other side, and to seek for ecumenical healing and forgiveness, being ready to suffer in one another's brokenness, opening to learning pardon and exchanging that in common witness, and through symbolic gestures of atonement and reconciliation. Like Lazarus in the tomb (Jn. 11:44), they cannot unbind themselves, but they can humbly and patiently begin to unbind one another.

This will demand the relinquishing of attachment to selective memory, one-sided truth claims, historical bias and tribal collusion. It will also require a willingness to keep truth connected to life in its dynamic diversity, beauty, and suffering, in all its cultural ambiguities and as gracious mystery.

Allied to this we need to explore new theological possibilities of atonement through the reconnection of justice to reconciliation. There has been some laudable experiment in the juridical arena on alternative choices for victim and perpetrator, with the aim of freeing social energy hitherto blocked by the exigencies of legal retribution, or trapped in cultural alienation or private loss. Within the purpose of collective responsibility and social freedom, a shared future can be imagined, where space is made for those on the wrong side of the law – for victims and perpetrators both as distinct persons and as existing *within* every person. Thus, hostility can be reconfigured as hospitality, and the practice of restorative justice give a new shape to the contact that might make forgiveness, change of heart and newness of life possible in society and Church spheres.[57]

---

[56] Cf., E. Schillebeeckx, The Church with a Human Face, op. cit., 4–6. The author urges a necessary interplay between theological and socio-historical perspectives, while warning of the baleful effects of a dualism of natural and supernatural in ministry (cf. 4–6).

[57] Cf., J. Consedine, Restorative Justice: Healing the Effects of Crime, Revised Edition, Christchurch, New Zealand: Ploughshares Publications, 1999, contrasts traditions and actual effects of retributive and restorative justice, distilling "restorative" insights from the Maori tradition but drawing on a range of cultural perspectives including the Celtic (132–145); also, J. de Gruchy, Reconciliation: Restoring Justice, Minneapolis: Fortress Press, 2002, 181–213;

Acknowledging Wounds: Beginning from Healing

Churches have some experience in what has been termed "the cure of souls." Even where they failed to be prophetic in inclusive outreach, Christian ministers have accompanied people pastorally in times of unspeakable sorrow. They have consoled the afflicted and buried the dead. Many priests and church members have shown themselves Christ-like with gestures of comfort and forgiveness, or in building bridges of reconciliation. In celebrating Eucharist, and baptism week in and week out, the communities of faith have entered into the saving mystery of the forgiveness of sin and the new life of grace, journeying through the darkness of loss, making manifest the hope of birth and grace in the midst of death and sin.

I have underlined that forgiveness and reconciliation are not achieved by forgetting, or by brushing aside persisting difficulty. But the churches in a spirit of reconciliation, can step forth in the humble authority of their call and mission to bring good news to the poor, to bring sight to the blind and bind up the broken, and announce a new year of the Lord's favour.[58] Such a mission invites patience, empathy and attunement (at-one-ment) to the slower rhythms of the soul. The churches may yet remember the deep inner knowledge of mourning and compassion. Robert Schreiter speaks of reconciliation as, "ultimately a spirituality and not a strategy,"[59] proposing the paradox that even where wounds do not completely heal or remain a handicap, emotionally or physically, this "has been discovered by some to be a spiritual resource."[60] Negatively, if left to fester, wounds do not heal. If attended with care they can become a source of healing for both sufferer and carer. While avoiding the temptation to cultivate pain,[61] re-living the memory holds out a hope that those grieving can find ways of reconnecting to themselves and to their personal and social agency. In

---

also, H. Zehr, The Little Book of Restorative Justice, Minneapolis: Fortress Press, 2002, 181–213, offers a succinct introduction to the principles and practice of restorative justice.

[58] R.J. Schreiter, Reconciliation: Mission and Ministry in a Changing Social Order, New York: Orbis Books, 1992, 18–27.

[59] Ibid., 70.

[60] Ibid., 77f.

[61] R. Williams likewise intimates the need for empathy in another's suffering, but suggests the need for a certain reserve, so as not to glorify pain, or through it endorse a cause, or compete for status. Cf., R. Williams, Interpreting the Easter Gospel, London: Darton, Longman & Todd, 2002 (1982), 75–76, 70f. This is challenging in the current Irish attempts to deal with the past – with the construction of a partisan "hierarchy of victims" a cultural temptation indulged in even by churches.

an ethos of empathy, they can find voice for what has not yet been said about their lost loved ones and about their own lives as not reducible to the label "victim." Thus, narrative identity is shaped by a subjective relationship to one's life-story – its history and hope of overcoming fate, and of entering into the élan of self-transcendence.[62]

Schillebeeckx's interpretation of the nature of the Gospel call to *metanoia* and Jesus's power to forgive sin, set in the context of his intercourse with sinners, transgressing of religious boundaries and eating with the disreputable, points a way for Christians today, centring on Jesus's prophetic summons to love in action and hope for new life. It is worth quoting at length:

"Jesus has 'de-classed' by eating with tax-collectors himself. His self-defence is that it is precisely to sinners, to those beyond the pale, that the invitation to communication must be carried: the sinners must be invited to God's table and his fellowship with human beings, in order to bring them out of their isolation. The sheep that is lost and isolated from the flock must be searched out (Lk. 15:1–8; 19"10; Mt. 9:36; 10:6; 15:24)[...] that Jesus seeks encounter with them, offering them this fellowship-with-Jesus, breaks through their isolation and gives sinners the chance 'to repent and be converted', the possibility of hearing about the invitation from the kingdom of God, first and foremost in actual fact. The Christian community, therefore, has in no way distorted its picture of his life on earth when it explicitly ascribes 'the authority to forgive sins' to the earthly Jesus [...]. This solidarity [...] his contact with sinful people, aimed at opening up communication with God and with men [...] his being delivered into the hands (Mk. 9:31 with 14:41) is for Mark at the same time the real import of Jesus's death: the saving gift to sinners."[63]

So too, Schillebeeckx leaves us in no doubt, when examining the earliest core of what Mark (2:15–17) is relating. This account of Jesus's engagement with Levi reveals Jesus's special care for sinners and outcasts. It was this very act of "making contact with the sinner, Levi [that] led to the man's *metanoia*," and thus, explains Schillebeeckx, "he turned himself into a disciple of Jesus."[64] So too, encountering the woman who was a great sinner, or in accounts of his eating with tax-collectors, Jesus's historically grounded action "is of a piece with the profoundest intentions of many

---

[62] Cf., G. Smyth, "Endangered Identity and Ecumenical Risk", in: A. Pierce / G. Smyth (eds), The Critical Spirit: Theology at the Crossroads of Faith and Culture, Dublin: Columba Press, 2003, 97–122, 111f.
[63] E. Schillebeeckx, Jesus, op. cit., 212.
[64] Ibid., 212.

of his parables as also of his mighty acts," eliciting Schillebeeckx's conclusion that "in Jesus' earthly career and ministry we are seeing demonstrated the praxis of the coming rule of God [...] already coming into view here on earth."[65]

A New Way of Life Together

Polarised interpretations of the past and the refusal to work for a changed and shared future, stand as a challenge to all leaders in Ireland to let go of sectarian mindsets and frozen patterns of division, and to begin together to envisage reconciliation, and ritually enacted forgiving, symbolically unbinding one another from over-confessionalised identifications. Observations made above about the direct influence of theology on the politics of forgiveness assume sharp moral and ecclesiological relevance in a culturally divided context like Northern Ireland. Since inter-community hostility is so systemically embedded, churches too need to give leadership in social and institutional change. Wilful essentialising of Protestant and Catholic theologies of conversion (and salvation) as necessarily and permanently oppositional is a scandalous counter-action to the Gospel of reconciliation. We need rather to search out and hold together visions of conversion as dramatic event of in-breaking grace, *and* as the spiritual call to live into the grace of reconciliation in the daily commitment to beginning again in love.[66]

Each community can benefit by listening and learning from the other's theological text in sufficient depth and subtlety as to allow it to modify and enhance that which is second-nature within each respective tradition, and indeed to call attention to neglected wealth therein. Political and religious leaders need to lead not from a place of power, but rather by making themselves vulnerable to one another after the example of Jesus who pleaded from the cross, "Father forgive them, for they know not what they do" (Lk. 22:34). Out of that vulnerability, a new interdependence may emerge, as we discover how our differences in approach or emphasis can manifest our ecumenical need, our hope that our whole Church will be made new and the whole creation will know the joy of reconciliation. As we tell out the Good News that all sufferings and joys are

---

[65] Ibid., 213.
[66] S. Schimmel, Wounds Not Healed by Time: The Power of Repentance and Forgiveness, Oxford: Oxford University Press, 2002, 158f. The author demonstrates this double pattern of conversion and renewal, faith and good works, highlighting their *coexistence* within Jewish, Catholic and Protestant traditions and in Jesus's own teaching (159).

gathered already into the memory of Christ's dying and rising, we will be *made one* in the *new covenant* of his blood shed for all so that sins may be *forgiven*.

Let the final words be left to our Dominican brother, highlighting the intentional New Testament association of the resurrection with the forgiveness of sins. There is no intention to co-opt Schillebeeckx's words to some spurious attempt at synthesis or conclusion, which would fly in the face of so much that his writing set itself to challenge. It stands rather as an act of gratitude for a continually inspiring brother Dominican, and an open statement of Easter faith in the impossible possibility of unbinding and unloosing (Jn. 20:22–23):

"The forgiveness of sins is a gracious Easter gift [...] In the experience of forgiveness as a gift of grace [...] lies the venture of faith [...] It is the individual's experience of new being that imparts to faith the assurance that Jesus is alive or is the coming judge of the world. "[67]

* * *

Zusammenfassung des Beitrags von Geraldine Smyth

Die letzten Jahrzehnte haben auf politischer und sozialer Ebene verstärkt Anstrengungen erlebt, die traumatische Zerrissenheit in postkonfliktiven Gesellschaften zu heilen. Mit der Hoffnung auf Vergebung und Versöhnung stehen dabei Begriffe im Mittelpunkt, die zum Kernbestand des christlichen Glaubens gehören. Der vorliegende Beitrag benennt signifikante wechselseitige Beeinflussungen der beiden Bereiche und fragt nach Möglichkeiten weiteren politisch-theologischen Zusammenwirkens.

In einem ersten Schritt wird hierfür der Blick auf die Entwicklung der Theologie gerichtet, die im Westen vielfach eine Verengung von Vergebung und Versöhnung auf die individuelle Gottesbeziehung erfahren hatte. Dieses Verständnis wurde in der (Folge-)Zeit des Zweiten Vatikanischen Konzils mit einer neuen theologischen Anthropologie und Soteriologie aufgebrochen, die sich Einflüssen aus Geschichte, Kultur und den Sozialwissenschaften öffneten und ein differenzierteres Verständnis der

---

[67] E. Schillebeeckx, Jesus, op. cit., 391f.

Beziehung von Sünde, Natur und Gnade ermöglichten. Zentral war die Betonung der theologischen Priorität der Gnade und von Gottes zuvorkommender Barmherzigkeit als fundamental für die christliche Vergebung auf individueller, sozialer wie sakramentaler Ebene.

Auf dem Hintergrund eigener Erfahrungen, wie Menschen mühsam zur Gewährung von Vergebung gelangen konnten, reflektiert die Autorin im Anschluss die gegenwärtigen Anstrengungen in Nordirland, das Erbe einer tief gespaltenen Vergangenheit und unzähliger unaufgearbeiteter Geschichten von Verlust, Gewalt und Schmerz durch narrative Reflexion zu bewältigen. Hierfür erweisen sich Schillebeeckx, Ricœur und Mackintosh aufgrund ihrer unterschiedlichen hermeneutischen Ausgangspositionen als hervorragende Gesprächspartner. Ihre Überlegungen zur narrativen Praxis, der Bedeutung der Erinnerung und dem Geschenkcharakter der Gnade im Geschehen von Vergebung und Versöhnung bilden zentrale Eckpunkte des vorliegenden Artikels.

Übersetzung aus dem Englischen: *Sabine Schratz*

Pierre-Yves Materne

METZ UND SCHILLEBEECKX – MYSTIK UND POLITIK

Komponenten für eine verantwortliche Theologie

Einführung: Mystik und Politik sind untrennbar

Edward Schillebeeckx und Johann Baptist Metz sind Theologen der gleichen Generation. Beide haben Thomas von Aquin studiert und die moderne Philosophie reflektiert. Wo Metz nur Fundamentaltheologie betreibt, nimmt sein Kollege die ganze Theologie in den Blick (Fundamentale Fragen, Christologie und Ekklesiologie). Metz hat nur kleine Schriften, meistens Aufsätze, der Dominikaner hingegen sehr umfangreiche Bücher verfasst. Schillebeeckx' Werke sind systematischer als die von Metz, er arbeitete sehr viel mit der modernen Exegese. Metz betreibt seine Theologie als Kampf, die Gottesrede in die Gesellschaft zu bringen. Metz hat die *neue Politische Theologie* als genuine Schule geschaffen. Schillebeeckx hat keine neue Schule gegründet, auch wenn der Dominikaner viele Schüler hatte. Die Theologie von Schillebeeckx steht stärker in der Linie der hermeneutischen Tradition als die von Metz, der sich als politischer Theologe eher mit der „Frankfurter Schule" auseinandersetzt. Die Erfahrungstheologie ist eher von Schillebeeckx bearbeitet, auch wenn klar ist, dass die Leidensfrage für beide Theologen ein wichtiges Thema ist.

Metz hat seine Theologie mit der Gerechtigkeitsfrage in Beziehung gesetzt und aus der Bibel begründet. Deshalb sind bei Metz Mystik und Politik zusammenzudenken. „Der christliche Glaube enthält deshalb immer eine Komponente, die sich von diesem Interesse an ungeteilter Gerechtigkeit leiten lässt; er ist in diesem Sinne mystisch und politisch zugleich: mystisch, weil er das Interesse an der Rettung vergangener, ungesühnter Leiden nicht preisgibt, politisch, weil ihn dieses Interesse an ungeteilter Gerechtigkeit immer wieder auch auf die Gerechtigkeit unter den Lebenden verpflichtet. Der Logos der Theologie ist von diesem Interesse, besser, von dieser Vision geleitet"[1]. Diese Zitat zeigt klar, dass bei Metz Mystik und Politik wesentlich für sein theologisches Denken sind. Es geht darum, die Gerechtigkeit im Namen des biblischen Gottes zu schützen. Das Heil ist nicht von der Weltgeschichte getrennt, auch wenn das Heil mehr als diese Geschichte ist. Man kann sehen, dass bei Metz Mystik nicht „entinkarniert" ist, sondern vielmehr eine Beteiligung an der Verbesserung der Welt bedeutet. Der deutsche Theologe empfindet eine gewisse Abscheu vor dem mythischen Denken, und zwar aufgrund der diesem Denken innewohnenden Tendenz, die Geschichte zu vernachlässigen: Die Kirche, so Metz' Forderung, „darf sich nicht aus der Spannung zwischen Mystik und Politik zurückziehen in ein geschichtsfernes Mythendenken"[2]. Metz bezeichnet die Kirche als „Tradentin der Hoffnung"[3], als „moralische Anstalt"[4]. Wenn man über Mystik und Politik spricht, darf man Theologie nicht auf Ethik reduzieren. Die Perspektive der neuen Politischen Theologie ist keine ethische, sondern sie ist eschatologisch ausgerichtet: „Theologie ist nicht primär eine Ethik, sondern eine Eschatologie"[5]. Dies meint, dass die Eschatologie die Gesellschaft gestalten soll. Anders formuliert: Das christliche Leben soll ein Zeichen der Hoffnung für heute sein. Auch wenn die Metz'sche Theologie pessimistische Akzente beinhaltet, bleibt doch, dass Metz Glaube als Hoffnung denkt. Die Spannung zwischen Mystik und Politik besteht besonders im Leben und auch in der Theologie. Wenn man über Eschatologie spricht, sollte man über die Welt in ihrer Wirklichkeit sprechen.

Edward Schillebeeckx hat vor allem die orthopraktische Dimension des Glaubens akzentuiert. In der Tat spielt die *Metanoia* eine wichtige Rolle, um das christliche Leben in der Welt zu verstehen. Die *Metanoia* ist nicht nur ein interner Prozess, eine Herz-Introspektion, sondern auch eine Handlung in der Welt – kurz gesagt: eine *Praxis der Solidarität*. Ich sehe mich nicht, ohne die Anderen im Blick zu haben, besonders die Leidenden. Die Christen sollen der Humanisierung der Welt dienen. Diese Humanisierung hat eine direkte Auswirkung auf den Glauben. Da in Schillebeeckx' Denken das Reich Gottes eine starke Kategorie ist, betont der

---

[1] J.B. Metz, Theologie angesichts des fremden Anderen. Zur neubearbeiteten Auflage von G. Gutiérrez' „Theologie der Befreiung", in: *Orientierung* 56 (1992), 4–6, hier 5.
[2] Ebd., 6.
[3] Ebd.
[4] Ebd.
[5] Ebd.

belgische Theologe vor allem den Dienst an der Realisierung des Reiches in der heutigen Gesellschaft. Besonders in seinen Buch *Weil Politik nicht alles ist* hat Schillebeeckx die Spannung zwischen Mystik und Politik herausgestellt: „Das christliche Glaubensleben hat neben der ethischen, der mitmenschlichen, der ökologischen und sozial-politischen auch eine mystische Dimension"[6]. Diese Verbindung zwischen Mystik und Politik war bei Schillebeeckx keine theologische Mode, sondern Ausdruck von Umkehr, Ausdruck einer Suche nach Heilung in der konkreten Welt.

Metz und Schillebeeckx sind gleichermaßen mit der *Befreiungstheologie* verbunden. Beide haben das Motiv der Befreiung der Menschen in der Geschichte (nach dem Impuls von Karl Marx) als seriöses Thema in ihre Theologien integriert. Wichtig dabei ist auch die Idee, dass die Kirche ein konkretes Volk in der Geschichte darstellt. In seinem Buch *Mystik und Politik* (zum 60. Geburtstag von Metz) schreib Schillebeeckx:„Theologie hat keinen Sinn, wenn sie nicht ‚befreiend' ist"[7]. Er hat auch hier an Metz gedacht: Es ist „unverkennbar, dass zum Beispiel J.B. Metz [...] Themen der lateinamerikanischen Befreiungstheologie in das Projekt seiner Politischen Theologie integriert hat"[8]. Trotzdem ist die Politische Theologie akademisch geblieben, ohne Volksbewegung von unten, wie es in der Befreiungstheologie der Fall war.

Leid als Kontrasterfahrung

Schillebeeckx hat in seiner Theologie das Konzept einer *Hermeneutik der negativen Kontrasterfahrungen* entwickelt. Demnach provozieren die universalen Erfahrungen von Leid, Gewalt und Unterdrückung eine Reaktion des Menschen. Es geht um den Protest gegen die Welt, wie sie ist, um eine Ethik der Entrüstung. Aber das Nein, der Protest, ist gleichzeitig ein Ja für etwas mehr Menschlichkeit.[9] Die Menschen wünschen eine humanere Umwelt, keine ungerechte und gewalttätige Atmosphäre.

Die Entrüstung „ist auch eine verfügbare Basis für Solidarität aller mit allen und für einen gemeinsamen Einsatz für eine bessere Welt mit einem

---

[6] E. Schillebeeckx, Weil Politik nicht alles ist. Von Gott reden in einer gefährdeten Welt. Aus dem Niederländischen von U. Ruh, Freiburg/Br. 1987, 92.
[7] Ders., Befreiende Theologie, in: ders. (Hrsg.), Mystik und Politik. Theologie im Ringen um Geschichte und Gesellschaft (Johann Baptist Metz zu Ehren), Mainz 1988, 56–71, hier 56.
[8] Ebd., 57.
[9] Vgl. ebd., 65f.

menschlicheren Antlitz"[10]. Dieses Zitat von Schillebeeckx könnte auch auf Metz zutreffen. Denn es geht um die Verantwortlichkeit gegenüber der Welt. Auch wenn Metz nicht wie Schillebeeckx von der Erfahrung der Menschen ausgeht, so besteht bei ihm aber doch eine Orientierung auf diese hin. Es geht auch bei Metz um die Universalität des Leidens. Metz sagt direkt: „Es gibt kein Leid in der Welt, das uns nicht angeht"[11]. Die Rationalität hat diese Realität mit zu bedenken. Metz unterstützt das Konzept einer *anamnetischen Vernunft*, um die Leidenserfahrung wahrzunehmen. Er erklärt, dass die Vernunft ein „Leidensapriori"[12] braucht. Es bedeutet, dass sich die Theologie von Leidenserfahrung irritieren lassen soll. Deswegen sind Solidarität und *Compassion* mögliche und notwendige Handlungen in der Welt. Ohne diese verbliebe man in einer fiktiven Gesellschaft, wo die wesentlichen Bedürfnisse des Menschen ignoriert würden. Um diese Idee stärker zu machen, spricht Metz über die Anerkennung der „Autorität der Leidenden"[13].

Man findet diese Kontrasterfahrung in jeder Kultur, auch wenn verschiedene Erklärungen dafür gegeben werden. Der Protest gegen Leid ist bei Metz eine Basis für *Compassion*; für ihn gehört die *Compassion* „zum Zentrum christlicher Praxis"[14]. Metz versteht sie „als Mitleidenschaft, als teilnehmende, als verpflichtende Wahrnehmung fremden Leids, als tätiges Eingedenken des Leides der Anderen"[15]. Deshalb eignet Metz in dieser Perspektive ein spezifisches Verständnis von Mystik: „Diese Mystik der *Compassion* ist keine esoterische Angelegenheit, sie ist allen vergönnt und allen zugemutet. Und sie gilt nicht nur für den privaten Lebensbereich, sondern auch für das öffentliche, das politische Leben"[16], Jesus hat diese Mystik inkarniert! Sie ist keine Privatsache, sondern eine Praxis des Reichs Gottes in der Gesellschaft.

Die Frage nach dem Leid wurde in der Theologie nach Auschwitz mit hoher Intensität gestellt. Die Katastrophe des Holocaust hat die Gottesrede in eine Krise geführt. Das Thema Auschwitz ist in der Theologie von Metz sicherlich ein stärkerer Brennpunkt als bei Schillebeeckx. Metz ist als Deutscher in seinem Ansatz sehr sensibel hinsichtlich der Verant-

---

[10] Ebd., 66.
[11] J.B. Metz, Wer steht für die unschuldigen Opfer ein? Ein Gespräch mit Johann Baptist Metz, in: *Orientierung* 72 (2008), 148–150, hier 149.
[12] Ders., Memoria Passionis. Ein provozierendes Gedächtnis in pluralistischer Gesellschaft, Freiburg/Br. 2006, 219.
[13] Ebd., 221.
[14] Ebd., 31.
[15] Ebd., 166.
[16] Ebd., 164.

wortung für den Holocaust. Kann man nach Auschwitz noch Theologie betreiben? Ja, wenn wir nicht mehr idealistisch, nicht mehr „mit dem Rücken zu Auschwitz" arbeiten.[17] Das heißt: Theologie soll die *Memoria Passionis* schützen und die Leidenden im Blick haben. Für Metz hat Theologie in der Perspektive der Opfer zu denken und zu sprechen, weil Gott immer auf der Seite der Opfer steht.[18] Metz hat zu seinen Studenten gesagt: „Fragt euch, ob die Theologie, die ihr kennen lernt, so ist, dass sie vor und nach Auschwitz eigentlich die gleiche sein könnte. Wenn ja, dann seid auf der Hut!"[19]

Aber auch Schillebeeckx hat das Problem von Auschwitz berücksichtigt. Der Dominikaner hat geschrieben: „Nach Auschwitz, Hiroschima [...] kann man nicht mehr in der gleichen Weise Theologie treiben und kirchlich sprechen wie zuvor. Es wird eine neue politische Vermittlung zwischen dem Evangelium und unserer politische Lebenswelt erfolgen müssen."[20] Auch wenn Schillebeeckx das Thema seltener als Metz angesprochen hat, gibt es in seinem Denken doch auch den Gedanken einer „Leidempfindlichkeit", welche nicht gewillt ist, die Opfer zu vergessen. Die Christologie von Schillebeeckx ist gut ausgearbeitet, expliziter als die seines Kollegen aus Münster. Metz hat die Christologie direkt in der Perspektive von Auschwitz ausgedrückt, als eine „Christologie nach Auschwitz" – das heißt, als eine Art *Karsamstagschristologie*. Es geht ihm darum, die Abwesenheit Gottes in Blick den zu nehmen: Wo ist Gott in der Leidenserfahrung? Metz glaubt an die *Memoria Resurrectionis*, die er an der *Memoria Passionis* festmacht. Ansonsten riskiere man, aus der Geschichte zu fallen. Für Metz ist Gott ein Vermisster. Wie Tiemo R. Peters richtig geschrieben hat: „Seine Theologie ist der trotzige und diskrete Ausdruck einer Verlassenheit; nicht eines Verlustes, nicht einer hoffnungslosen Verlorenheit: Theologie des vermißten Gottes."[21]

---

[17] Ders, Jenseits bürgerlicher Religion. Reden über die Zukunft des Christentums (Forum Politische Theologie Bd. 1), München – Mainz ⁴1984, 41.
[18] Vgl. ders., Memoria Passionis, a.a.O., 251.
[19] Ders., Jenseits bürgerlicher Religion, a.a.O., 41.
[20] E. Schillebeeckx, Befreiende Theologie, a.a.O., 68.
[21] T.R. Peters, Johann Baptist Metz. Theologie des vermißten Gottes (Theologische Profile), Mainz 1998, 156.

Ethik und Praxis der Anerkennung

Man trifft sicher sowohl bei Metz als auch bei Schillebeeckx auf eine *Ethik der Alterität*. Beide Theologen betonen tatsächlich die Relevanz der Alterität, um Glauben zu reflektieren. Sie beziehen sich dabei auf Emmanuel Levinas, um die Alterität der Menschen zu denken. In der Tat ist es wichtiger Punkt bei Levinas, dass die Beziehung mit Anderen nicht symmetrisch, sondern asymmetrisch konstruiert ist. Demzufolge spricht Metz sehr intensiv von der „Autorität der Leidenden", Schillebeeckx über das Gesicht des „Anderen", das Respekt und Gerechtigkeit fordert. Der Andere ist ganz anders – bzw. transzendent! Für Schillebeeckx ist dieser humane Imperativ wichtiger als alle religiösen Anforderung. Das heißt, keine religiöse Verpflichtung darf die Menschlichkeit des Menschen reduzieren.[22]

Metz hat eine klare *Praxis der Anerkennung* in seine Theologie integriert. Im christlichen Leben kann Gott nicht nur Denken sein. Die Beziehung mit den Anderen betrifft immer notwendig auch die Beziehung zu Gott (vgl. Mt 25): „Der uns in Jesus nahegekommene Gott ist offensichtlich nicht so sehr daran interessiert, wie und was wir zunächst einmal über ihn denken, sondern wie wir uns zu den Anderen verhalten; und erst dies, wie wir mit Anderen umgehen, lässt sich dann erkennen, wie wir über ihn denken und was wir von ihm halten"[23] Diese Aussage beinhaltet, dass Theologie immer auch eine ethische Komponente haben muss. Mehr noch: Die Ethik ist ein Weg, um die Hoffnung auf Gott zu überprüfen! Es ist wichtig dass die Christen eine „Kultur der Anerkennung der Anderen in ihrem fremden Anderssein"[24] fordern.

Schillebeeckx schreibt, dass Gott besonders in der Praxis von Gerechtigkeit erreichbar ist (vgl. Jer 22). Gott ist nach Metz eine „praktische Idee", nicht nur ein Konzept.[25] Und besonders die Erfahrung Gottes kommt aus der Begegnung mit den Anderen, besonders mit den Schwächsten. Wo Metz eher von Nachfolge spricht, insistiert der Dominikaner primär auf dem Reich Gottes. Was bei Schillebeeckx regelmäßig thematisiert wird, ist nicht – wie bei Metz – *Compassion*, sondern das „Reich Gottes": „Man kann Heil von Gott her nicht auf menschliche

---

[22] Vgl. E. Schillebeeckx, Weil Politik nicht alles ist, a.a.O.
[23] J.B. Metz, Religion, ja – Gott, nein, in: ders. / T.R. Peters, Gottespassion. Zur Ordensexistenz heute, Freiburg/Br. 1991, 14–67, hier 38.
[24] Ders., Memoria Passionis, a.a.O., 246.
[25] Vgl. ders., Glaube in Geschichte und Gesellschaft. Studien zu einer praktischen Fundamentaltheologie, Mainz 1977.

Praxis reduzieren. ‚Praxis des Reiches Gottes' oder ‚Jesu Nachfolge' ist mehr als ‚*nur Praxis*'. Aber ohne menschliche, von der Gnade getragene Praxis ist Glaube an eine eschatologische Zukunft ein leere Geschichte."[26] Es geht darum, das Reich Gottes in der konkreten Geschichte zu empfangen. Auch wenn der ‚eschatologische Vorbehalt' gilt, müssen die Menschen in der Praxis Jesu fortfahren. Schillebeeckx hat diese Idee stark gemacht: „Ohne eine Praxis des Reiches Gottes ist und kommt nie Reich Gottes."[27]

Wo Schillebeeckx von „Praxis des Reiches Gottes" spricht, spricht Metz von der „Praxis der Nachfolge", die nie hinter dem Glauben steht, sondern ihre wesentliche Komponente herstellt.[28] Die Kategorie vom Reich Gottes gehört nicht zur Grundlage der Politischen Theologie von Metz.

Hören der Welt als Welt Gottes

Gleichzeitig bleiben sowohl Metz als auch Schillebeeckx anderen Kulturen gegenüber offen. Man muss und kann von den Kulturen etwas über Gott lernen. Sie sprechen in diesem Sinn von „Fremdprophetie". Metz hat diese Idee klar ausgedrückt: „Fremde sind nicht Feinde, sondern – Engel; sie sind nicht nur willkommene Arbeitskräfte, sondern – und darin den Engeln gleich – Boten, Ratgeber. Wir hätten also auf die fremde *Prophetie* der Menschen aus anderen Kulturwelten zu achten."[29]

Heute ist jedem klar: Theologie ist immer in Kontexte eingebunden. Davon sind wir überzeugt. Zugleich jedoch darf man dabei nicht die universale Sicht aus den Augen verlieren. Schillebeeckx ist sich des kontextuellen Charakters des theologischen Diskurses bewusst, aber er bleibt der universalistischen Perspektive verbunden. „Regionale Formen von Theologie sind, als christliche Theologie, nie schlechthin regional. Denn es geht dabei um das – stets besonders situierte – Menschsein des Men-

---

[26] E. Schillebeeckx, Befreiende Theologie, a.a.O., 70.
[27] Ebd., 71.
[28] Vgl. J.B. Metz, Jenseits bürgerlicher Religion, a.a.O., 41 [Hervorhebung P.-Y.M.]: „*Doch auch das Christentum ist nicht in erster Linie eine Doktrin, die es möglichst ‚rein' zu halten gilt, sondern eine Praxis, die es radikaler zu leben gilt!* Diese messianische Praxis der Nachfolge, der Umkehr, der Liebe, kommt nicht nachträglich zum christlichen Glauben hinzu, sie ist realer Ausdruck dieses Glaubens."
[29] Ders., Das Christentum und die Fremde. Perspektiven einer multikulturellen Religion, in: F. Blake u. a. (Hrsg.), Schwierige Fremdheit. Über Integration und Ausgrenzung in Einwanderungsländern, Frankfurt/M. 1993, 217–228, hier 221.

schen in seiner Beziehung zu Mitmenschen in einer Welt, die letztlich eine ‚Welt Gottes' ist. Alle regionalen Formen von Theologie wollen in einer konkreten Situation das Evangelium zu Wort kommen lassen, vor allem im eigenen Lebensweg."[30] Für Schillebeeckx ist es wichtig, dass die Welt eine Welt Gottes ist.

Metz hat Angst davor, dass die Gottesrede kein universales Thema bleibt: „Gott ist entweder ein Menschheitsthema oder überhaupt kein Thema. Götter sind pluralisierbar und regionalisierbar, nicht aber Gott, nicht der biblische Gott. Er ist nur ‚mein' Gott, wenn er auch ‚dein Gott' sein kann, er ist ‚unser Gott' wenn er auch der Gott aller anderen Menschen sein kann"[31]. In diesem Sinne bleibt die Theologie „auf Universalität verpflichtet". Gott ist nicht das Privateigentum der Kirche oder der Theologie. „Die Gottesbotschaft der Kirche verträgt keine ekklesiologische Verschlüsselungen"[32]. Gott ist für alle Menschen. Deswegen hat jeder Mensch eine Gotteskompetenz. Diese Tatsache ist quasi ein Antidot gegen alle Formen von Klerikalismus oder Kommunitarismus.

Fazit

Die politische Theologie ist der „Versuch der christlichen Gottesrede mit dem Gesicht zur Welt, zur Welt in dieser Zeit"[33]. Dies könnte auch das Leitmotiv für Schillebeeckx sein. Mit anderen Worten: Der christliche Gott ist ein *Deus humanissimus*. Deswegen muss die Theologie die Erfahrung in der Welt von heute aus der Perspektive der Hoffnung analysieren. Metz und Schillebeeckx sind Theologen für die Welt, aber nicht im Sinne eines oberflächlichen Optimismus', sondern ausgestattet mit einer Sensibilität zum Leiden. Sie vertreten, dass die Theologie kein geschlossenes System sein darf. Es geht vielmehr darum, Mystik und Politik in dialektischer Weise zusammen zu denken. Politik wird als Engagement verstanden, um die Gesellschaft zu verbessern, in die die christliche Botschaft einen wichtigen Impuls einbringt. Die Gerechtigkeit hat mit dem Reich Gottes zu tun. Die Leidensgeschichte ist Teil der Passionsgeschichte. Die Anderen, besonders die Leidenden, bleiben ein wichtiger hermeneutischer Ort, von dem aus der Glauben zu denken ist. Metz hat diesen theo-

---

[30] E. Schillebeeckx, Befreiende Theologie, a.a.O., 67.
[31] J.B. Metz, Memoria Passionis, a.a.O., 160f.
[32] Ebd., 187.
[33] Ebd., 257.

logischen Anspruch *Mystik der Compassion* genannt. Er möchte, dass die Christen in der Welt sich vor diesem Horizont engagieren. Davon ist auch Schillebeeckx auf der Grundlage seiner Option für eine Praxis des Reiches Gottes in der Perspektive der Armen überzeugt. Auch wenn Metz einen sehr apokalyptisch-theologischen Stil an den Tag legt, spricht er kaum vom Reich Gottes, aber er steht der Hermeneutik von Kontrasterfahrung eines Schillebeeckx nahe. Der Dominikaner hatte vielleicht eine positivere Sicht auf die Welt, war mit mehr Hoffnung erfüllt, aber er stand trotzdem auf der Seite der Politischen Theologie.

Sicher stehen die zwei Theologen für eine verantwortliche Theologie, die der Gesellschaft gegenüber aufmerksam ist, besonders dort, wo eine Befreiung von Nöten ist. Die Mystik steht dabei nie außerhalb der weltlichen Realität, sondern schaut immer in Richtung der Menschheit. Gott ist für die Humanisierung der Welt, die seine Schöpfung ist, da. Um das Reich Gottes zu entfalten, braucht es aber auch die Mitarbeit der Menschen. *Gerechtigkeit, Befreiung* und *Liebe* sind nicht nebensächlich für unsere Gottesrede. Wenn jemand etwas über Gott denken und sagen möchte, muss man diese drei – *Gerechtigkeit, Befreiung* und *Liebe* – zusammen bringen und soll sie in der Perspektive der Anderen betrachten. Das haben wir vom Metz und Schillebeeckx gelernt.

* * *

Abstract of the contribution of Pierre-Yves Materne

This contribution to E. Schillebeeckx and J.B. Metz has also been made to bring in a comparison between these two major theologians of the same generation. They both were convinced that mysticism and politics are inseparable: the theological discourse is never external to the society as well as the call for justice and freedom belongs to the Revelation. Therefore they were very close to the liberation theology movement. They together pointed out strongly that the Christian praxis should be considered within the theological perspective in order to welcome the Kingdom of God to our world. Even though Schillebeeckx criticized Metz's "political theology" as remaining mostly on an academic level, he joined his German colleague on a field of theology preoccupied with the question of suffering. Schillebeeckx underlined "experiences of contrast," and a suffering as a particular kind of experience among them, as a way to think God in the world. On this basis he claimed to build a better society where the weakest people can be acknowledged and respected. On the other hand, Metz was credited with having introduced a theological theme of "Memoria Passionis," where he developed the idea of "compassion" to depict more precisely his theological project. Less dramatically than Metz, Schillebeeckx promoted the Kingdom of God as a key to the theological discourse aware of the sufferings but ready to hope for a better society. Concluding, what we can learn from these great theologians it is that Justice, Freedom and Love are never of the second importance in the heart of Christian theology.

Angel F. Méndez Montoya

PERFORMING THE REIGN OF GOD

The Mystical and the Political Co-Existing in Edward Schillebeeckx's Philosophical Theology

Perhaps one of the most revealing arguments by Schillebeeckx on the co-existence of the mystical with the political can be found in the following statement: "Without prayer or mysticism, politics soon becomes cruel and barbaric; without political love, prayer or mysticism soon becomes sentimental uncommitted interiority."[1]

To Schillebeeckx, mysticism tells about a relationship with divinity, an experience of encounter. For him, prayer is a paradigm of an astonishing encounter with God. Prayer is both invocation and evocation of the mystical or the religious, a *poietic* experience of "touching transcendence," implying not mere interior retreat, much less so absolute distance from the world and from the Other, but quite the contrary. This loving encounter with the Other is in itself a political action that moves the believer to love the others. Indeed, Schillebeeckx's insights into the meaning of the Greek word *polis* suggest that in the midst of the personal and communal shaping of identity, space and time are configured by an encounter with God, which subsequently leads towards loving the Other. The political does not express sheer human action empty of transcendence, for it would fall into cruelty and barbarity, becoming a simple rational equation, lacking the excess of divine caritas. To Schillebeeckx the mystical is already political, for it includes otherness, constructing time and space in community with the Other. Surely, not all politics are mystical. That is the reason why Schillebeeckx argues that politics achieves its plenitude and true vocation

---

[1] Cited by W.L. Portier, Interpretation and Method, in: C. Hilkert / R.J. Schreiter (Eds.), The Praxis of the Reign of God, New York: Fordham University Press, 2002, 18–34, 33.

within divine caritas, and in doing so becomes an alternative to an exclusively secular politics, without annulling secular discourse.

I argue that we can more concretely identify this general notion of the mutual implication of the mystical and the political in three key themes within Schillebeeckx's philosophical theology: 1) God's ineffability; 2) creation; and, 3) humanity/incarnation.

1. God's ineffability

Schillebeeckx follows a lineage within both the patristic and the medieval Dominican traditions, particularly after Thomas Aquinas and Meister Eckhart, who conjectured about the absolute transcendence of God. God is beyond any notion or linguistic category, and therefore exceeds all rational thinking. In the face of such a divine surplus, and as a strategy to unveil the limits of language, Schillebeeckx's philosophical theology opens up to the question on God, but following first an apophatic pathway, a negative or deconstructing attitude. The experience of encounter with God brings up the dilemma of God and the perplexity of the finitude of language, which simultaneously becomes evocation and epiphany of the infinite.

The astonishment from evoking the infinite tells of the mystery of God's presence in the finite. That is why it would be a mistake to label Schillebeeckx's philosophical theology as an exclusively apophatic discourse, lacking any affirmative language on God. His hermeneutical discourse is equally cataphatic. God is also absolute affirmation, divine resonance of the human *amen*. For God's ineffability, which makes us aware of our finitude, also reveals the presence of God with us: "the human experience of nothingness and finitude" is counterbalanced by the "absolute presence of God in and with the finite."[2]

Schillebeeckx's philosophical theology articulates the interweaving between silence and the word. The experience of encounter with God leads us to the most profound silence, from which the word bursts forth, or from which the word finds nourishment. Paradoxically, and despite the limits of linguisticity, language also signals sacramentality and symbol, since it mediates the presence of the infinite within human finitude. To

---

[2] E. Schillebeeckx, Interim Report on the Books *Jesus* and *Christ*, New York: Crossroad, 1981, 114, cited by Ph. Kennedy, God and Creation, in: C. Hilkert / R.J. Schreiter (Eds.), The Praxis of the Reign of God, op. cit., 37–58, 49.

be sure, from the horizon of Christian experience, this semiotic-sacramental presence of God is radicalized through Christ's incarnation, while the Holy Spirit promises the continuous advent of human history.

How then is this mysticism of God's ineffability that paradoxically reveals God's presence in the core of the finite also politics?

Political action emerges from the challenge faced after responding to God's presence. Responding to God's presence leads to making community with God, which further invites people to become present to one another. Moreover, God's ineffability is not apathy, for it is paradigmatically mediated as a sacrament of the Word made flesh, as Christ's incarnating in ecclesial communities, within human situatedness. From a Christian horizon, political action is a response to God's initiative and desire to make community with us. The resonance of such a desire is our response to the Other, including those who are beyond ecclesial borders, and beyond any religious institution, even reaching out towards those in particular who find themselves in a space of "God's absence," those who are abandoned or forgotten, the most vulnerable in our midst. The theopolitics of God's ineffability means responding to God's presence in the excluded ones.

2. Creation

Philip Kennedy's research is most helpful to understand the notion of creation in Schillebeeckx.[3] Very rightly, Kennedy considers that Schillebeeckx's theology of creation is the very oxygen of his entire thought. This oxygen is produced by the vitality and priority of grace, for creation is a gratuitous event initiated by God, it is God's gift. Creation is the gratuitous gift of God's overflowing love, God who is "new in each moment," God as "eternal youth," "a constant source of new possibilities."[4] As a creative expression of God, creation is thus perpetual newness, a constant unfolding process.

As expression of divine creativity, creation is an icon of the infinite in the finite, a paradigm of participation in God by the whole creation. Even deeper: since God is encountered in finite creation, then creation is simul-

---

[3] See Ph. Kennedy, Schillebeeckx, Collegeville: The Liturgical Press, 1993; ibid., God and Creation, op. cit.

[4] E. Schillebeeckx, God is New in Each Moment, New York: Continuum, 1983, 291; cited by Ph. Kennedy, God and Creation, op. cit., 55.

taneously *in* God. There is a mutual sense of participation. Time and space are not circumscribed by the past, but are a constant reiteration of God of the future, whose kenotic presence is given in the present, in the here and now of creation.

Schillebeeckx is influenced by Aquinas' semiotic and ontological arguments, which articulate creation as inherently good and not intrinsically evil. In the created order, evil is considered as something extrinsic to its being, as an ontological privation. As we shall see later, incarnation is an intrinsic – and not mere extrinsic – act, for the humanity *in* God affirms the goodness of creation, reorienting it towards greater harmony with the expression of divine creativity, promoting greater transparency of creation with itself.

We can find the politics of this "mysticism of creation" at the core of Schillebeeckx's philosophical theology of the gift. God gives God-self in the creative act, which constitutes creation as part of God: we are participants of divine goodness. Creation is an expression of God's desire to share divine self, inviting us to share this same gift with one another. Relationality does not only take place in human space, at a social and political level, but it furthermore includes a responsible and caring relationship with our environment, that is, an ecological relationship as well. This theopolitics of inclusion sets the motion to making community with a plurality of human communities, and urges to create harmonious community with the planet and the entire creation.

Creation intensifies – and not at all discards – the material world, situationality and contingency. For the ordinary displays the extraordinary: God is active in the world. Creation is the image and mirror of the glory of its creator. For the Christian mystic, creation is paradigmatically mirrored in Christ, who reveals the true meaning of creation as being God's plan par excellence, and as the space and time of making community with humanity. Creation is a profound political reality originated by God with us and for us.

The political expression of creation is also found at the heart of culture, which could be considered as an extension of God's creative act. Humanity, particularly in the midst of relationships of love, respect, justice, reconciliation and compassion, becomes co-creative with God's creative act.

3. Humanity/Incarnation

"God freely creates humanity for salvation and human happiness, but in this same action, in a sovereign freedom, he seeks himself to be the deepest meaning, salvation and happiness for human life."[5]

God makes an option to create humanity and desires to establish an intimate relationship with us. Again, to Schillebeeckx, God is not aloof, but rather maintains a strong intimacy with humanity. From the origins of creation, God is not indifferent to humanity, but rather establishes a relationship of affinity with humanity, for, since the beginning of creation, human beings were created as *imago Dei*. God's intimacy becomes more radical through incarnation, to the extreme of becoming human among humans. God takes the initiative of being among us in the most profound and primal dimension of being human: in flesh. Echoing the patristic mystic, Maximus the Confessor, Schillebeeckx also contemplates God as being the most human among humans. History then becomes the *ethos* and *pathos* of God with us, who is companion in humanity's historical pilgrimage.

Through incarnation, human story is also God's own story; it is God's narrative within human story. This implies that God becomes vulnerable and takes risks through a kenotic gesture of giving divine self to humanity. In a sense, for Schillebeeckx incarnation shows that God willingly renounces power opening up an autonomous space subject to human free will. That is why history is a project in a continuous creative process. Nevertheless, and beyond Schillebeeckx, one could argue that incarnation does not at all empty divine power, but rather, God's power, being a kenotic expression, manifests itself in a loving act of giving God-self to humanity – a perpetual divine *for you*, a gesture of solidarity that empowers humanity with the force and vitality of divine caritas. In this way, one could argue that paradoxically preserving the autonomy of humanity and creation, such autonomy is never antagonistic to divinity, but rather is affinity, co-creativity and interdependence with God.

As aforementioned, incarnation is an intrinsic act in creation, for the incarnated Christ re-integrates and re-orients creation, making it not a stranger to God. Schillebeeckx's soteriological anthropology leads – although timidly and without supremacist pretensions – towards a sense of *theosis*. Without annulling humanity, God divinizes; but this conjecture

---

[5] E. Schillebeeckx, On Christian Faith: The Spiritual, Ethical, and Political Dimensions, New York: Crossroad, 1987, 18.

can only be understood from an eschatological horizon. Insofar as humanity is open to encountering the God of the future, historicity could thus perform God's perpetual advent. As Kennedy points out, "the *humanity of God*: means that the realization and definition of humanity is ultimately to be found in God."[6] The political dimension of such an argument about humanity and the incarnation of Christ brings about another paradox that contemplates the beauty, superabundance, perfection and power of God in the face of the suffering Christ – the "monstrosity" of the crucified Christ. In the world, Christ's face incarnates in the most vulnerable (Mat, 25). God's *for-you* is a gesture of solidarity towards all humanity, although it privileges the most vulnerable, those who are the crucified in the world.

The mystical experience of encountering God propels political impulse. This is the imperative of encountering the Other, promoting the free responsibility of seeking common ethical criteria to engage in the world.[7] The mystical is political, for God is not extra-mundi, God is found in the heart of the world, being intrinsic to culture and human contingencies. Schillebeeckx is referring to a world that welcomes God, a world that builds and practices the reign of God, celebrating God's presence among us: "The kingdom of God is the presence of God among men and women, affirmed or made welcome, active and encouraging, a presence which is made concrete above all in just and peaceful relations among individuals and peoples."[8]

The practice of the reign of God unfolds a mystical experience of encountering the Other in the others, opening the time and the space of politics. The politics of the practice of the reign of God is a performance of time and space of God with us, God of the future that gives meaning and direction to humanity's here and now, God engaging with concrete individuals and communities through acts of solidarity and liberation.

Various liberation and solidarity themes resonate with influential Latin American liberation theologians inspired by Schillebeeckx's insights into the imperative of immanent social and political transformation. In transforming the world from violence into peace, from injustice to justice, from selfishness to divine caritas, the reign of God is ultimately performed. Schillebeeckx's affirmations of culture and social situatedness can also be reflected in Latin American liberationist approaches that insist on

---

[6] Ph. Kennedy, God and Creation, op. cit., 57.
[7] Idem, 52.
[8] E. Schillebeeckx, For the Sake of the Gospel, New York: Crossroad, 1990, 117.

celebrating polyphonic inculturations of culture and religion. Moreover, I propose we can move a step further regarding this genealogy of Latin American theologies that take the imperative of liberation seriously, and so recall the works by Marcella Althous-Reid and her "Queer theology."[9] Althous-Reid argues that a post-liberation and post-colonial theologian must include a responsible thinking on matters regarding corporeality, sexuality and gender, and move beyond homophobia, misogyny, and Western hegemony that at times some early liberation theologians reiterated without a critical approach. I personally believe that Schillebeeckx would approve of this movement forward in the shaping of diverse ecclesial communities of the twenty-first century.

* * *

Zusammenfassung des Beitrags von Angel F. Méndez Montoya

Obwohl Mystik und Politik von Theologien und Philosophien häufig als Gegenspieler betrachtet werden, entwickelt sich Schillebeeckx' Denken von einem Punkt aus, den William Cavanaugh als „theopolitische Imagination" bezeichnet: Raum, Zeit und menschliches Handeln werden durch gegenseitige Durchdringung und Herausforderung sowohl aus dem mystischen als auch dem politischen Bereich in ihrem Verhältnis zueinander geordnet. Schillebeeckx argumentiert, das Gott – obwohl er jenseits allen menschlichen Denkens verortet werden muss – dennoch in einer radikal intimen Beziehung zur Schöpfung und Menschheit steht. Gott existiert immer während *für Dich*, und lädt die Menschheit dazu ein, eine christliche und pneumatologische Praxis zu inkarnieren, die den Kreislauf von Gewalt und Ungerechtigkeit durchbricht und auf diese Weise eine gemeinschaftliche, alles umfassende Herrschaft des Friedens und der bedingungslosen Caritas errichtet. Diese Vision des Reiches Gottes ist zwar als protologisch und eschatologisch zu verstehen, wird aber durch eine kontinuierliche Bestätigung des Hier und Jetzt durch die Anwesenheit Gottes in der Menschheit und der Menschlichkeit in Gott vermittelt. Somit wird

---

[9] M. Althous-Reid, Teología indecente. Perversiones teológicas en sexo, género y política, Barcelona: Ediciones Ballaterra, 2005.

eine neue *polis* konstituiert, die paradoxerweise jenseits und gleichzeitig mitten in der menschlichen Vorstellungskraft und Kultur anzusiedeln ist.

Übersetzung aus dem Englischen: *Bernhard Kohl*

Bernhard Kohl

JENSEITS DES DISKURSES

Ethische Anstöße bei Edward Schillebeeckx

1. Erste Skizze: Ethik bei Edward Schillebeeckx

Für Edward Schillebeeckx gilt: Kriterien für die Festlegung von guter und geglückter Menschlichkeit bzw. von Handlungs- und Verhaltensweisen die diese Menschlichkeit fördern sind nicht einfach aus vorgegebenen Quellen deduzierbar.[1] Dieselbe Feststellung gilt für die Gewinnung ethischer Normen: „Frühere, aber auch heutige Formen der Ethik gingen und gehen von dem Naturgesetz aus. Sie setzen voraus, dass ‚die Ordnung' vorgegeben ist und dass daraus dann das Gebot kommt, diese Ordnung nicht zu verletzen. Darin liegt ein universaler Optimismus hinsichtlich der Interpretationskraft der ‚universalen' menschlichen Vernunft. Dass diese [...] abstrakt-universale Vernunft geschichtlich selbst auch in persönliche und gesellschaftliche Sündhaftigkeit und gierige Herrschaft verstrickt ist, wird dabei oft vergessen. Denn die Erfahrung lehrt, dass auch die sittliche Vernunft der Befreiung bedarf. Wenn wir genauer hinschauen, sehen wir, dass der konkrete Ausgangspunkt des Ethos nicht so sehr ‚die Ordnung' ist, die nicht gestört werden darf, sondern unsere Empörung über den geschichtlich konkreten, allenthalben schon verletzten Menschen: über die Unordnung, sowohl im eigenen Herzen als auch in der Gesellschaft und in deren Institutionen. Die tatsächliche Bedrohung und Antastung des gewünschten, aber positiv nie definierbaren ‚Humanum' – des Menschenwürdigen – führt zur Empörung und ist daher eine konkrete ethische Einladung und ein ethischer Imperativ, der in

---

[1] Vgl. E. Schillebeeckx, Christus und die Christen, Freiburg/Br. 1977, 712.

sehr situierte, negative Kontrasterfahrungen menschlichen Unheils und Unglücks, hier und jetzt, eingebettet ist."[2]

Neben dem Verzicht auf die Deduktion lehnt Schillebeeckx darüber hinaus ein positivistisches Normenverständnis zugunsten eines kontextualisierten Ethos ab, da Ethos und Normen faktisch nur innerhalb einer bestimmten Gesellschaft oder Gruppe von Menschen Geltung besitzen, diese faktische Gültigkeit aber niemals zum universalen Maßstab sittlichen Handelns erhoben werden kann. Ja, er geht so weit, dass er das Spezifikum einer christlichen Ethik darin sieht, keine zu sein. Das Christentum hat im Vergleich zu einigen anderen Religionen keine ihm eigene Ethik und erweist sich deswegen als offen „für das von allen Menschen gesuchte Humanum, hier und jetzt und immer wieder von neuem"[3]. Die vernünftige Urteilsfähigkeit des Menschen in Zusammenwirken mit der Kontrasterfahrung menschlichen Leidens ist hinreichend, um die ambivalenten Erscheinungen der menschlichen Geschichte und Gesellschaft abzuwägen, d. h. die situativ bedingte Gegenwart bildet den hermeneutischen Schlüssel zur Erfassung der *condition humaine*, da das menschliche Wesen nirgendwo anders als im Verlauf der Geschichte entdeckt werden kann, im Gegenteil: Wo Menschsein geschichtsvergessen erfasst werden soll, wird eine Grundbedingung menschlicher Existenz verneint, da Geschichte der Ort ist, wo über die Heilung oder das Heil von Menschen entschieden wird.[4]

Wenn auch Religion nicht auf das Ethos reduziert werden darf, so besteht doch ein enger, innerer Zusammenhang zwischen Glaube und Ethik, da ein Christ „die autonome Moral der Humanität konkret im Kontext einer Praxis gemäß dem Reich Gottes, auf das er seine Hoffnung gesetzt hat [sieht]"[5]. Auch wenn die christliche Ethik – ganz im Sinne einer autonomen Moral – einer auf den Menschen und seine Würde gerichteten Moral nichts hinzufügen kann und Gott nicht als unmittelbare Grundlegung des ethischen Handelns benötigt wird, da eine Moral, der es um die Menschenwürde eines jeden geht, an erster Stelle der kollektiven geschichtlichen Menschheit ein verantwortliches Mitspracherecht einräumen muss, gibt es für Edward Schillebeeckx keine Ethik ohne Gott, da diese gnadenlos würde.

---

[2] Ders., Menschen. Die Geschichte von Gott, Freiburg/Br. 1990, 54.
[3] Ebd., 54.
[4] Vgl. ders., Glaube und Moral, in: D. Mieth / F. Compagnoni (Hrsg.), Ethik im Kontext des Glaubens. Probleme, Grundsätze, Methoden (Studien zur theologischen Ethik Bd. 3), Freiburg/Ue. – Freiburg/Br. 1978, 17–45, hier 17.
[5] Ders., Menschen. Die Geschichte von Gott, Freiburg/Br. 1990, 54.

Diese Schlussfolgerung kann Schillebeeckx deswegen ziehen, weil er eine unaufhörliche Dialektik zwischen der Universalität des Evangeliums, welche jede Kultur kritisch herausfordert und transzendiert, und der doch immer kulturabhängigen Erscheinungsweise des Evangeliums sieht. Offenbarung, Glaube, Religiosität – das Theologale, das was Gott selbst zum Objekt hat – ereignet sich immer in einer bestimmten, kontingenten Kultur und muss in dieser artikuliert werden, damit sie für Menschen verständlich und relevant bleiben.[6]

Unter dem „Ethischen" hingegen ist all das zu verstehen, was die Humanisierung und die Förderung des Menschen als Mensch zum Objekt hat. Wie schon erwähnt besitzt es eine eigene, autonome Konsistenz, wird aber gleichzeitig zum Ausdruck des Religiösen bzw. Theologalen. Ein Ethos stellt für Schillebeeckx eine Form der Selbstverpflichtung dar, wonach Menschen sich selbst autonom eine Norm auferlegen. Dennoch würde eine Ethik ohne die Spiritualität des gottgläubigen oder theologalen Lebens den Menschen überfordern, da nur ein Leben im Gottglauben zum geschichtlichen Unternehmen einer menschlichen Befreiungspraxis führt und eine Reflexion hierüber hervorruft. In dieser Vermittlungsposition kann eine ethische Rationalität dann auch zur kritischen Instanz werden: Sie kann ideologisierende Aspekte des religiösen Lebens entlarven.[7] Umgekehrt wird das Ethische durch die Aufnahme des Theologalen transfinalisiert: Es verbleibt nicht in rein immanenten Dimensionen, sondern wird zu einem Ausdruck des kommenden Reiches Gottes. Kurz: Theologie ist im Verständnis Schillebeeckx' die Herstellung einer Korrelation zwischen der Botschaft des Glaubens und den menschlichen Erfahrungen in der Gegenwart.[8]

Diese beiden Pole weisen auf eine Gefahr hin, in welcher sich das Christentum in seiner spezifischen Wechselwirkung von Religiosität und Ethik ausgesetzt sieht: Es balanciert ständig zwischen einer Absorption des Menschlichen in das Göttliche und einer Reduzierung des Göttlichen auf das Menschliche bzw. Ethische. Diese Problematik hält Schillebeeckx aber im Rahmen einer inkarnatorischen Theologie für umgehbar, da gerade sie einer Polarisierung nicht erliegen darf und muss. Wenn man nämlich davon ausgeht, dass – theologisch gesprochen – Schöpfung und Inkarnation ein Ausdruck des Vertrauens Gottes in den Menschen dar-

---

[6] Vgl. ders., Gott – Die Zukunft des Menschen, Mainz 1969, 13.
[7] Vgl. ders., Menschen, 54f.
[8] Vgl. C. Barwasser, Edward Schillebeeckx. Eine Theologie der Erfahrung als Hermeutik christlicher Glaubenspraxis, in: Theologien der Gegenwart. Eine Einführung, Darmstadt 2006, 198–220, hier 214.

stellen, dann ist der Glaube an Gott nach aller geschichtlichen Erfahrung ohne den Glauben an den Menschen unmöglich. Eine christliche Anthropologie und Ethik kommt folglich ohne Dualismus und ohne Emanatismus aus.[9]

2. Zweite Skizze: Anthropologie bei Edward Schillebeeckx

Ähnliches wie für den ethischen Bereich gilt auch für den anthropologischen Ansatz Schillebeeckx': Der Mensch lässt sich nicht ontologisch definieren. Weder aus der sogenannten universalen menschlichen Natur, deren moderne Form das Naturrecht darstellt, noch aus der Schöpfungsordnung lässt sich das Sein des Menschen bestimmen.[10] Vielmehr sieht er mit Levinas die „absolute Forderung der Person des anderen in seiner transzendenten Andersheit"[11], die zur Bestimmung des menschlichen Wesens herangezogen werden kann. Hierfür müssten dann folgende Voraussetzungen gelten: Der Andere ist wirklich anders, d. h. transzendent; das Antlitz des Anderen stellt eine ethische Herausforderung für meine jeweils eigene, freie Subjektivität dar. Dabei wird dieser Andere nicht als „Alter Ego" gemäß kategorischem Imperativ, noch als Bestandteil einer Totalität, wie beispielsweise eines Staates verstanden, sondern als ursprüngliches, einzigartiges und somit transzendentes Wesen, zu dem das Ich in eine asymmetrische Beziehung gesetzt ist. Als asymmetrisch erweist sich die Beziehung deshalb, weil sich die absolute Forderung der Person des Anderen nicht dadurch ergibt, dass er wie ich frei ist, sondern weil seine Freiheit eine Überlegenheit genießt, die aus seiner Transzendenz herrührt.[12] Mit Levinas gesprochen: Das, was die andere Person von mir fordern kann ist keine Konsequenz dessen, was ich von ihr fordern kann.[13]

Diese Überlegung führt für Schillebeeckx zu der Erkenntnis, dass Gut und Böse, Gerechtigkeit und Ungerechtigkeit nicht als gleichberechtigt angesehen werden können und dass deswegen das Recht immer aufseiten des Guten liegt. Theoretisch vermittelt der Glaube an Gott zwischen die-

---

[9] Vgl. E. Schillebeeckx, Die Auferstehung Jesu als Grund der Erlösung (Quaestiones disputatae Bd. 78), Freiburg/Br. 1979, 129, 131f.
[10] Vgl. ders., Glaube und Moral, a.a.O., 24.
[11] Ders., Menschen, a.a.O., 128.
[12] Vgl. ebd., 128f.
[13] Vgl. E. Levinas, Totalität und Unendlichkeit. Versuch über die Exteriorität, Freiburg/Br. 1987, 327f.

ser menschlichen Hoffnung auf den endgültigen Sieg des Humanums und der konkreten Realität unserer Geschichte. Die praktische Vermittlung zwischen dieser auf Gott gegründeten Hoffnung und der geschichtlich erfahrbaren Welt erfolgt durch die gottgläubige Praxis der Weltveränderung und der Weltverbesserung, welche sich u. a. durch folgende Punkte auszeichnet:[14]

– Die Freiheit des Menschen, sich selbstlos für andere einzusetzen, in dem Vertrauen darauf, dass ein solcher Einsatz von Bedeutung ist.
– Die Freiheit des Menschen in der geschichtlich bedingten Welt ohne großes Misstrauen gegenüber dem Dasein leben zu können.
– Die Freiheit, Erfahrungen des Friedens, der Freude und der Kommunikation zu akzeptieren und sie als – wenn auch fragmentarische – Manifestationen der Heil bringenden Gegenwart des lebendigen Gottes zu verstehen.

Insbesondere die Gottebenbildlichkeit des Menschen sieht Schillebeeckx als Grund dafür an, die Welt zu verändern und zu verbessern, da durch eine von diesem Verständnis imprägnierte Auffassung des Schöpfungsgeschehens die Kontingenz jedes Entstehungsprozesses aufgehoben wird durch einen Begriff von Schöpfung, der sich selbst als Erklärung der Phänomene von Zufall und Notwendigkeit in Natur und Geschichte versteht.

Dies gilt dann auch für den Menschen: Wenn der Mensch nach dem Bild Gottes geschaffen wurden, dann muss dieser Mensch etwas anderes sein als ein Konservator, Restaurator oder Entdecker dessen, was schon gegeben ist. Dann wird er vielmehr selbst zum Prinzip dessen, was er aus der Welt und der Gesellschaft machen soll – und was hätte nicht sein können und faktisch doch ist, dank seines kontingenten freien Willens. Gott erschafft den Menschen als Prinzip seines eigenen menschlichen Handelns.[15] Der Ausspruch „Lasst uns Menschen machen als unser Abbild, uns ähnlich" kann in diesem Zusammenhang nur bedeuten, dass auch der Mensch in seiner Lebenswelt schöpferisch tätig sein muss.[16]

---

[14] Vgl. E. Schillebeeckx, Menschen, a.a.O., 174f.
[15] Vgl. ebd., 290f.
[16] Vgl. ders., Die Auferstehung Jesu als Grund der Erlösung, a.a.O., 138f.

3. Fazit: Autonomie, Pluralität, Diskurs, Weltverbesserung

Statt eines positivistischen oder eines historisch-notwendigen Entwurfs des Menschseins schlägt Edward Schillebeeckx „anthropologische Konstanten"[17] zur Charakterisierung des „menschlichen Wesens" vor. Diese offenbaren seiner Auffassung zufolge menschliche Werte, deren konkrete Normen von Menschen in den geschichtlich wechselnden Prozess kreativ eingetragen werden müssen, d. h. die anthropologischen Konstanten liefern nicht direkt ethische Normen, nach denen hier und jetzt menschenwürdige und ethisch lebbare Menschlichkeit ins Leben gerufen werden kann.[18] Vielmehr führen sie konstitutive, aus der Analyse der zeitgenössischen Situation immer von Neuem näher zu bestimmende Bedingungen, die in jedem menschlichen Handeln vorausgesetzt werden müssen, vor Augen und bilden somit eine Art Koordinatensystem, in welchem Normen in gemeinsamen Überlegungen gesucht und nach Analyse der ganz konkreten Gesellschaftsstrukturen in ihr gefunden werden können. Auf dieser Grundlage können dann anhand von Kontrasterfahrung, von Sinnerfahrungen und im Licht dessen, was eine Gesellschaft als anzustrebende Utopie betrachtet, Differenzen zwischen Ideal und Faktizität aufgezeigt werden, welche wiederum verschiedene Richtungen für die gesellschaftliche Entwicklung vorgeben. Somit kann bei divergierenden Differenzanalysen natürlich eine Pluralität von Normen auftreten, selbst wenn den anthropologischen Konstanten Gültigkeit zuerkannt wird.[19]

Eine weitere Konsequenz ist die der Säkularität: Normen, die früher Angelegenheiten der Religion oder des Christentums waren, werden heute als allgemeinmenschlich angesehen. Schillebeeckx verbindet hiermit aber keine Schwächung des Glaubens, sondern im Gegenteil eine Bestätigung der Richtigkeit der entsprechenden Normen.[20] Dies bedeutet auch, so Schillebeeckx, dass der Glaube dem Ethos eine gewisse Priorität vor dem Religiösen einräumen muss, was er damit begründet, dass das Ethos für ein menschliches Zusammenleben Dringlichkeit besitzt, und somit

---

[17] Zur vollständigen Ausführung vgl. E. Schillebeeckx, Christus und die Christen, Freiburg/Br. 1977, 715–725.
[18] Vgl. E. Schillebeeckx, Christus und die Christen, a.a.O., 714. An anderer Stelle unterscheidet Schillebeeckx auch zwischen formalen und inhaltlichen Normen, wobei die formalen Normen allgemeine, dynamische Richtlinien bezeichnen, die anzeigen, dass das Humanum gefördert werden muss. Sie sind also den anthropologischen Konstanten gleichsetzbar. Die inhaltlichen Normen verkörpern die materiale Umsetzung der formalen Normen in einer zeitlichen und räumlichen Weltsituation; vgl. ders., Glaube und Moral, a.a.O., 32f.
[19] Ders., Christus und die Christen, a.a.O., 723f.
[20] Vgl. ders., Die Auferstehung Jesu als Grund der Erlösung, a.a.O., 142.

nicht abgewartet werden kann, bis unter allen Menschen Einigkeit über sämtliche letzten Lebensfragen besteht.[21] „Auch dann, wenn ihre fundamentale Inspiration etwa aus einem religiösen Gottesglauben kommt, müssen ethische, das heißt die Menschenwürdigkeit fördernde Normen in einer intersubjektiv-gültigen, das heißt für alle vernünftigen Menschen zugänglichen, Diskussion rational begründet werden können. [...] Mit unterschiedlichen Auffassungen von konkreten Normen für eine hier und jetzt erforderliche Menschenwürde leben zu lernen wird zu den Aufträgen moderner lebbarer Menschlichkeit gehören. Die Trauer über diesen Pluralismus gehört zu unserer condition humaine, mit der wir fertig werden müssen, und zwar eben nicht durch diktatorische Ablehnung anderer Auffassungen."[22]

4. Kontextualisierung

Damit lässt sich der anthropologisch-ethische Ansatz Edward Schillebeeckx' folgendermaßen umreißen: Das „Ethische" ist – recht weit gefasst – all das, was die Humanisierung und die Förderung des Menschen als Menschen zum Objekt hat und zwar unter der Prämisse, dass das Ethische somit auch eine Förderung des Guten und Gerechten zum Ziel hat. Das Humane, Gute und Gerechte ist nur in geschichtlichen Kategorien erkennbar und wird nicht etwa als Prinzip aus dem Sein oder Wesen des Menschen deduziert, sondern der Mensch wird selbst zum intersubjektiv-diskursiven Gestaltungsprinzip der Gesellschaft und der Welt.

Diese „Säkularisierung" des Ethischen geht dann mit einer sich daraus ergebenden natürlichen Pluralität einher. Somit ist eine klare Distanzierung von einer Anthropologie und einer Methode der ethisch-moralischen Normgewinnung erkennbar, die davon ausgeht, dass in der Natur des Menschen und in der Schöpfung inhaltliche Forderungen für menschliches Verhalten zu finden, den geschaffenen Dingen also gleichsam eingeprägt sind. Hiermit ist verbunden, dass Normen nicht aus einem universalen und unveränderlichen Naturgesetz ablesbar sind und somit auch kein ein für alle Mal gültiger Normenkanon aufgestellt werden kann.

---

[21] Vgl. ders., Christus und die Christen, a.a.O., 638.
[22] Ebd., 724.

4.1. Autonomie

Schwieriger gestaltet sich die Bestimmung einer Zielrichtung bzw. die materiale Ausformulierung des anthropologischen und ethischen Ansatzes bei Schillebeeckx, da er, abgesehen von den o. g. anthropologischen Konstanten, keine dezidierte Anthropologie oder Ethik vorgelegt hat. Dennoch darf man wohl den Schluss ziehen, dass Edward Schillebeeckx' Impulse in diesen Bereichen der Theologie die Charakteristika einer autonomen und auch diskursiv geprägten Ethik aufweisen – Ansätze also, welche zur Zeit der Arbeit an den anthropologischen Konstanten noch nicht zum theologischen Mainstream gehörten.[23] Der Akzent verschiebt sich in einem solchen Ansatz von der Norm zur Verantwortlichkeit der handelnden Person, d. h., dass sich ethisches Handeln und Moralität nicht mehr durch das reine Befolgen von natürlichen Ver- und Geboten, sondern durch ein Handeln aus eigener Verantwortlichkeit auszeichnen. Nicht durch Heteronomie, sondern durch ein selbst gegebenes Gesetz erfolgt moralisches Handeln.[24] Die als kulturelle Leistung und als Erfüllung seiner Freiheitsgeschichte zu verstehenden ethischen Orientierungen des Menschen lassen sich somit nicht mehr ontologisch-objektiv verstehen. Ebenso wenig ist der Mensch nicht mehr bloß „Erfüller" einer sittlichen Ordnung, sondern normsetzende geschichtliche Freiheit.[25]

Ethische Normen werden damit aber nicht überflüssig, sondern im Sinne des Zweiten Vatikanischen Konzils stärker an das Gewissen des Menschen gebunden. „Durch die Treue zum Gewissen sind die Christen mit den übrigen Menschen verbunden im Suchen nach der Wahrheit und zur wahrheitsgemäßen Lösung all der vielen moralischen Probleme, die im Leben der Einzelnen wie im gesellschaftlichen Zusammenleben entstehen."[26] Das Gewissen bietet in diesem Verständnis eine objektive Rückbindung, weswegen die autonome Moral und in dieser Tradition stehend auch der Ansatz Schillebeeckx' nicht als Versuch einer subjektivistischen Gewissensmoral abgewertet werden können.

---

[23] Bspw. erschien A. Auers Werk zur autonomen Moral im Jahr 1971.
[24] Vgl. K.-W. Merks, Autonome Moral, in: D. Mieth (Hrsg.), Moraltheologie im Abseits. Antwort auf die Enzyklika „Veritatis splendor" (Quaestiones disputatae Bd. 153), Freiburg/Br. 1994, 46–68, hier 62f.
[25] Vgl. J. Römelt, Christliche Ethik im pluralistischen Kontext. Eine Diskussion der Methode ethischer Reflexion in der Theologie (Studien der Moraltheologie. Abtlg. Beihefte Bd. 4), Münster 2000, 99.
[26] Vgl. GS 16.

4.2. Pluralität und Diskurs

In dem beschriebenen Rahmen gehört es für ihn zur Normalität, dass sich in menschlichen Gesellschaften verschiedene Ansichten darüber herausbilden, welche Normen dem Erreichen dieser menschenwürdiger Zustände, d. h. der Weltveränderung und -verbesserung zuträglich sind. Aus diesem Grund stellt der rationale gesellschaftliche Diskurs über diese Normen einen wichtigen Faktor dar, um intersubjektiv gültige Einigkeit über die Verbindlichkeit von Normen zu erzielen. Damit greift Schillebeeckx erneut auf die Ergebnisse einer in den 1970er Jahren aktuellen Debatte um die Diskursethik und die damit verbundene Möglichkeit einer Neubegründung von Ethik zu, wenn er fragt, ob es eine universal-gültige, intersubjektiv bindende und trotzdem nicht-dogmatische, d. h. nicht autoritär auferlegte Auffassung von Normen geben kann, die von allen annehmbar wäre.[27] Damit betont Schillebeeckx gleichzeitig, dass ethische Normen, auch wenn sie ihre fundamentale Inspiration aus einem Gottesglauben beziehen, „in einer intersubjektiv-gültigen, d. h. für alle vernünftigen Menschen zugänglichen Diskussion rational begründet werden können. Keiner der Gesprächspartner kann sich dabei hinter einem ‚ich sehe etwas, was du nicht siehst' verstecken und trotzdem andere verpflichten, diese Norm einfach zu akzeptieren"[28].

In Bezug auf die Begründung von Normen ist in der Diskursethik vor allem der praktische Diskurs relevant, dessen Ziel es ist, zur Rechtfertigung eines problematisierten Richtigkeitsanspruchs von Normen zu gelangen. In diesem Ansatz sind auch die Geschichtlichkeit und kulturelle Bedingtheit und somit die Wandelbarkeit der Normen menschlichen Handelns, auf die Schillebeeckx einen Fokus legt, in angemessener Weise berücksichtigt. Schon Habermas wendet sich gegen eine „dogmatische Fassung des Konzepts der Gattungsgeschichte", die eine „einlinige, notwendige, ununterbrochene und aufsteigende Entwicklung eines Makrosubjekts"[29] annimmt und plädiert stattdessen dafür die Gesellschaft als Trägerin von Evolution zu sehen. Ähnlich argumentiert Schillebeeckx, wenn er davon ausgeht, dass ein gesellschaftliches Ethos und gesellschaftliche Normen nach einem längeren geistesgeschichtlichen Prozess in der Moderne als Kulturschöpfung des Menschen verstanden werden müssen, was nicht nur zu einer Lösung des Ethos von der Theologie, sondern da-

---

[27] Vgl. E. Schillebeeckx, Christus und die Christen, a.a.O., 641.
[28] Vgl. ders., Glaube und Moral, a.a.O., 37.
[29] J. Habermas, Zur Rekonstruktion des Historischen Materialismus, Frankfurt/M. 1976, 154.

rüber hinaus zu einer Loslösung des Menschen vom Ethos führt. Die neue Devise lautet sich experimentierend, also quasi evolutiv, auf die Suche nach den eigenen Grenzen zu machen und somit zu gesellschaftlichen Normen und einem gesellschaftlichen Ethos zu gelangen.[30]

In einem solchen Denkansatz kommt theologischer Ethik keine primäre Kompetenz in Bezug auf die Orientierung über gesellschaftliche Normen mehr zu. Vielmehr kann sie die Rolle einer Begleiterin der Suche moderner Kultur „nach einem angemessenen, nicht ins Abstrakte abgleitenden Verständnis des gesellschaftlichen Konsenses"[31] übernehmen und für eine Gestaltung des ethischen Gesprächs eintreten, in welchem der kommunikative Austausch verschiedene Traditionen und Einsichten moralischer Überzeugung achtet und dabei hilft, den moralischen Konsens der Gesellschaft immer neu zu erarbeiten.[32] Schillebeeckx scheint sich den Schwierigkeiten des praktisch-ethischen Diskurses durchaus bewusst gewesen zu sein, wenn er von einer Trauer über den Pluralismus spricht, die zu unserer *condition humaine* gehört, getragen werden muss und nicht durch diktatorische Ablehnung anderer Auffassungen eliminiert werden darf.[33]

4.3. Glaube und Handeln: Weltverbesserung

Allerdings weisen Ansätze autonomer Moral einen Schwachpunkt auf, den sie mit einer reinen Glaubensethik teilen: die Frage nach dem Verhältnis von Glaube und Handeln und die Trennung, die beide Ansätze hier vornehmen.[34] Eine solche Separation scheint nicht im Sinne Schillebeeckx' zu liegen, da er betont, dass in der Gottebenbildlichkeit des Menschen der theologische Grund für den Einsatz für Weltveränderung und Weltverbesserung zu finden sei.[35] Glaube und Handeln, Dogmatik und Ethik stellen komplementäre Faktoren da, die nicht auseinanderdividierbar sind.

Aus diesem Grund bieten Schillebeeckx' ethische und anthropologische Überlegungen Anklänge an Theoriebildungen der theologischen

---

[30] Vgl. E. Schillebeeckx, Christus und die Christen, a.a.O., 637.
[31] J. Römelt, Christliche Ethik im pluralistischen Kontext, a.a.O., 92.
[32] Vgl. ebd., 95.
[33] Vgl. E. Schillebeeckx, Christus und die Christen, a.a.O., 724.
[34] Vgl. E. Arens, Glaube und Handeln aus handlungstheoretischer Sicht, in: A. Bondolfi / W. Lesch (Hrsg.), Theologische Ethik im Diskurs. Eine Einführung (UTB Wissenschaft Bd. 1806), Tübingen – Basel 1995, 25–43, hier 28.
[35] Vgl. E. Schillebeeckx, Menschen, a.a.O., 290f.

Ethik, die über eine rein autonom oder diskursiv angelegte ethische Konzeption hinausweisen. Schillebeeckx scheint Ethik als christlich-kommunikative Glaubenspraxis aufzufassen, „die im Gespräch und in Auseinandersetzung mit der Diskursethik betrieben wird und mit deren Hilfe sowie ihr gegenüber die Grundstrukturen christlich-kommunikativer Praxis herausgestellt [werden], deren biblische Grundlagen sie im Ausgang von der jesuanischen Praxis der Gottesherrschaft und der kommunikativen Praxis der Jünger und Gemeinde Jesu Christi beleuchtet und als kommunikativ-ethische Glaubenspraxis bzw. Christopraxis identifiziert und expliziert. Eben damit gelangt sie zugleich zu einem integrativen Verständnis von Glaube und Handeln, das beide als kommunikativ und praktisch aufzeigt und entfaltet."[36]

5. Ausblick

Eine zusammenfassende Systematisierung der bisher dargestellten Grundlinien einer Ethik oder Anthropologie im Denken Edward Schillebeeckx' kann nur spekulativ bleiben. Dennoch sollen abschließend zwei Gedanken Schillebeeckx' herausgegriffen werden, die m. E. Impulse für eine zeitgenössische Moraltheologie bzw. theologische Ethik bieten können.

5.1. Trauer über die pluralistische condition humaine

„Mit unterschiedlichen Auffassungen von konkreten Normen für eine hier und jetzt erforderliche Menschenwürde leben zu lernen wird zu den Aufträgen moderner lebbarer Menschlichkeit gehören. Die Trauer über diesen Pluralismus gehört zu unserer condition humaine, mit der wir fertig werden müssen, und zwar eben nicht durch diktatorische Ablehnung anderer Auffassungen."[37]

Schillebeeckx betont, indem er der Trauer um die plurale *condition humaine* Ausdruck verleiht, dass gesellschaftliche Pluralität kein Ziel an sich sein kann. Zwar ist die Pluralität einer Gesellschaft und vor allem die Freiheit des Individuums, welche durch sie ermöglicht wird, ein in keiner Weise zu unterschätzendes Gut, allerdings stellt sich die Frage, ob Pluralität oder darüber hinaus das bewusste Offenhalten der Pluralität ausrei-

---

[36] E. Arens, Christopraxis. Grundzüge theologischer Handlungstheorie (Quaestiones disputatae Bd. 139), Freiburg/Br. 1992, 125f.
[37] E. Schillebeeckx, Christus und die Christen, a.a.O., 724.

chen kann, um die Herausforderungen und Ambivalenzen moderner Gesellschaften zu bewältigen. Auf den gesellschaftlichen Diskurs bezogen: einerseits kann ein innerhalb einer pluralen Gesellschaft erzielter Konsens einen Aspekt des Universalitätsanspruches aller Wahrheit besitzen, andererseits wird ein solcher Konsens aber nicht genügen, da Kommunikation zwischen Menschen häufig offene oder versteckte Unfreiheit in sich birgt. Schillebeeckx ging deswegen schon vor gut vierzig Jahren davon aus, dass globale Herausforderungen einer globalen Solidarität bedürfen,[38] also eines Faktors, der in der Lage ist, die pluralen Perspektiven zu einer gewissen Kohärenz zu führen, wenngleich auf diesem Wege – wie vermutlich auf keinem anderen – keine theoretische Letztbegründung menschlichen Handelns erreicht werden kann.[39] Selbstverständlich ist jeder einzelne Teil einer Gesellschaft aufgefordert sich auf die Suche nach den eigenen Normvorstellungen und Grenzen zu machen, doch wäre er ganz auf sich allein gestellt mit dieser Aufgabe überfordert.[40] Eine Beschränkung auf bereichsspezifische Anliegen scheint darüber hinaus angesichts globaler Herausforderungen auch nicht ausreichend, weswegen eine Vernetzung der vielfältigen Perspektiven innerhalb einer Gesellschaft erforderlich ist. Diese Vernetzung scheint im Sinne Schillebeeckx' als Transdisziplinarität denkbar, die historisch gewachsene und heute überflüssige Parzellierungen innerhalb der Gesellschaft aufheben kann. Somit ist es möglich zu einer paradoxen Einsicht der Moderne zu gelangen: „Gerade weil sie der Vielfalt freiheitlichen Lebens dienen will, bekommt sie es mit Antworten auf Fragen zu tun, welche das Leben einer Perspektive unterstellen, die größere Einordnungen und Deutungen wagen muss."[41] Theologische Ethik muss die Pluralität moderner Gesellschaften nicht scheuen, da sie Abschied nehmen kann von der einen Logik der Metaphysik der naturrechtlichen Tradition und in der Lage ist, die ethischen Positionen des Naturrechts in die heutige Zeit zu übersetzen. Somit wäre sie befähigt zur erwähnten erweiterten Perspektive im gesellschaftlichen Dialog beizutragen, allerdings nicht als außenstehende Wächterin, sondern als engagiertes, um Kompetenz bemühtes Mitglied der Diskursgemeinschaft. Außerdem ist es die Aufgabe theologischer Ethik darauf zu verweisen, dass die Transdisziplinarität zwischen den gesellschaftlichen Perspektiven immer

---

[38] Vgl. ebd., 641.
[39] Vgl. ders., Glaube und Moral, a.a.O., 30f.
[40] Vgl. ders., Christus und die Christen, a.a.O., 637.
[41] J. Römelt, Der kulturwissenschaftliche Anspruch der theologischen Ethik (Quaestiones disputatae Bd. 242), Freiburg/Br. 2011, 50.

ein normatives Ziel haben muss: die Erlangung einer größeren Humanität und den Anspruch, dass moderne Kultur gelingen möge.[42]

5.2. Vertrauen in das Dasein

„Durch Jesu Erlösung erfahren Christen die Freiheit, zu akzeptieren, dass wir trotz Sünde und Schuld von Gott angenommen sind, die Freiheit, in dieser irdischen Welt ohne großes Misstrauen gegenüber dem Dasein leben zu können [...]."[43]

Für Schillebeeckx sind Ethik und ethische Handlungsweisungen an den Gottglauben rückgebunden. Theologisch gesprochen hat sich Gott im Sterben seines Sohnes der Ambivalenz und Destruktivität menschlicher Existenz ausgeliefert und sie in seiner Auferstehung überwunden. Deswegen bestehen die Aufgabe und Kompetenz theologischer Ethik darin, nicht mit vorschnellen Antworten über die Untiefen moderner Welt hinwegzutäuschen, sondern im Gegenteil im Aushalten und Durchstehen der damit verbundenen Konflikte.[44] Die Erfahrung des christlichen Gottglaubens führt angesichts von Ambivalenz und Destruktivität menschlicher Existenz außerdem zu einer gewissen Gelassenheit und zu einem Optimismus, die es dem Individuum ermöglichen können ohne großes Misstrauen gegenüber dem Dasein zu leben.[45]

Die theologische Ethik schuldet der modernen Gesellschaft also den Dienst, „in den Konflikten der Gestaltung des modernen Freiheitsrechts die eigenen Fundamente nicht aus den Augen zu verlieren [...]. Denn moderne Kultur weist eine grundlegende Unsicherheit in Bezug auf die Verankerung in den sie tragenden Ressourcen auf"[46]. Dies bedeutet, dass eine wesentliche Aufgabe der theologischen Ethik und der Theologie überhaupt die bleibende Arbeit am fundamentalen Konsens der Gesellschaft sein muss, der um die Förderung der Humanität und somit um die Garantie der Menschenwürde kreist. Dabei darf sie sich im Sinne eines schöpfungstheologischen Optimismus im Prozess der gesellschaftlichen Konsensfindung auf gewisse Risiken und Unfertigkeiten einer lebensweltlichen Praxis einlassen, „die nicht nur auf eine naturwissenschaftlich-technisch, sondern auch moralisch bessere Lösung hin überwunden wer-

---

[42] Vgl. ebd., 83, 88, 51; vgl. auch E. Schillebeeckx, Glaube und Moral, a.a.O., 22.
[43] Vgl. ders., Menschen, a.a.O., 174f.
[44] Vgl. J. Römelt, Der kulturwissenschaftliche Anspruch der theologischen Ethik, a.a.O., 80.
[45] Vgl. E. Schillebeeckx, Menschen, a.a.O., 174f.
[46] J. Römelt, Umkämpfte Menschenwürde, in: *Stimmen der Zeit* 129 (2004), 579–588, hier 583.

den [müssen]"⁴⁷. Eine solche Interpretation der Aufgabe theologischer Ethik bedarf sicherlich in manchen Fällen der Nachsicht und Entsühnung, was sich aber, wie Johann B. Metz es formuliert, als zutiefst christlich erweist: „Alles geschichtliche Handeln bleibt selbst auf Nachsicht und Entsühnung angewiesen. Anders kommt es nicht aus der Paradoxie heraus, dass es unmöglich ist, unter den Bedingungen der Geschichte das Ende der Geschichte vorwegzunehmen, dass es unmöglich ist, unter den Bedingungen der Entfremdung die Entfremdung des Menschen vom Menschen zu überwinden [...]."⁴⁸

* * *

Abstract of the contribution of Bernhard Kohl

Edward Schillebeeckx emphasizes that there is no predefined notion of being human, no universal human nature and, hence, no simple deduction of a criteria for ethically responsible action derivative from the "nature of things" or from "divine order." On the contrary, it is the task of human reasoning and discernment to assess the ambiguous phenomena of historical human process, and to develop specific normative principles from such process, creatively incorporating historicity as the source of self-determined action, and in doing so, endeavoring to become God's image. This discursively and historically conditioned development of socially acceptable norms must relate to the social plurality of specific norms.

While deeply regretting this plural *condition humaine*, Edward Schillebeeckx simultaneously stresses that the many-voiced social discourse is not an achievement in itself, but has to show that it can be offered as an enhancement to the world, as a means of widening human capacities, and eventually making plural perspectives more coherent with each other.

Translation from German: *Tracy Rammler*

---

[47] Ebd., 587.
[48] J.B. Metz, Zur Theologie der Welt, Mainz ²1969, 129.

Thomas Eggensperger

„WEIL POLITIK NICHT ALLES IST" – SONDERN?

Eine sozialethisch ausgerichtete Relecture und Neubesinnung

Der Ausgangspunkt dieses Beitrags ist ein kleines Buch, das Edward Schillebeeckx im Jahr 1986 herausgab. In dem Band „Als politiek niet alles is ... Jezus in de westerse cultuur"[1] versammelte er seine Vorträge im Rahmen der Abraham Kuyper-Vorlesungen, die er in Amsterdam gehalten hat. Diese Vorlesungsreihe stellt eine Reminiszenz dar gegenüber dem protestantischen Theologen und Politiker Abraham Kuyper (1837–1920). Er war nicht nur Theologe (und als solcher Professor für Theologie in Amsterdam), sondern auch Politiker (als solcher sogar zeitweise Ministerpräsident der Niederlande). Von daher ist das Thema der Vorlesungsreihe, die in der deutschen Übersetzung publiziert wurde als „Weil Politik nicht alles ist. Von Gott reden in einer gefährdeten Welt"[2] seitens Edward Schillebeeckx durchaus im doppelten Sinne zu verstehen: Hier geht es um das Wechselverhältnis von Religion und Politik. Auf Kuyper allerdings bezieht sich Schillebeeckx nicht direkt. Vielmehr reagiert er auf die Thesen des niederländischen Theologen Harry Kuitert, von dessen kurz zuvor veröffentlichtem Buch „Alles is politiek, maar politiek is niet alles"[3] er sich offensichtlich herausgefordert fühlte. Kuitert sieht in seinem Buch Kirchen nur in Notfällen als kompetent an, gesellschaftliche Fragen mit einer gewissen Autorität ansprechen zu können. Dabei geht er davon aus,

---

[1] E. Schillebeeckx, Als politiek niet alles is ... Jezus in de westerse cultuur (Abraham Kuyper-lezingen), Baarn 1986.
[2] Ders., Weil Politik nicht alles ist. Von Gott reden in einer gefährdeten Welt. Aus dem Niederländischen von U. Ruh, Freiburg/Br. 1987.
[3] H.M. Kuitert, Alles is politiek, maar politiek is niet alles. Een theologisch perspektief op geloof en politiek, Baarn 1985 (Everything is Politics but Politics is not Everything. A Theological Perspective on Faith and Politics, übers. von J. Bowden, London 1985.)

dass in westlichen Demokratien ein solcher Notfall eher eine rein hypothetische Größe ist. Diese Art und Weise, Kirche aus politischen Fragen heraushalten zu wollen, kann Schillebeeckx offensichtlich nicht akzeptieren.

Dieser Beitrag setzt sich bewusst mit dem vierten und letzten Kapitel seines Textes auseinander, um sich anhand dessen an das Verhältnis von Politik und Religion heranzutasten. In einem weiteren Schritt wird die Position von Schillebeeckx gut eine Generation später im Blick auf die gegenwärtige Situation einer kritischen Relecture unterzogen. Hinsichtlich des methodischen Angangs wird die Lektüre unter sozialethischen Gesichtspunkten begangen.

1. Umkehr durch Sinnerfahrung

Das Wechselverhältnis von Religion und Politik ist für Schillebeeckx eng verbunden mit dem von Kirche und Ethik. Die sichtbare Kirchengemeinschaft Jesu Christi ist eine Schicksalsgemeinschaft von Menschen, die in einer bestimmten Tradition stehen, die sie gemeinsam bezeugen und die sich im alltäglichen Handeln an der Praxis des Reichs Gottes orientieren. Dafür ist nach Schillebeeckx die Ethik „Scharnier und Bindeglied" (68) zwischen der mystischen und politischen Dimension des christlichen Glaubens. Ausgangspunkt sind menschliche Sinnerfahrungen, die man sich nicht aussucht, sondern die über einen kommen. Im Rahmen dieser Sinnerfahrungen sind es vor allem die Erfahrungen von Leid und Unrecht, denen nach Meinung von Schillebeeckx „Offenbarungsbedeutung" (70) zukommt. Dabei scheint Schillebeeckx nicht allein auf die Negativschablone einer Erfahrung zu schauen, sondern vor allem auf die einer solchen Erfahrung zugrundeliegende widerständige Wirklichkeit. Es ist also vor allem dieses „Ärgernis" (70) einer Erfahrung, die die harmonische Lebenslinie, die Biographie zumindest stört, wenn nicht sogar in völlig neue Bahnen lenkt. Das Ärgernis wird zur „Metanoia" (71), das heißt, dass vorgegebene Identität sich wandelt in einer neue, eine „bessere" (ebd.) Identität.

2. Ethik

Hier kommt die Ethik ins Spiel. Schillebeeckx versteht darunter nicht unbedingt die klassische Variante einer Ethik, die von einer naturgesetzlichen Ordnung oder Schöpfungsordnung ausgeht, die qua Ordnung nicht verletzt werden darf und die vor allem durch eine wie auch immer geartete „universale" Vernunft begründet ist. Solcherart Vernunftdenken wird obsolet hinsichtlich des menschlichen Verstricktseins in persönliche und gesellschaftliche Sündhaftigkeit. Vielmehr lehrt die Erfahrung – so Schillebeeckx –, dass die sittliche Vernunft auf Befreiung angewiesen ist. Ausgangspunkt des Ethos ist nicht so sehr die Ordnung, sondern die Empörung über Unrecht, das an Menschen geschieht. Schillebeeckx nennt solche Situationen negative „Kontrasterfahrungen" (72). Es geht um die Un-Ordnung im Persönlichen, in der Gesellschaft oder in den Institutionen. Was ethisch gut ist, zeigt sich in der Praxis von Befreiung und Versöhnung. An dieser Stelle kristallisiert sich heraus, dass es für Schillebeeckx offensichtlich schwierig ist, sich eine Ethik ohne Gottesglauben vorzustellen, indem er sagt: „In einer autonomen Ethik, einer Ethik ohne Gottesglauben, steckt unverkennbar so etwas wie eine verzweifelte Utopie, die sich zumindest nicht an dem Unrecht und der Unfreiheit in unserer Welt mitschuldig machen möchte." (ebd.)

Er präzisiert: Religiöse Tradition kann man nicht auf Ethik allein reduzieren. Religion ist mehr als nur eine spezifische Ethik. Was die christliche Tradition angeht, so kann man auch nicht von einer spezifisch christlichen Ethik sprechen, was immerhin den Vorteil hat, dass sie offen ist auf das angestrebte (wenngleich unerreichbare) „Humanum" (ebd.) als religionsübergreifende und religionsunabhängige Ethik, das allen Menschen zugänglich ist. Eine autonome Begründung der Ethik braucht Gott nicht als unmittelbare Begründung für ethisches Handeln, sondern sorgt sich um die Menschenwürde eines jeden Menschen.

In einer Nebenbemerkung meint Schillebeeckx, dass dies im Islam anders sei (vgl. ebd.), da dieser nicht offen sei für eben jenes Humanum. Leider erklärt er diese Bemerkung an der genannten Stelle nicht weiter. Dies wäre interessant gewesen, schon allein, weil es „den" Islam bekanntlich sowieso nicht gibt. Allerdings muss man Schillebeeckx auch zugutehalten, dass der Islam zur Zeit der Abfassung seiner Vorlesung in dieser Zeit noch kein Schwerpunktthema der Theologie war, erst nicht der dogmatischen Theologie.

3. Ethik und Glaube

Aber ganz autonom will Schillebeeckx die Ethik nicht verstanden wissen. „Dennoch werden wir damit Gott im ethischen Leben nicht los!" (73) Es bleibt eine Verbindung zwischen Glaube und Ethik bestehen. Die christliche Ethik fügt zwar einerseits der autonomen Moral nichts hinzu, aber sie beruht auf dem „theologalen" Leben (vgl. ebd.), d. h. dem Einvernehmen mit Gott und der realistischen Hoffnung, dass er in der menschlichen Geschichte handelt. Das klassische ethische Prinzip, vernunftgemäß zu handeln, wird in den Kontext des Glaubens gestellt. Und dies gereicht zum Vorteil für alle: Einerseits bewahrt die sittliche Vernunft das glaubensorientierte Handeln vor Fanatismus, andererseits kann die glaubensorientierte Ethik der sittlichen Vernunft einen Aspekt erinnernd nahebringen, der sich ihr von allein nicht erschließt, nämlich die menschliche Leidensgeschichte.[4] Es ist Schillebeeckx klar, dass das Religiöse oder der Glaube nicht das Ethische sind. Aber der Glaube macht sich seines Erachtens nicht nur in Gebet, Liturgie und Ritual fest, sondern auch im menschlichen Ethos. Ethos ist eine Art der Selbstverpflichtung, d. h. Menschen unterstellen sich autonom einer Norm. Schillebeeckx lehnt dieses Ethos an sich nicht ab, aber er bedauert, dass dem Ethos Momente wie die der „Liebe" fehlen. „Ohne Spiritualität oder gläubige Ausrichtung auf Gott ist die Ethik oft gnadenlos, auf Rache und Vergeltung erpicht […]" (76).

Weiter heißt es: „Die Ethik braucht einen Gott, der mehr ist als Ethik." (77) Und Schillebeeckx liefert sein Gottesbild unverzüglich nach. Gemeint ist der christliche, der lebendige Gott, nicht ein unmenschlicher und strafender Gott. Er schließt seine einleitenden Ausführungen mit der These: „Folglich ist der Glaube an Gott Grundlage der welterneuernden Praxis" (90). Weil dieser Glaube affirmativ und befreiend ist, hat er eine kritische Kraft gegenüber Unheil und Unfreiheit. Damit ist er eine Antipode zur Gefahr menschlicher Hybris oder zur Geringschätzung der Möglichkeiten Gottes.

---

[4] Dazu ist zu verweisen auf die fundamentaltheologischen Ansätze von Johann B. Metz und Helmut Peukert. Vgl. J.B. Metz, Glaube in Geschichte und Gesellschaft. Studien zu einer praktischen Fundamentaltheologie, Mainz 1977 u.ö.; H. Peukert, Wissenschaftstheorie – Handlungstheorie – Fundamentale Theologie. Analysen zu Ansatz und Status theologischer Theoriebildung, Frankfurt/M. ³2009.

4. Die „politische Liebe"

Desweiteren geht Schillebeeckx auf das Verhältnis von mystischer und politischer Dimension ein. Das Bindeglied zwischen mystischer und politischer Dimension des christlichen Gottesglaubens ist für ihn die Ethik. Unter „Mystik" versteht er eine intensive Form der Gotteserfahrung oder der Gottesliebe. Unter „Politik" versteht er eine intensive Form des gesellschaftlichen Engagements im weiteren Sinne. (vgl. 99). Mit diesen recht naheliegenden Definitionen stellt Schillebeeckx klar, dass die eine nicht ohne die andere auskommt. Dafür benutzt er den Begriff der „politischen Liebe". Sie ist eine – aber nicht die einzige – Form der christlichen Nächstenliebe (neben anderen wie der caritativen Hilfe), die sich kontextuell abspielt und berührt ist von Leid und Unrecht, das anderen Menschen widerfährt. Und nicht nur das: Der gläubige Mensch erfährt in seiner politischen Liebe, in seinem Widerstand gegen Unrecht, intensiven Kontakt mit Gott, mit dem befreienden Gott Jesu. Edward Schillebeeckx sieht in dieser Form der politischen Liebe und der politischen Heiligkeit die größten Chancen der Gegenwart. Auch an dieser Stelle wird die Warnung ausgesprochen, dass ohne Gebet und Mystik die Politik Gefahr läuft, unerbittlich und barbarisch zu werden – so wie Mystik ohne politische Liebe sentimental werden kann.

Was bedeutet dies für die Kirche? Es gibt zwei sehr unterschiedliche Deutungsmuster. Eine Deutung – Schillebeeckx nennt sie „politischen Liberalismus" (104) – betont die absolute Neutralität der Kirche hinsichtlich sozialer und politischer Probleme. Eine andere Deutung meint genau das Gegenteil und betont, dass Kirche angesichts politischer und sozialer Probleme gar nicht neutral bleiben kann. Schillebeeckx versteht in diesem Zusammenhang die „politische Relevanz des Evangeliums" (106) nicht als Aufforderung an die Kirchen, Tagespolitik zu betreiben, sondern eine solche kritisch zu beobachten. Im Gegensatz zu Kuitert, der in seiner Darlegung der politischen Vernunft und der demokratisch verfassten staatlichen Ordnung gerne vertraut, ist Schillebeeckx in diesem Zusammenhang skeptischer und möchte auch diese scheinbaren Selbstverständlichkeiten kritisch hinterfragen können. Dabei ist evident, dass die Kirche sich hinsichtlich ihrer Artikulation dessen bewusst sein muss, dass die Berufung auf Bibel und Tradition für die politische Öffentlichkeit bedeutungslos ist, sondern sie vielmehr mit Argumenten sprechen muss, die auch Nichtgläubigen verständlich sind.

5. Die Zeichen der Zeit (1986–2010)

Der vorgestellte Text ist eine Generation alt, hat weitgehend historischen Charakter. Deshalb braucht es heute die Nachfrage, was von dieser Vorlesung aus dem Jahr 1986 für die Gegenwart relevant ist. Innerhalb einer Generation ist einiges geschehen. Nach dem Fall der Mauer sind die Kirchen mit einem völlig neuen Phänomen konfrontiert. Es ist nicht mehr der kämpferische Atheismus, der sich in West und Ost gegenüber der christlichen Tradition zu behaupten versucht. Er spielt heute praktisch keine Rolle mehr. M. E. handelt es sich bei dem so genannten „neuen Atheismus", teilweise verbunden mit dem Namen Richard Dawkins, im westlichen Raum um eine *quantité négligeable*. Die verschiedenen soziologischen Erhebungen zeigen, dass es in der Gegenwart vielmehr um Agnostizismus und zum Teil um Ignoranz im wahrsten Sinne des Wortes geht. Mit Agnostizismus bezeichne ich die informelle Haltung von Menschen, die Fragen des Glaubens überhaupt nicht als Herausforderung oder gar Provokation empfinden, sondern die ihnen leidlich egal sind. Genauso gut kann man den Agnostizismus mit dem Begriff der „religiösen Indifferenz" bezeichnen.[5] Mit Ignoranz gegenüber Glaubensfragen meine ich die Situation, dass nicht einmal mehr die *basics* von Glaube und kirchlicher Tradition bekannt sind. Kirche wird in diesem Fall wahrgenommen als eine nicht näher verständliche Weltanschauungsgemeinschaft mit einer zum Teil recht düsteren Vergangenheit. In Deutschland findet sich eine solche Einstellung vor allem im Ostteil, d. h. im Gebiet der früheren DDR. Die Distanz der Gesellschaft gegenüber Kirche und Glaube ist nicht nur das Ergebnis der 40jährigen Geschichte der sozialistischen Indoktrination, sondern begann bereits zu Beginn der 20. Jahrhunderts. Die heutigen christlichen Bestände im Osten von Deutschland beschränken sich zum großen Teil auf den Bereich der mehr oder weniger aktiven Pfarrgemeinden beider Konfessionen. In religionssoziologischer Hinsicht greifen hier sowohl die Säkularisierungsthese als auch die These der Individualisierung, die sich komplementär aufeinander beziehen.[6] Aber auch im Westen sind Traditionsabbrüche und Abwanderungen aus unter-

---

[5] Vgl. u. a. E. Tiefensee, Religiöse Indifferenz als interdisziplinäre Herausforderung, in: G. Pickel / K. Sammet (Hrsg.), Religion und Religiosität im vereinigten Deutschland. Zwanzig Jahre nach dem Umbruch, Wiesbaden 2011, 79–101.

[6] Die dritte These eines „ökonomischen Marktmodells" gilt in seiner Bedeutung als weniger bedeutsam. Vgl. dazu D. Pollack / O. Müller, Die religiöse Entwicklung in Ostdeutschland nach 1989, in: G. Pickel / K. Sammet (Hrsg.), Religion und Religiosität im vereinigten Deutschland, a.a.O., 125–144.

schiedlichen Gründen evident.[7] Trotzdem stellen die beiden großen Kirchen in Deutschland, wie vermutlich in den meisten europäischen Ländern, nach wie vor wichtige Akteure innerhalb der jeweiligen Zivilgesellschaft dar, die man ernst nimmt oder zumindest zur Kenntnis nimmt – auch und gerade, wenn sie sich hinsichtlich politisch relevanter Themen artikulieren (Bioethik, PID, Natur und Umwelt, Sozialpolitik).

„Weil Politik nicht alles ist", das ist nach wie vor *common sense* innerhalb und außerhalb der Kirche. Allerdings ist ebenso klar, dass Kirche und Glaube nicht alles ist in der Gesellschaft. Aber was ist es dann?

6. Relecture und Neubesinnung

Es gilt, die Thesen von Edward Schillebeeckx aus 1986 durchzubuchstabieren im Raster der gegenwärtigen Situation.

6.1. Sinnerfahrung als Offenbarungsdeutung

Es scheint heute eine gewagte These seitens Schillebeeckx zu sein, dass negative Kontrasterfahrungen, d. h. Unterbrechungen von Biographien, dermaßen als „Ärgernis" wahrgenommen werden, dass sie zu einer „Metanoia" führen. Das Problem liegt sicherlich nicht in der Annahme, dass Leid- und Unrechtserfahrungen dazu führen, dass die Betroffenen sie nicht einfach nur hinnehmen, sondern sich davon berühren lassen. Für die Gegenwart wird aber zu konzedieren sein, dass der theologale Charakter einer solchen Sinnerfahrung seitens der religiös Indifferenten und/oder Ignoranten kaum noch als eine religiöse Erfahrung wahrgenommen wird, erst recht nicht im Zusammenhang mit der christlichen Erfahrung von Offenbarung.

Man wird Schillebeeckx sicherlich gerecht, wenn man gemeinsam mit ihm annimmt, dass die Aufgabe von Kirche und Theologie darin besteht, eben diese scheinbar profane Erfahrung aufzugreifen, um dem Betroffenen das religiöse Potential einer solchen Unrechtserfahrung deutlich zu machen.

---

[7] Vgl. A. Gladkirch, Religiöse Vitalität und Religionslosigkeit bei jungen Erwachsenen in Ost- und Westdeutschland nach der Wende, in: G. Pickel / K. Sammet (Hrsg.), Religion und Religiosität im vereinigten Deutschland, a.a.O., 225–243. Sowohl im Westen als auch im Osten zeigt sich ein intergenerationeller Wandel von Kirchlichkeit und subjektiver Religiosität, wenngleich Kirchlichkeit und Religiosität im Osten geringer ausgeprägt ist.

6.2. Ethik und Religion

Edward Schillebeeckx geht vom Verständnis einer „autonomen Ethik" aus und impliziert eine auf Befreiung angewiesene sittliche Vernunft. Zudem anerkennt er die Tatsache, dass die autonome Begründung der Ethik Gott nicht als Begründung für ethisches Handeln braucht, es aber durchaus möglich und sinnvoll ist, das Vernunfthandeln in den Kontext des Glaubens zu stellen.

Gleichzeitig hat er Bedenken ob einer Ethik ohne Gottesglauben und befürchtet als Folge eine „verzweifelte Utopie". Es ist zu fragen, ob der Optimismus seitens Schillebeeckx berechtigt ist, dass glaubensorientierte Ethik der sittlichen Vernunft etwas Zusätzliches geben kann, nämlich den Rekurs auf die menschliche Leidensgeschichte. Indirekt unterstellt Schillebeeckx der autonomen Ethik das Unvermögen, Unrecht und Leid in ihrem Diskurs zu berücksichten. Für diese Befürchtung gibt es, wenn man sich die aktuellen Debatten zu Ethik anschaut, eigentlich keinen Anlass. Vielmehr steht die Frage ganz anders im Raum, die aber in diesem Beitrag nicht einfach beantwortet werden kann: Was ist innerhalb des ethischen Diskurses der Mehrwert einer religiös und/oder theologischen Anreicherung eben desselben, abgesehen vielleicht von einer alternierenden Terminologie? Dieses Problem stellt sich heute im Umfeld von Agnostizismus und Indifferenz massiver dar als noch zu einer Zeit, als man den Konflikt zwischen Glaube und Atheismus zu bewältigen hatte.

6.3. Mystik und Politik

Die Definition von Schillebeeckx der beiden Begriffe „Mystik" und „Politik" ist in seinem Buch dergestalt niederschwellig gehalten, dass eine Hinterfragung der Begriffe kaum möglich ist, bestenfalls eine Einladung, sie inhaltlich aufzufächern. Interessant ist seine Idee der „politischen Liebe", die nichts anderes bedeutet, als dass der gläubige Mensch auf der Grundlage seines Glaubens sensibel wird für Unrecht und Leid, dass es zu bekämpfen gilt.

Die Befürchtung, dass Politik ohne Mystik und Gebet „barbarisch" werden könnte, klingt ein wenig pauschal. Abgesehen von eindeutig theokratisch ausgerichteten Staatsformen wird keine Politik auf der Grundlage von Mystik und Gebet praktiziert – weder in den westlichen Demokratien noch in totalitären Regimes. Allerdings zeigt die Erfahrung der Geschichte, dass gezielt antireligiös orientierte Herrschaftsformen einen stärkeren Hang haben, totalitär und diktatorisch zu werden. Das gilt allerdings auch für Staatsformen wie der Iran mit einer starken Orientierung auf Religion. Heute braucht es hinsichtlich der säkularen Staatsform und des säkularen Europa eine differenziertere Betrachtung als in diesem Aufsatz von Schillebeeckx vorgelegt, inwieweit sich Politik in diesem Kontext „barbarisch" entwickelt. In diesem Zusammenhang sollte man auch Politik und das Politische näher differenzieren, weil (Tages-)Politik und das Phänomen des Politischen zwei unterschiedliche Dinge sind.

6.4. Die Rolle der Kirche und die „politische Relevanz" des Evangeliums

Es zeigt sich, dass die Kirchen nicht gut beraten sind, sich „politisch liberalistisch" zu geben, d. h. sich vollkommen aus den sozialen und politischen Gegebenheiten der Gesellschaft herauszuhalten. In der Tat engagieren sich die Kirchen in Deutschland und Europa durchaus politisch und nehmen Stellung zu grundsätzlichen Themen, zuweilen auch zu recht tagesaktuellen Ereignissen. Die Schwierigkeit besteht heute weniger darin, dass die Kirchen sich allzu neutral verhalten oder ihre Aussagen nicht wahrgenommen werden, sondern eher, dass sie im Inhalt und auch im Tonfall den Eindruck erwecken, sich einerseits vormodern zu artikulieren und sich andererseits verschätzen hinsichtlich der Bedeutung, die sie als *global player* in der Zivilgesellschaft heute haben.

7. Fazit

Politik ist tatsächlich nicht alles. Hier hat Edward Schillebeeckx einen Alternativentwurf vorgelegt – und keineswegs nur in den Amsterdamer Vorlesungen. Es ist keine Gegenposition, die er repräsentiert, sondern ein theologisch ausgerichteter Impuls, ein sinnvolles Wechselverhältnis von Religion und Politik, von Kirche und Staat zu skizzieren und dabei auf die „politische Relevanz" des Evangeliums zu rekurrieren. Politik ist zwar nicht alles, aber sie ist alles umgreifend; Theologie kann sich nur bewähren, wenn sie sich dem Politischen erfolgreich stellt und sie das Politische gewinnbringend bereichert.

* * *

Abstract of the contribution of Thomas Eggensperger

A socio-ethically oriented re-reading of the book "Als politik niet alles is ... Jezus in de westerse cultuur" (1986) on the one hand points to Edward Schillebeeckx's fundamental view that the ever-changing relationship between religion and politics is closely tied to that of the Church and ethics. Therewith autonomous ethics is understood as a desperate utopia unwilling to be complicit to the injustice and bondage of the world. Christian ethics adds nothing to this autonomous position, yet it touches a dimension of theological life, i.e., a communal understanding that God is an agent embedded in the history of humankind. For Schillebeeckx, ethics becomes the link between the mystical and the political, linking ethics with a Christian religious belief in God, namely "political love."

On the other hand, and after a later generation's re-reading of this same book, Schillebeeckx's text inevitably faced the signs of the times. The heated topic of today does not reflect a pugnacious atheism, but rather an agnosticism that shows total indifference to religious matters. In spite of such indifference, both the Church and theology continue interpreting every experience of injustice to victims from a religious perspective. At the same time, however, the question is whether a religiously and theologically charged discourse has any benefits to offer. Furthermore, the question regarding the importance mysticism holds for politics must be posed, but also whether the Church still continues being overtly premodern to the extent of affecting its role as a global actor in civil society. In conclusion: politics is not everything, but it is in everything.

Translation from German: *Tracy Rammler*

André Lascaris

SCHILLEBEECKX IN AN AGE OF „THE IMMANENT FRAMEWORK"

What does the future hold for the theology of Edward Schillebeeckx? No one can tell? His theology may turn out to be obsolete one day, but it still may be fruitful to do theology in his spirit. I am one of the few Dutch Dominicans who did not attend Schillebeeckx's lectures at Nijmegen University because I was sent abroad for my studies. I do not pretend to be an expert of Schillebeeckx's theology, yet he had a great impact on my life. I see him as one of those who helped me to accept today's world as the place of the encounter with God. The thirteenth century theologian Thomas Aquinas was already on his way to this position, but for instance his 'exitus et reditus' (exit and return) scheme shows that he never left the Neo-Platonist paradigm behind. For me, the theology of Schillebeeckx signifies the end of the domination of Neo-Platonism and a change of paradigm.

Revelation in and through human experience

In Neo-Platonism, reality is seen as a pyramid, with the highest spiritual being at the top and matter at the bottom. Reality itself is a great stream that emanates continually from the spiritual level downwards to the lowest level of reality: matter. Human beings are right at the border between the spiritual and material reality. They are supposed to leave the material world behind as much as possible and to come closer to the source of being by living according to reason, by suppressing passions, emotions and desires. In this way they will return to God who is their source.[1] Time is

---

[1] A. Lascaris, "Faith in God in a Postmodern Age", in: *Bulletin ET* 10 (1999), 25–28.

above all a circular movement: you come from God and return to him. Christian theology rejected the emanation and replaced it by creation. But the scheme of a hierarchical reality, in which the lower material world was suspect, remained. Though one of the intuitions of Thomas Aquinas was that 'there is nothing in the intellect that had not been first in the senses'[2], he did not take the consequences of this intuition sufficiently into account. In Neo-Platonism a person tries to connect with the spiritual world in order to see everything in its light. Knowledge was already present; one had to 'remember' it by relating to the spiritual reality.

Schillebeeckx accepted the empirical character of our knowledge. God's revelation does not come to us in heavenly concepts and signs but in words, concepts, images, acts and signs which are rooted in our human condition.[3] God's revelation, thus, comes to us through our senses. We experience something that strikes us and urges us to commit ourselves. 'The penny drops': a word, a deed, a feeling gets a new dimension, volume, depth. It is a disclosure: we receive a new insight, a vision, a discernment. We receive it more or less in the way of falling in love; it happens to us and we commit ourselves to it. Though it may be argued that this or that experience may well be a projection of ourselves, for us the experience comes from the outside; it goes beyond the psychological data. It may make us ready to live our lives in accordance with this experience.[4]

In one of his last theological articles, "Christian identity. Challenging and Challenged", published in 2005 in a book in his honour, Schillebeeckx confirms his loyalty to the earth and to the world. Human beings are citizens of this world.[5] They are born here and they die here. Time is a linear movement rather than a circular one and, moreover, this linear movement is interrupted at many places in different ways so that we need a hermeneutical approach towards today's texts – written texts, movies, pictures, photo's, people – and towards those of the past when we try to read them and to make sense of them. Hermeneutics are unavoidable.

---

[2] De Veritate 2, 3 obj. 19.
[3] E. Schillebeeckx, Openbaring en theologie, Bilthoven: Nelissen, 1964, 288; ibid., Gerechtigheid en liefde, genade en bevrijding, Bloemendaal: Nelissen,1977, 25–55.
[4] I.T. Ramsey, Religious language: An empirical placing of theological phrases, New York: MacMillan, 1957, 11–54.
[5] E. Schillebeeckx, "Christelijke identiteit, uitdagend en uitgedaagd. Over de rakelingse nabijheid van de onervaarbare God", in: M. Kalsky et al. (Red.), Ons rakelings nabij. Gedaanteveranderingen van God en geloof. Ter ere van Edward Schillebeeckx, DSTS: Nijmegen – Meinema: Zoetermeer 2005, 33–44.

This is one of the consequences of the insight that God's revelation takes place in and through human experiences.

Theology as a historical event

Another consequence is finding a new way to encounter and value other religions. Within the Christian tradition people already call on different experiences. This contributes to a richer and broader understanding of God and Jesus. The Islamic, Buddhist, Hindu and Theosophical traditions may point at experiences that Christians may not know, have forgotten or interpret in a different way. Meeting the other can become a religious experience and confront us with the narrowness of our images of God and of our interpretation of the world. An important consequence is to see that human experiences and their interpretations change in the course of time. Schillebeeckx's theology cannot be an exception. Topics that played an important part in the contribution of Schillebeeckx's theology in his time may have become less important issues at present, and the other way round. He never tried to form a school to safeguard his theological work into the future. In the article "Christian identity: Challenging and Challenged", Schillebeeckx himself states that today, people, 'we children of the Enlightenment', are looking for faith, while in the Middle Ages people were believers who were looking to understand their faith. They were looking for knowledge. When we are looking for faith, we are aware that faith – it may be Christian, Muslim, Buddhist or atheist – is always beyond rationality. However, it cannot exist without rationality. Today, people are living in a different historical situation. Schillebeeckx accepts that we cannot use the medieval paradigm any more. He shows that he is still a theologian in the spirit of Thomas Aquinas when he states that we cannot experience God. We only have human experiences. These make us realise that God is the one who cannot be experienced. God is transcendent. Each believer feels that they are being carried in life by love: that God is looking for them, rather than that they are looking for God. This emphasis on human experience runs counter to the attempts of Neo-Orthodoxy and Neo-Platonism to find other ways in which God's revelation can come to us and is one example of what Schillebeeckx's theology has to offer in the future.

Situation in the Netherlands

I was told that Schillebeeckx's theology is still very popular in the United States; students seem to come together to read parts of his articles and books to one another. I do not see this happening in the Netherlands and in Western Europe very much, but I may be mistaken. During Schillebeeckx's lifetime Western Europe became more secularized. In the Netherlands births, weddings and funerals are often celebrated outside the Church, in the circle of family and friends with new rites, created for this occasion. There are seventeen million people in our country; almost one million are Muslims, they come mainly from Morocco and Turkey; there are about 800,000 Christian migrants. At the beginning of the 20th century only 3% of the population in the Netherlands had no Church connection, but in the 21st century 60% do not have a relationship with a Church. Every year 80,000 people leave the Churches. Officially there are 4.5 million Catholics, of these, 300,000 attend mass every week, and most of these are elderly people. Church attendance is decreasing every year even in so-called flourishing parishes. In the near future, hundreds of church buildings will have to be closed and demolished. Christian faith is weakening, partly because it has become difficult to see that Churches are still witnesses to Christian love, considering the incidence of child abuse by priests and the way bishops dealt with this, and also, partly because society has moved from a situation where belief in God was unproblematic to one in which it is understood to be one opinion among others.[6]

The causes of the decline in Church membership are manifold; they are partly related to Dutch history and partly to international developments. The so-called 'pillarisation' system has come to an end: in the nineteenth and twentieth century Churches and movements such as socialism and liberalism each built a 'pillar' to support society by organising political parties, schools, the media, trade unions, youth movements around themselves. In this way, they offered safety to their followers. At present, we are in a process of decentralization. Membership of clubs, unions, political parties and Churches is decreasing. Individuals reject the hidden repression expressed in the rules of communities, groups, clubs, villages, cities, civil authorities, and Churches.

---

[6] Ch. Taylor, A Secular Age, Cambridge Mass.: Harvard University Press, 2007, 3.

A secular Age

Because the Netherlands are a small country with numerous worldwide connections, an international phenomenon such as the coming of the 'secular age' has had a great impact. One of the many books on this theme was published in 2007 by the Canadian Catholic philosopher Charles Taylor: *A Secular Age*.[7] He does not quote Schillebeeckx. He writes about this process in much detail in his book of almost nine hundred pages. It is impossible to do justice to this book in this article. I only try to mention some of his most important insights. Actually, he often admits that he has no answers, certainly not ultimate answers.

Taylor describes our world as a more immanent space than Schillebeeckx does. Taylor says that within various spheres of activity – economic, political, recreational etc., we do not normally refer to God at all.[8] We see the rise of a society in which, for the first time in history, a purely sufficient humanism becomes a widely available opinion. While in the past, the place of human fullness was understood to be outside and beyond human life, it is now to be found within human life. The great invention of Western civilisation was that of an immanent order in nature whose working could be understood on its own terms.[9] Individuals are a 'buffered self'; they are not open to signals from a reality beyond our world and our time any more. They are living within an immanent framework. If some people still talk about God within this framework, God has become impersonal and is more or less immanent. Taylor writes: "The paradox of Christianity is that, on the one hand, it seems to assert the unconditional benevolence of God towards humans [...] and yet it redefines our ends so as to take us beyond flourishing."[10] God places on us a demand which goes beyond human flourishing. Doing God's will is not the same as being nice to one another. 'Thy will be done' is not the same as 'let people flourish'. One may have to give up human flourishing and the fruit is that this becomes the source of flourishing to others and a collaboration with the restoration of a fuller flourishing by God.[11]

Taylor describes archaic religion as a situation in which human beings are embedded in society, society is embedded in the cosmos and the

[7] Ibid.
[8] Ibid., 2.
[9] Ibid., 15
[10] Ibid., 151.
[11] Ibid., 17.

cosmos incorporates the divine.[12] Religious life was inseparably linked with social life. What stands out is the ubiquity of relations to spirits, forces and powers which are different from the ordinary forces of animals. The primary agency of important religious activity was the social group as a whole or some specialized agency as acting for the group. The social order in which these roles were defined tended to be sacrosanct. It was impossible to think oneself outside of one's society. Embedding in society brings with it an embedding in the cosmos. The numerous spirits and forces are intricate in the world. Even high gods may be identified with certain features of the world. The third form of embeddedness is that people pray for prosperity, a good health, a long life, fertility, natural human flourishing. Evil is part of the cosmic and social reality. People endure this evil rather than trying to oppose it. Aboriginals still seem to try to live in assent with life, good or bad, and avoid quarrelling with life. The post-Axial religions initiate a break with the three dimensions of embeddedness: social order, cosmos, human good, at least to a certain degree. The Jews make a clear break by placing God above the created reality and above human flourishing. Buddhism undercuts the dimension of the cosmos or world, because the world is dominated by the wheel of rebirth that means suffering. Christianity states that our world is disordered and must be made anew. The transcendent world became unambiguously affirmative of the human good, but both the transcendent and the human good were reconceived in the process. The transcendent may be beyond or outside the cosmos as Creator or as Nirvana. Or if it remains cosmic, it exhibits an order of pure goodness. The most fundamental change is the understanding of human flourishing. Salvation takes us beyond human flourishing. It does not accept the order of things in which both goodness and evil are present. Evil has to be fought against. Christians are called to leave their family and society as they are becoming free individuals who are living within a new relationship, God, though they learn their identity in dialogue by being inducted in a certain language. The good Samaritan would never have saved the wounded Jew if he had followed the demands of sacred social institutions. Still, the outcome of this Christian turn was not an agape community, but a disciplined society, probably because Christians tried to achieve a community of love by making use of power and violence.

According to Taylor, the way up to the present reign of the humanistic outlook is Deism. The original orthodox idea that the world was de-

---

[12] Ibid., 146–158.

signed by God changed: God is supposed to have made a plan that is directed to the good of the creatures. This plan existed before human beings emerged. One interpreted creation as an event that took place at the beginning of the history of the cosmos.

The idea that God may have further purposes as well which we do not know disappears. We owe God essentially the achievement of our own good. We determine what God's purpose is. This is confined to the mutual happiness of his creatures[13], while in the past Christians believed that God was planning a transformation of human beings so that they would become partakers of the life of God and would go beyond the limitations of their present condition. By imitating God in Christ human beings became 'divine' as the Greek fathers put it. In Deism the notion of grace disappears. Because God designed the world on our behalf, we can realize his created order. This order is impersonal, but we can read God's purpose for us from the design of our nature. God's providence consists simply in his plan for us which we understand. God is given two roles: maker of this world and judge, distributing great rewards and terrible punishments. Jesus becomes less important; he is an example. Deism hardly invoked the saving action of Christ nor did it dwell on devotion and prayer.[14] Deism made the ground fertile for the humanistic idea of human flourishing. Once the religious belief had disappeared, we are left with ordinary human desires.[15] They should not be checked, but given freedom. Everybody is allowed to desire anything.

The deists and many 'orthodox' Christians tended to think that both science and theology offer an explanation of the origin and structure of the world. However, in Deism providential interventions became less important and disappeared, partly under the influence of the conviction of the existence of universal causal laws. Faith in an afterlife evaporated. Christianity became the object of hate with its original sin, reconciliation and the 'duty' to suffer. The representatives of Deism disliked the idea of a God who intervenes and acts as an arbitrary tyrant in the eyes of most people.[16] The discovery of history, the evolution theory and biblical criticism supported those who gave up their traditional Christian faith. The idea of God relating to us through an impersonal order seemed to be

---

[13] Ibid., 221–224.
[14] Ibid., 225.
[15] Ibid., 253.
[16] Ibid., 261–276.

more attractive than the orthodox view. We can create order ourselves and God is superfluous.

Taylor points out that many complain that our world lacks meaning and that young people particularly suffer from a lack of a strong purpose in their lives. They are often profoundly dissatisfied with a life encased in the immanent order.[17] Our age suffers from a threatened loss of meaning. The particular danger of a 'buffered identity' is that nothing significant will stand out for it. Many people who are unable to accept orthodox Christianity are seeking alternative spiritual sources. Today we are confronted by a plurality of opinions and views. Because we become like the other in almost everything, the difference in faith becomes an issue: why my way, and not his?[18]

However, it is possible to have a conversion and to break out of the immanent framework. People feel that they are breaking out of a narrower framework, into a broader field, which makes sense of things in a different way. Taylor seems to have a liking for a conversion that takes place because of a rediscovery of nature, but he also mentions mystics, writers and philosophers.[19] Actually, in my opinion (and Taylor presupposes this) a 'conversion' in the opposite direction is also possible and perhaps more likely: from the discipline of the Church to the freedom of the immanent framework. One future sees religion shrinking further and further. This point of view assumes that religious transcendent views have no plausible grounds. At this moment in history the Netherlands seem to be on the way to this future. Another future is based on the presupposition that in our religious lives we are responding to a transcendent reality. An earlier sense of fullness is given a new and deeper meaning.[20]

Traces of the transcendent

If the future will be one which sees religion shrinking further and further, Schillebeeckx's theology will have no future. His thinking is far removed from Deism and from atheism. For Schillebeeckx, God is always close by. God intervenes in human history. He calls this intervention an ongoing dialogue between God and human beings[21] and he would not have pro-

---

[17] Ibid., 506.
[18] Ibid., 302–304.
[19] Ibid., 728–767.
[20] Ibid., 768f.
[21] E. Schillebeeckx, *God en mens*, Bilthoven: Nelissen, 1965, 155–164.

tested against the model Ch. Taylor mentions: 'God is like a skilled tennis player, who can always return the service'[22], though he may have found the image of the tennis player too impersonal. God is always able to respond to whatever the universe and human agency throw up. As a (critical) reader of Thomas Aquinas, Edward Schillebeeckx has always tried to safeguard God's transcendence and to prevent turning God, in some way, into a part of the universe. Though he never published a work on creation, it is clear that to him the concept of creation is a theological interpretation of world, nature, and human nature. It does not offer any scientific explanation of the world and does not make any contribution to science. Creation does not explain the origins of the physical reality; it does not give any insight into the constitution of nature or its laws.[23] 'Creation' as such does not refer to a beginning either. It is the theological expression of the conviction that the universe, the world and human beings exist thanks to a relationship with God.[24] God takes the initiative to relate to people and the universe here and now so that they exist.

Schillebeeckx is looking for traces of God in our world. The world is disordered: the inhuman situation of the poor who become poorer while the rich become richer, the inequality of women over against men, and globalisation that can make many poor people victims. This is an old theme that remains new: every human being should get justice. God is a God of justice. Schillebeeckx believes that evil will not have the last and final word. Love is stronger than death. In God evil does not exist. In God there is no darkness at all. (1 John 1, 5)

At the end of this article, I would like to mention one possible trace of God in our world: unconditional forgiveness. It is not found in nature but in the daily living together. Schillebeeckx suggests in his book *Jezus, het verhaal van een levende* that after Jesus' death the experience of the disciples that they received forgiveness of their disloyalty led to the faith that Jesus was risen.[25] This experience thus is central to the Christian tradition. The experience of being forgiven and accepted can be an intensive experience of the presence of the transcendent. It is an anthropological necessity that every human being should be treated justly. Justice is conceived as a right balance between human persons. This search for justice,

---

[22] Ch. Taylor, A Secular Age, op. cit., 277.
[23] Ph. Kennedy, "God and Creation", in: M.C. Hilkert / R.J. Schreiter (Eds.), The Praxis of the Reign of God. An Introduction to the Theology of Edward Schillebeeckx, New York: Fordham University Press, 2002, 37–58.
[24] S. Theol. I, q. 45, a 3.
[25] E. Schillebeeckx, Jezus, het verhaal van een levende, Bloemendaal: Nelissen, 1974, 319–320.

for the right balance between human beings, is based on imitation.[26] Without imitation human beings and their culture cannot exist. Learning takes place by imitating other people. We learn a language by imitating. If a child is not able to imitate, we consider it as mentally retarded. We learn to become a citizen of our country by imitating the cultural heritage of our nation, changing it, and transmitting it to the next generation. A person who is harmed should be compensated, a person who gives a benefit, has a right to receive a benefit back. The Hungarian-American family therapist Ivan Nagy points out that every person keeps an ethical bookkeeping system in which all the benefits received are kept and compared with the benefits granted.[27] Again there should be a proper balance between debts and benefits received; this is based on imitation. Otherwise one tries to balance the ethical bookkeeping system by using violence and to force other people to do justice. The alternative to trying to get a proper balance is unconditional forgiveness. By forgiving one stops imitating the perpetrator, one does not demand compensation to the full and so transcends imitation. Forgiveness is not denying guilt or smoothing over the evil act, but tries to overcome evil with good. (Rom. 12:17–21) It is a promise: 'in spite of the harm you did to me, I shall not do you any harm'. Jesus offers to eat with the tax collector, Zacchaeus, before this man promised to change his ways (Luke 19:1–10). He forgives and this makes Zacchaeus free to make restitution and to pay compensation for the harm he has done. Jesus does not ask the murderer on the cross next to him to repent but promised him that today he shall be with him in Paradise. The later penitential discipline of the Church with the demand that people feel repentant, and to fulfil painful and humiliating penitential exercises, remained within the framework of human imitation and revenge. Actually in Scripture, repentance is not a feeling but a change of behaviour. The Church did not understand Jesus' new forgiving practice.[28] Receiving and granting forgiveness transcends our normal desire to be compensated. It is an Easter experience. It transcends the ordinary human justice. The issue of justice is basic. It has an impact on every day of human life which is a continuous process of dealing with partner, children, colleagues and other people. Such an experience may inspire people to break out of the immanent framework that is dominated by imitation.

---

[26] See for the mimetic theory: R. Girard, Des choses cachées depuis de la fondation du monde, Paris: Grasset 1978.

[27] I. Nagy Boszormenyi / B.R. Krasner, Between Give and Take: A Clinical Guide to Contextual Therapy, New York: Brunner & Mazel, 1986.

[28] A. Lascaris, Neem uw verleden op. Over vergelding en vergeving, Baarn: Ten Have, 1999.

It seems to me that the future of Schillebeeckx's theology in the Netherlands is rather bleak at this very moment. It may flourish in other parts of Europe and the world. However, people in this country may try to do theology in the spirit of Schillebeeckx, a theology open to the world and to their fellow men, open to science and history, open to social developments and open to a dialogue with God, waiting for a different future, looking for faith.

* * *

Zusammenfassung des Beitrags von André Lascaris

Schillebeeckx akzeptierte den empirischen Charakter unseres Wissens. Gottes Offenbarung erreicht uns nicht in Form von himmlischen Eingebungen, sondern in Worten, Begriffen, Bildern, Handlungen und Zeichen, welche in unserer *condition humaine* verwurzelt sind. Menschen werden hier geboren und sterben auch hier. Menschliche Erfahrungen und deren Interpretationen verändern sich im Laufe der Zeit. Jede Theologie hat ihre jeweils eigene Geschichte: eine Feststellung die auch auf Schillebeeckx' Theologie bezogen werden kann, deren Zukunft momentan zumindest in den Niederlanden sehr trostlos erscheint, da das Land in vielerlei Hinsicht Teil des „säkularen Zeitalters" ist. Eines der zahlreichen Bücher zu dieser Thematik wurde 2007 von dem kanadisch-katholischen Philosophen Charles Taylor unter dem Titel „A secular Age" (dt. 2007: „Ein säkulares Zeitalter") veröffentlicht. Die Menschen sind demnach nicht mehr offen für Signale aus einer Realität jenseits unserer Welt und Zeit. Sie wollen innerhalb eines immanenten Rahmens leben und wachsen. Wenn einige Individuen dann innerhalb dieses Rahmens immer noch von Gott sprechen, so handelt es sich dabei meistens um einen nichtpersonalen und mehr oder weniger immanenten Gott. In diesem Zusammenhang weist Taylor darauf hin, dass vielen Menschen ein Sinn und insbesondere jungen Menschen ein Ziel in ihrem Leben fehlt. Sie sind häufig zutiefst unzufrieden mit einem Leben, welches vollkommen in eine immanente Ordnung eingelassen ist, weswegen sich die Frage nach einer Umkehr und dem Ausbruch aus dieser vorgegebenen Rahmenordnung stellt. Es scheint mir, dass eine mögliche Spur Gottes in unserer Welt die der bedingungslosen Vergebung ist. Schillebeeckx bezieht sich in seiner Interpretation der Auferstehung hierauf. Dies könnte auch der neue Ausgangspunkt einer lebendigen Theologie sein.

Übersetzung aus dem Englischen: *Bernhard Kohl*

Maximilian Halstrup

THEOLOGIE 2.0!

Faktizität und Selbstrealisierung als Basiskategorien einer lebensweltlich verpflichteten Hermeneutik des Glaubens

Einführung: Honest to people

Der Titel meiner Ausführungen, Theologie 2.0, mag sperrig sein, kann doch der nicht geneigte Leser unterstellen, dass ich die Theologie 1.0 überwinden wolle. Der Internet- und kulturaffine Leser jedoch wird das perpetuierende Beta, das Nie-fertig-werden-können, und nicht etwa das Überwinden des Fertigen würdigen können. Inhalt dieser Ausführungen ist jedoch nicht die Differenz von Theologie 1.0 und 2.0, sondern vielmehr der *Kern* einer Theologie 2.0, die als lebensweltlich verpflichtete Hermeneutik des christlichen Glaubens relevant sein will.

Die Lebenswelt – und hier auch mitgemeint – die digitale Lebenswelt als Ausgangspunkt nachfolgender Überlegungen zu Grunde zu legen, ist meines Erachtens zwar angemessen, leider jedoch nicht komplexitätsreduzierend: So schrieb auch Edward Schillebeeckx „Konfrontiert mit den unverkennbaren Schwierigkeiten von den heutigen Christen in einer säkularisierten Welt, habe ich [...] die Tatsachen ruhig anschauen wollen, aber fühlte nichtsdestoweniger einen fast fieberartigen Andrang, weil es eine dringende Problematik von lebenden Menschen, Laien und Priestern, ist, die von allen Seiten auf uns alle zukommt."[1]

---

[1] „Geconfronteerd met de onmiskenbare moeilijkheden van de hedendaagse christenen in een ‚geseculariseerde wereld', heb ik de feiten rustig onder ogen willen zien, maar voelde niettemin een bijna koortsachtige aandrang, omdat het duidelijk een dringende problematiek is van levende mensen, leken en priesters, die van alle kanten op ons allen toekomt". E. Schillebeeckx, Het nieuwe Godsbeeld, secularisatie en politiek, in: *Tijdschrift voor Theologie* 8 (1968), 44–66, hier 44.

Stand in den 1960er Jahren noch die Problematik der Säkularisierung im Fokus theologischer Aufmerksamkeit und findet diese Thematik ihren Nachhall und Verschärfung in jüngeren Studien, die auch durch die deutsche Wiedervereinigung angeschärft wurden, so ist es ratsam, bei einer theologischen Grundlagenanalyse auch weitere *soziotechnische Faktoren* zu berücksichtigen. Wie der Titel *Theologie 2.0* insinuiert, ist die theologische Forschung vor die Aufgabe gestellt, die digitale (R)Evolution als zentralen Gegenstand theologischer Arbeit zu bedenken, weil dieses Existenzial auch ein wesentliches Merkmal eines heutigen Selbstverständnisses ist. Dieses Selbstverständnis ist von Theologen freilich zu adressieren. Edward Schillebeeckx charakterisierte diese Adressatenorientierung der Theologie: „Denn wenn ich die Voraussetzung für den Glauben in einer modernen Welt richtig sehe, bedeutet dies, daß Katechese und Verkündigung nicht nur die heutigen menschlichen Erfahrungen erhellen müssen, sondern daß sie auch so verantwortlich, so genau und suggestiv wie möglich entfalten müssen, was die christliche Daseinsorientierung in unserer Zeit für die Menschen konkret bedeuten kann. Menschen müssen wissen, mit welchem ‚Suchprojekt' sie sich befassen und worauf sie sich einlassen wollen."[2]

Somit sollte Theologie adressatenorientiert profiliert sein. „Versteht es auch die Kirche nicht, ein angemessenes Begriffssystem zur Erklärung der christlichen Botschaft und des christlichen Suchprojektes zu verwenden, so ist in der Tat den meisten Menschen von vornherein die Lust genommen, nach *diesem* Suchprojekt als möglicher Deutung ihrer Erfahrungen zu greifen."[3] Selbstverständlich gelingt dieses in der jetzigen Zeit nicht (mehr) durch eine faktische Selbstimmunisierung mittels apodiktischer Wahrheitsbehauptung, sondern nur im kritischen, in der Dimension menschlicher Erfahrung zu verortendem Dialog. „Irgendwie muß – mit dem ‚Suchprojekt' der kirchlichen Verkündigung als ‚Wünschelrute' – mit heutigen menschlichen Erfahrungen eine *christliche* Erfahrung gemacht werden"[4].

---

[2] Ders., Die Auferstehung Jesu als Grund der Erlösung. Zwischenbericht über die Prolegomena zu einer Christologie. Aus dem Niederländischen von H. Zulauf (Quaestiones disputatae Bd. 78), Freiburg/Br. 1979, 10.

[3] Ebd., 17.

[4] Ders., Gott – Die Zukunft des Menschen. Aus dem Niederländischen von H. Zulauf u. H.A. Mertens, Mainz 1969, 159. Vgl. zur Kulturtheologie einer lateinamerikanischen Perspektive L. Boff, Gott kommt früher als der Missionar. Neuevangelisierung für eine Kultur des Lebens und der Freiheit. Aus dem brasilianischen Portugiesisch von H. Goldstein, Düsseldorf 1991. Vgl. hierzu auch E. Schillebeeckx, Die Auferstehung Jesu als Grund der Erlösung, a.a.O., 46. Vgl. auch ebd., 74f: „Für den Christen, der im Licht der christlichen Erfah-

Wesentliche Elemente der Aufgabenstellung einer Theologie 2.0 nach Schillebeeckx sind damit klar benannt. Die konkrete, erfahrungs- und faktizitätsbezogene Intonation der Rede von Gott ist damit kein theologisches Surplus, sondern Bedingung der Möglichkeit einer angemessenen theologischen Artikulation. Wird diese wesentliche Form theologischen Arbeitens nicht befolgt, kann nur noch die hermetische Geschlossenheit der Welt des Glaubens und der Erfahrungswelt alltäglicher Lebenserfahrung und damit die gegenseitige Unvermittelbarkeit konstatiert werden. Weitsichtig beschreibt Schillebeeckx den Motivationsgrund seines Arbeitens: „Die Absicht ist, zu verhindern, dass für jemand, der von Herzen an der neuen Kultur teilnimmt, der Glaube eine nicht zu vollziehende Haltung bleibt, die ihn zu einem weltfremden Menschen macht, weil er gezwungen ist, in zwei Welten zu leben: in der Welt der Wissenschaft und der Technik, in der er seine weltliche Aufgabe erfüllt, und in einer Art Phantasiewelt, die er in seinem Glauben betreten muß. [...] Ich meine einfach bekennen zu müssen, dass wir als Gläubige nur innerhalb der Kultur, die die unsere ist, erwarten dürfen, mit dem Glauben ins reine zu kommen."[5]

Eine fertige Theologie 2.0 kann ich hier nicht anbieten. Ich unternehme lediglich den Versuch, die „dringende Problematik von lebenden Menschen [...] die von allen Seiten auf uns alle zukommt"[6], zu untersuchen. Ich bin mir aber sicher, dass eine Theologie nach Schillebeeckx eine auf die Zeit antwortende angemessene theologische Konzeption bereitstellen kann.

Konkretion: Digitale (R)Evolution

Die Bedeutung von Wiki-Systemen auch für die alltägliche Lebenspraxis dürfte dem interessierten Zeitgenossen bekannt sein: *Wikipedia, Wikileaks*

---

rungstradition mit seinen menschlichen ambivalenten Erfahrungen diese christliche Lebenserfahrung gemacht hat, ist das christliche Glaubens-Credo kein Suchprojekt mehr, sondern eine feste Lebensüberzeugung, die sich zu Mystik und entsprechender Lebenspraxis entwickeln wird. [...] Bei aller Überzeugung bleibt er ein offener Jemand. Mit anderen Worten, die feste Überzeugung wird im Hinblick auf neue Erfahrungen immer wieder zum ‚Suchprojekt', das in und an den neuen Erfahrungen getestet werden wird." Vgl. hierzu auch W. Schürger, Wirklichkeit Gottes und Wirklichkeit der Welt. Theologie im Konflikt der Interpretationen (Beiträge zur Dogmatik, Ethik und ökumenischen Theologie Bd. 12), Stuttgart 2002, 68–70.

[5] E. Schillebeeckx, Gott – Die Zukunft des Menschen, a.a.O., 158f.
[6] Ders., Die Auferstehung Jesu als Grund der Erlösung, a.a.O., 10.

und *Gutenplag-Wiki* seien hier stellvertretend für auch im industriellen Kontext vorzufindende Wikis genannt. Es sei bemerkt, dass gerade bei Wikileaks die digitale (R)Evolution ihr menschliches Antliz paradigmatisch offenbart. Selbiges gilt m. E. auch auf das Gutenplag-Wiki. Julian Assange kann als Ikone eines Paradigmenwechsels von der Industrie- zur Informationsgesellschaft verstanden werden – Transformation der Gutenberg-Galaxie zu hypermedialem Selbstverständnis –, mit gleichwohl allen noch nicht aufgearbeiteten und sich auch nur teilweise andeutenden Implikationen: Authentizität und technische Möglichkeiten sind hier zu nennen; Ebenso die kollaborative Suche nach dem wahren Kern (Gutenplag-Wiki), die aufgrund der Möglichkeiten digitaler Kommunikation auf Schwarmintelligenz setzen kann. Ein Phänomen, das in dieser Form bisher weder bekannt war – noch realistisch erschien. Ausgehend von dem Bewusstsein der Selbstrealisierungsmöglichkeiten des Menschen kann Josef Früchtl nach einer angemessenen Interpretationskategorie des oben genannten Sachverhaltes in der jetzigen Zeit fragen: „Wenn der affirmative Charakter der bürgerlich-idealistischen Kultur sich darin konzentriert, die Individuen zu Pflicht und Arbeit zu verhalten und ihnen Glück nur in Augenblicken des Kunstgenusses oder der industriell produzierten Unterhaltung zu gewähren, dann zeigt die gegenwärtige, im ideell-symbolischen Sinn verstandene Kultur einen deutlich postaffirmativen Charakter: das Alte, die Pflicht- und Arbeitsethik, wirkt noch nach, aber das Neue, die Authentizitätsethik, ist dennoch stärker."[7] Diese Koinzidenz von technischen Möglichkeiten digitaler Selbstrealisierung und dem Aufkommen der – auch durch die technischen Möglichkeiten entscheidend und nachhaltig ermöglichten – Authentizitätsethik bedingt die Herausforderung des Umgangs mit einer kategorial neuen Ausgangssituation. Diese Ausgangssituation ist von fundamental neuer Bedeutung für theologisches Selbstverständnis.

Die technischen Möglichkeiten sind auch im theologisch-philosophisch-kulturdiagnostischen Denkraum thematisiert worden. Es geht in den folgenden Ausführungen nicht darum, zu klären, ob das Internet vom ontologischen Status „schon die ganze Substanz" ist, wie Wolfgang Welsch insinuiert[8], sondern ausgehend von der Prämisse, dass

[7] J. Früchtl, Über den postaffirmativen Charakter der Kultur, in: Th. Düllo u. a. (Hrsg.), Einführung in die Kulturwissenschaft (Münsteraner Einführungen. Interdisziplinäre Einführungen Bd. 2.), Münster 1998, 39–58, hier 51.
[8] W. Welsch, Die Doppelnatur der Gegenwart. Virtualisierung und Revalidierung, in: G. Vattimo / W. Welsch (Hrsg.), Medien – Welten – Wirklichkeiten, München 1998. Vgl. hierzu auch H.-H. Gander, Interpretation – Situation – Vernetzung. Hermeneutische Überlegun-

das Internet als Raum des Lebens aufgefasst werden kann, sich – neben den oben angesprochenen Grundlagenproblemen – der weiteren Qualifikation der Möglichkeiten des Internet als vernetzter Kommunikation, als *shared spaces* (E. Borgmann) zu widmen.[9] Dies ist insofern von Bedeutung, da durch die Entwicklung des Internet auch unsere Weltsicht maßgeblich und nachhaltig modifiziert wird.[10] Unbestritten wird die Emergenz des Internet als eine wesentliche Entwicklung der letzten Jahrzehnte angesehen werden können. Von besonderem theologischen Interesse ist die Beschäftigung mit diesem Thema, da sowohl Kreativität und Kollaboration in besonderer Weise in der *virtuellen* Welt ausgeübt wird, die zudem aufgrund ihres eigenen symbolischen Universums bisweilen „neue Transzendenzerfahrungen" ermöglicht als auch Zeichen eines neuen Selbstverständnisses, des Verständnisses der Welt als einer *flat world*, ist.[11]

gen zum Selbst- und Weltbezug im multimedialen Zeitalter, in: U.H.J. Körtner (Hrsg.), Hermeneutik und Ästhetik. Die Theologie des Wortes im multimedialen Zeitalter, Neukirchen-Vluyn 2001, 19–33.

[9] Vgl. hierzu insbes. den Vortrag von T. Zondervan („Jongeren en religie in de netwerksamenleving. De betekenis van Schillebeeckx' ‚negative ecclesiologie'", 2005): http://www.dsts.nl/Zondervan_lezing.html [9.8.2011]. Zondervan erläutert hier die Bedeutung von Schillebeeckx' negativer Ekklesiologie als Interpretationsrahmen, der es ermöglicht, das gegenwärtig zu konstatierende Phänomen einer *connected society*, eines digitalen Lifestyles zu qualifizieren und damit für eine religiöse Interpretation zu öffnen. Vgl. zur digitalen Zeitsignatur auch die aktuelle Studie [2009] LIFE – Digitales Leben: www.studie-life.de [9.8.2011]. Diese Studie verbindet sowohl Experten- als auch Konsumentenmeinungen (56 Experten, 10.545 Konsumenten). Nur folgerichtig erscheint es, dass die CeBIT im Jahr 2009 die digitale Gesellschaft zu einem der Hauptthemen gemacht hat und mit dem Slogan „Webciety – Internet is coming home" beworben hat. Vgl. zu aktuellen Angeboten www.webciety.de [7.11.2011].

[10] Vgl. R. Reichert, Amateure im Netz. Selbstmanagement und Wissenstechnik im Web 2.0, Bielefeld 2008, 150: „Auf 70 Terabyte Bilddaten und 500 GB Indexdateien entfaltet das Computerprogramm Google Earth göttliche Perspektiven und allmächtige Übersichten. Die informationstechnischen Tools, mit denen man Geodaten erfassen, verwalten, visualisieren, manipulieren und ausgeben kann, gewinnen zunehmend an Bedeutung und beeinflussen maßgeblich unsere Weltsicht." Vgl. auch A.T.M. Reinders, Zugänge zur religiösen Dimension des Cyberspace (Literatur – Medien – Religion Bd. 16), Münster 2006, die konstatiert, dass der User ein Weltschöpfer sei; ebd., 136. Selbstverständlich muss der Schöpfer auch verehrt werden: „Dieses verehrungsähnliche Verhalten zeigt an, wie Menschen in der Gesellschaft mit einer selbstüberfordernden Tendenz, sich selbst als sinnproduktiv erweisen zu müssen, zu krankhaft scheinenden Gottessimulationen greifen können." Ebd., 138.

[11] J. Herrmann / A. Mertin, Die Herausforderung der neuen Medien für Theologie und Kirche, in: B. Heller (Hrsg.), Kulturtheologie heute? Hofgeismarer Protokolle (Tagungsbeiträge aus der Arbeit der Evangelischen Akademie Hofgeismar Bd. 311), Hofgeismar 1997, 116–124, hier 119. M. E. noch nicht systematisch-hermeneutisch erkundet und qualifiziert ist die Konsequenz des von Th.L. Friedman luzide herausgearbeiteten Genesismoments und dessen Konsequenzen; vgl. Th.L. Friedman, The world is flat: A brief history of the twenty-first century, New York 2005. Die mit der Emission der Netscape-Aktie am 8.9.1995 und der

An dieser Stelle muss ich die Benennung von einigen Aspekten soziotechnischer Analyse unterbrechen.[12] Dennoch: Aus vorangegangenen durch den Browser Netscape möglich gewordenen revolutionären Kommunikationsmöglichkeiten ermöglichten auch weniger technophilen Personen eine grenzen- und sprachüberschreitende, in der Regel kostenlose Kommunikation, und ließen die zukünftige Entwicklung vorausahnen. „When you take these first three flatteners together, what you get is the genesis moment for the flat world because what the Netscape revolution did was bring people to people, connectivity together like never before. People could connect with people thanks to that Netscape revolution like never before." http://www.imf.org/external/np/tr/2005/tr050408bf.htm [12.5.2009].

[12] Zugrunde gelegt wird hier der Begriff des sozio-technischen Systems (u. a. durch Thomas Herrmann), der in seiner begrifflichen Fassung – hier im Zusammenhang der Qualifikation des Internet – schon darauf aufmerksam macht, dass das Internet weit mehr ist als eine rein technische Plattform, sondern sich in seiner Vollgestalt wesentlich auch durch seinen Gebrauch realisiert. Für weitergehende Beschäftigungen sei auf die Begriffe *social computing* und *social software* verwiesen. In einer allgemeingültigen Definition der durch Nutzer generierten Internet-Enzyklopädie Wikipedia steht: „Social software enables people to rendezvous, connect or collaborate through computer-mediated communication. Many advocates of using these tools believe (and actively argue or assume) that these create actual community, and have adopted the term ‚online communities' to describe the social structures that they claim result." http://en.wikipedia.org/wiki/Social_software [11.1.2007]. Dass hiermit ein fundamentaler Unterschied zu herkömmlichen Massenmedien besteht, steht außer Frage. In diesem Zusammenhang hat sich auch der Begriff der virtuellen Präsenz herausgebildet: „Virtual presence means being present at virtual locations. In particular, the term virtual presence denotes presence on World Wide Web locations pages and Web sites which are identified by URLs. People who are browsing a Web site are considered to be virtually present at Web locations. Virtual presence is a social software in the sense that people meet on the Web by chance or intentionally. The ubiquitous (in the Web space) communication transfers behaviour patterns from the real world and Virtual worlds to the Web." http://en.wikipedia.org/wiki/Social_ software [11.1.2007]. Sämtliche Links verweisen auf Wikipedia.
Hier sind bisher die theologischen Implikationen nur unzureichend bedacht worden. Vgl. hierzu auch grundsätzlich Ch. Frey, Gottes Geist, Menschengeist und die Konstruktion der Wirklichkeit im Zeitalter der Information, in: J. Roloff / H.G. Ulrich (Hrsg.), Einfach von Gott reden. Ein theologischer Diskurs (FS F. Mildenberger), Stuttgart 1994, 111–123. Der Aktualisierungsbedarf der Grundannahme von Frey ist selbstevident. Vgl. zum Ganzen auch Ch. Fuchs, Internet and society: Social Theory in the Information Age, New York 2008. Fuchs beschreibt die durch die technische Entwicklung evozierte Veränderung einer *social theory*. Als zu favorisierendes Paradigma arbeitet Fuchs das Konzept der Selbst-Organisation heraus. Diese wird durch das Internet als *techno-social system* gefördert; vgl. ebd., 121–139. Die Dynamik der Entwicklung war auch in diesem Maße nicht vorhersehbar. In einer theologischen Analyse dieser Entwicklung geht es jedoch nicht nur um Gottesdienste im Internet, sondern viel eher um das Internet als Kulturraum. Die Diskussion kann inhaltlich weitergeführt werden ausgehend von der grundlegenden Positionsbestimmung, wie sie vorliegt bei St. Böntert, Gottesdienste im Internet. Perspektiven eines Dialogs zwischen Internet und Liturgie, Stuttgart 2005; vgl. hierzu auch http://mimaxxblog.blogspot.com/2005/10/gottes-dienst-stefan-bntert.html [15.6.2009]. Die digitale Ära wird unser menschliches Selbst- und Weltverständnis nachhaltig beeinflussen. Der Trend, die Sozialität des Internet als fundamentalen Faktor anzuerkennen, ist durch das Web 2.0-Phänomen deutlich sichtbar und deckt sich mit der konzeptuellen Beschreibung des Selbstverwirklichungsphänomens und

Überlegungen dürfte deutlich geworden sein, dass die Zeit – sowohl in der Kirche wie auch in der Theologie – reif für ein digitales Aggiornamento ist![13]

des postaffirmativen Charakters der Kultur. Dieser wird gerade hier in paradigmatischer Weise deutlich. In dieser Evolutionsstufenentwicklung ist in besonderer Weise die Relevanz des benutzergenerierten Inhaltes des Intranets von Bedeutung. Gleichwohl soll damit nicht die Rolle der technisch versierten und interessierten Inhaltsproduzenten der früheren Evolutionsstufe geschmälert werden. Ebenso muss die Rolle des Usenet seit den frühesten Tagen des Internet bei einer umfangreichen Würdigung in Anschlag gebracht werden. Vgl. hierzu auch http://de.wikipedia.org/wiki/Usenet [10.8.2011]. Unbezweifelbar ist die Bereitstellung eigener Inhalte in der gegenwärtigen Entwicklungsstufe des Internet auf einem noch nicht gekannten Niveau, das vermutlich mit dem Internet der Dinge und der fest verankerten lebensweltlichen Nutzung dieser Technologie mit Hilfe von Smart Clients wie Mobilphonen, Tabs, Netbooks etc. eine neue Qualität erreicht. Die hierdurch ermöglichten Modifikationen menschlichen Selbstverständnisses sind augenscheinlich und werden in verschiedensten Disziplinen wirtschaftlich-kultureller Selbstrealisierung in eine produktive Vorhabe gebracht. Die Evolutionsstufe vom Web 1.0 zum Web 2.0 ist m. E. als bedeutender zu bewerten als die sich abzeichnenden Weiterentwicklungen Web 3.0 (semantisches Web) oder Web 3d (dreidimensionales Web). Der zur Zeit Karriere machende Begriff des *user generated content* wird hier thematisch. Im Unterschied zu anderen Massenmedien geht es nicht nur um die hauptsächliche *top-down*-Bewegung, sondern auch wesentlich um die *bottom-up*-Bewegung und somit um neue Kommunikationsformen auch kirchlicher Selbstrealisierung, die bisher nur unzureichend genutzt werden. A.M.T. Reinders, Zugänge zur religiösen Dimension des Cyberspace, a.a.O., arbeitet wesentliche Aspekte der religiösen Dimension des Cyberspace sehr luzide heraus. Insbes. die Thematisierung Gottes unter den Gesichtspunkten *top-down* und *bottom-up* (ebd., 336) ist angesichts des hier thematisierten Horizonts sehr präzise. Reinders ist prinzipiell zuzustimmen, dass es hier insbesondere um *bottom-up*-Phänomene geht, die durch die Elaboration bzw. Nutzung des Cyberspace in den Fokus rücken können. M. E. ist diese Studie an diesem Punkt jedoch erweiterbar. Denn eine eingehendere offenbarungstheologisch-hermeneutische Untersuchung (über die ebd., 145–152, referierten Thesen hinaus) wäre an diesem Punkt zuträglich gewesen. Im Ergebnis richtig bestimmt Reinders die Notwendigkeit der Modifikation kirchlicher Kommunikation, ebd., 328: „Sind neue Medien ein Lernfeld für kirchliche Arbeit, dann auch im Stil der Kommunikation. Kirchliche Kommunikation hat eine Tendenz von oben nach unten, *top-down*. Nicht nur unter dem Aspekt der Deprivatisierung der Religion in der Postmoderne ist ein differenzierter Kommunikationsstil erforderlich. Die medialen Erfahrungen zeigen, dass ein hierarchischer Interaktions- und Kommunikationsstil im Cyberspace kaum akzeptiert wird – sieht man von hierarchischen Strukturen in Kirchenversammlungen virtueller Realitäten ab. Wenn das Internet ein Medium zur kirchlichen Verkündigung sein soll, ist eine Überprüfung, ggf. eine Korrektur des Kommunikationsstils geboten." Partizipation ist nicht nur ein im Zusammenhang der systematischen Rekonstruktion der Schöpfungslehre Schillebeeckx' beanspruchte Zentralbegriff, sondern auch ein Begriff, der in dem hier vorgestellten Kontext von zentraler Relevanz ist.

[13] St. Böntert, Gottesdienste im Internet, a.a.O., 290f. Vgl. zum Ganzen auch K. Müller, Verdoppelte Realität – virtuelle Wahrheit? Erkenntnistheoretische, sozialphilosophische und anthropologische Konsequenzen der „Neuen Medien", in: R. Funiok / U.R. Schmälzle / Ch.H. Werth, Medienethik – die Frage der Verantwortung, Bonn 1999, 75–92; A.M.T. Reinders, Zugänge und Analysen zur religiösen Dimension des Cyberspace, a.a.O. – So steht in der Tat, wie eine Webmasterin des Vatikans [http://www.vatican.va] [15.6.2009] in

Eckpunkte einer weiteren Ausarbeitung einer Theologie 2.0 sind mit den Begriffswelten Faktizität, Selbstverständnis und Selbstrealisierung, Erfahrung, und – mit Blick auf das virulente Postfix Theologie *2.0* – mit dem Begriff U*ser Experience* benannt. Gerade mit diesem *Terminus technicus* digitaler Selbstrealisierung und dem Design von sozio-technischen Systemen ist sowohl ein gemeinsamer Ausgangspunkt der Rede von Erfahrungen benannt – wie auch – durch die wirkmächtige Disziplin des User Experience Design (UX) ein konkreter Weg aufgezeigt, Erfahrungen angemessen als integrales Moment von Interaktions-, technischen und Selbstverständigungssystemen zu bringen. Ausgehend von diesem unhintergehbaren Ankerpunkt theologischer Methodik kann auch die Frage menschlicher Freiheit erneut thematisiert werden. Der in diesem Zusammenhang relevante Freiheitsbegriff ist jedoch in einem direkteren konstitutionslogischen Zusammenhang von Existenz und Kultur zu verorten: „Aus uns selbst sind wir nur Möglichkeit zur Freiheit und ist die Freiheit noch eine Leere, sie hat noch keinen Inhalt; durch die Kultur füllt die Freiheit kreativ diese Leere."[14] Und da Theologie ein interdependentes Geschehen ist, ist für eine angemessene Theologie die sorgsame Analyse des jeweiligen Kontextes einer sich stets verändernden Situation von besonderer Relevanz.[15]

---

einem Interview [http://www.podtech.net/home/2153/meet-the-techie-sister-behind-vaticans-website] [9.8.2011] konstatiert hat, die Hauptaufgabe der Webpräsenz des Vatikans darin, Informationen herauszubringen. Dennoch dürften auch hier mit mehr Mut und Offenheit die durch die Neuentwicklung des Internet, fast schon Inflationär unter dem Schlagwort web2.0 subsumiert, eröffneten Chancen für einen Dialog mit der Welt genutzt werden. Vgl. dazu auch St. Böntert „E-vangelisation" oder „mit Gott @ Internet"? Annäherungen zu einer theologischen Würdigung des Internet, in: P. Lüning / P. Neuner (Hrsg.), Theologie im Dialog (FS H. Wagner), Münster, 2004, 21–38. Bereits Heidegger hat auf den positiven Gehalt der Technik im Hinblick auf die Wahrheitsfrage aufmerksam gemacht; vgl. M. Heidegger, Die Technik und die Kehre, Pfullingen 1962, 12: „Die Technik ist also nicht bloß ein Mittel. Die Technik ist eine Weise des Entbergens. Achten wir darauf, dann öffnet sich uns ein ganz anderer Bereich für das Wesen der Technik. Es ist der Bereich der Entbergung, d. h. der Wahrheit." In der heutigen Zeit stellt sich dieses Problem mit zunehmender Virulenz. Vgl. dazu J. Werbick, Kirche. Ein ekklesiologischer Entwurf für Studium und Praxis, Freiburg/Br. 1994, 317: „In einer sich ausweitenden und zunehmend ‚vernetzten' Kommunikationsgesellschaft wird die Rede von der communio/participatio unweigerlich die ‚Kommunikation' als ekklesiologischen Grundvorgang mit ansprechen. Und sie wird die Frage aufwerfen müssen, welche verschiedenen ‚Kommunikationsrollen' das Kommunikationsgeschehen Kirche prägen und bei ‚seiner Wahrheit' halten."

[14] E. Schillebeeckx, Christus und die Christen. Die Geschichte einer neuen Lebenspraxis. Aus dem Niederländischen von H. Zulauf, Freiburg/Br. 1977, 796.
[15] Vgl. hierzu bes. R.J. Schreiter, The New Catholicity: Theology between the Global and the Local, New York 1997.

Fundamentalanalyse: Der Referenzrahmen der Faktizität

Zwei Gewährsmänner einer Theologie 2.0 sind mit Edward Schillebeeckx und Martin Heidegger zu benennen. Die Lebenswelt, die konkrete Kultur, in der Gläubige leben, sollte als systematischer Ausgangspunkt der Theologie referenziert werden, um die Theologie überhaupt als lebenspraktisch bedeutsam ausweisen zu können. Im ersten Schritt werden einige philosophische Implikationen des Erfahrungsbezuges weiter definiert werden. Ausgehend von diesem faktizitätsorientierten Erfahrungsbezug ist auch der Ort benannt, der Schillebeeckx als implizites Raster und wegweisender Horizont diente.

Heidegger

Der Erfahrungsbezug der Theologie muss gewährleistet sein und ineins damit ist auch ein sicherer Ausgangspunkt gefunden, der es ermöglicht, den Menschen als Hörer der Botschaft, ihrem Vermittler und wesentlichem Teil der Geschichte Gottes in seinem Kontext angemessen zu denken. So fragt auch Martin Heidegger konsequent in seinem sogenannten *Natorp-Bericht*[16], „(o)b nicht schon die Idee einer Religionsphilosophie, und gar wenn sie ihre Rechnung ohne die Faktizität des Menschen macht, ein purer Widersinn ist?"[17] Das Dasein ist In-der-Welt-sein. Dieses ist

[16] Im Herbst 1922 arbeitete Heidegger ein Bewerbungsschreiben für die Marburger und die Göttinger Philosophische Fakultät aus, einen sog. Natorp-Bericht, der zu seiner Berufung auf das Extraordinariat mit Stellung und Rechten eines Ordinarius an der Philipps-Universität zu Marburg führte. Diesen Bericht mit dem Titel „Phänomenologische Interpretationen zu Aristoteles (Anzeige der hermeneutischen Situation)" verstand er zugleich als Einleitung zu dem geplanten Werk über Aristoteles. Vgl. hierzu auch M. Heidegger, Phänomenologische Interpretationen ausgewählter Abhandlungen des Aristoteles zur Ontologie und Logik (Heidegger GA Bd. 62), Frankfurt/M. 2005.

[17] Ebd., 246. Vgl. hierzu auch B. Caspar, Die Gründung einer philosophischen Theologie im Ereignis, in: *Dialegesthai. Rivista telematica di filosofia* 5 (2003) [http://mondodomani.org/dialegesthai/bc01.htm] [9.8.2011]: „Bis zu Heidegger hat man das Menschenleben als Geschichte in einen a priori festliegenden zeitlichen Rahmen eingetragen, in dem die Gegenwart einem Punkt oder einer kurzen Strecke zwischen dem Früheren und dem Späteren entspricht; Heidegger, der diese Datierung keineswegs umstürzen will, macht darüber hinaus auf eine genuine geschichtliche Zeitlichkeit des Menschseins aufmerksam, die in gewisser Weise überholt und eine Quelle der Möglichkeit von Geschichte ist." H. Schmitz, Zeit und Freiheit, in: K. Cramer (Hrsg.), Theorie der Subjektivität, Frankfurt/M. 1987, 344–345, 360–372, 367, rekonstruiert, dass bei Heidegger die Anerkennung der Faktizität die Bedingung der Möglichkeit von verantworteter Rede vom Menschen und Geschichte überhaupt darstellt. Das von Schmitz inkriminierte Problem fundamentalontologischer Überhöhung der Existenz, welches sich gleichwohl bei Rudolf Bultmann noch deutlicher abzeichnet, kann an dieser Stelle nicht weiter geklärt werden. Vgl. ebd.: „Zugleich

seine „Grundverfassung"[18]. Es lebt in einer immer schon vorläufigen Ausgelegtheit: „das Dasein ist zunächst und zumeist *bei* der besorgten ‚Welt'"[19]. Es ist, da „von ihm selbst als eigentlichem Selbstseinkönnen zunächst immer schon abgefallen [...] an die Welt verfallen."[20] Schillebeeckx nimmt genau dieses diagnostische Moment in sein Konzept faktizitätsorientierter Theologie auf. „Wir sind, wie auch immer, selbst als endliche Wesen poniert, wie Heidegger es ausdrückt."[21] „Die Geworfenheit ist nicht nur nicht eine ‚fertige Tatsache', sondern auch nicht ein abgeschlossenes Faktum. Zu dessen Faktizität gehört, daß das Dasein, *solange* es ist, was es ist, im Wurf bleibt und in die Uneigentlichkeit des Man hineingewirbelt wird. Die Geworfenheit, darin sich die Faktizität phänomenal sehen lässt, gehört zum Dasein, dem es in seinem Sein um dieses selbst geht. Dasein existiert faktisch."[22]

Schillebeeckx

Auch Schillebeeckx hat sich in seiner Analyse des Wirklichkeitsbezugs im Prinzip an die Ausarbeitung des frühen Heideggers angelehnt. In den 1960er Jahren im engen theologischen Kontext dieser grundsätzlichen Suche nach einer angemessenen Denkform der Wirklichkeitserkenntnis konnte Schillebeeckx schreiben: „Im Licht der ‚Hermeneutik der Faktizität' Heideggers erhalten die alte Streitfrage um den ‚sensus litteralis' und den ‚sensus plenior' der Schrift sowie auch die ökumenische Frage nach dem Verhältnis des Dogmas (im katholischen Sinn) zur Schrift unerwartete Perspektiven. Es geht um die Zukunft der Schrift selbst."[23]

---

aber verstopft er [Heidegger; M.H.] diese Quelle, indem er die Geschichtlichkeit so überspitzt, daß sie sich mit wirklich verlaufender Geschichte nicht mehr verträgt, es sei denn durch Verfallen in Uneigentlichkeit." Da an dieser Stelle nur die geschichtliche Zeitlichkeit des Menschen beansprucht wird, ist der Rekurs auf Heidegger in dieser Studie nicht Abschluss des Denkens über eine angemessene und damit faktizitätsorientierte spekulative Entfaltung der Theologie im Gefolge Schillebeeckx', sondern damit vielmehr nur ein Anfang benannt.

[18] M. Heidegger, Sein und Zeit, Tübingen ¹⁷1993, 176. Vgl. hierzu auch M. Halstrup, Christsein ist zunächst und zumeist In-der-Welt-sein. Eine Implikation dialogfähiger Theologie, in: P. Lüning / P. Neuner (Hrsg.) Theologie im Dialog, a.a.O., 209–232.
[19] M. Heidegger, Sein und Zeit, a.a.O., 175.
[20] Ebd.
[21] E. Schillebeeckx, Menschen. Die Geschichte von Gott. Aus dem Niederländischen von H. Zulauf, Freiburg/Br. 1990, 112. Vgl. auch ders, Die Gläubigen, die anderen und die „Umwelt" [1960], in: ders., Gott – Kirche – Welt. Aus dem Niederländischen von H. Zulauf (Gesammelte Schriften Bd. 2), Mainz 1970, 62–79, hier 64.
[22] M. Heidegger, Sein und Zeit, a.a.O., 179.
[23] E. Schillebeeckx, Gott – Die Zukunft des Menschen, a.a.O., 39.

In einer Randbemerkung seiner frühen Löwener Vorlesung vermerkt Schillebeeckx handschriftlich: „Faktizität: Teilhabe → Teilnahme"[24]. Der Partizipationsgedanke ist hier von Schillebeeckx an menschliche Lebensrealität in einem thomistischen Interpretationsrahmen gegründet. Schillebeeckx ersetzt den wertneutralen Faktizitätsbegriff durch einen schöpfungstheologisch gefärbten Faktizitätsbegriff, jedoch ohne das durch diesen Begriff angedeutete originäre Potenzial zu desavouieren: „Nun, da der Mensch sich der Realität, dass er Person ist, bewusst ist, und dass sein Person-sein nur in menschlicher Mitpersönlichkeit zu sich selbst kommt und in der körperlichen Welt wächst, muss nun dieses Person-sein im Vollsinn seiner Faktizität bewusst gemacht werden, die ist: Geschöpf Gottes zu sein, als Person zu dem tiefsten von dem, was er ist, nach Gott gekehrt zu sein, dem er sich annähern will, aber eigenmächtig nicht annähern kann."[25] Das basale metaphysische Rahmenkonzept der Theologie Schillebeeckx', näherhin das schöpfungstheologisch orientierte Framework, findet sich auch hier, auf den Faktizitätsbegriff fokussiert, wieder. „Gottes innerliche, subsistente Freiheit und Selbstgenügsamkeit wird die ultimative Begründung der geschöpflichen Kontingenz und Faktizität. Und anders herum: aus der radikalen Faktizität der Geschöpfe können wir, metaphysisch, aufsteigen zu der Bestätigung von Gottes Selbstgenügsamkeit und Freiheit bei der Schöpfung."[26]

Ein robuster Rahmen faktizitätsorientierter Theologie ist damit skizziert. Dieser Rahmen wird durch folgende Kernelemente konstituiert:
- Schöpfungstheologischer Ausgangspunkt: *Deus Humanissimus*; – Gott und menschliche Freiheit,
- Verwiesenheit der Deutung von Schöpfung und Kultur; – von vorgegebener Faktizität auf menschliches Potential,
- Selbstrealisierung und Verantwortung,

---

[24] Vgl. Vorlesung Leuven „De Deo Creante II" [ca. 1949], 96: „faciticiteit: deelhebbing → deelneming".

[25] Vorlesung Leuven „Theologische Bezinning op het scheppingsgeloof" – „De Deo Creante", 19: „Nu de mens bewust is van de realiteit dat hij persoon is en dat zijn persoon-zijn slechts in menselijke medepersoonlijkheid tot zichzelf komt en groeit in deze lichamelijke wereld, nu moet dit persoonzijn bewust gemaakt worden van de volle zin van zijn faciticiteit, die is: Schepsel Gods te zijn, als persoon tot in het diepste van wat hij is naar God gekeerd die hij benaderen wil en eigenmachtig niet benaderen kan.".

[26] Vorlesung Leuven „De Deo Creante II", a.a.O., 139: „Gods innerlijke, subsistente vrijheid en zelfgenoegzaamheid wordt de ultieme begronding van de schepselijke contingentie en faciticiteit. En andersom: uit de radicale faciticiteit van de schepselen kunnen we, metaphysisch, opklimmen tot de bevestiging van Gods zelfgenoegzaamheid en vrijheid bij de schepping."

– Kontext und Situation. Weil uns im Folgenden wieder die sozio-technischen Konsequenzen eines faktizitäts-theologischen Referenzrahmens beschäftigen werden, sei kurz an einige zentrale Aspekte der Kulturtheologie Schillebeeckx' erinnert. In seinem bekannten Diktum schreibt Edward Schillebeeckx: „Menschen sind Subjekte des Glaubens, aber die Menschen haben auch Kultur, sind Kulturwesen. Deshalb ist die konkrete Kultur, in der Gläubige leben, *das, wonach* der christliche Glaube in Wirklichkeit modelliert wird, zugleich *das, wodurch* dieser Glaube lebendig assimiliert wird, und schließlich *das, worin* der Glaube konkret von hier und jetzt lebenden Menschen praktiziert wird."[27] Aber was verändert diese Feststellung in Bezug auf gegenwärtige Theologie? Kultur muss notwendig, schöpfungstheologisch grundgelegt, als basales Element theologischer Methode und konkreten theologischen Arbeitens in Anschlag gebracht werden.[28] Sie gehört zur *conditio humana* und bedingt letztlich alle gesellschaftlichen Phänomene.[29] Kulturtheologie muss aber auch stets konkret werden, da aktueller Glaube immer ein bipolares Geschehen ist. Es muss der Pol „der christlichen Offenbarungssituation (der Glaubens-, Erfahrungs- und der Interpretationstradition der jüdisch-christlichen Religion) und der Situation, in der Gläubige hier und jetzt leben", zusammengedacht werden.[30] Fokussiert auf die Existenz bedeutet dieses: „In einem Individuum lesen wir eine bestimmte Kulturgeschichte."[31] Ausgehend von der Verwobenheit des Glaubens in seine auch soziohistorische Konstitution anerkennt der

---

[27] E. Schillebeeckx, Menschen, a.a.O., 58f. Vgl. auch ders., Theologisch testament. Notarieel nog niet verleden, Baarn 1994, 69.

[28] Denn es sind ja in-der-Welt seiende Existenzen, die sowohl als theologietreibende Subjekte, als auch als Gläubige diese vorbereitete Weltvertrautheit, die Lebenswelt als den sie umgebenden Horizont innehaben. Vgl. hierzu auch M. Halstrup, Christsein ist zunächst und zumeist In-der-Welt-sein, a.a.O.

[29] Th. Sternberg, Kirche im Plural der Kulturen, Anmerkungen zum Verhältnis von Kultur und Religion, in: *Catholica* 54 (2000), 98–114, hier 99.

[30] E. Schillebeeckx, Menschen, 59. Insofern ist Theologie auch eine lebenspraktische Wissenschaft. Vgl. hierzu H. Wagner, „Crux probat omnia". Anstöße zur Bewältigung des Theodizeeproblems aus reformatorischer Theologie, in: ders. (Hrsg.), Mit Gott streiten. Neue Zugänge zum Theodizee-Problem (Quaestiones disputatae Bd. 169), Freiburg/Br. 1998, 131–150, bes. 134f.; H. Kessler, Was ist Theologie? Was heißt Theologie treiben? Zehn Thesen für den Grundkurs Theologie, in: J. Hainz / H.-W. Jüngling / R. Sebott (Hrsg.), Den Armen eine frohe Botschaft (FS F. Kamphaus), Frankfurt/M. 1997, 383–406: http://www.kaththeol.uni-frankfurt.de/funda_dogmatik/PDFs_kessler/was_ist_theologie. pdf [15.1.2009]; bes. Kap. V: „Eine lebenspraktische Wissenschaft". Vgl. zum Gesamtproblem auch K. Tanner, Theories of culture: A new agenda for theology, Minneapolis 1997.

[31] E. Schillebeeckx, Menschen, a.a.O., 77.

Gläubige, „daß auch in anderen Lebensüberzeugungen Wahrheit steckt"[32].

Radikalisiert wird diese kulturelle Bindung der Religion durch die gegenwärtige Zeitsignatur, die mit Ingolf U. Dalferth als „Endphase eines kulturgestützten Christentums" zu qualifizieren ist.[33] Und Werner Ross bemerkt in einem Artikel das Problem der Perspektive einer Kultur nur *innerhalb* des kirchlichen Raumes: „Es wäre übertrieben, von Ghettoisierung der Kirche zu sprechen, solange dieser kirchliche Raum so geräumig und lebensfreundlich ist, auch so ansehnlich und sich in vielerlei heilsamen Aktivitäten entfaltend wie heute. Trotzdem ist der Rückzug der Kirche aus der Öffentlichkeit erstaunlich, und am meisten auffallend in dem Bereich, der alles das umfaßt, was nicht im strikten Sinn Berufsleben, Wirtschaft, Technik heißt, weitgehend zum Beispiel der Freizeitaktivitäten."[34]

Ist eine Flucht aus dieser Ghettoisierung möglich? Unabdingbar ist meines Erachtens eine erfahrungsgebundene und lebensweltlich verantwortete Neuorientierung der Theologie! Elemente sind benannt worden. Die nachfolgende Konkretion soll eine erste Applikation dieser kulturtheologisch orientierten Applikation systematischer Aspekte einer angemessenen Theologie erproben.

Konkretion: User Experience und Design sozio-technischer Systeme

Faktizität ist Lebensraum. Leben ist Ausgangspunkt der Rede von Gott. Worin liegt das Unterscheidende einer gegenwärtigen Rede von Gott im Vergleich zu früheren Zeitaltern? Ohne Zweifel wird die jetzige digitale Zeitsignatur hier angeführt werden müssen. Nie dagewesene Möglichkeiten digitaler Selbstrealisierung eröffnen den Weg zu einer neuartigen und vor allen Dingen nie dagewesenen Nutzererfahrung und einem Bewusstsein dieser Möglichkeiten (Awareness). Ob nun einzelne Mitglieder der

---

[32] Ebd., 80.

[33] I.U. Dalferth, „Was Gott ist, bestimme ich!" Theologie im Zeitalter der „Cafeteria-Religion", in: *Theologische Literaturzeitung* 121 (1996), 416–430, hier 416.

[34] W. Ross, Art. Kultur und Kirche, in: Handwörterbuch religiöser Gegenwartsfragen, hrsg. von U. Ruh / D. Seeber / R. Walter, Freiburg/Br. 1989, 227–232. An dieser Stelle kann das brisante Verhältnis von Kirche und Kultur nicht weiter thematisiert werden. Sicherlich findet eine Verhältnisbestimmung unter den beiden Endpunkten der Beliebigkeit und der Ghettoisierung statt. Vgl. hierzu auch Th. Sternberg, Kirche im Plural der Kulturen, a.a.O., 105.

Digitalen Gesellschaft diese Möglichkeiten in Gänze angemessen durchdenken oder diese nur als Gegebene in Anschlag ihres Tuns bringen, soll hier nicht thematisiert werden.

Wichtig ist in diesem Zusammenhang lediglich das Faktum der wie auch immer auch gearteten Abkehr von der durch Marshall McLuhan konstatierten Gutenberg-Galaxie.[35] Zweifellos befinden wir uns, wie Norbert Bolz hellsichtig schon 1993 erkannte, „Am Ende der Gutenberg-Galaxis"[36]. Die Einsicht, dass reine Literalität durch *rich media* und ubiquitäres Internet bei gleichzeitiger fast uneingeschränkter Verfügbarkeit von digitalen, vernetzten Interfaces Garant einer bisher nicht dagewesenen Informationsvielfalt und auch sozialer Vernetzung (Awareness) ist, bedingt auch Theologie, der es darauf einkommt, die Kultur einer Zeit zu verstehen und sie im Lichte des Evangeliums zu deuten.[37]

Wenn Selbstrealisierung an konkrete Alltagserfahrung gekoppelt ist, Kultur faktizitäts- und schöpfungstheologisch zu bestimmen ist, stehen alltägliche (Nutzer-)erfahrungen im Zentrum theologischer Beschäftigung. Dass besonders die einlassende Erörterung aktueller technischer Phänomene nicht immer im Fokus aktueller theologischer Debatten stand, muss hier nicht weiter beachtet werden. Für die Konkretion der im Vorangegangenen skizzierten Analyse hilft es jedoch, den Blick auf den Methodenkasten und theoretischen Referenzrahmen von User Experience Designern zu fokussieren.

Nachfolgendes Schaubild nennt wesentliche Aspekte einer mobilen User Experience:

---

[35] M. McLuhan, The Gutenberg galaxy, Toronto – Buffalo – London 1962. So analysierte McLuhan eine Rekonfiguration der Galaxie, die sich nicht zuletzt durch den sich der Typographie bewussten Menschen als wesentliches Moment speiste.

[36] N. Bolz, Am Ende der Gutenberg-Galaxis. Die neuen Kommunikationsverhältnisse, München ³2008.

[37] Es geht hier um sowohl einfache, aber auch komplexe sozio-technische Systeme, ERP-Systeme, das Internet als *remote software interface* oder auch als digitaler Klingelbeutel, als Werkzeug; vgl. http://www.heroshopping.com [10.8.2011].

Abb. 1: Mobile User Experience:
http://www.beepoint.com.ar/blog/2007/10/mobile-user-experience.html [9.8.2011]

In der Community der User Experience-Designer wird Wert auf Diagramme als Unterstützung des Verstehensprozesses komplexer Sachverhalte gelegt. So konstatiert Andrew Meier: „Diagrams are of great use because they cut to the heart of the matter, taking away the ambiguity of words and visually depicting abstract concepts."[38] Es scheint nicht weiter verwunderlich, dass User Experience-Spezialisten ähnliche Bezugspunkte ihrer Arbeit als Ausgangspunkt ihrer konkreten Arbeit konstatieren, wie auch eine erfahrungsgeleitetete Hermeneutik des christlichen Glaubens dieses praktiziert.

In der „UX Honeycomb" von Peter Morville aus dem Jahr 2004[39] finden sich Nektartöpfe mit der Benennung *findable, accessible, credible, useful,*

---

[38] http://www.uxbooth.com/blog/8-must-see-ux-diagrams/ [9.8.2011].
[39] http://semanticstudios.com/publications/semantics/000029.php [9.8.2011].

usable, desirable, valuable. Den Ansatz von Peter Morville aufnehmend, jedoch systematisierend, entwickelt Magnus Revang das *UX Wheel*. Kern des Rades ist der Wert für Kunde und Anbieter. Die oben genannten weiteren Elemente augmentieren den Wert der User Experience. Weiter wesentliche Aspekte des Designs sozio-technischer Systeme sind komplettierend angeordnet.

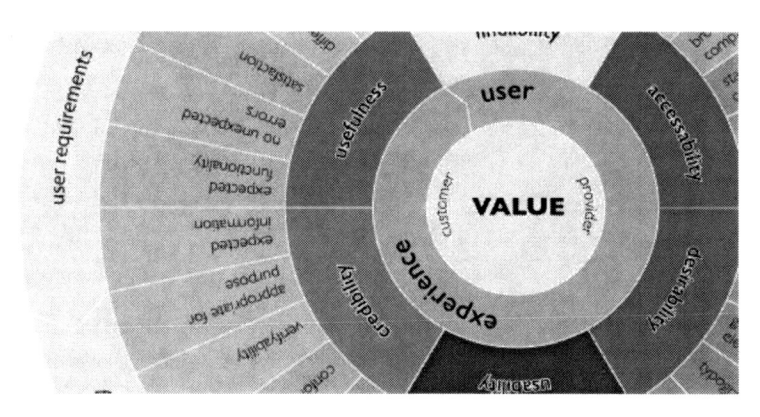

Abb. 2: The UX Wheel:
http://userexperienceproject.blogspot.com/2007/04/user-experience-wheel.html [9.8.2011]

Ausgehend von diesen ersten eher allgemein gehaltenen Annäherungen an Begriff und Inhalt kann nun detaillierter nach dem systematischen Gehalt von „User Experience" gefragt werden. Oben nicht thematisiert, aber unter den Schillebeeckx-Kennern bekannt ist der Zusammenhang von Erlebnis und Erfahrung; – letztere als (auch aufgrund eines spezifischen und wandelbaren Referenzrahmens) gedeutetes Erlebnis. Dieser zentrale systematisch-theologische Topos wird auch in gleichwohl anderem Zusammenhang durch nachfolgendes Diagramm (Ausschnitt) visualisiert.

Abb. 3: The Importance of User Experience diagram:
http://www.flickr.com/photos/bryce/106972762/ [9.8.2011]

Durch nachfolgendes letztes Diagramm schließt sich der Kreis. Das erste Diagramm ist fokussiert auf die individuelle Existenz. In dem gezeigten Ausschnitt des nachfolgenden Diagramms wird diese konkrete existentielle Situation systematisiert und abstrahiert.

Abb. 4: The Fundamentals of Experience Design:
http://www.poetpainter.com/thoughts/article/ia-summit-2009-the-fundamentals-of-experience-design- [9.8.2011]

Der hier angezeigte Ausschnitt dieses Diagramms führt uns zurück zur Antwort auf die Frage nach einer angemessenen Theologie; – kontextuell, erfahrungsbezogen und faktizitätsorientiert; für die Entwicklung einer gehaltvollen User Experience eine theoretische Basis und sachliche Notwendigkeit. Parallelen zu der Basiskonzeption von Schillebeeckx sind gleichwohl vorhanden.

Resümee: Theologie 2.0 – User Experience und Gott

Nur dann, wenn es gelingt, einen Plausibilitätsaufweis zu führen, der in der Regel erfahrungsgebunden veranlagt ist, wird es auch möglich sein aufzuzeigen, dass das, was auch wirklich angeht, thematisiert wurde. Die Zeit ist nicht (mehr) reif für Ideologien, die den existentiellen Lebensernst nicht mehr tangieren, sich nicht als authentische Lebensmaximen ausweisen können. Selbstrealisierung und User Experience, Lebensernst und Authentizität können als wesentliche Attribute eines angemessenen Referenzrahmens genannt werden. Dieser ermöglicht die Ausbildung wesentlicher Kriterien, die sowohl für den Umgang miteinander relevant sind, wie auch einen angemessenen Ort der verantwortbaren Gottesrede im Zeichen der digitalen (R)Evolution ermöglichen. Dies gilt m. E. sowohl im Diskurs über die Normen und Werte, aber auch im Hinblick auf die qualitative Bewertung von sozialen Aktivitäten und sonstigen Ereignissen. Theologie 2.0 ist eine auf die gegenwärtigen Herausforderungen angemessen antwortende Theologie, die sich den Leitthemen Faktizität, Selbstrealisierung und User Experience als grundlegenden Interpretationskategorien theologischer Arbeit und dialogischen Bemühens verpflichtet weiß. Sie kann damit als lebensweltlich verpflichtete Hermeneutik des Glaubens nach Schillebeeckx gelten können.

* * *

Abstract of the contribution of Maximilian Halstrup

This article recalls Edward Schillebeeckx's basic categories of a hermeneutics of faith that is engaged with all realms of life. Recourse to facticity and self-realization can expand our thinking and scope of creativity, which furthermore can help to make an up-to-date consideration of the concept of the wider realm of human experience. Even though a systematic reference to the space of digital experience [User Experience (UX)] is seldom an interest for theology, we may gain considerable knowledge through recourse to these digital places that involve human facticity and self-realization, as they regard the task of furthering the development of modern theological hermeneutics and of a narrative of God as being encountered within the whole realm of life experience.

"Theology 2.0" is a proposal with suitable answers to current challenges indebted to the ideas of facticity, self-realization and User Experience, which this essay considers as fundamental categories for theological hermeneutics, and for enabling a greater dialogical practice. It thus argues that these categories hold resonances of Schillebeeckx's hermeneutics of faith as it is engaged in all realms of human life.

Translation from German: *Tracy Rammler*

Manuela Kalsky

HEIL IM ALLTÄGLICHEN LEBEN

Weiterdenken mit Edward Schillebeeckx in einer multireligiösen und multikulturellen Gesellschaft

Theologie treiben bedeutet Mut haben zur konkreten Phantasie, zum konkreten Engagement, vor allem dann, wenn sich die Fragen und Schwierigkeiten türmen – und es bedeutet den aufrechten Gang in Kirche und Gesellschaft zu fördern unter dem Motto, „dass nur aufrecht Gehende auch freiwillig Kniende sein können."[1]

1. Umbruch im Theologietreiben

Diese Umschreibung dessen, was ein Theologe zu tun hat, stammt aus der Rede von Johann Baptist Metz, die er anlässlich des 75. Geburtstages von Edward Schillebeeckx am 11. November 1989 in Nimwegen hielt. Als theologischer Weggefährte skizziert er die ‚offensive Treue' zum Zweiten Vatikanischen Konzil und zur kirchlichen Tradition, die dieser große dominikanische Theologe sein Leben lang behielt, trotz aller Probleme mit der kirchlichen Autorität in Rom. Die Zeichen der Zeit deuten und sie als Herausforderung für die eigene Theologieausübung ernst nehmen, war das Anliegen, das beide Theologen in Freundschaft verband.

Metz beschreibt Schillebeeckx in seiner Rede als einen Theologen, der inmitten einer sich verändernden Gesellschaft an einer ‚neuen hermeneutischen Kultur der Anerkennung der Anderen in ihrem Anderssein' arbei-

---

[1] J.B. Metz, Kirchlichkeit in offensiver Treue zum Konzil, in: Mensen maken de kerk. Verslag van het symposium rond de 75ᵉ verjaardag van Edward Schillebeeckx, Baarn 1989, 13–26, hier 15.

tete. Mit dieser Skizzierung benennt er zwei Aspekte, die für die Theologie Edward Schillebeeckx' als auch für seine eigene in der zweiten Hälfte des 20. Jahrhunderts entscheidend wurden: die Entdeckung der Hermeneutik und den Einfluss befreiungstheologischer Ansätze im Zuge einer multikulturell werdenden Weltkirche.

Auch Erik Borgman weist am Ende des ersten Teils seiner Biographie über seinen theologischen Lehrer darauf hin, dass sich die Theologie Edward Schillebeeckx' nach dem Zweiten Vatikanischen Konzil einschneidend veränderte. Schillebeeckx selbst, so schreibt er, habe das Konzil als eine theologische Zäsur erfahren und sein Interesse in sein früheres theologisches Werk nahezu verloren, da er sich jetzt als nachkonziliarer Theologe in einem anderen theologischen Kontext verstanden habe.[2] Auch wenn Borgman meines Erachtens überzeugend aufzeigt, dass schon vor der Teilnahme am Konzil die Theologie Schillebeeckx' auf eine ‚Kulturtheologie' hin angelegt war, so unterstreicht diese von Schillebeeckx selber angebrachte Zäsur meines Erachtens die epistemologische Verschiebung, möglicherweise den Bruch, der sich in seiner Theologie vollzogen hatte. Je deutlicher ihm wurde, wie sehr jede Theologie von dem jeweiligen geschichtlichen Kontext, in der sie entsteht, geprägt ist, um so vehementer vertrat er die Überzeugung, dass „das Heil uns aus dem alltäglichen Leben heraus entgegen tritt und aus dem Arbeiten ‚in der Welt'"[3]. Mehr als zuvor verstand er seine Theologie als kontextuelle Theologie und zog hieraus den Schluss, dass das, was er ‚Heil von Gotteswegen' nannte, nicht länger in zeitlos theologischen Vorstellungen von Wahrheit zu finden sei, sondern sich immer wieder neu und anders im alltäglichen Leben von Menschen lokalisierte, mitten in der Welt und in einer Kirche, die im Anschluss an das Zweite Vatikanische Konzil ‚als das wandernde Volk Gottes und die lebendige Beziehung der Gläubigen (*communio*)' verstanden werden musste.[4] Wahrheitsfindung bedeutete für ihn jetzt im Sinne Heideggers *Enthüllung*, die allmähliche Entfaltung von Sinn. Was wir auch behaupten, es sind immer *wir*, die es behaupten. Und es hängt ab von der jeweiligen Brille, durch die wir die Wirklichkeit betrachten, was sich als Wahrheit vor uns auftut. Diese Situiertheit aller Wirklichkeits- und Wahrheitserfahrung, die Gadamers hermeneutischer Zirkel einsichtig

---

[2] E. Borgman, Edward Schillebeeckx: een theoloog in zijn geschiedenis. Deel I: Een katholieke cultuurtheologie (1914–1965), Baarn – Nijmegen 1999, 451–468.

[3] Ebd., 455.

[4] Wider die Entmündigung – für eine offene Katholizität. Kölner Erklärung katholischer Theologieprofessorinnen und Theologieprofessoren vom Dreikönigsfest, 6.1.1989: http://www.wir-sind-kirche.de/files/90_k%oF6lnerkl.pdf [6.7.2011].

macht, brachte Schillebeeckx schließlich im Anschluss an Habermas zu der Überzeugung, dass Glaubenswahrheit nur mit Hilfe von Kommunikation zustande kommen kann, im Austausch von Glaubenserfahrungen innerhalb der Glaubensgemeinschaft.[5]

2. Gott hautnah

Hermann Häring, der von 1980 bis zu seiner Pensionierung als Theologieprofessor an der Universität von Nimwegen tätig war und sich in vielem der Theologie Schillebeeckx verpflichtet weiß, rühmt ihn als einen der ersten katholischen Theologen, der die Hermeneutik in die katholische Theologie eingeführt habe. Nicht nur sei sie eine Art Gegengift gegen einen starren und rationalistischen Dogmatismus in der katholischen Theologie seiner Zeit gewesen, auch habe sie eine kritische Herangehensweise an die kirchliche Tradition gefördert, die den reaktionären und ideologischen Machtmissbrauch kirchlicher Autorität bloßgelegte. Häring unterstreicht, dass die prinzipielle Offenheit mit der Schillebeeckx Kirche und Welt miteinander in seiner theologischen Hermeneutik verband, in einer Verschiebung des Mottos *extra ecclesiam nulla salus* – außerhalb der Kirche kein Heil – hin zu: *extra mundum nulla salus* – außerhalb der Welt kein Heil – resultierte.[6] Gott lässt sich in der Welt erfahren als der Unerfahrbare, alle menschliche Erfahrung übersteigend und zugleich ‚rakelings nabij'[7]. Dieses Paradox der transzendenten Immanenz Gottes, eine den Menschen transzendierende Transzendenz im hier und jetzt, hat Schillebeeckx zu einer tastenden Theologie der Liebe Gottes für die Welt veranlasst, die sich sowohl im spirituellen Raum, im liturgischen Feiern

---

[5] Vgl. A. Houtepen, Edward Schillebeeckx, in: H. Achterhuis u. a. (Red.), Denkers en religie, Diemen 2010, 415–425, hier 418.

[6] Siehe hierzu das „In Memoriam" von Hermann Häring auf der Website der Schillebeeckx Stiftung: http://schillebeeckx.nl/overlijden-edward-schillebeeckx/in-memoriam [7.7.2011] und seinen Artikel zur ‚fundamentalen Hermeneutik' bei Schillebeeckx: H. Häring, God – puur verrassing. Edward Schillebeeckx' doorbraak naar een narratieve theologie, in: *Tijdschrift voor Theologie* 45 (2005) 13–31, bes. 23ff. („III. Een theologie op zoek naar humaniteit").

[7] „Rakelings nabij" ist ein von dem Liturgieerneuerer und Dichter Huub Oosterhuis benutzter niederländischer Ausdruck, der schwierig zu übersetzen ist, aber sehr treffend das Paradox der nicht beweisbaren Gotteserfahrung umschreibt. „Rakelings nabij" deutet eine Berührung an, die man meint gespürt zu haben, hautnah, sich aber zugleich nicht sicher ist, ob es auch wirklich so war. Man könnte sich auch getäuscht haben. Es bleibt ein Mysterium, was genau geschah.

und Beten als auch im praktischen Einsatz für Gerechtigkeit verortet.[8] Seine Theologie bleibt der christlichen Tradition im Sinne der biblischen Verkündigung treu und schreibt sie im Lichte dessen, was die Zeichen der Zeit heute fordern fort, ohne sich ihnen unkritisch auszuliefern.

3. Lehren und Lernen

Mit seiner hermeneutischen Herangehensweise richtete Schillebeeckx auch in Westeuropa den Blick in der Theologie auf die Marginalisierten und Bürger zweiter Klasse, womit er sich der Herausforderung befreiungstheologischer Ansätze und ihren kritischen Anfragen an die westeuropäische Theologie stellte. Im erkenntnistheoretischen Bereich bedeutete dies die Anerkennung des Primats der Praxis, wodurch die theologische Reflexion und Theorie zum zweiten Schritt im methodologischen Bereich wurden. Diejenigen, die bis dahin im theologischen und gesellschaftlichen Diskurs nicht gehört wurden, bekamen unter Berufung auf die biblische Option für die Armen und Ausgestoßenen eine Stimme. Ihre Erfahrungen traten in den Vordergrund und wurden zum *locus theologicus*. Neue theologische Einsichten entstanden. Scheinbar zeitlose, in sich geschlossene Systeme theologischen Denkens verloren ihren Ewigkeitswert und damit ihre Unantastbarkeit. Universell geglaubte Wahrheiten wurden als Verabsolutierung partikularer Einsichten und persönlicher Überzeugungen enthüllt, die zumeist männlich, weiß und der Mittelklasse zugehörig waren. Niemand, der sich heute als moderner wissenschaftlicher Theologe oder Theologin versteht und wie Schillebeeckx das *Adagium* der modernen Theologie *fides quaerens intellectum* unterschreibt, kann noch hinter die Einsicht zurück, dass Glaube und Theologie an Ort und Zeit gebundene Interpretationen sind.

Im Jahre 1982 wurde bestätigt, dass es Edward Schillebeeckx gelungen war, theologische Wissenschaft nicht nur mit kirchlicher Erneuerung zu verbinden, sondern auch mit gesellschaftlichen Fragen. Im königlichen Palast zu Amsterdam wurde er mit dem Erasmuspreis ausgezeichnet – ein Preis, der jährlich einer Person oder einem Institut zuerkannt wird, die oder das im europäischen Rahmen einen außerordentlichen Beitrag auf kulturellem, sozialem oder sozial-wissenschaftlichem Gebiet geleistet hat.

---

[8] Siehe die Einleitung zur Festschrift anlässlich des 90. Geburtstages von Edward Schillebeeckx: M. Kalsky u. a. (Red.), Ons rakelings nabij. Gedaanteveranderingen van God en geloof. Ter ere van Edward Schillebeeckx, Nijmegen – Zoetermeer 2005, 7–12.

Zum ersten Mal war es ein Theologe, der diesen Preis bekam. Auch war Schillebeeckx selbst kein Erstürmer der Bastille und hatten seine Bücher im kirchlichen Bereich oftmals ‚Übersetzer' nötig, so verfügte er doch über die Gabe der Empathie, die es ihm ermöglichte, sich in die Fragen und Nöte im täglichen Leben ‚ganz normaler' Menschen hinein zu versetzen. Er teilte und unterstützte ihr Aufbegehren gegen entmündigende und unterdrückende Strukturen innerhalb und außerhalb der Kirche und gab ihnen eine Stimme in seiner Theologie.

In diesem Sinne war Edward Schillebeeckx nicht nur ein großer theologischer Gelehrter, sondern auch ein großer theologisch Lernender, der dazu in der Lage war, mit offenem Visier und theologisch-wissenschaftlicher Neugier auf den Zeitgeist zuzugehen, sich ernsthaft mit ihm zu beschäftigen und von wissenschaftlich-theologischen Erkenntnissen und glaubend-intuitiven Einsichten geleitet, neue zeitgemäße Denkanstöße für Theologie und Gesellschaft zu formulieren wusste.

Weder kirchliche Autoritäten noch einschneidende Veränderungen im gesellschaftlichen Bereich konnten ihn einschüchtern oder zum Pessimisten machen. Sich auf Gott zu berufen, um die eigene theologische Position abzusichern, lag ihm fern und das Motto seines Ordens – *Veritas* – verstand er nicht als *superbia theologica*, sondern als dienende Suche nach den Spuren der Wahrheit Gottes im Leben von Menschen in dieser Welt.[9]

Ist die Theologie Edward Schillebeeckx, die so deutlich den Zeitgeist des 20sten Jahrhunderts atmet, zu Beginn des 21. Jahrhunderts noch relevant? Hat Sie Zukunft und wenn ja, auf welche Weise?

4. In den Spuren Edward Schillebeeckx'

Im nun Folgenden sollen diese Fragen mit Hilfe der Arbeit am „Dominikanischen Studienzentrums für Theologie und Gesellschaft" (DSTS) beantwortet werden. Dieses im Jahre 1988 von den niederländischen Dominikanern errichtete theologische Forschungszentrum bekam den Auftrag, einen Beitrag zu einer zeitgemäßen befreienden Theologie im westeuropäischen Kontext zu leisten. Im Laufe der Jahre hat sich das DSTS zu einem Institut entwickelt, dass mit seinen vierjährigen Forschungsprogrammen mitten im Zeitgeschehen steht und sich als Spieler auf dem Feld von Theologie und Gesellschaft in den Niederlanden einen

---

[9] E. Schillebeeckx, Theologisch testament. Notarieel nog niet verleden, Baarn 1994, 183.

Namen gemacht hat.[10] Wie die Arbeit am DSTS bei der zuvor benannten Theologieausübung Edward Schillebeeckx' anschließt und sie in seinem Geiste weiterführen möchte, soll nun mit Hilfe von zwei Punkten näher ausgeführt werden: das Verstehen der Zeichen der Zeit und die Suche nach Wahrheit als multimediale interreligiöse Kommunikation.

4.1. Das Verstehen der Zeichen der Zeit

Was sind die dringenden Fragen der Zeit in der wir leben und welche Antworten sind darauf aus theologischer Sicht zu geben? Eine Theologie, die keine rein akademische Angelegenheit sein will, sondern sich mit dem konkreten Leben der Menschen verbunden weiß, kommt um Antworten auf diese Frage nicht herum. Dies bedeutet, dass im methodischen Bereich keine binnentheologische Forschung betrieben werden kann, sondern nach interdisziplinären Verbindungen gesucht werden muss, um die Zeichen der Zeit in Religion und Gesellschaft zu deuten. Soziologische, religionswissenschaftliche, religionspsychologische, kulturphilosophische und literaturwissenschaftliche Studien werden darum in die vierjährigen Forschungsprogramme des DSTS mit einbezogen. Vorausgesetzt wird, dass der hermeneutische und erkenntnistheoretische Ort einer zeitgemäßen Theologie nicht in der Theologie selbst zu finden ist, sondern in den Lebens- und Glaubenserfahrungen der Menschen, die im Alltag einer multikulturellen und multireligiösen Gesellschaft leben, mit allen Vor- und Nachteilen, die dieser Pluralismus mit sich bringt. Nicht die Reinterpretation überlieferter theologisch-dogmatischer Begrifflichkeiten steht im Vordergrund der theologischen Arbeit, sondern die am Leben und Glauben der Menschen orientierten Fragen, wie beispielsweise: Wie vollzieht sich der alltägliche Umgang von Menschen mit unterschiedlichen religiösen und nicht-religiösen Weltanschauungen? Wie haben sich Glaubenserfahrungen und religiöse Identität im Laufe der Jahre verändert? Was wollen Menschen aus der jeweils eigenen religiösen Tradition bewahren, was inspiriert sie und was lassen sie hinter sich? Aus welchen religiösen und nicht-religiösen Quellen schöpfen sie? Was gibt heute Sinn und Richtung an ihr Leben und das Leben ihrer Kinder?

---

[10] Mehr Informationen zum DSTS unter www.dsts.nl [7.7.2011].

Wie bei Edward Schillebeeckx wird auch am Dominkanischen Studienzentrum vorzugsweise induktiv gearbeitet.[11] Kein dogmatisch-theologisch begrenzter Rahmen formt den Ausgangspunkt für die Theologieausübung, sondern eine für das Experiment offen stehende Multiperspektivität, in der die Kommunikation über zeitgemäße Erfahrungen von Unheil und Heil einen wichtigen Stellenwert einnimmt. Der Austausch von Einsichten und die Diskussion über erworbene Erkenntnisse stehen im interdisziplinär zusammengestellten Forschungsteam, das sich vier bis sechsmal im Jahr trifft im Vordergrund. In Kontinuität mit der dominikanischen Tradition wird die *circumspectio* ausgeübt, die nicht nur für Edward Schillebeeckx, sondern auch bereits für Thomas von Aquin wichtig war, um die Transformationen im religiösen Bereich aufzuspüren, zu verstehen und anschließend theologisch zu interpretieren. Die kritisch-theologische Deutung der Zeichen der Zeit und die Weitergabe der daraus gewonnenen Einsichten sind das Herz dominikanischer Spiritualität und kommt zum Ausdruck in dem Wahlspruch: *contemplari et contemplata aliis tradere*, sich der Betrachtung widmen und die Frucht des Betrachtens weitergeben. Es geht darum eine Wahrheit zu verkündigen, die nicht uniform und dogmatisch festgelegt ist, sondern die inmitten einer komplexen Welt leidenschaftlich nach Spuren des Reiches Gottes sucht.[12]

An dieser Spurensuche beteiligt sich auch das Dominikanische Studienzentrum mit seinen vierjährigen interdisziplinären Forschungsprogrammen. Inmitten einer stark säkularisierten, technisierten und individualisierten niederländischen Gesellschaft, die sich plötzlich, entgegen aller Erwartungen, erneut mit religiösen Fragen konfrontiert sieht, begibt sich das DSTS auf die Suche nach einem neuen ‚Wir' in den Niederlanden.[13] Bevor näher auf dieses Forschungsprojekt und die dazugehörige multimediale Website www.nieuwwij.nl eingegangen wird, soll zunächst ein Eindruck der gesellschaftlichen und kirchlichen Situation in den Niederlanden vermittelt werden, die den Kontext des heutigen Forschungsprojektes am DSTS formt.

---

[11] Zur induktiven Methode bei Schillebeeckx vgl. R.J. Schreiter, Edward Schillebeeckx. His Continuing Significance, in: M.C. Hilkert / R.J. Schreiter (Eds.), The Praxis of the Reign of God, New York 2002, 186–187.
[12] Vgl. hierzu die Ausführungen zum DSTS von P. Nissen, Verbeeldingen van verbondenheid en het verlangen naar ontgrenzing, in: J. Verheijen / J. Bekkenkamp (Hrsg.), Onszelf voorbij. Over de grenzen van verbondenheid, Almere 2011, 213–216.
[13] Zu den DSTS-Forschungsprojekten vgl. www.dsts.nl [7.7.2011].

4.1.1. Säkularisierung und Sakralisierung

Die religiöse Landschaft der Niederlande hat sich in kürzester Zeit einschneidend verändert. Während zu Beginn des 20. Jahrhunderts noch 98% der Niederländer und Niederländerinnen einer Kirche angehörten, sind das hundert Jahre später nur noch 40% der Bevölkerung.[14] Seit 1966 hat sich die Anzahl der Katholiken und Protestanten halbiert, ein Rückgang von 60% auf 30%.[15] Oberflächlich betrachtet, könnte man meinen, dass ein vom Calvinismus geprägtes christliches Land konform der Säkularisationstheorie sich mit steigender Wohlfahrt und fortschreitender Wissenschaft in hohem Tempo vom Glauben emanzipiert hat. Immerhin ist es eine Tatsache, dass jedes Jahr circa 80.000 Menschen das Institut Kirche verlassen. Religionssoziologen meinen, dass, wenn sich die Anzahl der Kirchenaustritte in den Niederlanden auf diese Weise fortsetzt, um das Jahr 2030 die letzte Kirche geschlossen werden wird. Aber, sind Kirchenaustritte auch ein Beweis für das Fehlen jeglicher Form von Religiosität? Keineswegs. Historische und soziologische Untersuchungen in den Niederlanden weisen neue spirituelle Entwicklungen vor allem im außerkirchlichen Bereich auf.[16] Auch wenn 60% der Bevölkerung nicht mehr einer Kirche angehört, so nennt sich doch ebenfalls 60% der Niederländer und Niederlanderinnen gläubig, aber nur 4 von 10 Personen meinen damit den traditionellen Glauben. Der Rest wird unter ‚postmoderne Spirituelle' subsumiert, die meinen, dass man Religion aus der Weisheit unterschiedlicher Traditionen zusammenstellen sollte.[17]

Nicht nur in den Niederlanden ist das Phänomen dieses ‚believing without belonging' zu beobachten.[18] Immer mehr Menschen kehren den

---

[14] G. Dekker, Heeft de kerk zichzelf overleefd?, Zoetermeer 2010, 18.

[15] T. Bernts / G. Dekker / J. de Hart, God in Nederland. 1996–2006, Kampen 2007, 14.

[16] Während die Protestantische Kirche der Niederlande (PKN) seit 1970 mehr als 50% ihrer Mitglieder verlor, lagen die Kirchenaustritte in der Katholischen Kirche um die 16%. Auffallend ist, dass kleine Kirchengemeinschaften von orthodoxem Zuschnitt seit 1970 Kirchenzutritte verzeichnen. So wuchs die Mitgliederzahl in den evangelischen Gemeinden und den Pfingstkirchen mit 138%. Ist hieraus der Schluss zu ziehen, dass die Kirchen, die neuen zeitgemäßen Entwicklungen in Kirche und Gesellschaft offen gegenüber stehen, aussterben werden? Oder anders gesagt: Kann die Kirche nur dann überleben, wenn sie sich in ein kulturelles und spirituelles Isolement zurück zieht? Vgl. zu kirchlichen und spirituellen Entwicklungen in den Niederlanden: J. de Hart, Zwevende gelovigen. Oude religie en nieuwe spiritualiteit, Amsterdam 2011, hier 235.

[17] Vgl. zum Umgang mit mehrfacher religiöser Identität: M. Kalsky, Religiöse Flexibilität. Eine Antwort auf kulturelle und religiöse Vielfalt, in: R. Bernhardt / P. Schmidt-Leukel (Hrsg.), Multiple religiöse Identität. Aus verschiedenen religiösen Traditionen schöpfen (Beträge zu einer Theologie der Religionen Bd. 5), Zürich 2008, 219–242.

[18] Dieser Ausdruck stammt von der englischen Religionssoziologin Grace Davie, mit dem sie zu umschreiben versucht, dass „das Heilige" in der Gesellschaft noch immer da ist, aber

religiösen Institutionen in (West-)Europa den Rücken zu. Viele von ihnen bleiben aber dennoch auf der Suche nach neuen Formen von Religiosität, nach dem, was ihnen Sinn und Werte in ihrem persönlichen Leben vermitteln kann. Der Glaube an einen persönlichen Gott nimmt ab und mit ihm der Glaube an dogmatisch-theologische Regeln der etablierten Kirchen. Im *Atlas of European Values*[19] ist nachzulesen, dass neben den Niederländern auch die Franzosen, Belgier, Dänen und Schweden die meiste Affinität mit der Umschreibung haben, dass es ‚etwas' geben müsse, eine Art Gott, einen Geist oder eine energetische Lebenskraft. Etwa 40% der Niederländer/-innen zählt sich zu dieser Gruppe sogenannter *Ietsisten* („*etwas*' heißt auf Niederländisch ‚*iets*'). Auch der Religionsmonitor 2008 der Bertelsmann Stiftung, der als interdisziplinäres und interreligiöses Projekt entwickelt wurde und mit dessen Hilfe 21.000 Menschen auf allen Kontinenten repräsentativ befragt wurden, um deren Religiosität zu messen, bestätigt diese Tendenz. In den von der Säkularisierung beeinflussten Kulturen ist eine spirituelle Dynamik festzustellen, die sich losgelöst hat von kirchlichen Institutionen und in der Gott oder das Göttliche sowohl als Person als auch als Energie aufgefasst wird.[20] Die Niederländer/-innen sind demnach in ihrer Suche nach einer holistisch geprägten und auf das Leben hin orientierten Spiritualität keine Ausnahme. Auch in anderen westeuropäischen Ländern ist diese Entwicklung zu beobachten und so gehen zur Überraschung aller, die meinten, dass mit der Säkularisierung Religion mehr und mehr verschwinden würde, auf paradoxale Weise Säkularisierung und Sakralisierung Hand in Hand.[21]

Die neue Spiritualität ist individuell geprägt, eklektisch von Art und aus traditionell theologischer Sicht eher synkretistisch orientiert, wodurch ihre multireligiöse Patchwork-Struktur oftmals aus kirchlicher und theologischer Sicht – ohne dass man meint sich wirklich damit beschäftigen

---

nicht mehr unbedingt in traditioneller Form: G. Davie, Religion in Britain since 1945. Believing without Belonging, Oxford 1994.
[19] L. Halman / R. Luijkx / M. van Zundert (Eds.), Atlas of Human Values, Leiden 2005.
[20] Vgl. P.M. Zulehner, Spirituelle Dynamik in säkularen Kulturen? Deutschland – Österreich – Schweiz, in: Bertelsmann Stiftung (Hrsg.), Religionsmonitor 2008, Gütersloh 2007, 143–157, bes. 152–154; St. Huber, Analysen zur religiösen Praxis. Ein Blick in die Schweiz, in: ebd., 158–166, bes. 163.
[21] Vgl. P. Heelas / L. Woodhead, The Spiritual Revolution. Why Religion is Giving Way to Spirituality, Oxford 2005; vgl. auch Bertelsmann Stiftung (Hrsg.), Religionsmonitor 2008, a.a.O., passim.

zu müssen – als oberflächliches Shoppen auf dem Markt der religiösen Möglichkeiten abgewiesen wird.[22]

So nicht Edward Schillebeeckx. In der Festschrift, die das Dominikanische Studienzentrum für Theologie und Gesellschaft anlässlich seines 90sten Geburtstages herausgab und die sich auf das Thema der Transformation christlicher Identität im Lichte kultureller und religiöser Vielfalt in Europa richtete, zeichnet er ein anderes Zeitbild als das der offiziellen Kirchen. Nüchtern und auch als 90jähriger die gesellschaftlichen Entwicklungen noch scharf wahrnehmend, konstatiert er: "Das Institut Kirche spricht nur noch wenige Menschen an. Andererseits stößt die seelenlose, kahle Säkularität viele ab. So begeben sie sich auf die Suche nach Spiritualität und ‚Religion', in welcher Gestalt auch immer. Religion ohne Gott kommt auf uns zu und rückt immer näher. Gleichzeitig ist unter denen, die sich zu Gott bekennen – Juden, Muslims und Christen, auch Katholiken – eine starke Tendenz zum Fundamentalismus zu verzeichnen, sodass das menschenfreundliche Gesicht von Synagogen und Kirchen, Moscheen und Pagoden sich verhärtet und verformt wird. Viele Christen erfahren nicht mehr, dass das Christentum an erster Stelle ein frohes und hoffnungsvolles Evangelium ist, ein Lebensweg und nicht eine Art philosophisches System mit für die Ewigkeit festgelegten Doktrinen. Aber die institutionelle Seite der Kirchen flüchtet in eine religiöse Ideologie, die, oftmals unbewusst, keinen Unterschied macht zwischen Gott und der eigenen Religion."[23]

Wiederum spricht hier ein Theologe, der die Zeichen der Zeit zu deuten weiß und dem Zeitgeist nicht apologetisch entgegentritt, sondern sich seinen Herausforderungen und den sich daraus ergebenen Veränderungen stellt. Mit der ihm eigenen empathischen Fähigkeit versetzt er sich in all die Pilger, die auf der Suche nach Wahrheit sind und von hierarchisch geprägten kirchlichen Instanzen nicht gehört werden. Es geht ihm nicht um die Verteidigung christlicher Identität als unveränderlicher Größe, die sich bereits durch Jahrhunderte hindurch als zeitlos manifestiert, sondern er stellt sie in seinem Artikel dar als einen dynamischen Prozess, in dem die Herrlichkeit Gottes (*kabood JHWH*) stets neue zeitgemäße Formen

---

[22] Vgl. T. Bernts / G. Dekker / J. de Hart, God in Nederland, a.a.O.; G. Dekker / J. de Hart / J. Peters, God in Nederland 1966–1996, Amsterdam 1997. Die Ergebnisse dieser Untersuchungen werden von dem Religionssoziologen Joep de Hart hilfreich zusammengefasst: J. de Hart, Zwevende gelovigen, a.a.O.

[23] E. Schillebeeckx, Christelijke identiteit, uitdagend en uitgedaagd. Over de rakelingse nabijheid van de onervaarbare God, in: M. Kalsky u. a. (Red.), Ons rakelings nabij, a.a.O., 13–32, hier 16 [Übersetzung MK].

annimmt, wodurch Kirche, Theologie und christliche Identität stets im Wandel begriffen sind.

Die Herausforderung des 21. Jahrhunderts für die europäische Theologie, liegt nach Schillebeeckx' Meinung nicht länger im *fides quaerens intellectum*, dem theologischen *Adagium* der modernen Zeit, sondern in der Frage, wie inmitten einer säkularisierten Gesellschaft Lebensinn und Glaube gefunden werden kann: *intellectus quaerens fidem*. Wie können wir im Zeitalter der Globalisierung und der damit verbundenen Migration die Frage nach Glaube und Lebenssinn beantworten inmitten eines stets deutlicher werdenden religiösen Pluralismus? Wie kann das Heil Gottes heute den Menschen verkündet werden, in der festen Überzeugung, dass dieser Gott ein *Deus humanissimus* ist, ein Gott für alle Menschen?

4.2 Die Suche nach Wahrheit als multimediale interreligiöse Kommunikation

Wie bereits erwähnt wird am Dominikanischen Studienzentrum zur Zeit ein interdisziplinäres Forschungsprogramm durchgeführt, das den Titel trägt: *Auf der Suche nach einem neuen Wir in den Niederlanden*. Aus dem Studium der Transformationen im religiösen Bereich, das in den vorhergehenden Jahren das theologische Forschungsinteresse am DSTS bestimmte und bei dem vor allem die Individualisierungstendenzen im Zentrum der Aufmerksamkeit standen, entstand nahezu organisch die Frage, wie sich diese inzwischen weit fortgeschrittene Individualisierung auf die Gruppenformung auswirkt. Wie steht es um die soziale Kohärenz der Gesellschaft, wenn die Institute nicht nur im religiösen, sondern auch im gesellschaftlichen Bereich abbröckeln? Gibt es neue, andere Formen der Bindung oder herrscht eine generelle Bindungsangst?[24] Hinzu kam, dass sich durch die weltweite Drohung terroristischer Anschläge extremistischer Muslime und die Ermordung des Cineasten Theo van Gogh im eigenen Land das gesellschaftliche Klima gegenüber dem Islam stets mehr verschärfte. Als Ausdruck der Angst vor dem Islam und der Unzufriedenheit der Bürger mit dem politischen Establishment ist der Wahlsieg der *Partei der Freiheit* (PVV) von Geert Wilders zu deuten. Sie wurde bei den letzten Landeswahlen die drittgrößte Partei in den Niederlanden. Auch in ande-

---

[24] Das erste Buch, das im Rahmen des neuen Forschungsprogramms herausgegeben wurde, thematisiert neben der Suche nach einem ‚neuen Wir' das Thema der Bindung/Bindungsangst: B. Brandsma / M. Kalsky (Hrsg.), W!J-land. Voorbij de bindingsangst, Kampen 2009. Die zweite Publikation, die neue Formen der Verbundenheit untersucht, erschien 2010: J. Bekkenkamp / J. Verheijen (Hrsg.), Als ik W!J word. Nieuwe vormen van verbondenheid, Almere 2010.

ren europäischen Ländern ist diese Tendenz sichtbar, aber in ‚Holland', das bis vor kurzem noch berühmt und berüchtigt war wegen seiner offenen und tolerante Haltung gegenüber vielem, was in anderen Ländern schier undenkbar war – man denke an die Regelung der Euthanasie und die Legalisierung bestimmter Drogen –, fällt die Wende hin zu einer nahezu xenophoben Politik besonders auf.

In einer komplex gewordenen Welt, sind auch Probleme komplex und einfache Lösungen eine Seltenheit. Alles scheint mit allem zusammen zu hängen. Ein Gefühl der Unüberschaubarkeit des eigenen Lebens macht sich breit, die die Menschen ängstlich und unsicher macht. Ständig müssen Entscheidungen getroffen werden, deren Konsequenzen nur schwer einzuschätzen sind. Alle Sicherheiten, bis hin zur Rentenversorgung im Alter, schmelzen wie das Eis am Nordpol. Es ist dann auch nicht verwunderlich, dass die Neigung besteht, sich auf ‚das Eigene' zurückzuziehen, auf das, was in früheren Zeiten Sicherheit und Geborgenheit gab oder das zumindest suggerierte. Dieser Retrotrend, der Rückgriff auf die Vergangenheit, ist in der Gesellschaft überall sichtbar, von der Mode über die Musik bis zum Essen.

Auch im religiösen Bereich ist diese Tendenz zu beobachten. Man begibt sich wieder auf die Suche nach der eigenen katholischen und protestantischen Identität als hätte es nie eine Ökumene gegeben. Abgrenzung gegenüber allem was anders ist, ist angesagt und es ist dann auch kein Wunder, dass der interreligiöse Dialog stagniert. Man kehrt der Zukunft den Rücken zu und sucht das Heil in der Vergangenheit. Verständlich, aber ist es auch vernünftig?

Die Antwort auf diese Frage muss ich schuldig bleiben. Nicht weil eine Antwort im Rahmen dieser Ausführungen zu weit führen würde, sondern weil ich sie ganz einfach zu diesem Zeitpunkt nicht weiß. Und bis jetzt habe ich sie auch noch bei keinem anderen Autor gefunden, zumindest keine zufriedenstellende. Das Paradigma der Diversität stellt uns vor eine neue Situation. Eine Situation, in der es vorläufig mehr Fragen als Antworten gibt. Das Paradigma der Vielfalt benötigt eine neue Denkweise, die die Anderen im Rahmen einer positiven Wertung der Vielheit partizipieren lässt und nicht, wie es bei der Suche nach Einheit häufig der Fall ist, ein- oder ausschließt. Es geht um eine Art des Denkens, die addiert und Beziehungen herstellt, die sich mehr im ‚Sowohl als auch' zu Hause fühlt als im ‚Entweder oder'. Kommunikation und gegenseitiges Verstehen sind heute von größter Wichtigkeit. Die Kunst das empathische Vermögen ein- und auszuüben in der Begegnung mit den Anderen und sich Wissen anzueignen, um die kulturellen und religiösen Weltanschauungen des Nachbarn zu begreifen, sind notwendig für das alltägliche Zusammenleben. Vertrauen aufbauen und eine beziehungsorientierte Integration fördern in der langsam ein ‚neues Wir' entstehen kann, ist jetzt gefragt.

Kurz und gut – es geht darum, Vielfalt als neues Paradigma für Europa zu umarmen[25] und die abgrenzende Haltung des ‚Wir und die Anderen' umzubiegen in ein auf Verbindung hin angelegtes Zusammenleben, dass die Unterschiede nicht zugunsten eines Einheitsideals negiert, sondern fruchtbar macht. Ein geht um ein Projekt, das sich auf die Zukunft hin orientiert und sich inspirieren lässt von den weisheitlichen Schätzen unterschiedlicher religiöser und humanistischer Weltanschauungen und Traditionen, wie beispielsweise dem Wert des Mitgefühls (*compassion*), das Karen Armstrong in ihrer *Charter for Compassion*[26] zu Richtlinien ausgearbeitet hat für Religion und Gesellschaft und die zur Zeit in den Niederlanden in vielen kirchlichen und gesellschaftlichen Kreisen diskutiert und praktisch umgesetzt werden.

4.2.1 Ein neues Wir

Bei der Suche nach Möglichkeiten, das Paradigma der Vielfalt als Zeichen der Zeit in Theologie und Gesellschaft ernst zu nehmen, entstand am Dominikanischen Studienzentrum die Idee, neben der wissenschaftlichen Arbeit des Forschungsteams, auch ein Internet-Projekt zu entwickeln, das die Kommunikation über dasjenige, was zu einem neuen Wir dazugehört, in der Gesellschaft fördert. Im Dezember 2009 ging die multimediale Webseite www.nieuwwij.nl online. Das Motto der Website, die mit finanzieller Unterstützung des niederländischen Ministeriums für Integration gebaut wurde, lautet: „W!J – verbind de verschillen!" (W!R – verbinde die Unterschiede!) Kein Einheitsdenken sollte auf dieser Site demonstriert werden, sondern sie sollte als Plattform fungieren für unterschiedliche Meinungen, Beiträge und Reaktionen. Um deutlich zu machen, dass es sich um ein neues, noch zu suchendes ‚Wir' handelte, wurde die Schreibweise W!R gewählt. Junge Websitedesigner entwarfen und bauten die Site nach den neusten ICT Erkenntnissen. Sie ist multimedial, interaktiv und umfasst einen Servicebereich, der alle Projekte in den Niederlanden vermeldet, die sich mit Fragen der interreligiösen Kommunikation beschäfti-

---

[25] Vgl. hiezu M. Kalsky, Embracing Diversity. Reflections on the Transformation of Christian Identity, in: *Studies in Interreligious Dialogue* 17,2 (2007), 221–231.
[26] Zum Inhalt des Manifests siehe www.charterforcompassion.org [7.7.2011].

gen. Ziel der Website ist es, Menschen in Bild und Schrift zu informieren, zu stimulieren sich mit den angegebenen Themen zu befassen und sich darüber eine eigene Meinung zu bilden. Auch können sie Fragen stellen und sich anschließen bei bestehenden Gruppen, die es bereits in ihrer Umgebung gibt. Jeden Monat steht ein neues Thema zur Debatte, das mit einem ‚neuen Wir' in den Niederlanden zu tun hat. Täglich werden neue Berichte und Beiträge hinzugefügt. Junge Generation Y-Mitarbeitern machen Videos, in denen bekannte und unbekannte Niederländer/-innen sich zu den Themen äußern und/oder Projekte sehen lassen, die mit einem ‚neuen Wir' zu tun haben. Es führt zu weit, an dieser Stelle auf die Gesamtkonzeption der Website einzugehen. Auf der Homepage ist ein Trailer zu finden, der das W!J Projekt umschreibt und die Möglichkeiten der Website näher erläutert.[27]

Die Zeichen der Zeit verstehen und ihnen mit offenem Visier entgegentreten, wie Edward Schillebeeckx das in seiner Zeit tat, bedeutet heute Gebrauch zu machen von den Möglichkeiten die das WorldWideWeb bietet. Für die ältere Generation ist dies möglicherweise weniger evident, aber um eine junge Generation zu erreichen, ist der Einsatz von Internet, Facebook und Twitter ein *must*. Den Puls der Zeit fühlen und mit beiden Beinen in der Gesellschaft zu stehen, bedeutet auch für Theologen sich den Herausforderungen der Globalisierung und der Migration zu stellen und die Begegnung mit Andersdenkenden und Andersgläubigen in einer säkularen Gesellschaft nicht zu scheuen. Konfrontationen die Stirn bieten und inmitten dieser nicht immer einfachen Begegnungen nach Momenten des Heils Gottes zu suchen, ist meines Erachtens die Aufgabe, die im 21. Jahrhundert auf die Theologie zukommt. Der Erfolg der Website, gemessen an 15.000 einzelnen Besuchern (*unique visitors*) pro Monat und die Verwendung vieler Beiträge von www.nieuwwij.nl auf anderen Sites und in anderen Medien, bestätigt diese Vermutung.[28]

Es sei deutlich, dass die Antwort, welche Zutaten ein ‚neues Wir' braucht, um allen Bürgern in Europa ein Gefühl der Geborgenheit und Sicherheit zu geben, nur in der gemeinsamen Suche danach gefunden werden kann. Viel hängt im religiösen Bereich davon ab, ob es gelingen wird, religiöse Unterschiede anzuerkennen und nicht zu bekämpfen. Timothy Radcliffe, der frühere Magister des Dominikanerordens, hat zur heutigen Rolle des Christentums in Europa beherzenswerte Dinge gesagt.

---

[27] Vgl. www.nieuwwij.nl [7.7.2011].
[28] Vgl. den DSTS-Jahresbericht 2010: http://www.dsts.nl/DSTS_Jaarverslag_2010.pdf [7.7.2011].

Für ihn ist die entscheidende Frage, ob die unterschiedlichen Religionen in der Lage sind, friedvoll miteinander zusammen zu leben oder ob sie Europa zerreißen werden. Vieles hängt seiner Meinung davon ab, ob die Menschen in Europa es zulassen, dass Europa zur Heimat aller Religionen wird. Radcliffe meint, dass das nur dann gelingen kann, wenn das Christentum dazu bereit ist, Menschen auf der Suche nach dem Guten, dem Wahren und dem Schönen zu begleiten. Begleiten bedeutet für ihn nicht in erster Instanz das Erstellen von Geboten, an die man sich zu halten hat, sondern die Vermittlung von christlichen Werten, von Tugenden als Lebensmittel für unterwegs. Zu diesem Zweck greift Radcliffe die vier Kardinaltugenden – Mut, Weisheit, Mäßigkeit und Gerechtigkeit – auf und fügt die drei theologischen Grundtugenden von Thomas von Aquin – Glaube, Liebe, Hoffnung – hinzu. Es gehe nicht um Regelgebung, sondern um moralisches Handeln, um eine christliche Ethik als Beitrag des Christentums für die Menschen, die in Europa Pilger sind. Kirche und Theologie, so fordert Radcliffe, müssen deren Wegbegleiter sein, sie dort abholen, wo sie heute stehen, egal ob der Ort übereinkommt mit den Normen der Kirche oder nicht.

Auch Radcliffe geht es um die Suche nach Wahrheit und um den Glauben daran, Wahrheit gemeinsam mit anderen Religionen finden zu können. Viel zu oft streiten Religionen seiner Meinung nach um Wahrheitsansprüche, was Intoleranz, Indoktrination und gewalttätige Auseinandersetzungen zur Folge hat. Stattdessen sollte es um den Mut gehen, Fragen zu stellen, ohne die Antworten schon im Voraus zu kennen; die „Anderen" nicht aus der eigenen christlichen Sicht heraus zu belehren, sondern selbst lernfähig zu sein. Außer dem Mut ihre eigenen Überzeugungen zu verkünden, müsse die Kirche auch den Mut haben zuzugeben, dass auch sie letztendlich nicht wirklich wissen und benennen kann, wer oder was Gott ist. Sie müsse die Bescheidenheit besitzen, von anderen Religionen lernen zu wollen und sich gemeinsam mit ihnen auf eine Pilgerreise begeben, auf der Suche nach Wahrheit.[29]

Auch bei Radcliffe ist die Stimme Edward Schillebeeckx zu hören, die dazu mahnt, christliche Wahrheit nicht mit einem inquisitorischen Wahrheitsanspruch zu verwechseln. Vielmehr geht es um eine Wahrheit, die uns als Christen im Leben Jesu als proleptisches Zeichen bereits vorge-

---

[29] T. Radcliffe, Godsdienst kan Europa verscheuren of samenbrengen, in: *Tertio* v. 10.8.2005 (Nr. 287), 6–7; vgl. ebenfalls M. Kalsky, Wahrheit in Begegnung. Die Transformation christlicher Identität angesichts kultureller und religiöser Pluralität, in: Christian Identity I / Christliche Identität I (Forum Mission Bd. 2), Luzern 2006, 29–52, bes. 45ff.

ben ist, sich jedoch im Horizont des Königreich Gottes immer wieder neu bewahrheiten muss. Wahrheit als die Realisierung des guten Lebens für alle, die im Zeitalter der Diversität nach Verbindungen zwischen Menschen von unterschiedlichen religiösen und nicht-religiösen Weltanschauungen sucht, ohne dabei die Unterschiede aus den Augen zu verlieren.[30]

5. Die Weitergabe des Feuers

Im Februar 2008 bekam ich die Gelegenheit noch ein Video-Interview mit Edward Schillebeeckx zu machen. Der Anlass hierfür war das 20jährige Bestehen des Dominikanischen Studienzentrums, das einen Monat später mit einem Symposium in Nimwegen gefeiert werden sollte. Das Video war als historischer Rückblick auf zwanzig Jahre DSTS gedacht. Desöfteren hatte Edward Schillebeeckx zu erkennen gegeben, die Arbeit am Studienzentrum mit Sympathie zu verfolgen. Zu seinem 90. Geburtstag hatten wir, wie bereits erwähnt, eine Festschrift herausgegeben, aber seine eigene theologische Arbeit war nicht direkt das Objekt unserer Forschung. Dennoch versteht und verstand sich das DSTS in seiner Theologieausübung im Geiste Edward Schillebeeckx', wie ich im Vorhergehenden versucht habe aufzuzeigen, und so wollte ich gerne von ihm wissen, was er für die Zukunft theologisch wichtig fand und worauf wir uns seines Erachtens konzentrieren sollten.

Er hatte sichtlich Mühe, alle theologischen Gedanken, die er als Vorbereitung auf das Interview in seitenlangen Aufzeichnungen niedergeschrieben hatte, so zu ordnen, dass sie sich in ein logisches Zusammenspiel fügten. Die Gehirn-Attacke, die ihn einige Monate zuvor getroffen hatte, hatte Hiate in seinem Sprachschatz hinterlassen und erschwerte das Finden der richtigen Worte. Im Hintergrund mahnte eine besorgte Hadewych Snijdewind mit Gebärden, das Gespräch zu beenden, da die vereinbarte halbe Stunde schon lange überschritten war und die Erschöpfung nach Ablauf des Gesprächs zu groß sein würde. Aber meine Versuche das Gespräch zu beenden, scheiterten kläglich. Er ließ sich ganz einfach nicht unterbrechen, geschweige denn stoppen. Gezeichnet von seiner Krankheit und dennoch mit fast jugendlichem Charme saß mir ein

---

[30] D. Strahm/ M. Kalsky (Hrsg.), Damit es anders wird zwischen uns. Interreligiöser Dialog aus der Sicht von Frauen, Ostfildern 2006.

94jähriger passionierter und ‚glücklicher' Theologe³¹ gegenüber, der mit dem, was er am liebsten tat, beschäftigt war: Theologie treiben inmitten des Zeitgeschehens. Und dann – ganz plötzlich war da wieder diese offensive kirchliche Treue, von der sein Freund Johann Baptist Metz in seiner zu Beginn des Artikels erwähnten Rede gesprochen hatte. Mit nahezu jungendlichem Kampfgeist sagte er fern: „Da kämpfe ich schon mein ganzes Leben lang gegen" – und ich fragte ihn ‚wogegen'? „Gegen die Kirche", antwortete er, „aber ich bleibe drin, gerade um etwas zu verändern und ich denke, dass das schwierig ist, aber wenn man raus geht oder irgendwo anders hingeht [...] wir müssen innerhalb der Kirche nach etwas Neuem suchen oder innerhalb der Gemeinschaften, denn es wird sich im Kleinen vollziehen müssen, kleine Bezirke [...] ich weiß nicht wie [...] aber in jedem Fall kommt es nicht aus Rom."³² Es klang als hätte er noch ein ganzes Leben vor sich.

Was bedeutet dies alles für die Suche nach einem neuen ‚Wir'? Nach einem ‚Wir', das sich in dieser Zeit möglicherweise weiter von der Kirche wegbewegt als Edward Schillebeeckx lieb gewesen wäre. Nach einem Wir, das nicht länger auf dem Paradigma der Einheit weiterbauen kann, sondern sich den Herausforderungen (nicht-)religiöser und kultureller Diversität stellen muss. Was hat Edward Schillebeeckx zukünftigen Theologen zu bieten? Bleibt seine Theologie auch in Zukunft relevant? Die wirkliche Antwort hierauf, können nur zukünftige Theologen und Theologinnen geben. Ich kann nur vermuten, worin die bleibende Relevanz seines Werkes für die Arbeit am Dominikanischen Studienzentrum liegt, nämlich:
– in seiner induktiven Methode, die Raum lässt für die alltägliche Erfahrung von Menschen und so anstelle theologischer Selbstbespiegelung, den Austausch und das experimentelle Zusammenspiel von Theologie und Gesellschaft fördert;
– in der Ausübung einer empathisch orientierten dominikanischen Spiritualität, die nicht ausgrenzt, sondern auf Verbindung und Kommunikation hin angelegt ist und so eine zeitgemäße anthropologisch-interreligiöse Ausrichtung der Theologie möglich macht;
– weil das Herzstück seiner Theologie das menschliche Sehnen nach der Praxis des Königreiches Gottes umfasst; die biblische Vision des gu-

---

[31] In einem Interview: E. Schillebeeckx, I am a Happy Theologian. Conversations with Francesco Strazzari, London 1994.
[32] E. Schillebeeckx im Gespräch mit M. Kalsky [Übersetzung MK], in: Film anlässlich des 20jährigen Bestehens des DSTS: http://www.dsts.nl/Film%20DSTS.htm [7.7.2011].

ten Lebens für alle, in der der Wolf neben dem Lamm liegt und die Letzten die Ersten sein werden.

Inwiefern diesen drei Punkten eine Exegese oder Eisegese der Theologie Schillebeeckx zu Grunde liegt, überlasse ich dem Urteil der Schillebeeckx-Expert/-innen.[33] Für die Arbeit am Dominikanischen Studienzentrum und dessen Suche nach Verbindungen zwischen Theologie und Gesellschaft sind sie eine bleibende Inspiration und theologische Herausforderung im Fortschreiben der dominikanischen Tradition, einer Tradition, die sich nicht ‚die Anbetung der Asche' zur Aufgabe gemacht hat, sondern ‚die Weitergabe des Feuers.'[34]

* * *

Abstract of the contribution of Manuela Kalsky

This article focuses on the relevance of Edward Schillebeeckx's theological work at the Dominican Study Centre for Theology and Society (DSTS). Before Manuela Kalsky demonstrates Schillebeeckx's insights within the interdisciplinary and multi-medial DSTS research project called "On the search for a 'new we'," she first describes how Schillebeeckx – using a hermeneutical method – reached his conviction that no salvation can be found outside the world.

Just like other DSTS scholars, Schillebeeckx was concerned with a contextual theological practice in search of a connection between theology and society. While we find no dogmatic arguments at the core of his theological work, his insights can nevertheless help us to search traces of God's truth embedded in people's living in the world. His inductive method, which draws on views of a theology of redemption, envisions everyday human experiences as being a *locus theologicus*. This method is one of the theological tools at the DSTS that echoes a Dominican spirituality

---

[33] Zur bleibenden Bedeutung von Schillebeeckx siehe auch R.J. Schreiter, Edward Schillebeeckx. His Continuing Significance, in: M.C. Hilkert / R.J. Schreiter (Eds.), The Praxis of the Reign of God, a.a.O., 185–194.

[34] Der Satz „Tradition ist die Weitergabe des Feuers und nicht die Anbetung der Asche" stammt von dem österreichischen Komponisten Gustav Mahler.

* Ich danke Leo Oosterveen für seinen Kommentar.

based on empathy-oriented and communication-based interpretations. Both interpretative aspects are at all times an inspiration for an up-to-date understanding of a practice-based theology that promotes the wellbeing for everyone, and which is expressed at the current DSTS inter-religious search for the "new we."

Translation from German: *Tracy Rammler*

Erik Borgman

„... LIKE A SACRAMENT"

Towards a theological view on the real existing church

The only time I was really shocked by one of Edward Schillebeeckx's texts, was in 1989 when the Dutch original of *Church, the Human Story of God* was published. In its introduction Schillebeeckx explained that he had not written the book he had envisaged as part three of his trilogy on the meaning of Jesus as the Christ – a sequel to *Jesus* (1974, English translation 1979) and *Christ* (1977, English translation 1980). He had intended to publish a book about the church as the historical and institutional embodiment of Jesus' message, but "[d]elight in belonging to this church, a delight which increased greatly during the Second Vatican Council and the years immediately following, has been sorely tested over the last decade."[1] What shocked me was Schillebeeckx's conclusion that given that situation, it would not be worthwhile to reflect theologically on the church. I, on the other hand, believed that the various forms of liberation theology had taught me that the liberating message of the Gospel could indeed be clarified by critically examining our own context, and by facing the struggle between the hopes and threats within that context. Why would not the same be true of the of the Roman Catholic church in the 1980s?

The entire first part of *Church, the Human Story of God* is dedicated to reflections on the continuing, ever renewing meaning of the Christian traditional notion of experience. In a sentence typical of Schillebeeckx, bursting at the seams because so much had to be said in the same breath, he states that, "The conclusion is that there is Christian identity *in* cultural breaks and shifts, and not an identity on the basis of what in a purely in-

---

[1] E. Schillebeeckx, Church, The Human Story of God, New York: Crossroads, 1990, xiii.

tellectualistic way used to be called 'homogeneous identity' (which cannot of course be proved historically)."[2] It does make one wonder even more acutely where the idea came from that any meaningful theological thought about the church would be dependent upon a clear institutional guarantee of Christian freedom as it is rediscovered at the Council. Towards the end of *Church, the Human Story of God*, Schillebeeckx himself writes that no one and nothing outside or inside the church holds a lease on the Spirit of God. All are dependent on and are put into perspective by "the living God, who brings his creation in Jesus Christ, through our history, to a final consummation after history."[3] This is not about a church that threatens to extinguish the Spirit, this is about a Spirit that keeps the church dynamic and inspires it to an existence in relation to the world and its history understood as the space of God's presence.

The central question of this article is, therefore, where this ambiguity in Schillebeeckx's vision on the church comes from. I aim to break away from it and present a theological vision on the real existing church. Where does it stand in our relation to God? This, in my view, necessarily entails a rather extensive discussion of God's presence in history, outside the church.[4]

1. The nature and role of tradition

The foreword to *Church, the Human Story of God* has not been written during a sudden attack of depression. It shows a curious impasse in the theology of the later Schillebeeckx. The first chapter of the book mainly concentrates on the revelatory power of the so-called contrast experience, experiences that tell us that the situation we live in is not right, and that seem to cry out for change. These experiences are revelatory. The good, towards which human existence is naturally oriented, according to Schil-

---

[2] Ibid., 1–45: "World History and Salvation History, History of Revelation and History of Suffering"; quote 44.
[3] Ibid., 228.
[4] L. Boeve, "The Enduring Significance and Relevance of Edward Schillebeeckx? Introducing the State of the Question in Medias Res", in: idem. / F. Depoortere / St. van Erp (Eds.), Edward Schillebeeckx in Contemporary Theology, London: T. & T. Clark, 2010, 1–24) suggests that in general my interpretation of Schillebeeckx regarding the theological meaning of the world and its history goes beyond what Schillebeeckx himself would have said. This article will show to what extent that may be true. In general, I feel supported in this by Schillebeeckx himself who, in a personal message he once wrote on a book of mine, that I was opening up 'new perspectives' for the future of theology, along the lines of his own work.

lebeeckx's anthropology (an anthropology that is ultimately based on that of Thomas Aquinas), comes to light in it in a negative, but real manner. To Schillebeeckx, this is a hint of the presence of God. Next, the second chapter deals with religious traditions as testimonies of encounters with God that can only be expressed in a human language, bound to concrete times and situations. Religions, when regarded as encompassing ways of dealing with the world in the light of that which reveals itself in contrast experiences, are the spaces in which the word 'God' can be used in a meaningful way. The third chapter focuses on the way in which this encounter, and God and man as the partners involved in this encounter, are regarded by Christianity in the person of Jesus. The fourth chapter then distils from all of this the basic outlines for 'a democratic rule of the church as a community of God.' In his treatment of these last two matters, developments in the real existing church after the apostolic age are of no importance.

1.1. The role of the histories of theology and of devotion

This is remarkable, particularly for Schillebeeckx. Already in *De sacramentele heilseconomie* and in his lecture notes from Leuven from the nineteen fifties, he had dwelt extensively on the development of theological thought outside the work of Thomas Aquinas, which at the time was still the norm for theological thinking. He was of the opinion that the entire history of theology, as an intellectual expression of the sense of faith of the faithful, forever developing in relation to their contemporary context, was constitutive of the contemporary situation. He concluded therefore, that detailed knowledge of this history was indispensable to theologians.[5] With this in mind, in *Christ* he painstakingly analyzed the various layers and movements within the Christian traditions, from the New Testament up to the great Christological councils of the fourth and fifth centuries. His aim here is no so much to rescue the original, pure unity of faith from the plurality of interpretations added later. He aims to provide insight into the new theologies developing within a Hellenistic context as fundamentally authentic forms of Christian confession within circumstances that are new compared to those in which Jesus lived.

Considering Schillebeeckx's ideas about theology and the importance of the history of theology, it would have made sense if – to limit myself

[5] Cf. E. Borgman, Edward Schillebeeckx: A Theologian in his History. Part I: A Catholic Theology of Culture (1914–1985), London: Continuum, 2003, 191–282.

here to the church – *Church, the Human Story of God* had provided a detailed investigation of the historical developments in the theological reflections on the church and its implicit vision on the unique identity to which Christians are called in relation to the world.[6] It seems that it would have confronted him rather acutely with the fact that, meeting with and reflecting on constantly changing contexts, the church has always regarded itself in terms of a continuity of tradition, of an anticipation of that which was promised as salvation, and as the actual presence of that tradition and that promise. The content and the nature of these three, the authorities they represent and the relation between them, have always been the subject of much debate. In line with Schillebeeckx's idea of hermeneutics, I believe we could say that this continuing struggle to formulate adequately what the church is, is in fact the hidden manifestation of the identity of the church. This identity cannot be unambiguously determined, however.

The Church with a Human Face, Schillebeeckx's study on ministry in the church published in 1985, does pay extensive attention to the history of theology. Earlier theologies of ministry are not discussed in their own right, however. They appear as either the causes of the current problems, or as the suppliers of possible solutions to those problems. Put differently, it is not the devotional and theological development of which the present is also part that gets the attention. The attention is focused on the contemporary problems involving ministry and priesthood that are regarded as pressing. And, undoubtedly, they are. It comes as a shock to see just how topical Schillebeeckx's description of the consequences of this issue still remains after 25 years: "'the word' is detached from 'the sacrament', Bible teaching becomes a secular occupation, the liturgist is cut off from the community which celebrates the liturgy; those who have to accompany the sick to their deaths have abruptly to hand over the sacramental sealing of this whole process to a strange priest summoned from elsewhere – to the disillusionment of the dying person; above all, the eucharist, so highly praised in Vatican II as a place where the heart of the community beats, must now suddenly give place to other liturgical celebrations (praiseworthy and welcome though they may be in themselves) for want of a priest, and many believers have to be content with a longing

---

[6] An attempt at such an approach had been made by R. Haight in his trilogy Christian Community in History. Part I: Historical Ecclesiology, New York: Continuum, 2004; Part II: Comparative Ecclesiology, New York: Continuum, 2005; Part III: Ecclesial Existence, New York: Continuum, 2008.

for the eucharist; and so on."⁷

Schillebeeckx refers to situations in which, as a result of the current criteria for ordination, people with a life-long commitment are nevertheless unable to officiate in the Eucharist, thus denying the community this sacrament for longer periods of time, as "difficult to place ecclesiologically" and speaks of a church of Christ that is "indeed stood on its head."⁸

In *The Church with a Human Face*, Schillebeeckx focuses on the problem of over emphasizing on the exceptionality of priesthood, as a result of which priests seemed to operate entirely separate from the community they should serve, as compared with the Biblical viewpoint.⁹ His aim is to return to the conditions as they were at the time of the New Testament, which he believes would ideally match the expectations of the modern faithful because of their informality and flexibility. This does make the many ages of reflection on ministry and on priesthood in the church seem an aberration, almost by definition. The idea by the Second Vatican Council that the church should first be regarded as the people of God before the office of the hierarchy can be regarded as sacramental within that church, thus can only be seen as the sudden and miraculous resurrection of a long lost truth.

It would have been different if Schillebeeckx had, for example, also pointed out that the starkly sacramental concept of office after the council of Trent actually made it possible to see the priesthood as a calling not just reserved for aristocrats and intellectuals who would take up the leading positions anyway, but also for common men.¹⁰ The strong emphasis on the qualitative difference between the people and the clergy at the same time paradoxically created a relatively close social proximity. In a rather more theological vein, Schillebeeckx could have pointed out that it was precisely the exalted idea of the priest as 'alter Christus' that made

---

[7] E. Schillebeeckx, The Church with a Human Face: A New and Expanded Theology of Ministry, New York: Crossroad 1985, 265.

[8] Ibid., 265. More than twenty years later, the Dutch Dominicans published their brochure 'Kerk en ambt: Onderweg naar een kerk met toekomst', Nijmegen: Valkhof Pers, 2007, which takes a similar point of view.

[9] See also E. Schillebeeckx, Ministry, leadership in the community of Jesus Christ, New York: Crossroad, 1981, of which 'The Church with a Human Face' is the extended second edition.

[10] The biography of Jean Marie Baptiste Vianney (1786–1859), the Saintly pastor of Ars, is an example of the remarkable combination of limited intellectual capacities, great personal piety, extreme dedication to the spiritual welfare of his parishioners, and a highly exalted concept of the priesthood. The statements he made about humankind being lost without priests because any real contact with God would not be possible and heaven would remain closed, should not simply be dismissed as an overestimation of the clerical identity. They are just as much testimony to a strong sense of responsibility and great devotion.

priests in the 1940s and 50s search for forms of 'incarnation' in the daily lives of the workers. They did not consider this to be a departure from the exalted idea of priesthood, but rather a radicalized form of it, in imitation of divine *kenosis*.[11]

Just how strongly Schillebeeckx regards everything in terms of a deadlocked struggle about church politics during the mid-1980s, is apparent from the way in which, in *The Church with a Human Face*, he talks of an ideological critique of the existing concept of priesthood, based on contemporary negative experiences because of this concept.[12] Much earlier, at the beginning of the 1970s, he had explicitly concluded that the traditions of the church and of theology handed on both meaningful and meaningless things, truths as well as lies. It is a constant task for theology to distinguish between the two in the light of new experiences.[13] A critique of ideology in this sense will have to be seen as part of a new hermeneutics aimed at establishing the correct interpretation of both the text that was handed down and the contemporary situation, to discover what can truly be called Christian tradition. In *The Church with a Human Face* however, Schillebeeckx seems to regard the critique of ideology as simply the exposure of a clerical power politics that unjustly tries to establish its legitimacy.[14]

1.2. The 'one subject church'?

The question of a legitimate place for criticism of the tradition of the church and particularly the question as to what extent the Second Vatican Council provoked a radically new interpretation of the Christian and catholic tradition that also corrected earlier interpretations, has been a constant issue with its documents. Time and again, the teaching authority made clear that new insight could only be legitimate to the extent that there were further explanations of earlier statements. This had led to the condemnation by pope Paul VI in 1965 of attempts in keeping with the

---

[11] For Schillebeeckx's connections to the worker-priests, see E. Borgman, Edward Schillebeeckx, Part I, op. cit., 126–132.
[12] E. Schillebeeckx, The Church with a Human Face, op. cit., 6–12.
[13] See idem, The Understanding of Faith: Interpretation and Criticism, London: Sheed and Ward, 1974, particularly the last part.
[14] All of this should however be read against the background of Schillebeeckx's conflict with the Congregation for the Doctrine of the Faith, concerning his theology of ministry. The developments in the conflict only served to strengthen his belief that the magisterium of the Roman Catholic church was not interested in a conversation about new possibilities, but mainly sought to bar these.

conciliar literary reform of the liturgy, particularly by Dutch theologians, to find entirely new words for the concept, which up to that point, had been referred to with the term 'transubstantiation', in view of the contemporary cultural and intellectual situation. Only further explanations of the exact meaning of this concept as confirmed by the Council of Trent, were considered to be authentically catholic.[15]

Almost from the very start of his pontificate, Benedict XVI has made the correct interpretation of the documents of the Vatican II a central issue. On 22 December 2005, approximately eight months after he took office and roughly forty years after the conclusion of the Council, Joseph Ratzinger used an address to the Roman curia and the prelacy to distinguish sharply between two interpretations of Council documents: "On the one hand, there is an interpretation that I would call 'a hermeneutic of discontinuity and rupture;' it has frequently availed itself of the sympathies of the mass media, and also one trend of modern theology. On the other, there is the 'hermeneutic of reform,' of renewal in the continuity of the one subject-Church, which the Lord has given to us. She is a subject which increases in time and develops, yet always remaining the same, the one subject of the journeying People of God."[16]

There is much more at stake than just the adequate interpretation of ecclesiastical documents: their relation to other documents and the greater part of history to which they are connected, also need to be considered. In the end, to Ratzinger this is about the correct understanding of the church and its relation to modernity.

As early as ten years after the Council, in 1975, Joseph Ratzinger, who at that time was neither bishop nor cardinal, but merely professor at the University of Regensburg, protested against the way in which the pastoral constitution on the church in the modern world, *Gaudium et Spes*, had been used to justify a strong identification of the church with secular de-

---

[15] Cf. the encyclical *Mysterium fidei* of pope Paulus VI (3 sept. 1965); see E. Borgman, Edward Schillebeeckx, Part I, op. cit., 337–345.

[16] See http://www.vatican.va/holy_father/benedict_xvi/speeches/2005/december/documents /hf_ben_xvi_spe_20051222_roman-curia_en.html [07/11/2011]. As far as it refers to the interpretation of Vatican II, this address is quoted as Benedict XVI, 'A Proper Hermeneutic for the Second Vatican Council', in: M.L. Lamb / M.W. Levering (Eds.), Vatican II: Renewal within Tradition, Oxford: Oxford University Press, 2008, ix–xv. Ratzingers approach also involves an attack upon the history of the Council by G. Alberigo / J.A. Komonchak, History of Vatican II, Maryknoll: Orbis – Leuven: Peeters 1996–2006, 5 parts, which supposedly overemphasizes the contradistinctions and the struggle both during and after the Council.

velopments.[17] He considered this tendency, which was especially strong in the Netherlands, he explicitly states, to be mistaken, because it would mean that the church surrendered its critical distance regarding modernity. Ratzinger thought that the introduction of *Gaudium et Spes* in particular was too optimistic about modernity, but that this one-sidedness is later remedied by this document. However, just like in his address of 2005, Ratzinger's key point in 1975 was that the church can only rightly be considered the dwelling place of God's truth if it is independent from its worldly context. He believes that only if the church contains the truth within itself, the faithful can see themselves as true 'co-operators of the truth' – Ratzinger chose 'cooperatores veritatis' (cf. 3 John 8) as his motto at his investiture as archbishop of Munster and Freising in 1977.

In the end, Ratzinger rejects a 'hermeneutic of discontinuity' of the documents of the Second Vatican Council for the same reason that leads him to reject a 'hermeneutic of discontinuity' for biblical texts in his books about Jesus.[18] The church's credibility as a faithful witness to the truth entrusted to it by God in Jesus Christ would be endangered. In his 2005 address, he is clear about this: to him, the church is "a subject which increases in time and develops, yet always remaining the same"[19]. To a large extent, this means a return to the opposition that determined the Roman Catholic Church's self-image and attitude from Leo XIII to Pius XII. This distinctions sharply between an internally divided modernity, torn by contradictory tendencies on the one hand, and the Catholic church on the other, the latter being able to redeem mankind from its destructive powers because it remains outside modernity.[20] At Christmas of 2009 during his blessing *urbi et orbi*, and referring to the introit of the daylight mass of Christmas, "A light will shine on us this day, the Lord is born for us," Benedict XVI characterized the church as the 'us' which carries the divine light and offers it to the human family "profoundly affected by a grave financial crisis, yet even more by a moral crisis, and by the painful wounds of wars and conflicts."[21] The church is a subject that

---

[17] J. Ratzinger, "Der Weltdienst der Kirche: Auswirkungen von 'Gaudium et Spes' im letzten Jahrzehnt", in: *Internationale katholische Zeitschrift Communio* 4 (1975), 439–454.

[18] Cf. E. Borgman, "Opening Up New History: Jesus of Nazareth as the Beginning of a New History", in: *Concilium* 44 (2008) no. 3, 64–72.

[19] Benedict XVI, A Proper Hermeneutic for the Second Vatican Council, op. cit., x.

[20] This sharp distinction can be found throughout the works of Ratzinger; cf. T. Rowland, *Ratzinger's Faith: The Theology of Pope Benedict XVI*, Oxford: Oxford University Press, 2008; L. Boeve / G. Mannion (Eds.), *The Ratzinger Reader*, London: T. & T. Clark, 2010.

[21] http://www.vatican.va/holy_father/benedict_xvi/messages/urbi/documents/hf_ben-xvi_es_20091225_urbi_en.html [7.11.2011].

carries the truth in itself and shares out the riches it has received from God, in a world that would be devoid of this truth without the church.

Thus, only two days after his death, Schillebeeckx seemed to be right all along: this is indeed a completely different spirit than that of the solidarity in which *Gaudium et Spes* is introduced. That document declares that the church is intimately connected with the "joys and the hopes, the grief and the anxieties of the men of this age, especially those who are poor or in any way afflicted" (nr. 1). The vision presented by the pope on Christmas Day on the other hand, is characteristic of a church that maintains its distance from the insecure world of man and like the Virgin Mary, offers to the world Jesus, the Son, whom she herself has received as a gift, the One who came to set mankind free from the slavery of sin. Like Mary, the Church does not fear, for that Child is her strength. But she does not keep him for herself: she offers him to all those who seek him with a sincere heart [...]

So according to this view, the church is anything *but* connected to the anxieties of the men of this age. Its connectedness with the world is not one of solidarity, but one that entails the church giving the world what it lacks by itself: God's presence and closeness. This is diametrically opposed to the words of *Gaudium et Spes* which speaks of a "world which the Christian sees as created and sustained by its Maker's love, fallen indeed into the bondage of sin, yet emancipated now by Christ, Who was crucified and rose again to break the strangle hold of personified evil, so that the world might be fashioned anew according to God's design and reach its fulfillment" (nr. 2). According to *Lumen Gentium*, the church is not the mother or the birthplace of this redeeming presence, as the pope's analogy with Mary seems to suggest, but 'like a sacrament', that is: 'sign and instrument' (nr. 1).[22] The world testifies to God's love in a hidden way, has been redeemed by Jesus Christ and is in a state of transformation and completion. The church serves this process by making it visible and by advancing it.

This view of the church, which he believes is the most adequate, is what Schillebeeckx seeks to promote. That is why, in the 1970s and 80s he expressly focuses on Jesus and his mission in life. He believes that this

---

[22] For an analysis of the break with the commitment of especially *Lumen Gentium* and *Gaudium et Spes* during the pontificate of John Paul II in particular, largely under the intellectual supervision of Joseph Ratzinger in his capacity as the Prefect of the Congregation for the Doctrine of the Faith, see E. Borgman, "The Rediscovery of Truth as a Religious Category: The Enduring Legacy of the Second Vatican Council", in: *Bulletin ET* 17 (2006) no. 2, 53–66.

is the criterion for what it really means to be the church, and this renewed encounter with him can break open deadlocked frames of mind and forms of organization.

2. ... like a sacrament: sign and instrument

We would be justified in saying that this was a central aim of Schillebeeckx's Christological project: breaking with the assumption that the Jesus of Nazareth that the faithful confessed to as the salvation from God would by definition be the same as the one the church offers to the world for its salvation. If the Savior and the Son of God the church confesses to has nothing to do with the Jesus that walked upon this earth, Christianity becomes nothing more than an unhistorical 'myth' that has lost its specific and critical meaning. It will then have to be restored.

2.1. Belief in Jesus' message and acts, and belief in Jesus as Christ

This is why the attention to exegetical details that is so typical to *Jesus, An Experiment in Christology*, is of theological importance, according to Schillebeeckx. "[I]f we ask what is meant by the 'eschatological salvation' given to us by the crucified-and-risen One, to give substance and content to this we have to point to Jesus of Nazareth himself, his person and his whole career and course of action up to and including his death."[23] Schillebeeckx believes that, apart from the faith he evokes right up to this day, it is possible to attain imperfect, yet genuine knowledge of Jesus through historical-critical investigation.

Schillebeeckx's aim is not to found Christian faith on that 'historical Jesus,' because just like the 'dogmatic Christ' constructed by theology, this is an abstraction, determined in this case by the possibilities and limits of the historical method.[24] Christian faith is ultimately about a personal encounter with a concrete human being. Why and how a person is encouraged to see a 'Parable of God' in Jesus in such an encounter remains a mystery which can ultimately not be justified theoretically, according to Schillebeeckx.[25] The concrete situation of the person that experiences the

---

[23] Cit. E. Schillebeeckx, Jesus, An Experiment in Christology, New York: Seabury Press, 1979, 52.
[24] Idem, Jesus, op. cit., 64–76.
[25] Ibid., 650.

encounter as part of the encounter itself, is in accordance to Schillebeeckx's hermeneutical concept of faith. He realizes that his own Christology is also very much connected to his time, by keeping with the mentality of the first half of the 1970s and orienting it towards reforming the world in the image of the Kingdom of God, by active solidarity with the poor and the excluded.[26] Only such a faith is believable to modern man, he feels.

In my view, Schillebeeckx's Christology is mainly aimed at bridging a double chasm. Firstly, he wants to show that it is possible to reasonably justify the transition from a faith in Jesus' message to a faith in Jesus as the Christ and the Son of God. The faith in Jesus as Christ is not opposed to Jesus' faith in the Kingdom of God, but its extension. According to Schillebeeckx, Jesus' message and life were based on a close relationship to God as his 'Abba.' That is why the rejection that was implied in his death on the cross demanded a corrective confirmation by God: the apparent break that Jesus had turned into a final prophetic sign of faith by voluntarily submitting to it, had to be healed by God. This is what happens through Jesus' resurrection and his ascension, and it is reaffirmed by the faithful when they confess to him as Christ and the beloved Son of God. Secondly, Schillebeeckx attempts to show that anyone who says he or she is no longer a believer, yet feels inspired by the person of Jesus, is not as different from the believing Christian as either of them might think. The aspects of Jesus that appeal to the faithful are comparable to the inspiration non-Christians can derive from him, Schillebeeckx says. What is most pertinent to this article however, is that faith in Jesus as the Christ is for Schillebeeckx a way of joining Jesus in his faith in the Kingdom of God.

There is a third chasm that is of interest to Schillebeeckx: the chasm between Jesus as a child of his time and the way the New Testament talks about him, and Twentieth Century men and women as children of their time, to whom that same Jesus can still become a means of salvation and of redemption. His vision differs from current followers of Bultmann's program of de-mythologisation. According to Schillebeeckx, we do not need a special method to free Jesus from his captivity in a mythical view of the world that did allow for direct divine intervention in history and even considered this to be likely. According to Bultmann, our fundamen-

---

[26] Ibid., 61; Schillebeeckx quotes the words of the Church as sacrament from Gaudium et Spes, 'that is, as sign and intermediary, of a profound union with God and of unity between all human beings.'

tal break with this worldview – not just theoretically but also and mainly practical: our use of electricity and radio, our faith in modern medicine – makes Jesus' message and acts irrelevant, and it requires a special method of 'de-mythologisation' to recover this relevance.[27] It is typical of Schillebeeckx that is his view the chasm between present and past is continually bridged, namely whenever people testify to having been appealed to by Jesus. The 1960s and 70s witnessed to a minor *boom* in new, popular interpretations of Jesus, showing that Jesus was of evident interest to modern people.[28] The fact that Jesus' message and acts can still be regarded as redeeming by his contemporaries, to Schillebeeckx is a confirmation of the Christian confession which confirms that he is still the Living One.

Do believers within the church and those inspired outside that church actually feel the appeal of Jesus? Popular, contemporary images of Jesus are often just as different from what we read New Testament or what we are able to reconstruct of the historical Jesus, as the images in the church. In 1983, this caused Schillebeeckx to formulate a radical point of view in his valedictory speech as a professor at Nijmegen University, a radical point of view he would develop further in 1989, in his *Church, The Human Story of God*. He introduces the idea of a 'proportional identity': the message contemporary people get from Jesus should relate to their situation in the same way as Jesus message and acts related to his situation.[29] Schillebeeckx suggests that this is a way to *assess* attempts to express the contemporary meaning of Jesus and his message. What is revolutionary about this, as Schillebeeckx himself puts it, is that the model of proportional identity does not merely introduce 'the social-cultural present' 'into the concept of revelation,' but ultimately also into revelation itself. After all, it is not simply a moment of revelation in the past that needs to be reinterpreted time and again: the revelatory aspect of Jesus Christ's life, death and resurrection continually needs to be addressed within the ever-changing historical contexts.

This does, however, initially lead to an aporia. What is clear is that the community of faith cannot simply be the foundation for the continuity

---

[27] Cf. R. Bultmann, Neues Testament und Mythologie: Das Problem der Entmythologisierung der neutestamentlichen Verkündigung, München: Kaiser, 1985 (original 1941).

[28] Cf. W. Kapser / J. Moltmann, Jesus ja – Kirche nein? Zürich: Benziger, 1973.

[29] E. Schillebeeckx, Theologisch geloofsverstaan anno 1983, Baarn: Nelissen, 1983, 14–17; idem, Church, the Human Story of God, op. cit., 40–45. The idea matches that of C. Boff in his Theology and Praxis: Epistemological Foundations, Maryknoll NY: Orbis, 1987 (revised edition), 146–150; cf. also H.J. Pottmeyer, Theologische Erkenntnislehre als kritische Hermeneutik, in: J. Kirchberg / J. Müther (Eds.), Philosophisch-theologische Grenzfragen: Festschrift für Richard Schaeffler, Essen: Ludgerus, 1986, 205–210.

between Jesus and the interpretation of his meaning. Schillebeeckx does sometimes suggest that the continuity with the origin is a given when a contemporary individual allows himself or herself or when a community allows itself to be inspired by Jesus. That would mean a complete reversal of the main aim of Schillebeeckx's Christology, however. The only difference with the views of Ratzinger we looked at earlier then would be that to the latter, the doctrine as formulated and handed down by teaching authority of the church is the indisputable starting point, and that to Schillebeeckx, it is the actual religious consciousness of the church as a community of the faithful, or of the individual that is inspired by Jesus. However, the basis of this continuity can no longer be the exact same Jesus as he has spoken and acted in the past, died and was affirmed in his resurrection as God's ultimate self-revelation either. Schillebeeckx keeps suggesting that the latter is indeed the case. But if we as contemporary human beings depend entirely on the heritage received from the life of Jesus, our own present does not really enter into revelation itself. It would imply that, with the Christian tradition, we receive a message from the past, which, by definition, never really equates the questions and dilemmas of our present.[30]

I would suggest that Schillebeeckx makes a *theological* rather than a *methodological* argument in what he says about the 'proportional identity' of message and context between Jesus and us. Speaking of proportional identity clarifies that the foundation of continuity is neither one-sidedly the Jesus as he still speaks to contemporary people and inspires them from his history, nor is given in the institutionalized church and the apostolic succession. This continuity is theological and lies hidden in the Christ who lives within God and still manifests himself through God's Holy Spirit. The Christ who makes his presence felt in the Spirit is not simply an object of faith and theology from the past or in the church's confession, but the source of an ever-unexpected dynamic which cannot be anticipated. Truly speaking, in faith, about Jesus is forever new and renewing, and he himself is the one that makes this possible time and again through the Spirit.

---

[30] In my published dissertation, Sporen van de bevrijdende God, Kampen: J.H. Kok, 1990, I have tried to show that, by starting from the contemporary context as a place of God's nearness, the various forms of liberation theology have succeeded in breaking this impasse of western theology as it is taught at universities. That is their true theological significance.

2.2. The God of Jesus as an ever-new presence in the Spirit

In *Jesus, An Experiment in Christology*, Schillebeeckx mainly tries to show that there is no break between Jesus' historical existence (to the extent it can be established by means of the historical-critical method), and the believer's confession that he is the Christ of God. This probably explains why all the emphasis in this book, and in the second and largest section of *Christ, The Experience of Jesus as Lord,* is upon the fact that what is said about Jesus later can be regarded as the effect of the revelatory force that emanated from him during his life.[31] According to Schillebeeckx, the 'history of God with man in Jesus, handed on and put into practice by the "community of God"', is a 'history without a historical end' that continues at least until today.[32] It is the revelatory force that lay hidden in Jesus' verbal and practical preaching of the Kingdom of God by means of his historical acts, which can still be felt in our day and age when it is confessed.

This is in line with the idea that Schillebeeckx developed earlier, during his time at Leuven, when his theological work was still entirely determined by his interpretation of Thomas Aquinas. In 1952, Schillebeeckx proposes in his *De sacramentele heilseconomie* that, according to Thomas, the power of the sacraments does not stem from their specific properties, but from the fact that they refer to the salvation that took place in the life, death and resurrection of Jesus. They have no power by themselves, but they pass on the grace that lay hidden in what Jesus did and in what happened in and to Jesus.[33] Accordingly, in *Jesus, An Experiment in Christology*, Schillebeeckx talks of Jesus' resurrection as the divine confirmation of what has happened in Jesus' life. It implies a correction: the rejection of Jesus' message implicit in his death on the cross was undone. The message, however, that in God the salvation for humankind is stronger than a decline and death, is in his view intrinsically a continuation of Jesus' testimony in both words and actions to the imminent Kingdom of God. There has been considerable debate about the question whether Schillebeeckx actually fully confesses to the real resurrection of Jesus, but there is in fact little doubt about this, particularly after he added five pages to

---

[31] E. Schillebeeckx, Christ: The experience of Jesus as Lord, New York: Crossroad, 1980, 112–462.

[32] Ibid., 641–642.

[33] Idem, De sacramentele heilseconomie: Theologische bezinning op S. Thomas' sacramentenleer in het licht van de traditie en van de hedendaagse sacramentsproblematiek, Bilthoven: H. Nelissen, 1952, 142.

the third edition of Dutch edition of *Jesus, An Experiment in Christology* in 1975. There he explains extensively that this divine correction of Jesus' rejection implies that the same Jesus who was killed earlier, does truly live thanks to God. Schillebeeckx summarizes this as follows: "Jesus' resurrection, acknowledged and confessed in and through the apostolic conversion or Easter experience, is: (a) God's legitimation, ratifying and sanctifying of Jesus' person, message and life of service 'unto death'; (b) it is also exaltation and new creation, that is to say, God's *corrective* triumph over the negativity of death and man's history of suffering, in which Jesus participated; in other words, there is life after death; (c) the resurrection is at the same time the sending of the Spirit and, in being that, the founding of the Church, a living fellowship, now renewed, of the personal, living Jesus Christ with his people on earth."[34]

So, Jesus' resurrection is not identical to the news that his message goes on, which reunites his disciples, as sometimes has been suggested – even though, according to Schillebeeckx, this community-restoring message is indeed an aspect of the resurrection.

In view of their content, however, Schillebeeckx interprets the stories about the revelation of Jesus after his death as pertaining first and foremost to the conversion of his disciples. Those who had earlier abandoned Jesus out of fear or lack of faith came to see this as a form of treason. They mend their ways by aligning themselves with him again, and they are gracefully offered a chance to do so. According to Schillebeeckx, the disciples experience at Easter is that they are being converted, by Jesus' initiative, to Jesus as Christ and, thus, finding definitive salvation in him.[35] The content of this conversion is that they return to doing what they did before, something they had erroneously allowed themselves to be distracted from by their failure and guilt: recognizing salvation coming from God in the acts and words of Jesus. This illustrates just how strongly all meaning is encompassed in the acts of the historical Jesus in Schillebeeckx's vision of faith and of the church, regardless of how hard he tries to incorporate and emphasize contemporary interpretations of these acts.

It is obviously beyond the scope of this article to develop a different

---

[34] Idem, Jesus, op. cit., 649; cf. his earlier comments on Jesus' resurrection, 329–398. For the debate on Schillebeeckx's views on the resurrection, see idem, Interim Report on the Books *Jesus* and *Christ*, New York: Seabury Press – London: SCM Press, 1980, 74–93; for the confrontation on this with the Congregation for the Doctrine of Faith, see T. Schoof (Ed.), The Schillebeeckx Case: Official Exchange of Letters and Documents, New York: Ramsey, 1984.

[35] E. Schillebeeckx, Jesus, op. cit., 379.

exegesis of the stories of Jesus' appearances. Yet, I do believe that Schillebeeckx is hard-pressed to do justice to the new, expectation-bursting aspect of the acts of the Risen One in these stories. Rather than referring back to past acts, these stories, like the stories about the Holy Spirit in the Acts of the apostles, seem to express mainly that what has started with and in his live, starts to create history in new and unprecedented ways. At the original end of the gospel of Marc (16:1–8), the women at the grave are told to go to Galilee, not in order to remember what Jesus did there before, but to meet him again. In Acts, the mission that Jesus started within the borders of the land of the Jews expands to the ends of the earth.[36] As far as I am concerned, the image of the Risen One breaking in on his disciples, and the revitalizing Spirit, contradicts the idea that the church mainly exists on what it has received through Jesus' words and acts in history and through God's affirmation of them. It is not simply about the 'story of God with people in Jesus, handed on and practiced by the "communion of God."'

Schillebeeckx has always strongly emphasized that, from a Christian point of view, the fullness of God's presence is not in the past or the present, but in the future.[37] If the church does indeed believe in God's future, this ultimately implies that the church has not just being initiated within history by Jesus, but that it is also, time and again, opened up and appealed to by the Anointed One and his Spirit to render its services to the coming Kingdom of God, which is ever near. Put differently, the radical reinterpretation and recreation in the light of God's near future, the breaking open of set conditions, is typical of Jesus' actions. If he is forever the Living One after the resurrection and the Ascension, his main task is to remain active among us, breaking open and recreating, rather than coinciding with the church as it has become, or with the memory of his actions and his message as they have been. I believe this is in accordance with the idea that is central to *Gaudium et Spes*: "The People of God believes that it is led by the Lord's Spirit, Who fills the earth. Motivated by

---

[36] For further explanation of the idea that Jesus' message, oriented towards a future in God, continues after his death and, guided by the Spirit, finds new and previously unseen forms, entirely in tune with the future-oriented character, see E. Borgman, Wortelen in vaste grond: Een cultuurtheologisch essay, Zoetermeer: Meinema, 2009. It is my intention to systematically develop this view on the work of the Spirit, and its consequences for theology, in the coming years.

[37] Cf. esp. E. Schillebeeckx, The Understanding of Faith, op. cit., where Schillebeeckx protests against an interpretation of Christian faith that is too one-sidedly oriented towards contemporary relevance. See also the title of his book: God the Future of Man, New York: Sheed and Ward, 1968, which reprints partly the same articles.

this faith, it labors to decipher authentic signs of God's presence and purpose in the happenings, needs and desires in which this People has a part along with other men of our age" (no. 11).

By showing God's ever-new presence with the world as references to a God of whom Jesus is the pre-eminent icon, the Holy Spirit keeps revealing the God who is forever new.[38] The church is 'sign and instrument' of the world as the place of God's commitment as shown in Jesus, because of, and insofar, as it is continually opened up by the Spirit.

3. The church, appealed to and broken open by the Spirit

Joseph Ratzinger as pope Benedict XVI and Karol Wojtyla as pope John Paul II, have always emphasized the first sentence of paragraph 22 of *Gaudium et Spes* in their interpretations of the document: 'The truth is that only in the mystery of the incarnate Word does the mystery of man take on light.' In a way, Schillebeeckx's Christology can also be regarded as an attempt to interpret human existence in light of – and we need to use a different terminology here, just like Schillebeeckx does – Jesus of Nazareth as the embodiment of salvation from God. Schillebeeckx does this in a way that allows him to take into account the last sentences of the same section of the text quoted above, in a much better way than the doctrine developed during the pontificates of the last two popes: "Pressing upon the Christian to be sure, are the need and the duty to battle against evil through manifold tribulations and even to suffer death. But, linked with the paschal mystery and patterned on the dying Christ, he will hasten forward to resurrection in the strength which comes from hope. All this holds true not only for Christians, but for all men of good will in whose hearts grace works in an unseen way. For, since Christ died for all men, and since the ultimate vocation of man is in fact one, and divine, we ought to believe that the Holy Spirit in a manner known only to God of-

[38] It is particularly emphasized in orthodox Christianity, the dynamics of the Spirit and the idea that it is the task of the Spirit to reveal the full presence of the living Christ among us. For the Second Vatican Council as modest and incomplete, but very real break-through regarding this issue in the Church of the West, see Y. Congar, I Believe in the Holy Spirit, The Complete Three Volume Work in One Volume, New York: Crossroad Herder. 2000, I/167–173 (originally in French: Je crois en l'Esprit Sainte, Paris: Cerf, 1979–1980); Th.J. Norris, The Trinity – Life of God, Hope for Humanity: Towards a Theology of Communion, Hide Park N.Y.: New York City Press, 2009. Cf. also E. Borgman, "Altijd ongekend: Gods Geest als Gods aanwezig komende toekomst", in: H. Bakker e.a. (Eds.), De werking van de Heilige Geest in de Europese cultuur en traditie, Kampen: Kok, 2008, 7–18.

fers to every man the possibility of being associated with this paschal mystery."

According to Ratzinger, people outside the church are indirectly gathered up into the mystery of Easter because the church shares the salvific effects of divine revelation with the world outside. According to Schillebeeckx, people outside the church can be gathered up into the mystery of Easter because they are part of creation and therefore share in what he calls 'the inexhaustible surplus of creation.'[39] This focus on and longing for a good life, put into human being by God, is the condition for them to be open to the story of Jesus. That is why Schillebeeckx proposes reversing the old adage, there is 'no salvation outside the world'. That is also why the so-called contrast experience, in which the realization that things are not right the way they are, leads to a longing for a situation that is right, is not an absurd paradox but a testimony to God's presence that creates a future.[40]

Schillebeeckx however, keeps emphasizing the restored continuity: anytime history seems to end, that which comes from the past turns out to have a future after all. The story of Jesus confirms the orientation of creation on the fullness of life, in spite of and after numerous failures. Jesus' resurrection affirms his salvific life, which at first seemed to be a dead end, and the hope for resurrection is a continuation of the hope that was given with creation itself. That is why in 2000 it was possible for Schillebeeckx to identify the celebration of God's continuous, future-giving presence among humankind without reserve as the 'ritualization of religious moments in daily life.' In his view an explicit Christian interpretation of these rituals in the light of the Christian story was not necessary, because the Christian meaning is implicit in the dynamic orientation of human existence towards salvation.[41]

However, this suggests that the new is merely a confirmation of that which had already been given in the old – which does not suffice, theologically. The fact that the creator of heaven and earth shows his face in a vulnerable and weak human being who realizes fragments of goodness

---

[39] E. Schillebeeckx, Interim Report, op. cit., 121.
[40] Idem, Church, op. cit., 5f.
[41] Idem, "Naar een herontdekking van de christelijke sacramenten: Ritualisering van religieuze momenten in het alledaagse leven", in: *Tijdschrift voor Theologie* 40 (2000), 164–187; partly translated as Towards a Rediscovery of the Christian Sacraments: Ritualizing Religious Elements in Daily Life, in: D.G. Lange / D.W. Vogel (Eds.), Ordo: Bath, Word, Prayer, Table, Akron: OSL Publications, 2005, 6–34. See also E. Schillebeeckx, Verzet en inzet, overgave en viering, in: idem, Theologisch testament: Notarieel nog niet verleden, Baarn: Nelissen, 1994, 185–191.

amidst overpowering evil, and who is moreover subjected to suffering, death and rejection, does fundamentally change the meaning of confessing God as Creator. Likewise, the fact that Jesus' life ends in a violent death and then has an unexpected future beyond death, itself changes the image of what constitutes salvific action. We have to move further than that, however. Among the Spaniards in Santo Domingo, Antonio de Montesinos (approx. 1480–1540) discovered that Jesus could not be found with the Christians who introduced his message to the New World by means of violence, but with the original population they abused and exploited. This reveals a uniquely new aspect of what it means that Jesus, as the Letter to the Hebrews puts it, has suffered 'outside the city gate.' 'Let us, then, go to him outside the camp, bearing the disgrace that he bore' (Hebrews 13:13–14). Analogous to this, I think, is the discovery that the Shoah is partly the product of Christian history and a specific concept of the Christian message, posing unprecedented questions to the traditional self-image of the church as the new people of God.

Its seem to be part of the specific way the Christian message relates to its context, that the one in, by and for whom everything has been created – 'things in heaven and on earth, visible and invisible, whether thrones or dominions, or principalities, or powers' – nevertheless speaks from the margins of all of this. He who is 'the head of the body, the church' (cf. Colossians 1, 16.18), reveals himself time and again as surprisingly unknown, even to the church. Salvation is the restoration of creation in its orientation towards the good life; the eschaton is the complete breakthrough of the liberation that took place in Jesus, but only this eschaton will fully reveal what creation and salvation really are. The Spirit keeps representing this eschaton in new ways and shows us anew how the words and the acts, the life, the death and the resurrection of Jesus Christ are anticipations of it.[42]

Let us now return to the real existing church and its relation to the Spirit. The church does not encompass the Spirit, and cannot keep her alive. Nor can the church extinguish the Spirit. This Spirit stays alive and brings life, and during their lives, people testify to this in various ways. It is the church' task to be open to this Spirit, to be prepared to become a

---

[42] This implies that the question whether it is really Jesus Christ and his Spirit that present themselves, is more difficult to answer. After all, the criterion is no longer simply the recovery of Jesus from the past, but the fullness of revelation in the future. The touchstone is that we should be able to see a plausible connection between the things the Bible tells us about Jesus as the embodiment of the imminent Kingdom of God and that which presents itself in his Spirit as an anticipation of the future.

sign and an instrument of her presence, again and again. I agree with Schillebeeckx that the Second Vatican Council took a number of significant steps in the direction of a church that really would do these things, and like him I deplore the fact that the process has now stalled and is often actively reversed. Nevertheless, the church is ever-present time and again, it is only partially and never wholly, possessed by the Spirit, called into action and brought to new insights.

Let us look at two examples, rather randomly. Firstly, through its hierarchy, the Roman Catholic church uses all sorts of dubious and sometimes rather strange arguments to forbid the use of condoms to combat AIDS, and actively tries to frustrate this use. Even to those who realize that a wider availability of condoms will not solve the problem of AIDS, it is shocking that the question as to what this standpoint actually means for the struggle against AIDS is never really debated. Yet, at the same time, there are a large number of AIDS-victims mainly being cared for by religious women who represent that same church, at great risk to their own life. Despite all cultural and religious pressure, and enlightened by the Spirit, they see the face of Christ in the faces of their patients. Secondly, the twentieth century saw the rise of a new form of martyrdom within the church, a new practiced vision of testifying by risking one's own life. It has not been planned by anyone, nor has it been conceived by an explicit new theology, but it does manifest itself in a most impressive way. The new martyr is not someone who dies a heroic dead, his of her blood explicitly testifying to the gospel, they are people who stay in dangerous places and do not flee, in solidarity with others who are threatened but cannot flee.[43] This is the incarnation of the opening words of *Gaudium et Spes:* "Joy and hope, sadness and fear of today's people, particularly of the poor and of those who in any way suffer, are just as much the joy and the hope, the sadness and the fear of the disciples of Christ: there really is nothing in mankind that does not resonate in their heart." (no. 1) The church that tries, on the one hand, to weaken its ties with the world in which it lives, on the other strengthens these in surprising ways.

My goal is not to show that, next to disappointing developments there are also other developments that could justify optimism. The point is that, in fact, the church is still alive until this day because of this breaking in of the Spirit. It dos not live from the fire it keeps going in the inside, but the fire that keeps getting rekindled and stirred up from outside. This is how the church handed-down testimony of a God who came powerful-

---

[43] Cf. A. Riccardi, Il secolo del martirio: I cristiani nel Novecento, Milano: Mondadori, 2009.

ly intimate in the weakness of Jesus the Anointed, is expressed in ever-new ways. Contrary to what the pope suggested, the salvation of the church will be that it does *not* offer something to the world from outside, but instead, that it is appealed to form within the world and with the world through the Spirit to free it from its inward-looking stance, and thus it enables the church to start speaking and acting again. Thus, it will become sign and instrument of God's salvific engagement and find new ways to testify to this, despite itself. To quote Schillebeeckx by way of conclusion: the church is a "living testimony of the *humanity* of the transcendent God and, at the same time, of the religious, *transcendent* dimension of our human reality."[44]

* * *

Zusammenfassung des Beitrags von Erik Borgman

In seinem Buch *Menschen. Die Geschichte von Gott (1990; original 1989)* kommt Edward Schillebeeckx zu dem Schluss, dass er nicht so über die Kirche schreiben könne, wie er es ursprünglich geplant hatte, da der Geist des Zweiten Vatikanischen Konzils, welcher für ihn der Heilige Geist war, zum größten Teil aus der Kirche verschwunden sei. Andererseits jedoch, so argumentiert er, sei inner- und außerhalb der Kirche alles von der Präsenz des lebendigen Gottes abhängig, welcher die menschliche Geschichte auf ihr post-historisches Ende hinführt. Der vorliegende Artikel stellt den Versuch dar, die Ambivalenz in Schillebeeckx' Ansätzen zur Kirche zu verstehen und zu überwinden:

Zuerst, so vor allem in seinen Reflexionen zur Kirche und ihren Ämtern aus den 1980er Jahren, versteht Schillebeeckx die Geschichte entweder als Quelle oder Lösung zeitgenössischer Probleme. Eine Betrachtungsweise, die kaum mit seinen eigenen Maßstäben übereinstimmt, wonach die ekklesiologische Gegenwart nur einen kleinen Teil einer umfassenderen Geschichte darstellt. Zweitens soll verdeutlicht werden, wie die lehramtliche Betonung der einen „Subjekt Kirche", die eine autar-

---

[44] E. Schillebeeckx, "Bij het eerste eucharistisch voorgaan van een tot priester gewijde vrouw in de Anglicaanse Kerk", in: idem, Theologisch testament, op. cit., 163–167, quote on 167.

ke Existenzweise aus sich selbst heraus beansprucht, zu fundamentalen Problemen führt. Drittens wird der Ansatz vertreten, dass Schillebeeckx diese Probleme zu lösen versucht, indem er sich verstärkt dem historischen Jesus zuwendet und die wachsende Abhängigkeit von ihm betont. Diese Argumentation führt dann allerdings zu einer Aporie, welche in Schillebeeckx' Konzept der „proportionalen Gleichheit" zum Ausdruck kommt: Die Beziehung der Kirche zu ihrem jeweiligen Kontext sollte dieselbe sein, wie die Beziehung Jesu zu seinem Kontext. Weder Jesus als historische Figur, noch das gegenwärtige Verständnis von Christus in der Kirche kann hier als Kriterium der Authentizität herangezogen werden. Viertens kann deshalb formuliert werden, dass die Kirche in bleibender Abhängigkeit zum lebendigen, aktiven Christus steht, der sich selbst in jeweils unerwarteten und beispiellosen Weisen zeigt.

Abschließend wird deshalb auf die Notwendigkeit hingewiesen, von der Tendenz in Schillebeeckx' Werk abzusehen, eine Kontinuität direkt vom Ursprung her zu betonen, da die Fülle der Gnade Gottes zwar in der Schöpfung und die Fülle seiner Offenbarung in Jesus Christus gegenwärtig ist, die Bedeutung dieser Aussagen allerdings erst im Geist verständlich wird, welcher die Gegenwart und die Vergangenheit zu Orten macht, an welchen die Zukunft Gottes beginnt. Damit ist auch gesagt, dass die entscheidende Frage nicht darin besteht, wie die Kirche ihre eigene Sendung in Bezug auf den Jesus der Vergangenheit und den im Geist gegenwärtigen Christus auffasst, sondern wie sie unerwartet und beispiellos vom Geist überwältigt wird. So *ist* sie auch nicht, sondern *wird* immer wieder neu Sakrament, wie es das Zweite Vatikanische Konzil formuliert, „Zeichen und Werkzeug für die innigste Vereinigung mit Gott wie für die Einheit der ganzen Menschheit."

Übersetzung aus dem Englischen: *Bernhard Kohl*

Ulrich Engel

DOMINIKANISCHE PREDIGT

Eine hermeneutische Rekonstruktion in ekklesiopraktischer Absicht

Rom, 1957: Im Rahmen eines internationalen Treffens zum Thema „Predigt" präsentierte Edward Schillebeeckx „Anstöße zur Erneuerung dominikanischer Predigt im Licht ihrer geschichtlichen Ursprünge"[1]. Ausgehend von diesem nunmehr über ein halbes Jahrhundert alten Text, der so etwas wie eine kurz gefasste Genealogie der *praedicatio ordinis praedicatorum* darstellt, präsentiere ich hier einige grundlegende Reflexionen zum Thema „Dominikanische Predigt"[2]. Über den römischen Vortrag hinaus beziehe ich mich in meinen Überlegungen auf den hermeneutisch bedeutsamen Gedanken einer kritischen Interrelation zwischen göttlicher Offenbarung und menschlicher Situation. Diese Denkfigur hat Schillebeeckx vor allem in seinem Buch „Mensen als verhaal van God"[3] aus dem Jahr 1989 entfaltet.[4]

---

[1] Eine von P. Thibault OP verantwortete englische Übersetzung des ursprünglich auf Latein gehaltenen Vortrags wurde zehn Jahre später in Washington D.C., USA, publiziert: E. Schillebeeckx, Dominican Preaching. Suggestions for up-dating Dominican Preaching in the light of its historical origins, in: *Dominicana* 52 (1967), 102–109. Eine von M. Brink OP erstellte deutsche Arbeitsübersetzung blieb bislang unveröffentlicht.

[2] Zum Thema dominikanische Predigt vgl. auch meine früheren Beiträge, u. a. U. Engel, Predigt „von unten". Zum Charisma dominikanischer Spiritualität, in: *Geist und Leben* 79 (2006), 161–169; ders., Predigt als Übersetzung. Gottes Wort hören und weitersagen in einer postsäkularen Gesellschaft, in: ders., Gott der Menschen. Wegmarken dominikanischer Theologie, Ostfildern 2010, 41–56.

[3] E. Schillebeeckx, Mensen als verhaal van God, Baarn 1989. Ich zitiere im Folgenden nach der deutschen Ausgabe: Menschen. Die Geschichte von Gott. Aus dem Niederländischen von H. Zulauf, Freiburg/Br. 1990.

[4] Zum Thema insges. vgl. jetzt neu J. Díaz Sariego, Teología y Predicación. Aportaciones de Edward Schillebeeckx al quehacer teológico, in: *Ciencia Tomista* 102 (2011), 7–44.

Mein leitendes Interesse hinsichtlich des gewählten Themas ist ein ekklesiologisches, insofern ich der dominikanischen Predigt einen spezifischen, von der amtlich-homiletischen Verkündigung unterschiedenen und folglich kirchlich-theologischen *eigenständigen* Ort zuweisen möchte. Dazu werde ich mich neben den genannten Schillebeeckx-Texten vor allem auf Überlegungen von Gianni Vattimo zur philosophischen Hermeneutik, von Melchor Cano zur theologischen Topologie und von Thomas von Aquin zur praktischen Spiritualität beziehen.

Erst in der Markierung eines von der amtlichen Predigt unabhängigen Ortes wird es – so meine Überzeugung – möglich, die theologisch unzweifelhafte Berufung *aller* Dominikanerinnen und Dominikaner zum Predigtdienst auch ekklesiopraktisch zu entfalten.

1. Dominikanische Predigt im Feld profaner Heiligkeit

Dominikus hat seine Gemeinschaft „für die Predigt und das Heil der Menschen gegründet"[5]. Deshalb heißt sie „Predigerorden" – oder besser: „Neuer Predigerorden"[6]. Denn als zeitlich erster Prediger-Orden hat die Gemeinschaft der Bischöfe zu gelten; ihr ist das Predigtamt [„Praedicationis munus"] zur Hauptaufgabe [„praecipuum {munus}]" gegeben, wie knapp 250 Jahre nach Dominikus das Reformdekret des Konzils von Trient (1545–1563) formulierte.[7] Bis zur Gründung des Dominikanerordens also war das Predigtamt den Bischöfen vorbehalten. Andere Prälaten und Priester konnten nur in Ableitung von diesem episkopalen *ordo praedicatorum* predigen; sie bedurften unabdingbar der bischöflichen Delegation.[8]

---

[5] Liber Constitutionum et Ordinationum Fratrum Ordinis Praedicatorum, Roma 1986, Constitutio Fundamentalis, 1, § II.

[6] F. Martínez Díez, Die dominikanische Predigt in der medialen Welt. Theologische und anthropologische Überlegungen. Aus dem Spanischen von B. Watzling, in: *Wort und Antwort* 40 (1999), 73–78, hier 73.

[7] Sessio XXIV – De reformatione, can. IV (11.11.1563): „Praedicationis munus, quod episcoporum praecipuum munus est [...]" (Conciliorum Oecumenicorum Decreta, cur. von G. Alberigo u. a., hrsg. vom Istituto per le Scienze religiose, Bologna ³1973, 763.) Vgl. dazu auch W. Löser, Die Lehre von der Kirche in den Dekreten des Konzils von Trient, in: Ch. Barnbrock / W. Klän (Hrsg.), Gottes Wort in der Zeit: verstehen– verkündigen – verbreiten (FS V. Stolle) (Theologie: Forschung und Wissenschaft Bd. 12), Münster 2005, 339–358, bes. 354f.

[8] Vgl. F. Martínez Díez, Espiritualidad Dominicana. Ensayos sobre el carisma y la misión de la Orden de Predicadores, Madrid 1995, 92.

Wie die Mitglieder des ersten Prediger-Ordens – sprich: die Bischöfe – sind auch die Mitglieder des Neuen Predigerordens – die Dominikaner – niemals je einzeln, sondern immer ausschließlich aufgrund ihrer Zugehörigkeit zur jeweiligen Körperschaft – *ordo* – zur Predigt beauftragt. In diesem Sinne gilt: Die dominikanische Predigtberufung „hat ihr Fundament in dem ursprünglichen Ziel, für das der Orden gegründet worden ist. Deshalb haben diejenigen, die ihre Profess auf die Mission des Ordens abgelegt haben, durch eben diese Profess am Predigtauftrag teil"[9].

Mit der historisch gewordenen Doppelung der Predigerverbände ist jedoch ein Problem auf uns gekommen: das Problem der zwei in der Kirche miteinander konkurrierenden Predigtaufträge. Seit dem 13. Jahrhundert stellt sich diese Konkurrenz in der Dualität zwischen zwei Predigttypen dar. Auf der einen Seite steht die dem Amtsträger (Bischof – und von ihm abgeleitet: Priester und Diakon) vorbehaltene Homilie in der Eucharistie; auf der anderen Seite der qua Profess übertragene spezifisch dominikanische Predigtauftrag. Die eine Predigt ist „Teil des bischöflichen oder hierarchischen Amtes"[10]; in diesem Sinne bezeichne ich sie als *amtliche Predigt*. Die andere, *dominikanische* Gestalt bestimmt Schillebeeckx als „didaktische Predigtweise"[11] bzw. „lehrhafte Predigt"[12].

Wegen ihrer Genese aus der und in ihrer Bindung an die bischöfliche Korporation wird die amtliche Predigterlaubnis gemäß gültigem Kirchenrecht bis heute ausschließlich Männern zuerkannt: „Die heilige Weihe empfängt gültig nur ein getaufter Mann."[13] Andersherum formuliert: Aufgrund der in der römisch-katholischen Kirche nur Männern vorbehaltenen Weihe zum dreifachen Amt (Diakon, Priester und Bischof) bleiben Frauen also von der amtlichen Homilie ausgeschlossen. Die dominikanisch-lehrhafte Predigt hingegen, begründet in der Bindung an die Gemeinschaft durch Professversprechen, ist allen Mitgliedern des Ordens als

---

[9] M.C. Hilkert u. a., The Dominican Charism of Preaching: An Inquiry [May 2001], unter: http://www.op.org.au/texts/preaching.pdf [7.11.2011].

[10] E. Schillebeeckx, Dominican Preaching, a.a.O, 102: „[...] the office of preaching belongs properly to the episcopal or hierarchical order [...]".

[11] Vgl. ebd., 103: „[...] didactic form of preaching [...]"; ebd.: „[...] didactic manner of preaching [...]".

[12] Vgl. bspw. ebd.: „[...] doctrinal character of Dominican Preaching [...]".

[13] C. 1024 CIC 1983. – „Ordinatio sacerdotalis" hat darüber hinaus betont, dass zumindest die Frage der Gültigkeit der Priesterweihe von Frauen keine rein kirchenrechtliche Frage ist. Vgl. Johannes Paul II., Apostolisches Schreiben „Ordinatio Sacerdotalis" über die nur Männern vorbehaltene Priesterweihe (22.5.1994) (Verlautbarungen des Apostolischen Stuhls Bd. 117), Bonn 1994, Nr. 4.

Verpflichtung und Aufgabe übertragen: Frauen und Männern – und zwar unabhängig, ob ordiniert/geweiht oder nicht!

Vor dem Hintergrund der hier von mir im Anschluss an Schillebeeckx stark gemachten Unterscheidung zwischen dominikanischer und amtlicher Predigt kann der Charakter der *praedicatio ordinis praedicatorum* mindestens in dreifacher Hinsicht bestimmt werden:

– Der Ort genuin dominikanischer Verkündigung ist (anders als der Ort der amtlichen Predigt) gerade *nicht* eindeutig im sakralen Raum verortet. Vielmehr hat sie ihren Platz im weiten Feld „profaner"[14] bzw. – um Schillebeeckx zu zitieren – „weltliche[r] Heiligkeit"[15].

– Der Ort dominikanischer Predigt kann (anders als der der eucharistischen Homilie) gerade *nicht* primär oder gar ausschließlich liturgisch qualifiziert werden. Vielmehr hat sie ihren bevorzugten Platz im „Außen" der innerkirchlichen Sozialgestalt.

– Der Ort der *praedicatio ordinis praedicatorum* ist (anders als der Ort der klerikalen Auslegung des Evangeliums) definitiv *nicht* in geschlechterausschließender Weise nur (zölibatär lebenden) Männern vorbehalten. Vielmehr markiert sie einen Platz, der in genderspezifischer Weise inkludierend wirkt.

2. Dominikanische Predigt als hermeneutischer Akt

Neben der oben skizzierten kirchen*geschichtlich* gewordenen und kirchen*rechtlich* festgelegten Differenz zwischen amtlicher und dominikanischer Predigt werde ich im hier folgenden Abschnitt – bezugnehmend auf den italienischen Philosophen Gianni Vattimo[16] – die geschichtlichen und praktischen Implikationen des hermeneutischen Aktes in den Blick nehmen. Dabei gehe ich davon aus, dass die Predigt ein Geschehen zwischen der Situation der Menschen auf der einen und dem Wort Gottes auf der anderen Seite darstellt.[17] Vor allem die nachkonziliare Homiletik hat die-

---

[14] Vgl. Ch. Bauer, Heiligkeit des Profanen? Spuren der „école Chenu-Schillebeeckx" (H. de Lubac) auf dem Zweiten Vatikanum, in diesem Band, 67–83.
[15] E. Schillebeeckx, Kirche und Welt im Licht des Zweiten Vatikanischen Konzils, a.a.O., 236.
[16] Vgl. U. Engel, Philosophie (im Licht) der Inkarnation. Zu Gianni Vattimos Religionsdiskurs im Zeitalter der Interpretation, in: G. Vattimo / R. Schröder / U. Engel, Christentum im Zeitalter der Interpretation, hrsg. von Th. Eggensperger (Passagen Forum), Wien 2004, 41–78; Th. Eggensperger, Sich Reiben an der Religion. Gianni Vattimos Blick auf Christentum und Kirche, in: *Zibaldone. Zeitschrift für italienische Kultur der Gegenwart* 51/2011, 127-132.
[17] Zur Deutung des Predigtgeschehens als hermeneutischen Akt vgl. K. Müller, Homiletik. Ein Handbuch für kritische Zeiten, Regensburg 1994, bes. 109–137.

sen Konnex stark gemacht und dazu beispielsweise Hans-Georg Gadamer mit seinem *Opus Magnum* „Wahrheit und Methode"[18] „zu einer Art katholischem Hausphilosophen"[19] geadelt. Anders als die Vertreter dieser (auch kritisierten[20]) theologischen Rezeption der philosophischen Hermeneutik beziehe ich mich hier auf den (ebenfalls in Kritik stehenden[21]) italienischen Hermeneutiker Gianni Vattimo[22] – und zwar aus zweifachem Grund, interessieren mich doch im Blick auf die Predigt sowohl die *geschichtlichen Implikationen* des hermeneutischen Aktes, als auch die ihm innenwohnende *praktische Dimension*. Beide Aspekte zielen m. E. eindeutig auf das, was Schillebeeckx die „Eigengesetzlichkeit dieser Welt"[23] bezeichnet hat.

2.1. Geschichtliche Implikationen des hermeneutischen Aktes

Wichtig im vorliegenden Zusammenhang ist vor allem die Frage nach der *geschichtlichen* Verankerung des hermeneutischen Geschehens. Klaus Müller hat die Figur einer ungeschichtlich auftretenden Hermeneutik m. E. zu Recht als verkapptes metaphysisches Denken kritisiert und um der Ret-

[18] H.-G. Gadamer, Wahrheit und Methode. Grundzüge einer philosophischen Hermeneutik, Tübingen ⁶1990.
[19] K. Müller, Herbst der Hermeneutik? Eine philosophische Debatte von theologischer Brisanz, in: E. Garhammer / H.-G. Schöttler (Hrsg.), Predigt als offenes Kunstwerk. Homiletik und Rezeptionsästhetik, München 1998, 137–148, hier 137f.
[20] Zur Kritik einer in der katholischen Theologie weit verbreiteten unreflektierten Gadamer-Beerbung vgl. H.-G. Stobbe, Hermeneutik – ein ökumenisches Problem. Eine Kritik der katholischen Gadamer-Rezeptzion (Ökumenische Theologie Bd. 8), Zürich – Köln – Gütersloh 1981; ders., Schädliche Einheit. Ein Beitrag zur Wiederbelebung der hermeneutischen Debatte, in: K. Müller (Hrsg.), Fundamentaltheologie. Fluchtlinien und gegenwärtige Herausforderungen, Regensburg 1998, 121–149.
[21] Zur (mit recht unterschiedlichen Begründungen aufwartenden) theologisch motivierten Kritik an Vattimos Ansatz vgl. Papst Johannes Paul II., Enzyklika *Fides et ratio* an die Bischöfe der katholischen Kirche über das Verhältnis von Glaube und Vernunft (Verlautbarungen des Apostolischen Stuhls Bd. 135), Bonn 1998, Nr. 48; G. Vergauwen, Wider die schwache Vernunft. Notizen am Rande der Enzyklika „Fides et Ratio", in: A.R. Batlogg / M. Delgado / R.A. Siebenrock (Hrsg.), Was den Glauben in Bewegung bringt. Fundamentaltheologie in der Spur Jesu Christi (FS K.-H. Neufeld), Freiburg/Br. 2004, 308–319; L. Osterveen, De zwakke identiteit van het geloof. Een theologische kritiek op Gianni Vattimo's interpretatie van het christendom, in: *Tijdschrift voor Theologie* 46 (2006), 333–354.
[22] Vgl. G. Vattimo, Jenseits der Interpretation. Die Bedeutung der Hermeneutik für die Philosophie. Aus dem Italienischen von M. Kempter (Edition Pandora Bd. 36 / Europäische Vorlesungen 8), Frankfurt/M. – New York 1997, bes. 111–139 („Die Wahrheit der Hermeneutik") und 140–158 („Rekonstruktion der Rationalität").
[23] E. Schillebeeckx, Kirche und Welt im Licht des Zweiten Vatikanischen Konzils, in: ders., Gott – Kirche – Welt. Aus dem Niederländischen von H. Zulauf (Gesammelte Schriften Bd. 2), Mainz 1970, 228–242, hier 234.

tung der Hermeneutik selbst willen (im Anschluss an Gianni Vattimo) für ihre geschichtliche Zuspitzung plädiert: „Begnügte sich Hermeneutik mit dem Befund, daß es verschiedene Hinsichten auf die Welt gibt, bliebe sie bei ihrem Abschied von der Metaphysik dadurch auf halbem Wege stehen, daß sie deren objektivistisches Wahrheitsideal reproduzierte. Neuzeitliche Hermeneutik (qua Philosophie der Moderne par excellence) muß sich dagegen ihrerseits so radikal geschichtlich verstehen, daß nur noch eine Geschichte, sowohl im Sinne von *res gestae* als auch in dem von *historia rerum gestarum* [...] als Beweisinstanz für ihren eigenen Anspruch in Frage kommt und sie sich selbst folgerichtig selbst nur als eine Interpretation präsentieren kann."[24] Die hier angesprochene geschichtliche Legierung der Hermeneutik ist also keine ‚starke', denn „der Horizont, innerhalb dessen die Welt sich jeweils den geschichtlichen Menschheiten ergibt, [ist] keine stabile Struktur, sondern *Ereignis* [...]. Der *geschichtliche Horizont* ist [...] kein Grund, keine stabile Struktur"[25]. Damit ist auch Wahrheit – im Sinne einer Kette von Verweisungen – als „geschichtliche Überlieferung"[26] zu verstehen.

2.2. Praktische Implikationen des hermeneutischen Aktes

Zugleich formuliert Vattimo im Zuge seines so genannten ‚schwachen' Denkens („*pensiero debole*"[27]) einen „Letztbegründungsgedanken"[28], der den hermeneutischen Ansatz gegen den Vorwurf des Relativismus schützt. Im Zuge seiner These, dass erst der christliche Gedanke der Selbsterniedrigung Gottes in die Gestalt des Menschen hinein (Inkarnation bzw. *kenosis*) die philosophische Abschwächung starker, d. h. objektivistischer Ansprüche ermöglicht, kann Vattimo behaupten, dass „die Norm der Säkularisierung die christliche Liebe ist"[29]. Der Prozess der

---

[24] K. Müller, Herbst der Hermeneutik?, a.a.O., 139.
[25] F. Giacobbe, Das „schwache Denken" Gianni Vattimos und die Wahrheitsfrage, in: Th. Eggensperger / U. Engel (Hrsg.), Wahrheit. Recherchen zwischen Hochscholastik und Postmoderne (Walberberger Studien. Philosophische Reihe Bd. 9), Mainz 1995, 116–129, hier 125 [Hervorhebungen U.E.].
[26] Ebd.
[27] G. Vattimo / P.A. Rovatti (Hrsg.), Il pensiero debole, Milano 1983.
[28] K. Müller, Herbst der Hermeneutik?, a.a.O., 145.
[29] G. Vattimo, Glauben – Philosophieren. Aus dem Italienischen von Ch. Schultz, Stuttgart 1997, 101. – Vgl. dazu auch in verblüffender Ähnlichkeit die von Ch. Bauer (Heiligkeit des Profanen?, a.a.O., hier 77) zit. Aussage Chenus, nach der „es in der innersten Gesetzmäßigkeit des Christentums liegt, die Welt zu desakralisieren"; M.-D. Chenu, Les laïcs et la ‚consécration' du monde, in: ders., Peuple de Dieu dans le monde, Paris 1966, 69–96, hier 81.

kenotischen Säkularisierung mündet also in die christliche „*caritas*"[30]. Die in der inkarnatorischen Logik angelegte Selbstentäußerung führt somit gerade nicht in ein abgründiges „Nichts". Vielmehr eignet dem hermeneutischen Prozess der Erniedrigung – quasi am Boden der Abwärtsbewegung – ein normatives Moment. Als „Norm"[31] – so Vattimo wörtlich – lässt sich dieses Moment nicht völlig auf die zu interpretierenden Zeichen reduzieren. Die *caritas* als limitierender Faktor bringt sich „in einem Dementi jeglicher metaphysisch verstandenen Letztheit als unhintergehbare und insofern ‚letzte' (in Anführungszeichen) Bedingung der Möglichkeit eines (kenotischen) ‚pensiero debole' sich zur Geltung bringt."[32] Vattimo versteht also *caritas* bzw. Liebe als ein ‚letztes' Prinzip, das seinem Wesen nach aber gerade nicht letztgültig ist. Es ist – wie Klaus Müller formuliert – „nicht-letzt"[33]: „Die Interpretation, die Jesus von den Prophezeiungen des Alten Testaments gibt, ja: die Interpretation dieser Prophezeiungen, die er selbst *ist*, enthüllt deren wahren Sinn, der am Ende nur einer ist: die Liebe Gottes zu seinen Geschöpfen. Und dieser ‚letzte' Sinn ist eben dadurch, daß er die *caritas* ist, niemals der wahrhaft ‚letzte', hat nicht die Letztgültigkeit des metaphysischen Prinzips, über das man nicht hinausgeht und vor dem jedes Fragen aufhört."[34]

Im Sinne des *pensiero debole* Vattimos kann der hermeneutische Akt nun als Beziehungsgeschehen zwischen *Geschichte* und *caritas* schematisiert werden:

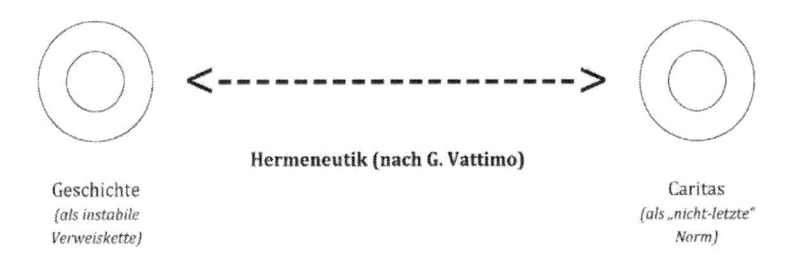

Hermeneutik (nach G. Vattimo)

Geschichte
*(als instabile
Verweiskette)*

Caritas
*(als „nicht-letzte"
Norm)*

---

[30] G. Vattimo, Glauben – Philosophieren, a.a.O., 87.
[31] Ebd., 114.
[32] K. Müller, Herbst der Hermeneutik?, a.a.O., 141.
[33] Ebd.
[34] G. Vattimo, Glauben – Philosophieren, a.a.O., 69.

3. Dominikanische Predigt als kritische Interrelation

Im Blick auf das Predigtgeschehen ist vor dem skizzierten Hintergrund ein Zweifaches festzuhalten: Zum einen muss der Akt des Predigens als hermeneutisches Geschehen eine *geschichtliche Signatur* mit sich führen. Und zum anderen kann das hermeneutische Predigtgeschehen nicht ohne ein *praktisches Moment*, konkret: der *caritas* gedacht werden. Beide Aspekte stehen in einer spannungsvollen Relation zueinander.

Zu zeigen ist im Folgenden, wie das von Vattimo her skizzierte hermeneutische Verhältnis bei Schillebeeckx ausgeführt wird. Meine These lautet dazu: *Die amtliche Predigt legt das Wort Gottes auf die Situation der Menschen aus. Die dominikanisch-lehrhafte Predigt interpretiert die Situation der Menschen auf das Wort Gottes hin.* Inspiriert zu dieser These hat mich ein (wenn auch partiell anders intendierter) Gedanke von Tiemo R. Peters, der da lautet: „Predigt als öffentliche Rede ist primär gerade nicht Schrift-, sondern Wirklichkeits-, Gesellschafts-, Weltauslegung"[35]. Im Sinne einer einfachen Schematisierung kann meine hier thetisch behauptete Unterscheidung wie folgt gefasst werden:

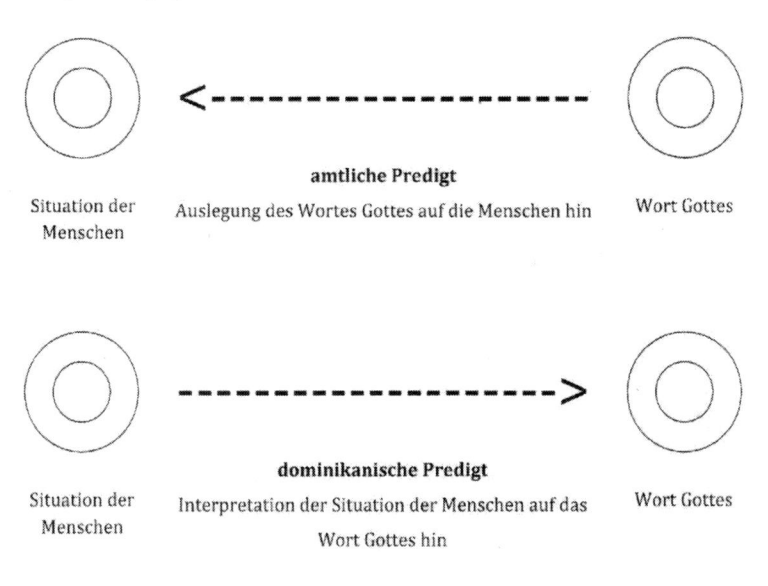

amtliche Predigt

| Situation der Menschen | Auslegung des Wortes Gottes auf die Menschen hin | Wort Gottes |

dominikanische Predigt

| Situation der Menschen | Interpretation der Situation der Menschen auf das Wort Gottes hin | Wort Gottes |

---

[35] T.R. Peters, Predigt als öffentliche Rede, in: *Zeitschrift für Gottesdienst und Predigt* 3,2 (1985), 17–22, hier 20.

In der Terminologie von Edward Schillebeeckx handelt es sich hier um eine „Interrelation"[36] zwischen Offenbarungstradition (= Wort Gottes) und Erfahrung (= Situation der Menschen). Im Unterschied zum üblicherweise gebräuchlichen Begriff der Korrelation betont die Rede von der Interrelation auch *Brüche* und *Diskontinuitäten*[37] in der Beziehung zwischen der Offenbarungstradition auf der einen und dem – wie Schillebeeckx formuliert – „kultur-gesellschaftlichen und existentiellen Kontext der Menschen"[38], kurz: der „Situation"[39], auf der anderen Seite. Somit besteht das „bleibende ‚Offenbarungsangebot', das aber jeweils in einer bestimmten Kultur akklimatisiert wird, während dieses Angebot nie ungeschichtlich und überkulturell in den Blick kommt. Es geht um die *geschichtliche Identität* dessen, was *gerade in* dem haften bleibt, was wegen seiner Kontingenz zerfließt und vorbeigeht."[40] Diese Relation beschreibt Schillebeeckx als eine „reziprok-kritische Begegnung"[41].

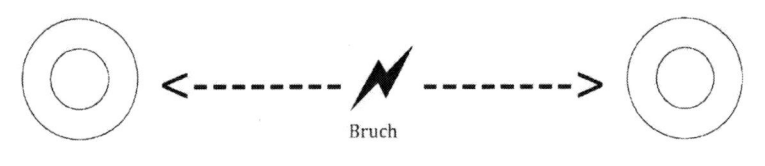

◯ <--------- **N** ---------> ◯
　　　　　　　　Bruch

Situation der　　**kritische Interrelation (nach E. Schillebeckx)**　　Wort Gottes
Menschen

---

[36] E. Schillebeeckx, Menschen, a.a.O., 61. – Zum theologischen Gehalt des Begriffs „Interrelation" bei Schillebeeckx vgl. auch B. Grümme, Vom Anderen eröffnete Erfahrung. Zur Neubestimmung des Erfahrungsbegriffs in der Religionsdidaktik, Gütersloh – Freiburg/Br. 2007, 129ff. („Erfahrung als Kritische Interrelation"); H.-G. Ziebertz, Tradition und Erfahrung: Von der Korrelation zur kritischen Interrelation. Hans-Georg Ziebertz im Gespräch mit Edward Schillebeeckx anläßlich dessen 80. Geburtstag am 12. November, in: *Katechetische Blätter* 119 (1994), 756–762; A. Odenthal, „Kritische Interrelation" von Lebens-Erfahrung und Glaubens-Tradition? Überlegungen zu einem Diktum von Edward Schillebeeckx im Hinblick auf einen symboltheoretischen Ansatz als integratives Paradigma der Liturgiewissenschaft, in: *Theologische Quartalschrift* 187 (2007), 183–203.

[37] Vgl. E. Schillebeeckx, Breuken in christelijke dogma's, in: ders. u. a. (Red.), Breuklijnen. Grenservaringen en zoektochten. 14 essays voor Ted Schoof bij sijn afscheid van de theologische faculteit Nijmegen, Baarn 1994, 15–49; weiterhin siehe L. Boeve, Experience According to Edward Schillebeeckx: The Driving Force of Faith and Theology, in: ders. / L.P. Hemming (Ed.), Divinising Experience. Essays in the History of Religious Experience from Origen to Ricœur (Studies in philosophical theology vol. 23), Leuven 2004, 199–225.

[38] E. Schillebeeckx, Menschen, a.a.O., 60.
[39] Ebd.
[40] Ebd., 62.
[41] Ebd.

Selbstredend beeinflussen solche Differenzen nicht bloß die *relatio* zwischen Offenbarungsangebot und Erfahrung (und *vice versa*), sondern ganz wesentlich auch die Erfahrungen der Menschen *per se*. Diskontinuitäten gehören zu den signifikanten Charakteristika – konzilstheologisch gesprochen: zu den „Zeichen der Zeit" (Gaudium et spes, 4) – der späten Moderne. Solcherart Brüche können ausnahmslos alle Lebensbereiche des Subjekts betreffen:
- Lebensentwürfe, die in sich als nicht kohärent erfahren werden,
- Praktiken, die von verschiedenen Akteuren völlig widersprüchlich gedeutet werden,
- und Sinnzuschreibungsversuche, die immer nur vorläufig bleiben und deshalb stetig reformuliert werden müssen.

Vor dem Hintergrund solcher Differenz- oder gar Brucherfahrungen spricht m. E. einiges dafür, den „Ansatzpunkt"[42] von religiöser Kommunikation im Allgemeinen und der Predigt im Speziellen in den konkreten geschichtlichen Erfahrungen der Menschen zu verorten. Eine spezifisch *dominikanische Predigt* – so meine nun auch auf Schillebeeckx Bezug nehmende These – wäre also zu charakterisieren als *interrelational zu denkende Auslegung menschlicher Situationen auf das Wort Gottes hin*.

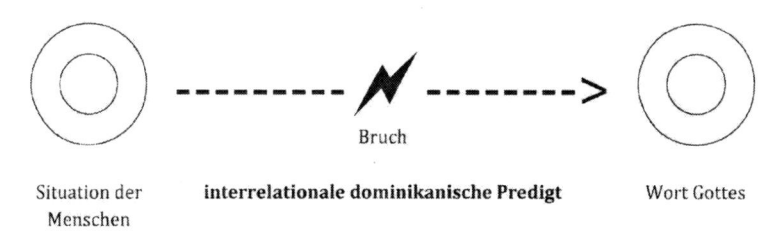

| Situation der Menschen | **interrelationale dominikanische Predigt** (Bruch) | Wort Gottes |

Damit auch würde sich Predigt als hermeneutisches Geschehen im Sinne der ersten Forderung Gianni Vattimos in der Geschichte verankern. Und es wäre der kirchlichen Verkündigung eine Zeitsignatur eingeschrieben, die sie – gerade ob dieser ihrer geschichtlichen Legierung – vor der Verkündigung theologisch-metaphysischer Gemeinplätze bewahren könnte.

Als *dominikanisch* kann eine solche Predigt, die von den disparaten und in sich oft widersprüchlichen Lebenserfahrungen (inkl. ihrer Glaubenser-

---

[42] B. Schwarz-Boenneke, Erfahren in Widerfahren und Benennen. Zu Verständnis und Relevanz von Erfahrung in den christologischen Prolegomena von Edward Schillebeeckx (Studien zur systematischen Theologie und Ethik Bd. 48), Berlin 2009, 295.

fahrungen) der Menschen ausgeht[43], deshalb qualifiziert werden, weil sie einer zentralen Denkbewegung des Thomas von Aquin verpflichtet ist. Thomas fragt – etwa im Rahmen seiner so genannten Gottesbeweise, den *quinquae viae*[44] – von den Phänomenen der sichtbar-kontingenten Welt her nach der jeweiligen Ursache: der Ursache, die das Ganze übersteigt und die wir in hermeneutischer Weise, wie es in den *viae* vier und fünf heißt, als Gott *interpretieren*, die wir Gott *nennen*: „et hoc *dicimus* Deum"[45].

Auf diesem Weg, der seinen Anfang immer in den *phantasmata*[46], d. h. in den Situationen und Lebenserfahrungen der Menschen nimmt, wird Gott gerade in der Differenz zwischen Endlichem und Unendlichem, zwischen Geschöpf und Schöpfer, zwischen Situation und geoffenbartem Wort erkannt. Alessandro Cortesi hat im Rückgriff auf Schillebeeckx diese Gegebenheit m. E. sehr treffend formuliert: „[...] die menschliche Erfahrung an sich [ist] der Ort, an dem durch das Wirken Gottes Heilsgeschichte geschieht, und die Geschichte ist der Ort, an dem Gott seine Geschöpfe schafft und befreit."[47]

Nach Schillebeeckx ist Erfahrung der erste Ort der Offenbarung, insofern „Gott sich, in und durch menschliche Erfahrungen, selbst als derjenige zu erkennen gibt, der alle genau beschriebenen Erfahrungen übersteigt."[48] Indem Schillebeeckx solchermaßen „die menschliche Erfahrung und die menschliche Lebensrealität als Ort der Offenbarung anerkennt"[49], macht er (in gut dominikanischer Tradition) vor allem das Geheimnis der göttlichen Menschwerdung theologisch stark. Denn „Offenbarung als Menschwerdung Gottes macht die Welt zum Ort des Evangeliums."[50] Damit – das sei nur nebenbei angemerkt – knüpft Schillebeeckx dezidiert an das inkarnatorische Denken seines Lehrers Marie-Dominique Chenu (1895–1990) an.[51]

---

[43] Vgl. ebd., 76.
[44] Vgl. STh I 2, 3 (DThA Bd. 1).
[45] Ebd. [Hervorhebungen U.E.]. Vgl. insgesamt zu dieser Interpretation E. Schillebeeckx, Verlangen naar ultieme levensvervulling. Een kritische herlezing van Thomas van Aquino, in: *Tijdschrift voor Theologie* 42 (2002), 15–34.
[46] Vgl. U. Engel, Conversio ad phantasma. Fundamentálno-teologicky náčrt k dominikánskej spiritualite, in: *Listy* 15,3 (2003), 39–42.
[47] Vgl. (mit Bezug auf E. Schillebeeckx, Menschen, a.a.O., 34) A. Cortesi, Das Heil der Menschheit in einer Welt der vielen Religionen. Anregungen aus dem Werk von Edward Schillebeeckx, in diesem Band, 39–52.
[48] E. Schillebeeckx, Menschen, a.a.O., 51.
[49] B. Schwarz-Boenneke, Erfahren in Widerfahren und Benennen, a.a.O., 299.
[50] Ebd., 303.
[51] Vgl. z.B. M.-D. Chenu, La Parole de Dieu. II: L'Évangile dans les temps, Paris 1964, 87–107; 109–132. – Siehe dazu auch U. Engel, Theologale Mystik im Konflikt. Marie-

4. Dominikanische Predigt unter den Bedingungen normativer Pluralität

Der hier von mir präferierte Ansatz stellt ganz im Sinne Schillebeeckx' eine hermeneutische Grundentscheidung dar, nach der die skizzierte kritische Interrelation eben bevorzugt aus der erfahrungsbasierten Perspektive der Menschen und der Zeichen, die ihrer konkreten Zeit konstitutiv sind, her zu lesen ist. Damit schließe ich mich der Schillebeeckx'schen Überzeugung an, nach der göttliche Heilsbotschaft „nicht nur aus der Schrift zu uns spricht, sondern ebenso aus jeder menschlichen Existenzerfahrung, die auf irgendeine Weise immer mit der Huld des lebendigen Gottes konfrontiert wird."[52]

Mit diesem Plädoyer für eine in den geschichtlich bedingten, d. h. immer auch gebrochenen Erfahrungen der Menschen und ihrer real gelebten Lebensentwürfe ansetzende Predigthermeneutik leugnen weder Schillebeeckx noch ich die Normativität der Heiligen Schrift.[53] Gleichwohl kann im Rahmen eines hermeneutischen Ansatzes, der sich dem schwachen Denken Vattimos und dem interrelationalen Ansatz Schillebeeckx's verpflichtet weiß, auch das Wort Gottes ‚nur' als „nicht-letzte" Norm verstanden werden, unterliegt doch auch die Heilige Schrift als *norma normans* des Glaubens (neben der katholischen Tradition) hinsichtlich der Möglichkeit menschlichen Verstehens unabdingbar der Interpretation. Damit bleibt die selbstverständlich anzuerkennende Autorität der Schriftoffenbarung begrenzt. Geschichte und Wort Gottes stehen in einer unaufhebbaren Spannung zueinander. Im Rahmen eines inkarnationstheologischen Denkens kann die *Zweiheit* von Gottes Wort in der Schrift und menschlicher Erfahrung in der Geschichte nicht ohne weiteres auf eine *Einsheit* reduziert werden.

Schon Melchor Cano (1509[1506?]–1560)[54] hat mit seiner *Loci theologici*-Lehre eine plural zugeschnittene theologische Topologie vorgelegt.[55]

Dominique Chenu OP und die Grundintuitionen seiner Theologie, in: M. Delgado / G. Fuchs (Hrsg.), Die Kirchenkritik der Mystiker – Prophetie aus Gotteserfahrung. Bd. 3: Moderne (Studien zur christlichen Religions- und Kulturgeschichte Bd. 4), Fribourg – Stuttgart 2005, 351–369, bes. 360–362.

[52] Vgl. E. Schillebeeckx, Kirche und Welt im Licht des Zweiten Vatikanischen Konzils, a.a.O., 235.

[53] Zum spannungsreichen Verhältnis von Offenbarungsangebot und Glaubensinterpretation vgl. auch Schillebeeckx' entsprechende Zurückweisung der Kritik L. Duprés an seinem Ansatz: ders., Menschen, a.a.O., 64f.

[54] Vgl. Melchioris Canis Episcopi Canariensis ex Ordine Praedicatorum Opera, a P. H. Serry, o.O. 1754. Siehe dazu auch B. Körner, Melchior Cano, De locis theologicis. Ein Beitrag zur

Ihm gemäß kommt nicht nur der Schrift und der Tradition, sondern neben den verschiedenen kirchlichen Instanzen (Kirchenvätern, Schultheologen, Päpsten, Konzilien etc.) auch außen angesiedelten Anders-Orten, den so genannten *loci aliieni*, theologische Autorität zu. Max Seckler hat m. E. überzeugend dargelegt, wie die verschiedenen Orte sich im Modus eines hochkomplexen, pluralen und diskursiv angelegten „Interaktionsgefüges"[56] gegenseitig bedingen und – das ist wichtig: sich gegenseitig begrenzen. Allen *loci theologici* kommen also „Wächterfunktionen"[57] zu. Das gilt auch für den theologisch relevanten Ort der menschlichen Erfahrung, insofern dieser – wie gezeigt – unhintergehbar geschichtlich situiert ist. Insofern nun die Geschichte (*Humanae auctoritas Historiae*) nach Cano einer der drei theologisch relevanten *anderen* Autoritätsorte ist, kann Seckler argumentieren: „Selbst den *loci alieni*, der Vernunft, den Philosophen und der Geschichte, war und ist ihr Wächteramt [...] nicht zu nehmen."[58]

In dieser Linie schrieben die vom damaligen Ordensmeister Timothy Radcliffe (1992–2001) eingesetzten Mitglieder der Kommission „The Dominican Charism of Preaching" – Mary Catherine Hilkert, Benedikta Hintersberger, Hervé Legrand, Mary O'Driscoll und Paul Philibert – in ihrem Abschlussbericht vom Mai 2001: „Die grundlegende Idee [der Predigt; U.E.] verweist auf die Verantwortung der Kirche, die ‚Zeichen der Zeit' zu analysieren und im Licht des Evangeliums zu deuten. ([...]) Die Fundamentalkonstitution (§ V) drängt uns, das Verständnis unseres Predigtauftrages ‚im Hinschauen auf die Menschen in ihrer unterschiedlichen Situation von Zeit und Raum' permanent zu erneuern."[59] Ähnlich formuliert auch Rolf Zerfaß in seinem m. E. homiletisch immer noch maßgeblichen „Grundkurs Predigt": „Frage bei jedem theologischen Begriff: Welche Erfahrung hat zu diesem Begriff geführt? Welche Geschichte hat in

---

theologischen Erkenntnislehre, Graz 1994; E. Klinger, Ekklesiologie der Neuzeit. Grundlegung bei Melchor Cano und Entwicklung bis zum Zweiten Vatikanischen Konzil, Freiburg/Br. 1978.

[55] Zum Ansatz einer toponomischen Pragmatik vgl. M. Seckler, Die ekklesiologische Bedeutung des Systems der „loci theologici". Erkenntnistheoretische Katholizität und strukturale Weisheit, in: ders., Die schiefen Wände des Lehrhauses. Katholizität als Herausforderung, Freiburg/Br. 1988, 79–104. Seckler erkennt den verschiedenen *loci theogici* „Wächterfunktionen" (ebd., 99) zu. Jeder der zehn *loci thelogici* kann bis zu neun andere Autoritätsorte für oder gegen sich haben – „mit entsprechenden Allianzen" (ebd., 104). Weiterhin siehe P. Hünermann, Neue Loci Theologici. Ein Beitrag zur methodischen Erneuerung der Theologie, in: *Cristianesimo nella storia* 24 (2003), 1–21.

[56] M. Seckler, Die ekklesiologische Bedeutung des Systems der „loci theologici", a.a.O., 101.

[57] Ebd., 99.

[58] Ebd., 101.

[59] M.C. Hilkert u. a., The Dominican Charism of Preaching, a.a.O. [15.7.2010].

ihm ihren Niederschlag gefunden? Und dann erzähl diese Geschichte, und beschreibe diese Erfahrung. Dann kannst Du Dir diesen Begriff sparen."[60]

5. Dominikanische Predigt als partizipatorische Messiaspraxis

Hier nun gilt es noch einmal den zweiten Grundgedanken Gianni Vattimos zur Bestimmung des hermeneutischen Geschehens aufzugreifen. Vattimo definiert, so wurde gezeigt, *caritas* bzw. Liebe als ein ‚letztes' Prinzip, das seinem Wesen nach jedoch ‚nicht-letzt' ist. In dieser Perspektive eignet dem (dominikanischen) Predigtgeschehen unbedingt ein *praktisches Moment*. Eingebunden ist dieses in den biblisch gegründeten Verkündigungsauftrag an *das ganze Volk Gottes*. Felicisimo Martínez Díez verweist in diesem Zusammenhang auf die kollektive Berufung zum prophetischen Predigtdienst in Num 11,29: „Wenn nur das ganze Volk des Herrn zu Propheten würde [...]"[61] Allein von diesem biblisch angezielten Predigtdienst aller her und nur in der Rückbindung an ihn kann sich letztlich auch der spezifisch dominikanische Predigtdienst legitimieren! Und analog gilt dies dann auch für den kirchlich-amtlichen Predigtauftrag. Damian Byrne, von 1983 bis 1992 Ordensmeister der Dominikaner, umschrieb dies einmal so: „Viele in der Kirche sind zum Dienst der Predigt berufen; gerade aber deswegen ist ein Predigerorden notwendig, um die Kirche permanent an ihre ureigenste Mission zu erinnern, nämlich das Evangelium zu verkünden."[62]

In Num 11,29 kreuzen sich die Einbindung der spezifischen dominikanischen Predigtberufung in die *vocatio praedicationis* des gesamten Gottesvolkes und die theologische Qualifizierung der *praedicatio ordinis praedicatorum* als eine prophetisch-praktische. Diesen Zusammenhang gilt es abschließend näher zu beleuchten.

Thomas Staubli weist in seinem Kommentar zum 4. Buch Mose darauf hin, dass die Episode der Austeilung des Geistes auf die Siebzig in Num 11,24–30 „gegen zu enges priesterliches Denken gerichtet"[63] ist.

---

[60] R. Zerfaß, Grundkurs Predigt. 1: Spruchpredigt, Düsseldorf 1987, 149.
[61] Vgl. F. Martínez Díez, Espiritualidad Dominicana, a.a.O., 92.
[62] D. Byrne, A Pilgrimage of Faith, Dublin 1991, 21, 81.
[63] Th. Staubli, Die Bücher Levitikus, Numeri (Neuer Stuttgarter Kommentar. Altes Testament Bd. 3), Stuttgart 1996, 247. – Grundsätzlicher zur prekären Relation von Prophetie und Institution vgl. U. Bechmann / J. Kügler, Biblische Prophetie. Exegetische Perspektiven auf ein heikles Phänomen, in: R. Bucher / R. Krockauer (Hrsg.), Prophetie in einer etablierten

Die hier von Mose (gegen Josua) gewünschte Demokratisierung des geistgewirkten Verkündigungsauftrags findet sich analog auch in Joël 3,1f. (in Bezug auf ganz Israel) und Apg 2,17f. (nach Petrus die Erfüllung dieses Wunsches im Pfingstereignis).[64] Genauerhin qualifiziert Staubli die avisierte *vocatio praedicationis* des gesamten Volkes als eine spirituell-praktische: „Der Wunsch des Mose, daß doch alle zu ProphetInnen werden mögen, zeigt, worum es geht, sind doch die ProphetInnen jene, die die Weisungen im Herzen tragen *und* danach handeln."[65] Das Bindeglied „und", das an dieser Stelle das „im Herzen tragen" mit dem „danach handeln" verbindet, darf allerdings nicht als eine konsekutive Relation gelesen werden – etwa nach dem Motto: die Praxis ist nicht mehr als eine abgeleitete Anwendung einer vorab schon vorhandenen Spiritualität. Stattdessen eröffnet nur eine integrale Lesart des „und" die beide Pole miteinander verbindende Dialektik einer spirituellen Praxis resp. praktischen Spiritualität der Predigt.

In seiner spezifisch dominikanischen Variante ist dieser Zusammenhang von Spiritualität und Praxis schon bei Thomas von Aquin vorformuliert, wenn er in der *Secunda Secundae* seiner Theologischen Summe schreibt: „Denn wie es besser ist, zu erleuchten, als nur zu leuchten, so ist es auch größer, *das in der Beschauung Empfangene an andere weiterzugeben*, als bloß in der Beschauung zu leben."[66] Thomas begründet seine These mit einem Vergleich zur Differenz zwischen leuchten (*lucere*) und erleuchten (*illuminare*), wobei nach Überzeugung des Aquinaten das *illuminare* höher zu bewerten ist als jedwedes *lucere solum*. Mit dieser These rekurriert Thomas (zwar ohne den Vers zu zitieren) direkt auf Mt 1,15 („Man zündet auch nicht ein Licht an und stülpt ein Gefäß darüber, sondern man stellt es auf den Leuchter; dann leuchtet es allen im Haus.") und verknüpft auf diese Weise das *contemplata aliis tradere* programmatisch mit der Reich-Gottes-Verkündigung Jesu in der Bergpredigt (Mt 5,1–7,29), insofern exakt in deren Kontext die herangezogene Vergleichsgröße des Leuchtens/Erleuchtens ihren genuinen Platz hat.

Kirche? Aktuelle Reflexionen über ein Prinzip kirchlicher Identität (Werkstatt Theologie. Praxisorientierte Studien und Diskurse Bd. 1), Münster 2004, 5–23; U. Engel, Ordensleben als prophetisches Zeichen? Eine systematisch-theologische Skizze, in: *Ordenskorrespondenz* 49 (2008), 446–450.

[64] Vgl. J. Scharbert, Numeri (Die Neue Echter Bibel. Kommentar zum Alten Testament mit der Einheitsübersetzung Lfg. 27), Würzburg ²2000, 50.

[65] Th. Staubli, Die Bücher Levitikus, Numeri, a.a.O., 247 [Hervorhebung U.E.].

[66] STh II-II 188, 6 (DThA Bd. 24): „Sicut enim majus est illuminare, quam lucem solum videre, ita majus es *contemplata aliis tradere*, quam solum contemplari" [Hervorhebung U.E.].

Die *vocatio praedicationis* des gesamten Volkes ist – so sei das Ergebnis der Numeri-Lektüre noch einmal erinnert – ist eine spirituell-praktische. Neutestamentlich weitergeführt und über den Aquinaten als spezifisch dominikanisch ausgewiesen kann die bislang noch relativ allgemein formulierte spirituell-praktische Charakteristik des Predigtauftrags nun genauer gefasst werden als eine aktive Bewegung hin auf die von Jesus in der Bergpredigt angesagte messianische Praxis der Gerechtigkeit (vgl. bspw. Mt 5,20) und der Liebe/*caritas* (vgl. z. B. Mt 5,44). Ziel der dominikanischen Predigt ist demnach „Gott als Woraufhin der Erkenntnis, der Erfahrung und der humanen Aktion"[67]. Insofern dieser Verkündigungsauftrag nach Numeri dem ganzen Gottesvolk gilt, ist auch die Ansage der messianischen Zeit praktische Aufgabe aller Predigerinnen und Prediger. In diesem Sinne verstehe ich Gerd Theißens These von einer „partizipatorischen Messianität"[68], die grundsätzlich allen Menschen eine aktive Teilhabe an der Heraufkunft des Gottesreiches zuerkennt. Damit kann nun abschließend die prophetische Predigt in ihrer demokratisierten Form noch exakter gefasst werden: nämlich als partizipatorische Messiaspraxis!

Eine solchermaßen qualifizierte Predigt, die von ihrem Ansatzpunkt bei den Erfahrungen der Menschen als „dominikanisch" zu bestimmen ist, stellt – so mein Fazit – gerade keine abgeleitete oder gar defiziente Form der amtlichen Predigt dar. Im Gegenteil: Auch wenn ich das theologische Spezifikum dominikanischer Verkündigung aus seiner Differenz zur amtlichen Predigt herausgearbeitet habe, so markiert die *praedicatio* von Dominikanerinnen und Dominikaner als partizipatorische Messiaspraxis dennoch einen *eigenständigen* Platz im Gesamt des ekklesiopraktischen Feldes.

* * *

---

[67] T.R. Peters, Spirituelle Dialektik. Thomas von Aquin grüßt Karl Marx, in: ders., Mystik, Mythos, Metaphysik. Die Spur des vermissten Gottes (Gesellschaft und Theologie. Forum politische Theologie Bd. 10), Mainz – München 1992, 26–39, hier 26.

[68] G. Theißen, Gruppenmessianismus. Überlegungen zum Ursprung der Kirche im Jüngerkreis Jesu, in: ders., Jesus als historische Gestalt. Beiträge zur Jesusforschung, Göttingen 2003, 255–281, hier 278.

Abstract of the contribution of Ulrich Engel

This article presents fundamental reflections on the subject of Dominican preaching. It is mainly based on a reading of Schillebeeckx's lecture on the renewal of the Dominican Homily (1957), and on his book "Mensen als verhaal yan God" (1989), both of which shed light on hermeneutically meaningful considerations about the critical interrelationship between divine revelation and human situatedness. This is an area that always carries a precarious tension between divine revelation and human experience.

Our guiding interest regarding this subject is primarily ecclesiastical, for the Dominican Homily shows a particular articulation that differs from other official sermons, and therefore holds its own independent ecclesial-theological space. Along these aforementioned works, we will include a reflection on the arguments of Gianni Vattimo on philosophical hermeneutics, of Melchor Cano on theological topology, and of Thomas Aquinas on practical spirituality.

By being positioned within an independent space of profane holiness, which is distinct from official sermons, the unquestionable call to *all* Dominicans to preach can be developed systematically and theologically, anchored spiritually and practically, and demanded ecclesial-politically.

Translation from German: *Tracy Rammler*

Stefan Knobloch

EDWARD SCHILLEBEECKX' TRILOGIE ALS DENKANSTOSS MEINER THEOLOGIE

Eine Dankesbezeugung

Zu Edward Schillebeeckx ist hier aus vielerlei Perspektiven fast alles gesagt worden. Mit meinem Statement will ich keine weitere Perspektive hinzufügen. Ich möchte lediglich dartun, wie Schillebeeckx' Trilogie auf mein theologisches Denken Einfluss nahm und meinen theologischen Horizont erweitert hat. An vier Topoi sei das in gebotener Kürze aufgezeigt.

1. Schillebeeckx' Exegese

In den 1970er Jahren faszinierten mich in Schillebeeckx' Werken „Jesus. Die Geschichte von einem Lebenden" und „Christus und die Christen. Die Geschichte einer neuen Lebenspraxis" seine kenntnis- und aufschlussreichen exegetischen Darlegungen. Und das, obgleich ich in Rudolf Schnackenburg in Würzburg in den 1960er Jahren einen der damals namhaftesten deutschsprachigen Exegeten als Lehrer hatte. Um es nur an einem Beispiel zu erläutern[1]: Ich hatte bis dahin kaum bemerkt, dass es in der Apostelgeschichte drei „Berichte" zum Damaskuserlebnis des Paulus gab, nämlich in Apg 9,1–22, in Apg 22,6–21 und in Apg 26,12–23. Schillebeeckx arbeitete am ersten Bericht überzeugend heraus, dass es sich bei ihm, obwohl man dort dem Satz begegnet, Paulus werde „den Namen Jesu vor Völker und Könige tragen", um eine Bekehrungsvision und nicht

---

[1] Vgl. E. Schillebeeckx, Christus und die Christen. Die Geschichte einer neuen Lebenspraxis, Freiburg/Br. 1977, 319–335.

schon um eine Sendungsvision handelt – um die Vision einer Bekehrung also, die Leid und Verfolgung einschließe. Der zweite und dritte „Bericht" gehen mit der Vorlage aus Apg 9 in ihren anderen Kontexten interpretierend um. Sie wählen, erkannte Schillebeeckx, eine „Metasprache". Der zweite Bericht legt den Akzent auf die Sendung des Paulus, der dritte verleiht der Damaskusvision den Charakter einer Ostererscheinung.

Das Interessante für mich war, dass Schillebeeckx die drei Momente der Damaskusberichte – Bekehrung, Sendung und Ostererscheinung – in den Ostererscheinungen der Evangelien wiederfand. Nach ihm liegt das Moment der Bekehrung in der Aufforderung des Auferstandenen an die Jünger, an ihn als Auferstandenen zu glauben. Eine „Bekehrung", die ihnen nicht einfach leicht fiel, wie man den Ostererzählungen unschwer entnehmen kann. Das Moment der Jüngersendung liegt daneben ohnehin auf der Hand. Beide Momente aber, so Schillebeeckx, sollen die tragenden Säulen auch unseres Auferstehungsglaubens bilden.

2. Erfahrung und Offenbarung: Ohne Erfahrung keine Offenbarung

Der Begriff der Erfahrung war, etwas vergröbert gesagt, während meines Theologiestudiums ein Fremdwort. Oder lag das nur an dem verengten Blickwinkel, unter dem ich die Theologie wahrnahm? Bei Schillebeeckx lernte ich etwas anderes. Nach ihm rezipieren wir die Offenbarung nicht anders als in der Dimension unseres Erfahrungshorizontes. Er brachte das auf die Formel: „Keine Offenbarung ohne Erfahrung"[2]. Das aller Erfahrung eigene Moment der Widerständigkeit und Widerborstigkeit der Wirklichkeit[3] haftet auch der Erfahrung der Offenbarung an. Es ist ihr immanent in Gestalt des die, paulinisch gesprochen: ‚hamartia' (im Sinne von Einzel- wie struktureller Sünde), überwindenden und das Heil von Gott her ansagenden Charakters. Schillebeeckx meinte eine gewisse Annäherung des Konzils an die Formel „ohne Erfahrung keine Offenbarung" und damit an die Rolle der menschlichen Erfahrung im Rezeptionsprozess der Offenbarung feststellen zu können. Aus der Offenbarungskonstitution *Dei verbum* spreche die Vorstellung einer unvermittelten Offenbarung, eine Vorstellung, die sozusagen an der Feinmechanik des

---

[2] Ebd., 38.
[3] Vgl. B. Schwarz-Boenneke, Die Widerständigkeit der Wirklichkeit als erstes Moment des Erfahrens, in diesem Band, 94–109.

Vermittlungsprozesses der Offenbarung an den Menschen wenig Interesse hat. So heißt es dort: „Durch seine Offenbarung wollte Gott sich selbst und die ewigen Entscheidungen seines Willens über das Heil der Menschen kundtun und mitteilen, ‚um Anteil zu geben am göttlichen Reichtum, der die Fassungskraft des menschlichen Geistes *schlechthin* übersteigt'" (DV 8). ‚Omnino' heißt es hier im Lateinische – als komme der menschlichen Erfahrung im Prozess der Offenbarungsrezeption keinerlei Bedeutung zu. Demgegenüber räumt die Pastoralkonstitution *Gaudium et spes*, wenn auch nur zögernd, der Erfahrung des Menschen einen gewissen Raum ein. Nach *Gaudium et spes* 41 ist es der Kirche anvertraut, das Geheimnis Gottes dem Menschen offenkundig zu machen und ihm das Verständnis seiner Existenz zu erschließen. Hier fungiert die Kirche als Vermittlungsinstanz der Offenbarung, aber sie kann diese Funktion nicht ausüben, wenn sie nicht selbst die Offenbarung menschlich, unter Einsatz menschlicher Erfahrung, rezipiert hat. Das Nämliche gilt dann für die Weitervermittlung der Offenbarung durch die Kirche an die Menschen. Schillebeeckx bringt das auf die präzise Formel: „Gott offenbart sich selbst, indem er den Menschen *ihm selbst* offenbart."[4] ‚Ihm selbst': Das geht schlechthin nicht ohne die Aktivierung der menschlichen Erfahrung.

Von daher stellt sich als weitere Einsicht ein, dass auch die Heilige Schrift nicht die Offenbarung selbst ist, sondern die Schrift *über* die Offenbarung, eine Schrift, in der sich unter der Führung des Heiligen Geistes Erfahrungen der Menschen mit der Offenbarung widerspiegeln. Wenn das der Punkt ist, dann sollten wir in der Heiligen Schrift den *Erfahrungen* der ersten Zeugen nachspüren und nicht bei den *Begriffen* hängen bleiben, in denen sich die Erfahrungen versprachlicht haben.

Eine weitere Assoziation sei noch angefügt. Wenn man bezüglich der Offenbarungsrezeption und damit bezüglich des Glaubens die Bedeutung der Erfahrung in all ihren Dimensionen hoch ansetzt, dann stellt sich die Frage, ob nicht die Enzyklika *Fides et ratio* von Johannes Paul II. über das Verhältnis von Glaube und Vernunft und Benedikt XVI. in seinem Bemühen um die Rationalität des Glaubens die menschliche Erfahrung auf die Dimension der *ratio* verkürzen und Johannes Paul II. wie Benedikt XVI. damit die Multidimensionalität der Erfahrung ausschlagen?

---

[4] E. Schillebeeckx, Christus und die Christen, a.a.O., 38.

3. Der theologische Topos der Wehrlosigkeit

Im dritten Band seiner Trilogie, „Menschen. Die Geschichte von Gott", öffnet Schillebeeckx im Begriff der Macht- bzw. Wehrlosigkeit Gottes einen interessanten, um Nuancen, gegenüber dem Bisherigen, anderen Blick auf den Tod Jesu am Kreuz. Wehrlosigkeit ist nach Schillebeeckx eine durchgehende Perspektive des Lebens Jesu, und deshalb auch seines Todes. Jesus trat nicht als machtvoller Messias auf, um die Menschen zu blenden und zu beeindrucken. Er hatte seinen Platz an der Seite der gesellschaftlich Marginalisierten, der Ausgestoßenen, der Verworfenen, an der Seite des einfachen Volkes, dem das religiöse Establishment keine Chancen vor Gott einräumte.

In dieser Wehrlosigkeit nimmt Jesus auch seinen Tod am Kreuz an. Dieser Tod – so tragisch er nach menschlichem Ermessen ist – desavouierte nicht sein Lebenswerk, er bagatellisierte nicht sein Leben. Sein Tod trug in Kontinuität mit seinem Leben das Merkmal der bewusst auf sich genommenen Wehrlosigkeit. Nur dürfen wir diese Wehrlosigkeit nicht in einem bloß ethisch-moralischen Sinn deuten. Sie hat vielmehr Offenbarungscharakter. In ihr wird an Jesus ansichtig, wie Gott ist. Der Wehrlosigkeit Jesu am Kreuz korrespondiert deshalb das Schweigen des Vaters beim Sterben des Sohnes.

Dieser Wehrlosigkeit aber wohnt eine Leben schaffende Dialektik inne. Sie ging nicht als Wehrlosigkeit unter, sie erstickte nicht sozusagen an sich selbst. Sie entpuppte sich als Lebenskraft, als eine dem Leben neue Kräfte zuführende Dynamik. Bereits Jesu wehrloses Lebenswerk wies „antizipative Merkmale"[5] der Auferstehung auf. Von daher darf man seine Auferstehung nicht gewissermaßen als Kompensation eines letzten Endes verfehlten und vergeblichen Lebens ansehen. Anders herum war die Auferstehung die Bestätigung und Erfüllung seines Lebens. Und es scheint ein wesentlicher Aspekt der Nachfolge Jesu zu sein, wenn auch nicht gleich der zentralste, der Spur der Wehrlosigkeit Jesu zu folgen.

Schillebeeckx hat im Topos der Wehrlosigkeit eine zentrale Herausforderung der Theologie benannt, der in seinen vielen Dimensionen immer wieder theologisch zu reflektieren ist.

---

[5] Ebd., 169.

4. Das Verhältnis der christlichen Religion zu den anderen Religionen

Auch in einem hier letzten Punkt gingen von Schillebeeckx entscheidende Anregungen aus, nämlich hinsichtlich des Verhältnisses der christlichen Religion zu den anderen Religionen der Welt. Davon war bereits im Statement von Alessandro Cortesi die Rede.[6] Ich darf nur noch einmal an den von Schillebeeckx vorgenommenen kühnen Perspektivenwechsel von „extra ecclesiam nulla salus" zu „extra mundum nulla salus" erinnern. Schillebeeckx knüpfte die Gabe des Heils von Gott *an* die Welt der Menschen.

So heißt es in 1 Tim 2,4: „Gott will, dass *alle* Menschen gerettet werden und zur Erkenntnis der Wahrheit gelangen. Und Schillebeeckx fügt hier erläuternd an: „[...] auch dann also, wenn sie Jesus Christus nicht kennen gelernt haben."[7] Damit wird dem Absolutheitsanspruch der christlichen Religion als *einzig wahrer Religion* der Abschied gegeben. Nicht aber der durch sie bezeugten Universalität des Heils für alle Menschen. Denn die universale Reichweite des Heils lag dem Wirken Jesu zugrunde. Wenngleich es da beim historischen Jesus, dem Juden, diesbezüglich einen Lernprozess gab. Man denke an seine Begegnung mit der kanaanäischen Frau, die ihn um die Heilung ihrer von einem Dämon gequälten Tochter bat.[8] Jesus lehnte ab. Er sei nur zu den verlorenen Schafen Israels gesandt. Auf ihr weiteres Insistieren hin blieb Jesus weiter bei seiner ablehnenden Haltung. „Es ist nicht recht, das Brot den Kindern wegzunehmen und den Hunden vorzuwerfen." Eine geradezu menschenverachtende Metapher. Und auf ein erneutes Insistieren der Frau lenkt Jesus ein. Er heilt die vom Dämon gequälte Tochter der Frau.

Die universale Befreiung, die Jesus brachte, wurde in seiner historischen Partikularität, in der geschichtlichen Eingebundenheit seines Lebens präsent. Die Kirche repräsentiert das universale göttliche Heil als „Sakrament", das heißt, als Zeichen und Werkzeug dieses Heils. Und sie ist dabei, wie der historische Jesus, in ihrer Partikularität begrenzt. Aber sie ist sich bewusst, dass das universale göttliche Heil auch in den anderen Religionen der Welt zugänglich ist. Auch sie sind Wege der Menschen zu Gott. Die Religionen stellen in ihrer Vielzahl einen Reichtum der

---

[6] Vgl. A. Cortesi, Das Heil der Menschheit in einer Welt der vielen Religionen. Anregungen aus dem Werk von Edward Schillebeeckx, in diesem Band, 39–52.
[7] E. Schillebeeckx, Menschen. Die Geschichte von Gott, Freiburg/Br. 1990, 190.
[8] Vgl. Mt 15,21–28.

Menschheit dar. Aufgrund der verschiedenen Perspektiven, unter denen sie die Wirklichkeit der Welt wahrnehmen, kommen sie bezüglich der Heilswirklichkeit zwar zu divergierenden Anschauungen, die aber spiegeln „keine kontradiktorischen Widersprüche" und keinen Relativismus, sondern einen „perspektivenrelativen Realismus" wider.[9]

5. Fazit

Meine vier Gedankenschneisen zu Schillebeeckx bieten nicht mehr als flüchtige Andeutungen. Sie machen mir aber – und sicher darüber hinaus auch einem großen Kreis – exemplarisch deutlich, wie dankbar Theologinnen und Theologen, ja, wie dankbar die Kirche Edward Schillebeeckx sein darf. Er bereicherte die Theologie unserer Tage nachhaltig.

* * *

Abstract of the contribution of Stefan Knobloch

Edward Schillebeeckx is a blessing for theology. This subjective outline highlights the influence of Schillebeeckx has on the theological themes explored from his "Trilogie." He was a thorough theologian who in his thoroughness uncovered new exegetical cross-references. One of his merits is the evaluation of human experience in the context of the reception of God's revelation. His insights on the defenselessness of Jesus as a sign of God's own defenselessness is thought provoking. However, it is also interesting to find in Schillebeecx an understanding of the necessary relationship between Christianity and other religions, and of living in the midst of globalization, on the same planet, and yet with a wide diversity of cultures and religions. Overall Schillebeckx's works invite current theo-

---

[9] Vgl. P. Schmidt-Leukel, Das Problem divergierender Wahrheitsansprüche im Rahmen einer pluralistischen Religionstheologie. Voraussetzungen zu einer Lösung, in: H.-G. Schwandt (Hrsg.), Pluralistische Theologie der Religionen. Eine kritische Sichtung, Frankfurt/M. 1998, 39–58.

logians to be thankful and appreciative, while bestowing new tasks on them.

Translation from German: *Tracy Rammler*

MITARBEITER/-INNEN | CONTRIBUTORS

Christian Bauer OPL
  Dr. theol.
  Universität Tübingen (D)
Erik Borgman OPL
  Prof. Dr. theol.
  Universiteit Tilburg (NL)
Alessandro Cortesi OP
  Prof. Dr. theol.
  Centro Espaces „Giorgio La Pira", Pistoia; Istituto Superiore di Scienze Religiose „Ippolito Galantini" – Firenze (I)
Vera Donnelly OP
  Dr. theol.
  Sion Hill, Dublin (IR)
Thomas Eggensperger OP
  Dr. theol., M.A.
  Institut M.-Dominique Chenu, Berlin; Philosophisch-Theologische Hochschule Münster (D)
Ulrich Engel OP
  Dr. theol. habil.
  Institut M.-Dominique Chenu, Berlin; Philosophisch-Theologische Hochschule Münster (D)
Stephan van Erp
  Dr. theol.
  Universiteit Nijmegen (NL)
Maximilian Halstrup
  Dr. theol., Dipl. Arb.-Wiss.
  interface medien GmbH, Münster (D)

Manuela Kalsky
>Dr. theol.
>Dominicaans Studiecentrum voor Theologie en Samenleving, Nijmegen; Project W!J, Amsterdam (NL)

Stefan Knobloch OFMCap
>Prof. em. Dr. theol.
>Universität Mainz (D)

Bernhard Kohl OP
>Dipl.-Theol.
>Institut M.-Dominique Chenu, Berlin; Universität Erfurt (D)

André Lascaris OP
>Ph.D (Theology)
>Dominicaans Studiecentrum voor Theologie en Samenleving, Nijmegen (NL)

Michael Lauble
>Dr. theol.
>Übersetzer | Translator, Düsseldorf (D)

Pierre-Yves Materne OP
>Dr. theol., Lic. iur.
>Institute Catholique, Paris (F); Cabinet d'Avocats Philippe & Partners, Bruxelles (B)

Angel F. Méndez Montoya OP
>PhD (Philosophical Theology), Prof.
>Universidad Iberoamericana, México D.F. (MX)

Johann Baptist Metz
>Prof. em. Dr. phil., Dr. theol., Dr. h.c. mult.
>Universität Münster (D)

Rebecca Pohl
>Erstes Staatsexamen Lehramt | Master of Education
>University of Manchester (UK)

Tracy Rammler
>B.A.
>Englischlehrerin | English Teacher, Leipzig (D)

Sabine Schratz
>Dr. theol., M.A.
>Novizin | Novice, Cabra Dominicans, Tallaght (IR)

Robert J. Schreiter C.PP.S.
    Prof. Dr. theol.
    Catholic Theological Union, Chicago IL (USA)

Bernadette Schwarz-Boenneke
    Dr. theol.
    Herbert Quandt-Stiftung, Bad Homburg (D)

Geraldine Smyth OP
    Ph.D (Theology), Dr. h.c., Prof.
    Trinity College Dublin (IR)

Perspektiven dominikanischer Theologie

ULRICH ENGEL
Gott der Menschen
Wegmarken dominikanischer Theologie

Ulrich Engel
Gott der Menschen
Wegmarken dominikanischer Theologie

Format 14 x 22 cm
176 Seiten
Paperback
ISBN 978-3-7867-2839-9

Die nun bald 800 Jahre währende Geschichte des Dominikanerordens ist auch eine Geschichte des Ringens darum, wie Barmherzigkeit und Menschenfreundlichkeit Gottes angemessen verkündet werden können.
Die Spannungsfelder von Innen und Außen, Kirche und Welt, Glaube und Politik sind die Orte, an denen sich (nicht nur) dominikanische Theologie bewahrheiten muss. Theologen wie Thomas von Aquin, Albertus Magnus, Marie-Dominique Chenu oder Edward Schillebeeckx sind Zeugen für dieses Ringen, das Ulrich Engel geistlich inspirierend und intellektuell herausfordernd vorstellt.

GRÜNEWALD   www.gruenewaldverlag.de

Erschienen bei

topos taschenbücher

THOMAS EGGENSPERGER /
ULRICH ENGEL
Dominikanerinnen
und Dominikaner
Geschichte und Spiritualität

topos taschenbücher

Thomas Eggensperger/Ulrich Engel

Dominikanerinnen und Dominikaner

Geschichte und Spiritualität

216 Seiten

Band 709
ISBN 978-3-8367-0709-1

www.toposplus.de